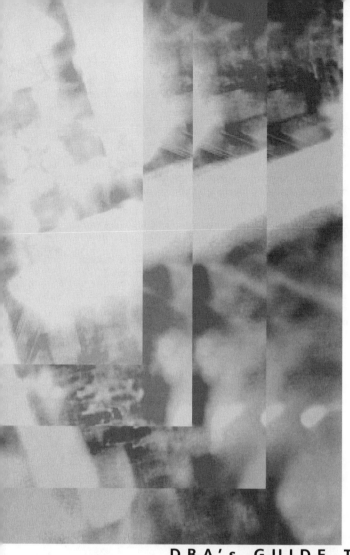

DBA's GUIDE TO
DATABASES
ON LINUX

SYNGRESS®

KEY	SERIAL NUMBER
001	9TRP52ADSE
002	XPSTRA7TC4
003	CLNBC28FV7
004	DC5C8N4RL6
005	Z745Q81DBR
006	PF62RT6XMB
007	DTPLA5ZX44
008	XRDF743RTG
009	6532M941DS
010	SMWR8PSMRN

PUBLISHED BY
Syngress Media, Inc.
800 Hingham Street
Rockland, MA 02370

DBA's Guide to Databases on Linux

Printed in the United States of America

1 2 3 4 5 6 7 8 9 0

ISBN: 1-928994-04-0

Copy edit by: Adrienne Rebello
Technical edit by: Chris Rogers
Index by: Jennifer R. Coker
Project Editor: Mark A. Listewnik

Proofreading by: Lynette Crane
Page Layout and Art by: Craig Enslin
and Katharine Glennon
Co-Publisher: Richard Kristof

Distributed by Publishers Group West

Acknowledgments

We would like to acknowledge the following people for their kindness and support in making this book possible.

Richard Kristof, Duncan Anderson, Jennifer Gould, Robert Woodruff, Kevin Murray, Dale Leatherwood, Shelley Everett, Laurie Hedrick, Rhonda Harmon, Lisa Lavallee, and Robert Sanregret of Global Knowledge, for their generous access to the IT industry's best courses, instructors and training facilities.

Ralph Troupe and the team at Rt. 1 Solutions for their invaluable insight into the challenges of designing, deploying and supporting world-class enterprise networks.

Karen Cross, Kim Wylie, Harry Kirchner, John Hays, Bill Richter, Kevin Votel, Brittin Clark, Sarah Schaffer, Luke Kreinberg, Ellen Lafferty and Sarah MacLachlan of Publishers Group West for sharing their incredible marketing experience and expertise.

Peter Hoenigsberg, Mary Ging, Caroline Hird, Simon Beale, Julia Oldknow, Kelly Burrows, Jonathan Bunkell, Catherine Anderson, Peet Kruger, Pia Rasmussen, Denelise L'Ecluse, Rosanna Ramacciotti, Marek Lewinson, Marc Appels, Paul Chrystal, Femi Otesanya, and Tracey Alcock of Harcourt International for making certain that our vision remains worldwide in scope.

Special thanks to the professionals at Osborne with whom we are proud to publish the best-selling Global Knowledge Certification Press series.

From Global Knowledge

At Global Knowledge we strive to support the multiplicity of learning styles required by our students to achieve success as technical professionals. As the world's largest IT training company, Global Knowledge is uniquely positioned to offer these books. The expertise gained each year from providing instructor-led training to hundreds of thousands of students worldwide has been captured in book form to enhance your learning experience. We hope that the quality of these books demonstrates our commitment to your lifelong learning success. Whether you choose to learn through the written word, computer based training, Web delivery, or instructor-led training, Global Knowledge is committed to providing you with the very best in each of these categories. For those of you who know Global Knowledge, or those of you who have just found us for the first time, our goal is to be your lifelong competency partner.

Thank your for the opportunity to serve you. We look forward to serving your needs again in the future.

Warmest regards,

Duncan Anderson
President and Chief Executive Officer, Global Knowledge

Contributors

Tom Bascom is an Enterprise Architect for EDS responsible for providing business and information technology consulting to EDS and customer enterprises. His duties include formulating enterprise-wide strategies and providing recommendations in the design, development, implementation and management of appropriate products and solutions. Tom has been involved with products using the Progress database since 1986 and Linux since 1994 and is a frequent contributor to public forums such as PEG and the comp.databases.progress newsgroup. Tom is also an occasional speaker and author of industry specific and technical articles in the Progressions newsletter.

Jamieson Becker is a Linux/UNIX and Windows NT engineer and owner of Ring0.com, a Web services engagement firm. Since starting programming in 1980, Jamieson has become an accomplished consultant, completing engagements with IBM, Compaq, Carrier, Brown & Williamson, VoiceStream, Cargill, and Citizens. Jamieson specializes in large Web applications using Linux. He lives with his wife, Jennifer, and cat, Angie, in Atlanta, GA. He can be reached at jamiebecker@ring0.com.

Geoff Crawford heads New Jersey-based consulting company Innov8 Computer Software, LLC. (www.innov8cs.com). He has been using Progress since its commercial release 15 years ago. Geoff is a regular contributor to the Progress E-mail Group, author of the Progress ODBC FAQ, and a regular speaker at Progress user conferences. In his spare time, Geoff enjoys the unlikely combination of researching his Pennsylvania Dutch roots and listening to Pantera.

Marc Connolly has worked with relational databases since 1987. He has extensive experience with DB2, Informix, and Oracle, and has worked with each in various capacities, as a DBA, product developer, product manager, and marketing specialist.

Brad Dietrich (B.S. Computer Science and Electrical Engineering) has worked professionally and academically on the Internet since its earliest days. He is currently one of the founding Software Engineers for ChannelDot Networks in San Francisco, CA. Before joining ChannelDot, he founded and ran DefTech Contracting (www.deftech.com), a successful Internet and Web application development business, where he developed world-class Web applications for many clients including Mattel and Spyglass. He worked on projects ranging from e-commerce solutions to legacy system integration and terabyte databases. He has provided support to application development in the open-source community for the Linux environment ranging from viable middleware to bug workarounds in closed-source drivers. Prior to starting his Internet application development business, he worked to develop Web-based network management applications at FORE Systems as well as developing Web-based distance learning systems at Carnegie Mellon University.

David Egan (P.Eng.; BASc Engineering, University of Toronto; MCT; RHCE) has lived in several countries and worked with computers since the early days of the Apple and IBM-type PC's. David's first "hobby-turned-job" was a five-year position as a Z80 Assembler and C Language programmer. David shifted gears somewhat to become a VMS/UNIX/NT/PC Systems Integration Consultant and Technology Instructor over the past 15 years. David is still consulting and writing the occasional book, but mostly contracts as a Course Director and Course Writer of Unix-, NT- and Linux-based courses for Global Knowledge Inc. of Cary, NC: http://www.globalknowledge.com. When not on the road preaching the virtues of Linux and NT from his stage, he resides outside Vancouver, BC with his lovely wife Deborah, daughter Vanessa and son Callen. They can be reached at either egand@istar.ca or egand@wwdb.org or through http://home.istar.ca/~egand.

Brent Gilmore (Sun Certified Solaris Administrator and Sun Certified Network Administrator) is an Oracle DBA and Programmer/Analyst for San Diego State University. He has been working in the IT industry since 1989 and has received a B.S. degree in Information Systems and a M.S. degree in Business Administration Management. Brent started using Linux in 1996 and began using Oracle in 1997. He is currently involved in Internet application development and database design using Oracle8/8i, Linux, Perl, PL/SQL, OAS, and Apache.

Bryan Schwab (B.S. Computer Engineering, Florida Atlantic University) is a Principal Engineer with Billpoint, an eBay company, and is responsible for developing its back end eCommerce system, including shipping and ordering servers, security specifications, monitoring systems and the integration of major strategic partner applications. With over 10 years as a software engineer, Bryan specializes in developing back end database architecture on Linux, Solaris, FreeBSD, OpenBSD and Windows NT/9*x*. He has designed and implemented mission-critical information systems and large-scale business processes for companies such as Wired Digital and NetGravity. He has authored articles for *Wired Magazine* and *Webmonkey*.

Tim Schaefer is an Informix Data Base Administrator and IT data warehousing consultant, currently working with Galaxy Latin America DirecTV, in Ft. Lauderdale, Florida. He has worked on Informix databases of all sizes, ranging from the Standard Engine on Xenix 80286 machines to large-scale data warehouses with Informix Extended Parallel Server (XPS). He has been in the computer business since 1985, attending college at Webster University in St. Louis in 1985, and has been working with Informix products since 1988. Among his many successes, Tim participated in an international group of developers and business professionals chosen to promote the benefits of Informix on Linux. He also runs the InxUtil Web site, http://www.inxutil.com, a Web site dedicated to Informix tools and is actively involved with the South Florida Informix Users Group of Ft. Lauderdale. Tim is an avid scuba diver and can be found many weekends in the spring and summer off the coast of Ft. Lauderdale, FL diving among the fish, the many shipwrecks, and reefs. You can reach Tim at tschaefe@bellsouth.net.

Alavoor Vasudevan "Al Dev" (B.E. Osmania University, M.S. University of Texas at El Paso) started his computer science career in 1985. Since then, he has worked extensively with Unix/C/C++/SQL databases. He also has experience in E-commerce, HTML and Linux. His hobbies include writing a good amount of documentation for Linux/Unix as well as software development for Linux/Unix. Al Dev lives in Pearland, TX and works as a consultant for companies in downtown Houston and the surrounding area.

Paul Zikopoulos is a senior member of the DB2 information and development team, specializing in DB2 installation and configuration issues. He has more than five years experience with DB2 Universal Database and has written numerous magazine articles and books about DB2. Paul is an IBM Certified Advanced Technical Expert (DRDA and Cluster/EEE) and an IBM Certified Solutions Expert with DB2 Universal Database. You can reach him at paulz_ibm@yahoo.com. Paul would like to thank IBM developers Susan Williams and Darin McBride for their help and passion for DB2 and Linux.

Technical Editors

Chris Rogers has been configuring Linux servers since 1994. To give an idea of how long that is in terms of the computing industry, the Web browser was Mosaic, Netscape 0.9 had just hit the FTP sites, and the Slackware distribution without X-windows could still fit on only three 3.5" diskettes. Chris is now CEO of PowerStreak Networks, a Management Services Provider that specializes in managing customer networks using Linux servers. Chris may be e-mailed at crogers@powerstreak.com.

David C. Niemi is a senior network engineer at a large financial company. He is also president and co-founder of Tux.Org, a nonprofit company devoted to education and support for free software. He has been contributing to the Linux kernel and other free software projects.

Contents

Chapter 4: An Informix Installation on Linux — 115

Chapter 6: Installing DB2 Universal Database Version 6.1 on Red Hat Linux

Chapter 7: MySQL on Linux

Preface

It is hard to believe that Linux is less than 10 years old. In that short timeframe, the fledgling operating system that was written as an experiment by a Finnish graduate student has exploded in function and usage. The similar explosion of the Internet fueled the growth of Linux.

Nowadays, Linux is rapidly gaining popularity as an enterprise-level, mission-critical server platform. Since its first general release, Linux has proven itself as a stable and scalable operating system. However, only recently have the major software vendors begun porting their applications onto the Linux platform. The most notable advance in this area came in 1999 when the four major database vendors—Oracle, Informix, Sybase, and IBM—announced general support for the Linux platform. Linux had other databases available to it before then, but the participation of these highly respected vendors gave it the final push into the limelight that it needed.

About This Book

Many of the chapters walk you through the installation of various databases, as well as how to test and utilize some critical features for maintaining the databases. The decision is left to the reader as to exactly which database is best for a given project, but a few pointers will be given in the introduction and along the way to help you choose.

Organization of This Book

This book covers the installation and configuration of several major databases. It is intended primarily as a reference and, as such, there may be some readers who may not necessarily read the book cover to cover. With that in mind, each chapter is written to stand on its own as a reference for each particular database.

Chapter 1: The Linux Operating System is a summary of Linux in general. This chapter explores a bit of history and some of the logistics of Linux, and is a good background chapter for those unfamiliar with Linux and the Open Source movement.

Chapter 2: Basic Red Hat Linux Installation is a step-by-step review of installing the most popular flavor of Linux, Red Hat. If the database server in question is to be a production server, a clean operating system install is recommended for new hardware, which will result in the most stable configuration.

Chapter 3: Installing and Running Oracle on Linux Oracle tends to be the most popular and widely recognized database on the market today. It is highly scalable and extremely reliable. However, it is rather expensive and may not be appropriate for small businesses.

Chapter 4: An Informix Installation on Linux Informix closely follows Oracle in scalability and reliability. Usually the choice between the two databases falls simply to personal preference.

Chapter 5: Installing and Utilizing Sybase on Linux Sybase has a very loyal following. If you are familiar with Microsoft SQLServer, Sybase follows as a logical choice for the Linux environment. Microsoft's design for SQLServer closely follows the Sybase design.

Chapter 6: Installing DB2 Universal Databases Version 6.1 on Linux DB2 is the most under-appreciated of the major databases. While it is still mostly used on mainframes, the DB2 port to Linux is powerful and scalable. You should not discount DB2 as a viable alternative without carefully examining this chapter.

Chapter 7: A MySQL Installation on Linux MySQL is the most popular of the freeware databases. It is easy to set up and configure, and lends itself well to Web-based applications. However, it tends to be less scaleable for extremely large databases.

Chapter 8: Installing and Managing Progress on Linux Progress is usually overlooked by most DBAs. Progress often embeds itself in third-party applications but is a very capable database on its own.

Chapter 9: PostgreSQL on Linux PostgreSQL comes installed with several Linux distributions. It is open source like MySQL, and offers a very easy startup for a small database application. Its scalability is limited, however.

Chapter 10: Developing a Web-Based Application provides a sample database application. Once a database is installed, there are many things that can be done with it.

Online Usenet groups, white papers, and user groups are valuable resources for computer professionals to network and share ideas. To that end, throughout the book, we've provided valuable links and resources to access on the Web.

Databases on Linux

Presumably, you have already made the decision to implement a database solution on Linux. The stability and reliability of the Linux operating system suits a database well. As an open source operating system, Linux is well supported and constantly updated. The user must realize from the beginning that the major kernel releases and the minor bug fixes must be applied to the operating system with regularity. Care must also be given to the actual hardware for the database server. Redundancy should be built in. Strongly consider multiple disks in some sort of Redundant Array of Independent Disks (RAID) configuration. Different databases like different configurations. It goes without saying that as much memory as possible should be installed; the best database available would fail miserably if it is not deployed on sufficient hardware.

With the operating system and server in hand, several questions should now be asked:

- What do you want your database to do?
- What specific production environment do you have: small, medium, or large?
- Is this a mission-critical application?
- Will there be support needs for this application?

Each of the databases covered in this book has its strengths and weaknesses. If the decision has not already been made, or even if it has, each should be considered carefully. A little extra thought never hurts before the solution is implemented.

Oracle always rises to the top as one of the leaders in scalability and reliability. Oracle also requires highly qualified DBAs and support contracts from the company. This combination, along with the high cost of commercial licenses for Oracle, usually makes it out of reach for smaller companies with smaller database needs. Informix follows this same pattern. It is a highly functional and reliable database, but the cost of acquiring and supporting it is often too high.

Sybase comes out as a good middle of the road solution. It may not have quite as rich a feature set as Oracle or Informix, but it is certainly not lacking in the essentials. Its cost is more manageable, and, if the user is familiar with Microsoft SQLServer, its configuration is very straightforward. Sybase scales to most applications, and provides good stability. Much the same can be said for DB2. It can be a bit more challenging to support, but it is just as feature-rich and scalable as Oracle. The cost for commercial applications is lower as well. Progress also fits into this category.

The freeware databases like MySQL and PostgreSQL are very good entry-level solutions. The cost is very nice, of course... free. These databases are easy to implement and easy to maintain. A novice user with the help of this book could be up and running in just a day or two. The main drawback with these databases is scalability. Usually the freeware databases have performance problems with more than a million records. Still, it is a perfectly viable solution to start with one of these freeware databases and then migrate to one of the larger ones. Exporting the tables into SQL and then importing the SQL into a different database usually works very well. Spending time on a solid database design and a good data model from the very start will save a great many headaches if you plan on taking this route. This is, of course, true for any database implementation, but is especially pertinent in a data migration situation.

This book should be used as a resource to help you decide which will best suit your needs. In the end, only you can decide which one is right for your purposes.

More Database for Your Buck

Yesterday's databases are a shadow of the powerful applications currently being produced by today's top corporations. Managers and DBAs have many options to choose from today. The standardized nature of SQL makes the data very portable. The use of BLOBs (Binary Large OBjects) makes it possible to store images and executables in a database. The relatively new technology of XML allows the data that was once locked behind two or three application layers to be served instantly out to the Web. In general, the databases covered in this book can fit into two categories: traditional and open source.

Traditional Databases

Databases are traditionally programmed and supported by large software companies. The most notable advantage to this model is product support. For an annual maintenance fee, the software vendor is readily available for product support, troubleshooting, and upgrades. Most large companies that heavily rely on extremely large databases absolutely refuse to give up the extra layer of accountability that this support model offers. One obvious disadvantage of the traditional model is the slowness of the software vendor to change its product and add new features. The latest technology is often months to years in the development cycle before it makes it into the hands of the end user. A significant disadvantage is that these companies, like any other corporation, are forced to watch their bottom line. The cost of the individual licenses can be prohibitive for many users. The vendor is usually subject to intense competition. As a result, products come out too early, and patches are often needed. A prime example is Oracle 8i. The long-awaited version of Oracle was programmed to be Internet-ready, but was filled with bugs. Oracle 8i, Release2 fixes those bugs, but was released one year later. This is a scenario that many software vendors deal with all the time.

Open Source Databases

The newer software development model is open source. Open source has the large advantage of its development community. There are usually one or a few people that are responsible for the code with basically the entire Internet as a developer base. The resulting software is updated and revised often. The latest release of a particular piece of software has the latest features and the newest technology. This, of course, leads to the disadvantage that those features may not be entirely tested yet. The system administrator must keep on top of the new changes and additions, and a more advanced user is required to maintain the system. Larger companies balk at the fact that traditional support and accountability is not available. The support falls on the administrator. In all honesty, that is exactly how most corporate systems are supported anyway. The administrator uses his or her own knowledge and applies the knowledge that can be gained from Web sites and newsgroups on the software in question.

Utilizing and Maximizing Your Database

Having a database on a Linux server is a great thing, but what should you do with it? For the most part, the answer is: "The sky's the limit." Tracking employee data, managing customer requirements, correlating marketing data, improving the efficiency of an ordering system, and a host of other applications can be conceived and programmed.

Basic Features

All databases speak SQL (Structured Query Language). This basic standard assures compatibility from one database to another. Some databases implement more or less of the standard, so be careful in the migration. As an example, don't try to migrate an Oracle database using BLOBs into a PostgreSQL database that does not support those types of objects. All databases support the basic four SQL constructs: SELECT, INSERT, UPDATE, DELETE. In addition, all should support the basic user and table schema that is used to create and manage database tables and user permissions.

Advanced Features

The two most notable advanced features are BLOBs and XML. BLOBs allow large binary objects, such as images, to be stored in the database. Oracle and several other databases support BLOBs. XML (eXtensible Markup Language) is a relatively new technology. Similar to HTML, XML is a subset of SGML (Standard Generalized Markup Language). Unlike HTML, which is a document formatting markup language, XML is a data vocabulary markup. XML allows data to be dumped directly into a Web page. If the browser or application server speaks XML, the data is formatted and displayed with a minimum of programming. Most every database that is on the market today now supports XML in some fashion.

Databases and Beyond

The Web has exploded onto the scene over the past three years. Utilizing databases on the Web is already the order of the day. Housing user and customer information, accessing personal profiles, sorting and cataloging product information and data for customer access will be the new standard—the model that will drive e-commerce. Data mining, portals, and shopping carts are the buzzwords in the golf conversations of CEOs everywhere.

For the purposes of this book, we have presented a shopping cart scenario to illustrate some of the potential uses for your database. Web servers are a key element in utilizing databases on the Web, and we have provided a short overview of many of the most popular ones today.

Overall, we hope you find this book a useful reference that will assist your efforts in bringing up a database on Linux for whatever purpose.

Audience

This book is intended primarily for database administrators and Linux users who want to improve their skills and understanding of various databases. We hope you will come away with a better understanding of database design and implementation in general. A mechanical set of instructions to install and configure a database is all very well, but this book attempts to give you a better understanding of the Linux operating system when it is used as a database server.

Other Books by Syngress

In addition to this book, Syngress Media Inc. has produced a number of other titles for IT professionals. Please check our Web site at www.syngress.com for the latest announcements.

## Chapter 1

The Linux Operating System

Solutions in this chapter:

- **A Brief History of Linux**

- **The Linux Kernel**

- **The Difference between Linux and Other Operating Systems**

- **Why Choose Linux?**

- **Distributions of Linux**

- **Considerations Before Upgrading or Migrating**

- **How to Begin the Process**

A Brief History of Linux

Linux has been in continuous development since its creation in 1991, when Linus Torvalds began writing a UNIX-based operating system for the Intel PC environment.

As a graduate student at the University of Helsinki, Finland, Linus saw the advantages of a basic PC as a desktop system over the high cost of dumb terminals. At that time, however, the cost of the desktop software and the required desktop operating system prohibited the average student and user from being able to afford a PC with all the necessary software products. In an effort to alleviate this problem, and extend the resources of the school at which he was working, Linus decided that he would work to redevelop Minix code (a microkernel-based clone of Unix) to create few simple utilities for himself. He felt it would be a worthwhile project even if it simply allowed the school to use some old PCs as dumb terminals to connect to the main servers.

Linus opened his project to the Internet community for additional development ideas and resources. In early 1992, only a few hundred people were using Linux. The original Linux kernel was very compact and had only the most basic functionality. The Internet community quickly latched onto this project and helped supplement its development in a truly grassroots fashion. Soon, hundreds and then thousands of programmers collaborated to help with code and break out on their own to develop their own Linux code. This provided a very fast development with many eyes debugging and testing the code. Before long, Linus had replaced all the Minix code with his own code plus the contributions from other development volunteers. Taking advantage of the Open Source community, which was still in its infancy, Linus released Linux to the world.

In terms of the development of utilities, there was and still is no "best design" of a utility. Anyone can contribute whatever he or she feels might be a useful utility. This is evident in the fact that there are several utilities that perform the same basic function; many were designed so that if you were already familiar with a specific utility, Linux would provide a fully functional counterpart for you. For example, there are a dozen or more file editors supplied in text-based and X Window versions.

Nearly a decade later, Linux is beginning to find its place in the business community as a viable, and often superior, replacement to many other server and desktop operating systems. Linux has entered into and excelled at a newer area—that of a database server—as proven by the many alliances between various Linux vendors and some of the big database vendors like Oracle and IBM, to name a few. This book introduces the strengths of Linux as a database server platform, examines several database solutions, and introduces a few examples of real-world applications.

The Linux Kernel

Linux was originally developed for recreational use and was always intended to be distributed for free. The Linux kernel and the related source code are made available to everyone and will continue to be free as long as Linus holds the copyright to the kernel source. Linux is a registered trademark of Linus Torvalds and is collectively written under the terms of the General Public License (GPL) by its hundreds of contributing authors. The GPL allows anyone to freely distribute the full source code in its entirety, make copies thereof, and sell or distribute it (with a few exceptions) any way he or she wishes. The GPL is supplied along with the Linux kernel (**usr/src/linux/COPYING/** directory on the Linux CD-ROM), or it can be downloaded and viewed from many sites on the Internet.

NOTE

Software under the GLP provides almost unlimited flexibility to users of the software, and frees them from the expensive license purchasing and tracking.

The Linux kernel is just one small part of the whole thing collectively known as Linux. The kernel, as its name would imply, is the central, core piece to the operating system. You can think of the kernel as the engine of your PC; that which "makes it all run." The kernel handles I/O, performs memory management, and is basically the brains of the operating system. The kernel, though compact, is one of the key reasons why Linux is such a powerful and efficient OS.

In addition to these central parts, you need many other components to build a complete and usable operating system. The power of an operating system can't be fully tested without utilities to accomplish work like creating documents, sharing files, and installing, displaying, and printing files and documents. These utilities are freely available on the Internet, the same as the Linux kernel. Table 1.1 provides a very small sample of the utilities supplied with Linux.

Table 1.1 Basic UNIX Utilities Supplied with Every Linux Distribution

Operation	Command Line or File
File Manipulation	cp, mv, rm, ln, touch, ls, cat, more, >, >>, 2>, <
Setup	ifconfig, mount, showmount, /etc/printcap, /etc/hosts
Stats	ps, vmstat, nfsstat, innstat, netstat, top, who, users, pac, du
Utilities	vi, pine, pico, sed, awk, grep, find, netscape, tar, cpio, compress
Network Services	DHCP, http, SMB, ftp, telnet, talk, pop3, imap, fingerd, sendmail

All of these utilities and hundreds more are freely available on the Internet. You can download and install each one individually, or you can download the kernel and all of the required utilities in a single (albeit large) file. Instead of downloading, many software companies offer their versions of Linux on CD that can be bought at a local store. This is what the commercial versions are—a collection of these programs and utilities, along with some of their own homemade utilities that make up their version or distribution of Linux.

The Future of Linux Development

All the source code is freely available; even if Linus decides to stop working, someone else can easily take the source and continue the development. The kernel is one small, but very important part of the whole community that is Linux. Most of the hundreds of utilities have been contributed from the GNU project and elsewere in the Open Source arena.

Linus is not the only kernel developer in the world. There were many contributors up to this point and there will be many more. Alan Cox is one notable contributor to kernel development in such areas as dealing with additional hardware and new CPU design requirements. Specifically, AMD is providing all the processor nuts and bolts of the Athlon processor to Alan Cox. Kernels released in the very near future should process at record speeds, as they will be optimized to run on an Athlon machine.

Linux Distributions

Whenever you get a copy of Linux, either commercially or for free, you get what collectively is called a *distribution*. A distribution is one company's collection of utilities for Linux along with the kernel and possibly some of their proprietary products, like database managers, firewall software, etc. A typical Linux distribution contains hundreds of standard UNIX-like utilities as well as an excellent set of development tools, games, databases, graphical display, and control utilities, as well as a windowing Graphical User Interface (GUI) called the X Window System.

Some of these Linux distributions are not entirely free. The base of their system may be free but they charge for the extras that make it their special version of Linux. There are commercial versions of Linux produced by companies like Debian, Red Hat, VA Linux, SuSE, and others. Under the terms of the General Public License, you can download a full copy of these Linux distributions at no cost. Distributions can usually be found on each company's Web site, as well as from any one of the many mirror sites on the Internet.

Why Pay for a Commercial Linux Version?

The commercial versions offer added bonuses that are not available with the free versions, although the actual media that is supplied may seem identical. The difference is usually in some value-added product or service that is included with the commercial product. For example, Red Hat Linux, when bought commercially from a retailer, includes 30–180 days of free installation support as well as a subscription to their update central Web service. The Debian Distribution provides unlimited support from its Web and ftp sites. You can also buy this support and update service on a yearly contractual basis from Red Hat and other providers. This is how Red Hat makes its money and continues to pour that money back into developing additional features for their product.

Commercial versions are also more likely to be kept current and usually have a simplified installation and unified interface prepared for you. In the early days of Linux, you were given a basic set of instructions on how to get the supplied Linux distribution to install. You then had to configure your files and printers, network and sound cards individually. Current releases almost always have an installation interface that may be color-oriented and menu-based (most common), or it may be GUI-oriented (X Window) like the current release of Red Hat.

The Difference between Linux and Other Operating Systems

Linux is a UNIX clone that is written to be POSIX-compliant wherever possible. Linux was originally written for the Intel platform but there are ports to PowerPC, Macintosh, Amiga, some Atari computers, and even the Palm Pilot. If you know the basic commands, file system layout, and general utilities of any other UNIX variant, you know them for Linux. If you are Microsoft Windows- or Macintosh-oriented, you may not be as comfortable at first, but you will find that almost everything is similar.

Feature Rich

Not every Linux distribution has exactly the same set of utilities, but in general, the base features supplied with Linux are quite impressive to say the least. Since Microsoft Windows has had almost no competition at the desktop, their advertisements almost always speak to the improvements over their previous offerings, not their competition. Linux is a competitive operating system for the Intel or clone-based PC as both a workstation and server operating system. In fact, most of the improvements added to Windows NT over the past four years have been UNIX-like services that Linux has always supported.

Some of the many features included with most Linux variants that make Linux a great database server are the following:

- Multitasking
- SMP
- 32- and 64-bit virtual memory models
- Protected kernel mode
- ELF standard binaries
- Multi-user
- Free GUI
- Binary compatibility with other UNIX variants
- Extensive network protocols and services support
- All the standard UNIX network services like HTTP, FTP, Telnet, etc.

Multitasking

Multitasking is an essential requirement of any server, especially a database server. With a true 32-bit Intel multitasking environment (64-bit on supported RISC CPUs), Linux has the ability to run multiple programs apparently "simultaneously" even on a single processor. The process, in reality, is a very fast round-robin — that is, each process waits its turn in line for the required resources. The particular method that Linux uses to handle the requests gives the impression of true multitasking. Many process threads can be started simultaneously and execute in parallel, thus offering excellent performance and optimization of I/O channels.

Symmetric Multiprocessor Support

Out of the box, Linux will support between one, and in some cases, up to 16 CPUs, depending on the variant. This multiprocessor support makes Linux an excellent platform for a database server, able to handle many threaded processes simultaneously. Almost all major vendors sell multi-processor servers specifically for database and Web services. The Linux kernel is well-designed to handle these multiple processors, providing nearly full utilization of each additional processor instead of a declining utilization ratio as each new processor is added.

32-Bit (and 64-Bit RISC) Virtual Memory

Linux uses the full processor 32-bit memory management services to provide virtual memory of 4GB on Intel platforms and 16 exabytes when using 64-bit Linux on any RISC processor. Each new process gets an independent user-level process with 2GB of virtual space (available if required; in reality, it uses only enough RAM as needed to support the process). This provides security and independence between every process on the system.

Binary Compatibility: Standard Executable and Linking Format (ELF) Binaries

Linux has embraced the standardized ELF-based binaries' and shared libraries' (similar to dynamic link libraries (DLL) but not compatible) application design strategy. This allows applications to run on multiple operating systems without need of recompilation. SCO UNIX 4.2, SVR4, AIX, Sun, and most Linux Intel-based versions are among the many UNIX variants that are moving toward this compatibility design. For example, Corel Draw! for SCO also runs under Linux.

Multi-User

True multi-user capabilities provide for multiple users to run multiple processes on a single Linux server host. This should not be confused with "multiple access capability," which is what Microsoft Windows NT provides, in which multiple threads and processes run but without complete, separate user contexts.

Fully Protected Kernel Mode Operations

The Linux operating system runs all applications in fully protected mode (no process can circumvent the operating system). No user application can interfere with any other user application unless it is specifically allowed, and there is no direct access to any hardware in Linux. These are the two main problems with DOS-type operating systems, which exacerbates their vulnerability to viruses and other security problems.

Free X Window GUI

The Linux Graphical User Interface is a completely free GUI, based on an XFree86 standard version of the X Window System (most existing X-based programs will run under Linux without any modification). The X Window System has been around since the early 1980s, predating the Microsoft Windows design. You may even notice that the new look of Win9x / NT is very similar to the X Window standard that has been around for quite a bit longer.

Limited DOS / Windows Application Support or VMWare

Supplied with most versions of Linux is a DOS Emulator package called DOSEMU and a Windows Emulation package called WINE. Both of these packages provide Support for basic, "well-behaved" applications which don't try to bend any rules like directly accessing hardware or using undocumented APIs.

Another bright spot for Linux is a Virtual Machine Emulation package called VMWare. VMWare offers *full* Windows 3.*x* / 9.*x* / NT support by allowing Linux to be a host operating system with one or more of these guest operating systems installed in a virtual world, sharing with the Linux OS the local memory and hardware resources equally and at the same time. You literally can have both Linux and one or more Windows Operating Systems running at the same time on the same machine in different X Window Panes! This means you could provide either desktop to all users on the network on any relatively powerful PC (i.e., with the proper hardware: 266+ MHz, 96+ MB RAM, plus disk space). Note that VMWare offers the equivalent virtual machine product for NT. You can install Linux as a guest OS onto NT and run both desktops together from a Windows window. You can download a 30-day free trial version from www.vmware.com for either OS.

Extensive Networking Support

Perhaps the biggest selling point for most any Linux version is the extensive networking support provided. This includes native protocols and application-level support for almost all other network operating systems commonly used on PC hardware. Additionally, there is extensive media support for various types of interfaces other than standard Ethernet and Token Ring, like ISDN and even Ham Radio support.

Full native protocol support is supplied for Macintosh, DOS, Windows NT / 9*x* /3.*xx*, Novell, and OS/2 networking through various add-on packages, making Linux appear like a local native server or client to these other OS versions.

Standard Web Services

Internet services support is provided with the Apache Web server, the most dominant Web server product running http services on the Internet, as well as full versions of the latest CGI interfaces: Perl, Java, etc. Linux is an excellent Web server; Apache is a top-of-the-line Web application that has integration hooks for all the major database services using these CGI interfaces. The only Web interface not supported locally is Active Server Pages (ASP). ASP support is available via a number of third party vendors.

Standard UNIX Services

Linux supports all the standard UNIX services: e-mail, FTP, UseNet news, Telnet, POP, IRC, NFS, DNS, NIS, SNMP, Kerberos, etc., as would be expected of any Internet OS. For a much more detailed overview of what Linux is and is not, you can check out the Linux International Web site at http://www.li.org/li/index.shtml.

Why Choose Linux

Any operating system has the same basic set of requirements: reliability, security, features, and cost. When you add these together, Linux is hard to beat. Few other operating systems boast the breadth of applications, the proven track record of reliability, and the latest networking features for little or no cost. The initial software is free. The on-going costs of support and staffing are no different than normal, but someone has to install, manage, and maintain it. The total cost of ownership with Linux is very low, and, while qualified systems administrators are not always easy to find, Linux doesn't require very much attention once it is up and running.

When to Use Linux

The most common and best uses of Linux are as a router, dynamic host control protocol (DHCP), Web, file transfer protocol (ftp), database, file or print server, for almost any operating system. Then you can migrate it to desktops.

Linux is a noted firewall server with the latest security offerings of advanced packet filtering and TCP Wrappers services. Linux can provide network address translation (NAT) as well as proxy services for intranet hosts accessing the Internet more securely. With Apache and WS-FTP services, you have a very secure and robust Web and ftp site with extensive security, auditing, and management features to match, and which exceeds any other competing products on the market. Various Linux versions have created alliances with major database servers to ensure optimal integration and performance. One such alliance has been created between Red Hat and Oracle and there are others; check the home Web site of any version for the particulars.

Servers and Workstations

There is no real separation between a workstation and a server version, as Linux is still the same operating system when used in either capacity. However, Linux may be packaged and sold with those distribution assigned classifications; for example, TurboLinux Workstation version retails for less than the TurboLinux Server package. The only difference is how much and what type of software you get to install with it. A workstation usually means it includes the main Linux network services that pertain to a user and additional productivity applications like an office suite. A server version might not include these user productivity applica-

For IT Professionals

Odd Incompatibilities

In one recent class, we were working with a few local machines. They contained a common network interface card (NIC) that was assumed to work with Linux. Sadly, all this NIC did was cause frustration. A quick check of the NIC manufacturer corporate Web page gave us a glimmer of hope. The Frequently Asked Questions (FAQ) section provided a Linux-specific section with a helpful hint that required a download of their DOS Setup utility disk files. The site stated "This NIC works best when not in Plug and Play mode with Linux." The setup utility, however, did not have any way to change this status on these particular NICs, though the NIC worked fine under Windows and NT. No amount of coaxing or begging helped. It was eventually replaced by a really old 8-bit NIC that worked just fine on the first try. Just goes to show, you that you never know for sure.

The Web site did indicate that their newer NIC cards were indeed Linux-compliant, and that there were even some Linux drivers available for them. Thankfully, Linux is becoming another OS that hardware manufacturers are spending increased development time on to ensure compatiblity.

tions by default, but this would not preclude you from installing them at a later time.

If you are using your Linux host primarily as a file, print, Web, and ftp service, then this host would be considered a server. If you add an office productivity suite like Corel WordPerfect, StarOffice, or Applixware (basically all Office97 equivalents), then you have a workstation again. This "workstation" and "server" designation is more a perceived use than a restriction put on the software. Most Linux versions come with all possible applications for both server services and user applications; you get to pick and choose what you want to install every time. You can even automate the installation to a single diskette bootup that connects to a central installation service with a script identifying what disk partitions to create, of what size, and what packages should be installed. The Red Hat distribution provides the Kickstart automated installation service for multiple installations of Red Hat Linux onto similar machines.

Recommended Hardware

Linux servers run well on older equipment and are an excellent way to get added mileage out of older equipment as a firewall, file and print (nfs, SMB, Novell, Mac), or Web or ftp server. But for the desktop, last year's models are the best. You *do not* always want the latest and greatest hardware; many times they are very specific to Windows only, like WinModems. Generally speaking, name-brand peripherals or peripherals that use well-known chip sets work with Linux the best. Linux has a large following and there is usually a driver for most common equipment easily available at some Internet site.

Finding Drivers

A great place to begin looking for drivers is at the Web site of the Linux distribution; for example, www.RedHat.com, a small part of the main Red Hat Web site, or www.debian.org/distrib/ftplist, a small part of the main Debian Web site. You can also use your favorite search engine from any Web browser and type in the keywords "Linux" and "your hardware name." You should come up with a number of links to sites with drivers and maybe run down some favorites like video cards, network cards, and SCSI cards. Most sites will also include their latest hardware compatibility HOWTO for additional hints. In general, the Internet should be your best source for Linux documentation, updates, and support.

Migrating to Linux Workstations

Anytime an enterprise shifts operating systems, the change will be some-what traumatic. You may have to retrain some users in some cases. The basic GUI interface skills will remain the same, but the applications may appear different for some things, like your office suite. But if this is a dedicated database client desktop, the look and feel should be very simi-lar, and the reliability will be very high. For your end users, you may want to check out the StarOffice productivity suite supplied free from Sun Microsystems found at www.sun.com/products/staroffice/get.cgi. StarOffice comes bundled with many versions of Linux including Red Hat 6.1 and TurboLinux 4.0. You can find these and other products like the new GNU Office Suite products by visiting sites like www.slashdot.org and www.freshmeat.net for Linux community news and the latest software downloads of games, applications, patches, and upgrades in most cases for all the different Linux versions.

Distributions of Linux

There are numerous commercial and noncommercial distributions of Linux. Some of the most popular are listed in Table 1.2.

Table 1.2 A Sample List of Available Linux Distributions

Web Site	Distribution
www.caldera.com	Caldera Systems OpenLinux
www.conectiva.org	Conectiva Linux
www.debian.org	Debian GNU/Linux
www.libranet.com	Libranet
www.linux-mandrake.com	Linux Mandrake
www.linuxppc.com	LinuxPPC (PowerPC)
www.phatlinux.com	Phat Linux
www.Red Hat.com	Red Hat Linux
www.slackware.com	Slackware Linux
www.stampede.org	Stampede GNU/Linux
www.suse.de	SuSE Linux
www.turbolinux.com	TurboLinux
www.yellowdoglinux.com	Yellow Dog Linux (PPC, RS6k)

Many of these distributions are are available in different language versions. Not all versions support all possible languages, so be sure to check with the main Web site for each distribution for more details.

Quick Distribution Reviews

These reviews are not meant to replace your own testing and evaluation of the various Linux distributions but are intended to get you started in the right direction.

All versions listed run a 2.2 series kernel, provide the KDE and Gnome desktop, provide NFS and SAMBA additional network support services, and use Apache as their Web server. All versions except Corel and Mandrake provide sendmail for their e-mail services. All these versions provide some form of written documentation when you buy the product commercially, and all provide documentation in electronic format (you print it).

NOTE

The version numbers after each distribution name was current as of this document. Subsequent releases usually will use higher or longer numbers in all cases.

Debian GNU/Linux 2.1

Debian is a volunteer effort distribution of Linux of more than 500 programmers cooperating over the Internet. Debian is sponsored by VA Linux Systems Inc., O'Reilly and Associates Inc., and Silicon Graphics Inc. Its packaged price is $20 which includes a free book on learning Debian GNU/Linux and a CD-ROM with the distribution on it. If you register your copy, you can receive a free copy of StarOffice. The main Debian Web site provides unlimited access to files and support, free updates forever, free software from their archives, and even free advice!

Caldera OpenLinux 2.3

Caldera has a very slick installation that multitasks the pieces and lets you play Tetris while you wait for the package installation to finish. The list is $49 and includes tech support. Caldera also supplies many office suites such as WordPerfect, StarOffice, Koffice, and Applixware. Caldera Linux was originally derived from Red Hat and shares many features.

Turbo Linux 4.0

Turbo Linux is a solid performer with a cheap price as low as $20 (lists at $49) and a $199 server edition that includes some commercial products like BRU as well as excellent support services. This is also a Red Hat-based distribution with its own set of installation and management utilities.

Red Hat Linux 6.1

Red Hat Linux 6.1 is the preferred version with most of the market share according to almost all the surveys on Linux. The X-based installation is very slick (some details shown earlier) and includes some Red Hat specific utilities such as DiskDruid and Kickstart to name a few. Red Hat has created many alliances with the big-name PC makers and most of the big-name database vendors like Oracle and IBM's DB2. The base version is $29, but the deluxe version with a better support option is $79. Red Hat also announces new partnerships with major hardware and software vendors regularly, so you may want to keep an eye on the press releases if there's a particular vendor or software product you're interested in.

Linux Mandrake PowerPack 6.1

Mandrake is based on the Red Hat distribution with additional features and lots of additional packages at a slightly lower price ($55) than the Red Hat deluxe version ($79). Mandrake comes on six CD-ROMs which ties it with SuSE for the most CD-ROMs in any distribution listed here.

SuSE Linux 6.3

SuSE Linux 6.3 is the most popular version of Linux in Europe with a multitude of applications, desktops, and bundled name-brand software, similar to Mandrake. The tech support is above average and their installation is also GUI oriented. In addition, you get a copy of VMWare along with the StarOffice and Applixware office suites.

Database Server Roundup

As a final database-oriented roundup, Table 1.3 provides a quick overview of the main server-based Linux versions, along with the level of tech support for each and the supported database servers which are included with their distributions.

Table 1.3 Selected Linux Distribution Comparison

	Caldera	Debian	TurboLinux	RedHat	Mandrake	SuSE
Install	GUI	GUI	Text	GUI	Text	Text
System Setup	Lizard	Debian Installer	Turbocfg	linuxconf	linuxconf	Yast2
Package Installer	COAS, kpackage	Get-it, corel pkg installer	Apt-get	RPM, GnoRPM	RPM, GnoRPM	RPM, GnoRPM
Database Server	IBM DB2	Postgress SQL	IBM DB2	MySQL, Postgress SQL	MySQL	MySQL, Sybase, Informix
Tech Support	90-day phone, e-mail, Web	Web	60-day phone, e-mail, Web	30-day phone, 30/90/180-day ftp, and Web (depends on price)	100-day phone, Web	60-day phone, e-mail, Web

The following distributions were not included in the preceding review, but are worth mentioning briefly.

SPIRO-Linux

The SPIRO-Linux version is 100 percent Red Hat- and Mandrake-compatible, supports 16 languages just like the others do, and even provides Palm Pilot synchronization software. This distribution is aimed at Intel and Sun Ultra Platforms with five different server-installation configurations, three workstation configurations, as well as a custom and an upgrade option. SPIRO includes the KOffice Suite and it can import Word documents into Linux. More information can be found at www.spiro-linux.com.

Corel Linux

Corel Linux is more of a workstation version with a strong commitment to the new user with a flashy GUI-based installation utility. Corel Linux is based on the Debian distribution and includes a copy of WordPerfect 8 (not a full port of the full office suite available for Win9x/NT). Lack of included support for sendmail or any database server is not a concern as it will still support connections to any database server. You could also install PostgresSQL which is included the Debian distribution.

Considerations Before Upgrading or Migrating

Upgrading a large user client base will take resources and time. No matter how you try to tackle it, it will be a major undertaking. You will need to take into account the current state of your network, network cabling, and network bandwidth to ensure that proper performance specifications are met. Training users will be required only if their current application or applications are from a completely different database server type.

If the database server product is not going to change (for example, it remains Oracle, just on a new platform), then the applications should not have to change. If this is a new database server service, as in a migration from Access or Dbase to Oracle or Informix, then there will be a lot of training involved for the new interface and associated applications.

If you have to migrate legacy databases to this new service, you will need to retrain users accessing the relocated data with the new interfaces. Retraining users for any new or upgraded product will require resources. This is just part of any new development or improvement project. Other resources to consider include the database administration itself, user development tools, interface development, additional network bandwidth requirements, and ongoing support and help services.

For Managers

Cheap Is Still Cheap

A test system purchased a year ago that was just behind the leading edge at the time had a complete power supply failure one year and one month after going into continuous but very light-duty service. The warranty was one year. The replacement part retails for $30 but the aggravation of being down for one day was not worth the small savings for the cheap power supply used in the tower box.

In comparison, the older 200 MHz machines, which have been in continuous service for over two years have not had a power failure yet, nor have the many 100 MHz workstations purchased five years ago. You get what you pay for and there is a reason why the big, name-brand companies are selling specific server-style hardware—it is designed to last longer. It is a niche market and hence fewer are built, so the price is higher. Be prepared to purchase server quality products.

Hardware Compatibility

The first consideration should be hardware compatibility, availability, and the time needed to research the compatibility issues. You can usually check for hardware compatibility information at the main Web site of each of the distributions as illustrated in Table 1.2, earlier. In general, older is better in most cases. Extremely out and seemingly "outdated" hardware can be used in some cases for general purposes like e-mail, routing, firewall, file and print services, but the support issue of older hardware for replacement parts must be weighed against the relative cheapness of last year's model of computer, often an excellent choice to run Linux on. Linux has less overhead as an operating system and should provide more bang for the buck in optimizing older hardware.

In most cases, your database server will be dealing with mission-critical data. You want to put the best hardware you can without having to deal with finding drivers for the very latest hardware designs. You also want reliable hardware that will survive the rigors of 24 by 7 service. The under $1000 PC currently available does not have the best high-reliability parts in it and is not as likely to run 24 by 7 for more than a year or two—it is designed to last a minimal amount of time and get replaced often. The components will be inexpensive, in general.

Most name-brand server vendors today (IBM, Compaq, Dell, HP, and others) offer Linux pre-loaded on at least part of their product line. Several vendors specialize in Linux-based servers (VA Linux Systems, Cobalt Networks, and Penguin Computing to name a few). Either of these approaches can save you a lot of time and effort in getting a well-configured Linux system up and running.

Your main concern is to ensure you have enough in the way of processing power and RAM. A database server optimally should have multiple CPUs, twice the RAM you think you need, the fastest NIC possible with a direct connection to the biggest network switch available, and four times the disk you need on multiple SCSI controllers!

Test Environment

You should have a test environment consisting of at least one server machine and a few client machines. Have some knowledgeable users test the first few upgrades. Get a plan of action for training, deployment, and troubleshooting, and then stick to it. The test environment all too often is skipped to meet deadlines. Proper planning and implementation using a test environment will smooth the final rollout for all concerned.

Upgrading

There is an Upgrade Option for most Linux installations. This usually entails re-installing the newer versions of all currently installed products, including the kernel files. Any dependencies are also installed if necessary. Some distributions of Linux keep track of every package installed and where the related files are installed. This database is queried for all current packages, and any related new packages will overwrite them as well as install any new dependency packages.

NOTE

If you already have some version of Linux, you need to be aware that the Workstation installation option on some versions of Linux (like Red Hat) deletes ALL Linux partitions (and leaves any other OS partitions alone), then creates and installs everything new, whereas the Server installation on some versions of Linux (again, notably Red Hat) just wipes out ALL partitions on all drives and proceeds to install everything fresh.

Migrating from Another OS

A big question regarding any migration strategy is what to do with the old files of information. You may wish to leave it on a disk partition (FAT, FAT32, NTFS, etc.) and make it available to the Linux system. You do not have to delete the old OS or any of the file system if there is available file system space for Linux. You can even keep the old OS intact (in a dual boot configuration) until you are ready to complete the migration. This is not the recommended method for hundreds of workstations, because this may require two visits to each machine. You need to test the transition, plan it carefully, roll it out, and allow for some hiccups.

However, if this is truly to be a database server only, you do *not* need any other OS or their old files using up disk space. Convert the data and use all the available disk space on the new box for this server. Keep a backup if you want, but once you have moved on to the new service, you will most likely *not* need to access the old data.

Choosing a Distribution

Deciding on the distribution will always be a difficult decision. This may depend more on who you hire rather than what is the best known. You can use the one that suits your needs, that you have someone trained for or whichever you can download free first. If you are like most, you will probably want one that offers free and fee-based support services like Red Hat, Caldera, SuSE, Turbo Linux, or one supported by a commercial organization like Compaq, IBM, VA Linux, and others. Most commercial versions offer support of some sort. There are also support companies that are version-independent, like LinuxCare.

How to Begin the Process

Generally, you want to devise a plan, get your people on board, carefully test your plan, and then keep to it. The assumption is that you already have a project that you are working on that requires a dedicated database server. As discussed earlier, Linux is an excellent choice for that underlying server. You should include in your plan some testing of the database server as early in the development phase as possible. Do not let the procurement of the hardware be a last minute or rash decision—plan ahead. Hardware changes daily, and new releases of Linux occur semi-annually in many cases. If this is a really big project, go to the big hardware vendors and let them show you their hardware running with Linux on it. Test bed your initial designs with them and get a feel for what you will need long term.

How to Get Your People Started

There are many training companies that provide brand-name training such as Global Knowledge Inc., found at www.globalknowledge.com. Others include the training offered by the Linux distributions themselves. Doing a search for "Linux Training" on any Web search engine will provide many listings for organizations like www.linuxtraining.org, www.learningtree.com, www.linuxsystemsgroup.com.

Proper training of the users, and of the support and administrative staff cannot be overemphasized. Understand too that, just because a course title begins with "Introduction to . . ." (some with no prerequisites), you cannot send just anyone into the course as a student. Any big corporate training company is going to offer very high-level courses—even the introductory courses are going to begin at a fairly advanced level.

Issues to Present to Your Manager

Cost. No doubt about it, zero operating system licensing cost is a big advantage. When calculating licensing costs for competing platforms, be sure to calculate the licensing costs for clients that utilize that server, and the license cost of future upgrades. They can be tremendously expensive for some other operating systems. But zero licensing cost does not mean there is no support; commercial support is available. The big names in computer manufacturers are starting to offer their PCs preconfigured with Linux, usually Red Hat. This is a big plus in favor of using Linux if companies like Compaq, Dell, and IBM are deciding to support Linux on their hardware.

Reliability. There is almost never a reason to reboot Linux; drivers and applications can be reloaded anytime. Most Internet server operating systems are powered by Linux and other UNIX-style operating systems because they are extremely reliable. UNIX dominates the high-end market for production servers and high-end graphics workstations because it has the reliability and resilience to keep going.

Security. Another reason for the strength of Linux and Unix on the Internet is their mature and robust security model. The kernel is well protected from direct access by any user, and the file system is designed to be secure and has been proven secure for years on the Internet. Most security breaches are not from weaknesses that the average or even above average user would be able to exploit in any operating system—it comes from poor security practices of the users. Win98 has no real security built-in. Linux has security built into the file system and available on every file.

Doing a Proper Cost Analysis

You need to do a proper cost analysis of bringing in another operating system into your network, the support needed (staff training; client training should be minimal), integration issues (few if any), interface issues (different type of window interface but same basic concepts), and cost savings.

You will need to provide test resources, training resources, retraining resources, and helpdesk resources long-term with any operating system. By using a reliable, secure, and powerful operating system like Linux, you can cut down on some resource drain.

Summary

The phenomenon that is Linux is here to stay. The grassroots feelings that center around Linux, and the new ease of installation and integration make Linux a very attractive product. It is a robust alternative to any Windows operating system as long as you remember it is NOT Windows per se. Linux is at home in the server arena as well as in the desktop environment. Keep in mind that Linux is a version of UNIX, and you will need someone with UNIX or Linux experience to manage it. The interface is very similar to Windows but not exactly the same in all cases, but there is nothing you can do in Windows that you cannot do in Linux. There are plenty of user-type applications available for Linux that do all the same functions, albeit differently at times. The main benefits are the cost, reliability, and security that Linux offers as an operating system, not to mention the steady increase in support from the big players on the block like Oracle, Informix, IBM, Sun, Dell, Compaq, and many more.

FAQs

Q: Will I lose access to Windows?

A: Yes and no. Yes, you can if you want to, and no, you do not have to if you do not want to. This will be made more evident in the installation section. Basically, you can add Linux as an alternate operating system to most any PC without losing the current configuration if you have available, unused disk space. You can also decide to remove all traces of any other operating system if you desire and use this machine with Linux only. Realistically speaking, you want to eliminate any other operating system on the database server. You would not be utilizing your disk space in having more than one when only one can run at any one time (except in the case of running VMWare—VMWare is best used on a work station rather than a server because of the overhead of running two operating systems at once).

Q: Do I need to keep Windows?

A: Yes, if you absolutely cannot live without it. No, if you want to move on or if this machine is for development. Like any operating system, you can always rebuild it later. In general, for a database server, you should only use one.

Q: How do I make it dual (triple, quadruple, etc.) boot with my current operating system(s)?

A: Remember, unless this is a development system, you do not need nor want to have two operating systems on a machine that will be a server. However, during installation, you can elect to have the system add a dual boot feature using **lilo**, or you can add the Linux boot to almost every known boot manager for the Intel-based PC.

Q: Can it run Microsoft Office 97?

A: Not really, as it is not native. By using an emulator, like WINE, you may be able to get some or all of Office97 to run. You can use one of the many alternates that are similar but *not exactly* the same, like StarOffice or WordPerfect. Each of these can read and write the Office97 format on most documents.

Q: What about support?

A: For support, start by thinking about who supports you now. Find someone similar, just like you did when you first started with Win9*x* or Win NT. Give someone a chance to shine, promote from within, or ask for a volunteer. You may actually find someone who is already playing with it at home or used it in school. Support is available free via news services and user groups on the Internet, and paid commercial support is available from many organizations. See the vendors listed in Table 1.3.

Q: How do I remove Linux?

A: Technically, you just need to repartition the disk, make one of the new partitions active, transfer some OS-like DOS to this active partition, and then reboot. Voilà, Linux is gone forever. You can do this to any operating system on a PC to get the same result.

If you left Windows 9*x* on, then you can use a Win 9*x* boot disk, and run the command:

```
A:> FDISK /MBR
```

This will eliminate the **lilo** bootup and automatically start Windows 9*x* again. You can then repartition or reformat any previous Linux partitions to be FAT format.

If you left NT on another partition, it is a little harder to rebuild the NT MBR but you can do it by using the rescue option and forcing NT to rewrite the MBR block.

Q: What applications run on Linux?

A: Lots of applications are out there somewhere on the Internet. As far as most Linux distributions are concerned, the applications must be specifically Linux-oriented, just like Windows 9*x*/NT applications must run on their own platforms. There are several thousand products available for the Linux OS that are just not sold via (Windows-based) PC magazines, mostly because they are free, so there are no advertisements. You look them up on the Internet or you can look for commercial versions advertised in your favorite magazine or Web search engine. Are you aware that all the big server services run on Linux-like database managers, network management, firewalls, Web services, e-mail services, and so on.

Q: I have never installed an operating system, is it difficult?

A: Anything can be difficult without the proper knowledge or tools. Linux has been made as user friendly as any installation out there, with a lot less advertising as well. Put the CD-ROM in your machine and power up. Most new machines will start the installation automatically, while others need to be started manually. Even then, it is not that hard. Chapter 2 will cover the installation of Red Hat 6.1 in detail.

Q: Do I have to know something about UNIX to use Linux?

A: Yes, I'm afraid so. Although the GUI world of windows is nice, it is only one method of management. And management is the difference between all versions of operating systems. You need to get a clear idea of how UNIX/Linux does something before you can tackle the problem. Once you know the basics, you can hunt and peck with the best of them.

## Chapter 2

A Basic Red Hat Linux Installation

Solutions in this chapter:

- **Introduction**

- **Preliminary Installation Decisions**

- **Installing Red Hat**

- **Custom (Manual) Installation**

- **Other Flavors of Linux**

Introduction

This chapter will introduce the basic concepts you need to know to install any Linux distribution, and will specifically use specific examples from a Red Hat Installation. Linux distributions usually provide a plethora of utilities and products; you must decide which you need and which you do not. Many include a free or sample version of a database server.

Linux is also a server of many network and productivity services so you must decide how you will use this server before you plan your installation. Technically, you can run any combination of the following services: dynamic host control protocol (DHCP), Domain Name Server (DNS), ftp, a database product such as Oracle (not supplied with most distributions), or the PostgrsSQL server (free version supplied with some versions of Linux). You can do all of these services from one physical machine or you can spread them out to any combination of machines you want.

NOTE

The screen shots used in this chapter were obtained during an installation of Linux onto a host NT 4.0 machine using VMWare. They are for illustrative purposes; be aware that the title bars such as those in Figure 2.2, Figure 2.3, and others which follow, do not appear during the installation.

Separate Physical Machine

Naturally, a separate server for your database is highly recommended. This provides the best responsiveness, security, and reliability. Most common database applications are very complex in design and are very CPU-, memory-, and disk-intensive. You do not want your database server competing for CPU cycles or disk I/O with any other services (Web, ftp, file, and print, for example), as this would greatly reduce the performance of all services in general.

By separating the database service, you are also better able to secure the system from intrusion, and keep the data and its backups completely separate and secure from other processes. The general types of system attacks are mostly in standard network services. If you keep these services on another machine, intruders are unlikely to be able to get to your database server. Even the administrative passwords should be different between these systems for additional security against intruders who do breach one of the other servers on your network.

Choosing a Distribution of Linux

Next to consider is which distribution version of Linux to use. There are many to choose from; they will all probably support any database certified on Linux to some extent, but the more commercial versions will probably already have a support service or an alliance with the database product company already. Red Hat has support for many database vendor products such as Oracle, and from such hardware vendors as Dell, Compaq, and IBM to name a few.

Preliminary Installation Decisions

Your project should be designed with every step in mind. In this section, you will be introduced to some of the basic topics you should plan for before the installation takes place. This includes the performance levels you want for now and the future, and will lead to the hardware and software decisions prior to the actual installation.

The most critical part of the server is the various hardware aspects as outlined in the next few sections. This would be true no matter what operating system you decided to use.

Hardware

Although it may sound odd in this period of cheap home computers, the big-name server vendors are big because their high-end servers are just that—designed to run 24x7, with fail-over features and easy maintenance and serviceability features. This is where you need to spend some time and get a machine that can handle extended periods of high I/O, run lots of processes simultaneously, move lots of data between disk and memory and from memory to CPU, keep most processes memory resident, and have some form of hardware RAID for fail-over contingencies. Make sure your new system can be expanded easily in the areas of disk controllers, disk drive bays, and RAM.

Multiple CPUs

Database servers need lots of CPU power. The cheap processors can be run in parallel to provide amazing throughput and peak load levels. Although you do not get 100 percent of each additional CPU, the added benefit of keeping everything in local memory outweighs the additional cost for the server that supports multiple CPUs.

RAM

The most critical factor after deciding on the CPU (or CPUs) is the amount of RAM—you need to get a lot. You should do a preliminary analysis of the expected database needs and add a reasonable extra margin. A reasonable minimal amount of RAM to start with is probably 256MB for most basic databases.

Disks

The next most important feature is the disk subsystem. Multiple controllers provide better throughput and Redundant Array of Independent Disks (RAID) level 5, Disk Striping with Parity, provides even better performance in many but not all instances. In some cases, especially with databases, RAID level 0, Disk Striping without Parity, and RAID level 1, Disk Mirroring, are the recommended options. One more thing to note is the cost associated with each of these RAID levels as discussed in the next section on RAID.

In absolute terms you do not need RAID—any good quality, high-speed disks with lots of on-board cache will do. As long as you have an adequate backup and the down time to recover is not too expensive to your business, you can use anything you want. Just remember that if your server is your order entry system and it goes down, everyone waits until it is up again—*everyone*, including your staff and your clients. Can you really afford not to have it up? Measure the meager cost of the hardware against the possible revenue losses and you will probably want to go for some form of RAID that offers easy recoverability if not assured 24x7 availability.

RAID

RAID level 1, Mirroring, is a good option for your system disks, where your operating system resides. Your database files should be on separate disks entirely from the OS and should be hardware RAID 5 to get the best throughput and reliability.

Cost of RAID

The most expensive RAID level is 1. In this case, if two disks of the same size are used, you end up with only the space of one for your system; the other is a duplicate. This is a 50 percent realized utilization of the two disks. If three disks are used for mirroring, then you effectively get 33 percent as only one disk is actually available—in essence, the other two are just duplicates of the first one.

With RAID 0, you get 100 percent realized utilization of the disks with usually improved read and write speeds. This is because all disk space is available but there is *no recovery*. If any one disk fails, they all are lost and you must rebuild them all and then recover all data back to all disks. This is *not recommended* for mission-critical data, but could be used for scratch and temporary data. Alternatively, a set of hardware RAID services underneath providing the multiple disks is an acceptable option. You can use this software RAID 0 to combine them into one really big disk as far as the server is concerned.

RAID level 5 effectively uses the space on one of the disks (on a rotating basis throughout all the disks in the RAID group) to provide a parity block that is used to regenerate the data missing by the loss of any one disk at a time. Only one disk can fail at any one given time and must be recovered before any other disk fails; usually, there are exceptions. The minimum is three disks, the maximum is 32, depending on the operating system used. With three disks, you effectively get two of the three for 67 percent utilization. With four disks, you get three of four for 75 percent, four of five for 80 percent, and so on until the best utilization is 31 of 32 for about 96 percent realized utilization with built-in recoverability. This is the recommended solution for mission-critical data.

Hardware or Software RAID

Linux does provide for software-based RAID levels 1 and 5. This is an excellent option if the hardware solution is not chosen. This is implemented with two and three minimum disks, respectively, and with **mdrecoverd** daemon service. You can select entire disks or just similar-sized partitions to implement the RAID sets. The setup is clearly outlined in the HOWTO-RAID documentation.

Network Interface(s)

A network interface will be another bottleneck in your system. The bigger the *pipe* (data throughput rate), the better. The slowest part of any system is the disk drive system. It runs in milliseconds of average seek time, the system memory runs in nanoseconds, and the network falls in the middle, usually at microseconds. Get 100 megabit cards and a switch instead of a hub, or get two network interface cards (NICs) to two separate hubs if possible and spread the load. After the disk system, this is the next bottleneck to contend with in getting data between your server and your clients.

Backup Issues

The biggest tape drive gets bigger every month. A good top-of-the-line but basic single-tape backup can back up a maximum of about 80GB. Get at least 2GB, for redundancy and speed. There are many options for backup other than tape drives; for example, CD-R, CD-RW, DVD-ROM, and Jaz disks, which may offer better availability than tapes at a slightly higher cost. You can also go for the newest disk management systems that offer data migration from high-need RAM disks, to medium-need disk drives, to low-need CD-ROM or Jaz-type disks, to rarely needed archive levels on tape, all in one big system that appears to your machine as just one big disk. This is a truly awesome product for availability of your data to the server. Tapes are the traditional way, but you can buy two Jaz disks or you can buy another 6–10GB of disk drive (and this is constantly growing), which has a much higher recovery time. Stick these disks on another server and use them as backup media—fast to back up and fast to recover, and cheaper. If the other server is off-site, you also have disaster recovery built–in, depending on distance. Check out all your options before proceeding, remembering that recovery time is a truly important aspect of your decision. Also, don't forget to verify your backups and to test your recovery procedures.

Support Issues

Every big hardware vendor and many Linux vendors make a vast majority of their income by providing support services to companies like yours. You pay a premium price for a premium product and most would agree it is worth the extra cost.

TIP

A variety of support services are available for different versions of Linux.

- If you purchased either the Deluxe or Professional official products, Red Hat offers 180 days free ftp support, 90 days web-based support, and 30 days of installation phone support.
- Debian GNU/Linux provides unlimited access to their Web and ftp support sites.
- Purchasers of TurboLinux get 60 days of technical support.

Installation Preliminaries

For a development machine, you could simply add some extra disk to an existing machine and then install Linux onto that extra disk, set the system for dual bootup, and then reboot into whichever OS you prefer. This is a common scenario for many administrators that want to try it first, prove it under a simulated load, and then deploy it to the field.

For a real, full-time, dedicated mission-critical server, you need to dedicate the machine to the serving of the database and, preferably, nothing else.

Installing Red Hat

Red Hat Linux is the single largest distribution, and several other leading distributions are derived from it to varying degrees. Red Hat was one of the first commercial versions of the Linux distribution that offered support services and added additional user-friendly features and will be covered here for the above reasons.

A Quick Installation Run-Through

Insert the CD-ROM marked #1 into a bootable CD-ROM drive and reboot your machine. You will see your system carry out its normal sequence that includes hardware peripheral identification, memory test, and basic systems check.

At this point, your CD-ROM or diskette will begin the boot process. If your system does not detact and boot off the CD-ROM at this point, you will need to tell your BIOS setup to add the CD-ROM first in its boot sequence; and, for some older machines, you may need to use a boot floppy to start the process.

After the initial files have been loaded into memory, you are presented with a Red Hat welcome screen and four options (not shown here). Press **Enter** at this point to continue with the installation. You could type **Text** to go to a text mode installation, but that is not covered here specifically; although the questions asked are identical, the interface is different. Figure 2.1 shows the typical output from the initial startup of a Linux kernel.

Figure 2.1 Typical Linux startup (after preliminary startup screen).

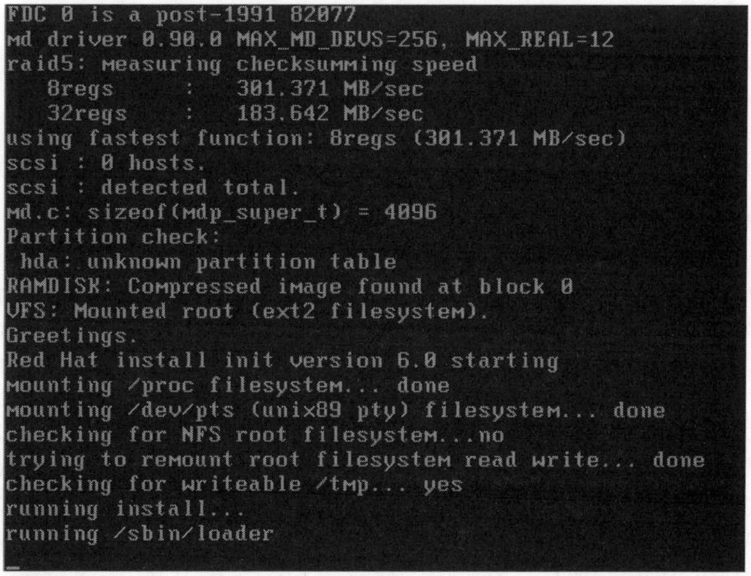

```
FDC 0 is a post-1991 82077
md driver 0.90.0 MAX_MD_DEVS=256, MAX_REAL=12
raid5: measuring checksumming speed
   8regs     :    301.371 MB/sec
   32regs    :    183.642 MB/sec
using fastest function: 8regs (301.371 MB/sec)
scsi : 0 hosts.
scsi : detected total.
md.c: sizeof(mdp_super_t) = 4096
Partition check:
 hda: unknown partition table
RAMDISK: Compressed image found at block 0
VFS: Mounted root (ext2 filesystem).
Greetings.
Red Hat install init version 6.0 starting
mounting /proc filesystem... done
mounting /dev/pts (unix89 pty) filesystem... done
checking for NFS root filesystem...no
trying to remount root filesystem read write... done
checking for writeable /tmp... yes
running install...
running /sbin/loader
```

The installation will test for X Window-compliant hardware and will then start an interactive X-based GUI setup. The GUI setup will first display the Red Hat logo and name before proceeding.

The first step in the installation is the language selection as depicted in Figure 2.2. Notice that Linux can be installed with many language variations. Note also that the CD-ROM provided in the USA *does not* contain the other language setups; you actually would need to get the files from either the Red Hat Web/ftp site or order the language-specific CD-ROM version.

Figure 2.2 Select a language.

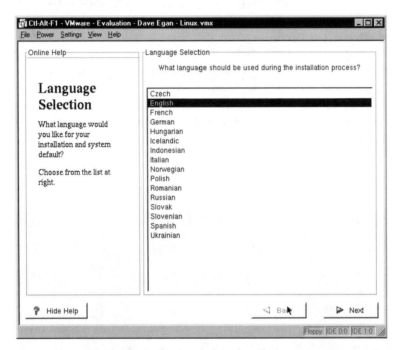

The next screen combines what used to be three separate text mode screens into one screen, where you can select everything about your keyboard and mouse. Notice that Linux has detected the basic hardware for your system as shown in Figure 2.3, as well as in many subsequent screens.

Figure 2.4 shows the Mouse selection option. Linux prefers a 3-button mouse. However, you probably have a 2-button mouse so you want to change the selection to a 2-button mouse of the same type, either bus (also known as PS/2—it has a small-as-a-pencil connector), or the serial mouse (9-pin connector).

NOTE

You need to select the right mouse settings since the X Window system prefers three buttons. You simulate the middle button by pressing the other two buttons together as one event.

Figure 2.3 Keyboard selection.

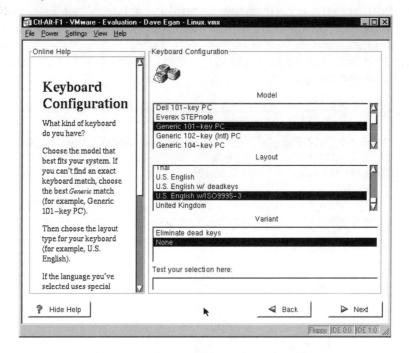

Figure 2.4 Mouse selection: 2-button, auto-selects emulate 3-button.

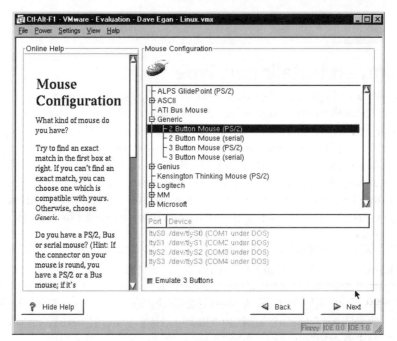

The next screen to appear again has the Red Hat logo. This indicates you are about to set up your software and the related choices of disk partitions, if needed. You have the option at this point to go back and make changes if necessary.

Figure 2.5 Installation type.

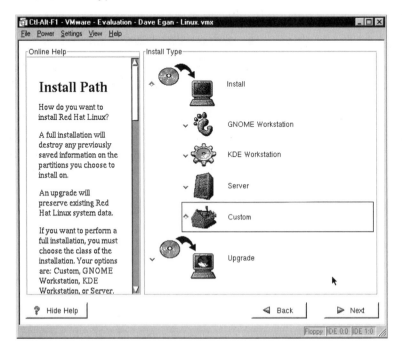

Choosing an Installation Type

The Installation Type, as shown in Figure 2.5, is *very important*. This is when you are asked to make a big decision about how to install your Linux. For Red Hat, you have three basic options: Server, Custom, or the two versions of Workstation, either with Gnome or KDE desktops. A fourth option, *Upgrade*, is chosen only if you already have an earlier version of the same Linux version on this machine. You cannot upgrade any other version of Linux except an earlier version of the same Linux; in this case, you could upgrade only an earlier version of Red Hat Linux.

A Workstation Installation

The workstation options may be sufficient mainly for your clients or your test machine; they are not recommended for a real server. They will install a base Linux for you with an X Window interface of either Gnome or KDE. They are predefined to partition available disk space into three partitions and to install everything into the biggest partition of the three. If you were to add disks after this, you technically could use this choice. If you had lots of disk space, you could create a development machine with this and install your database onto this one big partition or onto another disk, your choice. By default, if there were another OS on this machine, it would be retained automatically and offered as an optional bootup choice (albeit not displayed, you just have to know it is there). This is not the recommended installation type for your server.

A Server Installation

The server installation is another possible choice, as it does a much better job of partitioning the disk into a more desirable management-oriented design. It also installs a lot of server software and *does not* install the X Window system by default. This installation also removes all previous operating system partitions of any type, creates six partitions with minimal sizes for most, and then installs all the server packages and few of the user packages. For ease of getting started with a Linux-based server offering all the network services ready to go, this is the easiest option for a new machine. Make sure you have lots of extra space for your database application and its data.

The Upgrade Installation

The upgrade installation is obviously intended only for a system that already contains a previous version of Red Hat. This is not applicable to any other version of Linux. Upgrades only replace the currently installed software sets with the newer versions plus any new dependency-related software sets.

A Custom Installation

The custom installation is the best choice for someone who knows exactly what he or she wants. You can implement a specific design for your disks—what size partitions on what disks, then define the directory location for each of these partitions in your file system—and finally, you can decide on the software sets you want to install.

Custom (Manual) Installation

The remaining steps assume you are following a *custom installation* procedure, and take you through each of the basic steps with helpful hints and suggestions. This is the recommended installation method for a database server, so that you can select the additional services you need. It is highly recommended *not* to include any other services on your database server. Of course, if you have no other server for them, or if this will not be a heavily burdened server, then you can add them during this installation process easily and quickly.

Creating the Partitions to Your Specifications

The next step provides a graphical disk partition and assignment tool called *Disk Druid*. Unfortunately, this tool is available only during installation. When the system is running, you can use the **fdisk** utility to perform partition changes, but not the partition to directory assignments.

WARNING

As a database server, the separation of the data into distinct partitions will provide for better overall management later on. You are encouraged to keep the system files and database files on separate partitions.

For IT Professionals

Disk and Memory Issues

Technically, you can use FAT16 and FAT32 formatted drives with Linux, but this would be a poor choice for a database server. The optimal type of file system is the Linux Native for all data drives. You also need disk space allocated to swap drives. You can have a maximum of 4GB of swap space spread across eight partitions with any one partition not to exceed 2GB in size. The recommendation is to have two to three times your RAM size as swap. This is a good rule of thumb until you get up into the gigabytes of RAM. You are unlikely to swap at this point and even less likely to swap out all 2GB of RAM. There are exceptions, for example, if you have really big single processes configured like big resident database files, then you need the large amount of swap. If you are more designed toward smaller transaction oriented processes, then you can have less total swap space. Remember, if you have big processes in memory, disk is cheap, use it for swap. At this point, stick to two to three times the RAM until you can do some system analysis.

Multiple Swap Partitions

Swap is where the system puts certain memory-resident process sets when RAM becomes full. You need it for the system to work properly but you really *do not* want the system to use it because it is incredibly slow compared to RAM. It is there for emergencies when your RAM is overwhelmed, and it is fine for occasional use. Steady use is a clear indication that you do not have enough RAM. Upgrade immediately if you detect or notice extensive use of swap space. Since any disk activity is improved by spreading the requests out over multiple disks or controllers, the same goes for swap space—spread it out to improve performance and spread the load out to all disks evenly.

Delete a Partition

You would delete a partition if you were starting with a machine that may already have had an operating system on it. If you want to start fresh, that is, you do not need to keep this OS, then delete every partition you see. If you want to keep the old OS and just add Linux to some free space or reuse a disk partition that is free to use, you should delete the old partition first.

You can delete any currently existing partition on any disk at this point within Disk Druid. Select the partition in the upper box and then click **Delete** and confirm the action.

Edit a Partition

You can change a partition parameter setting at a later time if desired by using the **Edit** option.

Add a Partition

Click the **Add** button to add a new partition. You will need to do this for each partition you want to set up. If there is more than one physical disk, you should select the specific disk in the lower box first.

Partition Mount Point

When you click **Add**, you are presented with a parameter setting screen. There are four parameters to set. The first parameter is the mount point. Unlike DOS-based systems that define a **drive letter** for each partition (currently, this is changing in Microsoft Windows 2000), in UNIX and Linux, there is one file system that uses directory names to connect them together. These directories are called *mount points*. UNIX has had some historical mount points that Linux has continued with. You can either enter a directory name of your choice or pick from one of the preconfigured directory names in the drop-down list. Figure 2.6 shows the preconfigured mount point options available. This is not a limitation, just a beginning point.

Figure 2.6 Mount point options in Disk Druid.

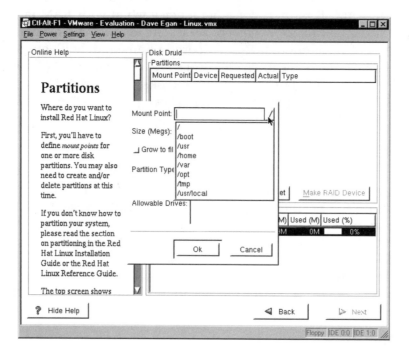

Size of Partition

The second parameter to decide on is the size. You should enter the approximate value you want the partition to be in megabytes. Note that the actual size will depend on physical drive characteristics (sizes are rounded to the nearest disk cylinder) and and may vary by a few megabytes from the sizes you specified.

The size option also has a radio button that you can use to let the partition size "Grow to fill disk." This option will allow this partition to use all available remaining disk space or share equally with any other partitions on the same physical disk, all the remaining disk space. This is a great option on the last partition created or on multiple partitions where you want to share all remaining disk space. This option always uses all remaining disk space. You can put any value in the Size parameter box if you select this Grow button. Disk Druid will deal with the real size when it actually does the partitioning after you have finished configuring all partitions (this is all done in memory; nothing actually will be created until you finish with this screen). Figure 2.7 illustrates the Size value field as well as the Grow to fill disk radio button.

NOTE

The X Window system uses colored buttons instead of the Windows checkmark. If the button appears dark (appears to be pushed in), then it is deemed to be **on**, or selected. Figure 2.7 illustrates the **off** position, light colored, for the Grow to fill disk? option.

Figure 2.7 Disk Druid—Partition type selection options.

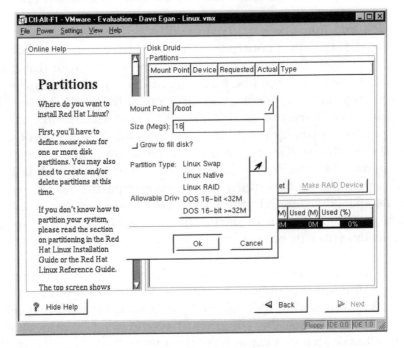

Partition Type

Other than the swap partitions requiring you to set them as Linux Swap, you should *always* pick Linux Native for all other partitions that you create. *Do not* choose any DOS partitions; they are not optimized for data-base files in any way.

WARNING

Linux Native is a very fast file system, well-optimized for data files. Linux can use DOS, HPFS, NTFS, and other types of partitions, but not in an optimized fashion. Avoid them all—you *do not* need them. However, several new, even higher performance, file systems are being developed for Linux and should be considered when they are ready; these include Ext3, Reiserfs, and XFS.

Hard Drive Selection

The hard drive option is an issue *only* if you have more than one physical drive to choose from. If your system has a single IDE drive available, it will be called **hda** (hard disk a). This would be the name for the first hard drive on the IDE type first controller. The next drive would be **hdb** on the same IDE controller. On the second IDE controller, the first drive would be **hdc** and the second would be **hdd**. On each of these drives the partitions are simply numbered from 1 to 16. Hence, the partition the DOS world would usually refer to as **C:** on the first partition, Linux calls **hda1**. The next partition primary partitions would be **hda2**, then **hda3**, and **hda4**. However, due to the original bizarre partition scheme design, there is one designated Extended primary partition, and it can be **hda2**, **hda3**, or **hda4**, depending on how many other primary partitions already exist. Within this special Extended primary partition, you can create up to 12 additional partitions. These 12 partitions start as **hda5** and go to **hda16**. So, technically, you can have up to 16 partitions on any one physical IDE drive.

For a SCSI disk, the moniker is **sda** for the drive; the partitions are **sda1** to **sda15** (supports only 11 partitions within the extended drive).

Figure 2.8 shows what a completed partition table with respective mount points would look like when you have finished creating and assigning all disk space to various partitions.

TIP

You need to create partitions for management purposes. There is a very valid set of reasons in a secure operating system for splitting the disk drive into these smaller partitions: ease of management; ease of recovery of just what failed, not everything; selective backup levels; selective auditing and disk quota management; and security policy implementations.

Figure 2.8 Completed partition table example.

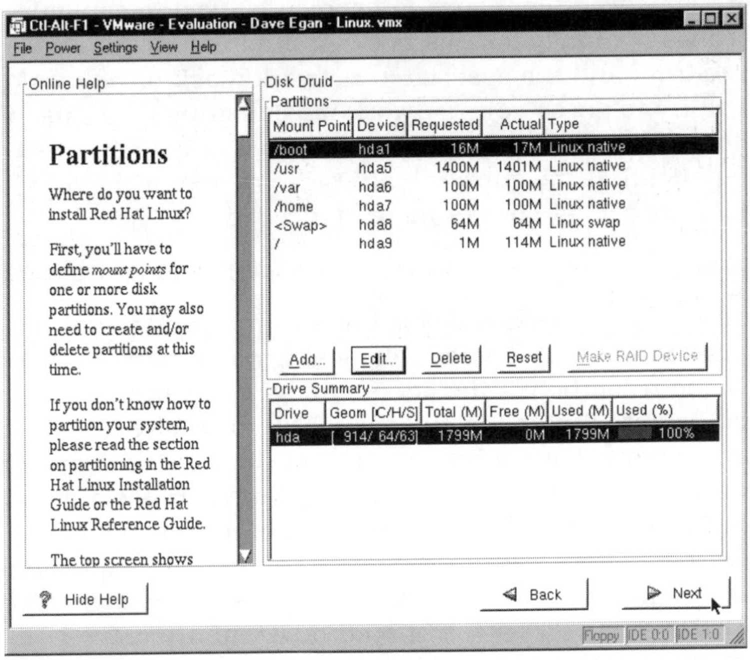

Network Setup

Linux, like UNIX, is centered around the TCP/IP protocol suite. This is the main network protocol and needs to be configured accordingly. You have the option of selecting each network adapter that was discovered and configuring all parameters for each card separately. On a single network adapter machine, as depicted in Figure 2.9, the first network card is called **eth0**.

Using DHCP

The first option button when configuring a network adapter is the choice to use DHCP (Dynamic Host Configuration Protocol) to configure all TCP/IP related information automatically from a central DHCP server service that can be running on any other OS, as long as it is RFC-compliant.

Activate on Boot

The second option button when configuring a network adapter is the choice to activate this network adapter on boot. If this is the only network adapter, this will be selected for you. If this is an interface that is dial-in or dial-out oriented, you may not want it to activate on bootup. You can make this a demand-activated service, but that is beyond the scope of this installation.

Not Using DHCP

The rest of the network configuration screen is used to configure the TCP/IP settings manually for this host. At a minimum, you need to supply the IP address and the associated network mask or *netmask*. The interface will try to guess your network mask setting if you use the **Tab** key to go to the next field (it may pause a short time to do this calculation, so be patient). If the guessed values are correct, you can simply move to the next field or correct them as needed.

Hostname

The hostname is just a reference for this machine and is not necessarily the same name used to reference this host from anywhere else on the network. Name resolution is the act of changing a name to an IP address. Linux uses the **/etc/hosts** file and then DNS to resolve a host name to an IP address before doing a broadcast. But the local naming scheme is neither shared nor specific; every other machine can use any name it wishes locally for the IP address of your machine. Only when you use a central service like DNS are you restricted to a specific name, and even this can be circumvented. In summary, this hostname does not have to be unique on the network, but it should be if you are using DNS.

Figure 2.9 shows a completed setup for one network adapter card with manually entered IP information, hostname, gateway, and DNS (Domain Name Service, often just "Name Service") entries.

Figure 2.9 Network configuration.

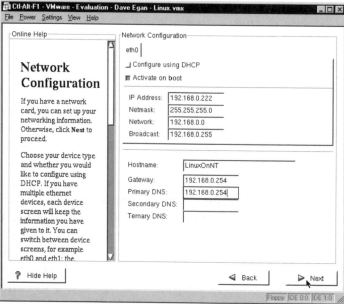

Time Zone Selection

Although there are many cute things in Linux, this has to be one of the nicer ones. All the little yellow dots you see represent city names, few of which are common. Not only that, but if you move your cursor over the map, a little green arrow appears, as depicted in Figure 2.10, that shows the closest named spot to that location with a known time zone, such as Gambier Islands in the southern Pacific Ocean. If nothing else, you can get a quick geography lesson before you move on.

Figure 2.10 System time configuration.

root Account Configuration

Every distribution of Linux has one special account, usually denoted as *root*, which is sometimes referred to as *superuser*. The root account has permission to do anything on a Linux or UNIX system, at least in theory. You must configure the password. On some Linux versions, you also are given an opportunity to install any other users you may wish to include. For instance, with Red Hat Linux, you can easily add one or more additional users during the installation, as shown in Figure 2.11. You do not have to add another user but it is *highly* recommended that you create one un-privilege account (i.e., other than the root) for day-to-day work on a workstation. You *should not* be root while doing basic user tasks! Mistakes made as root can destroy crucial files or compromise the security or stability of the system.

Figure 2.11 Configure *root* and additional accounts (at least one).

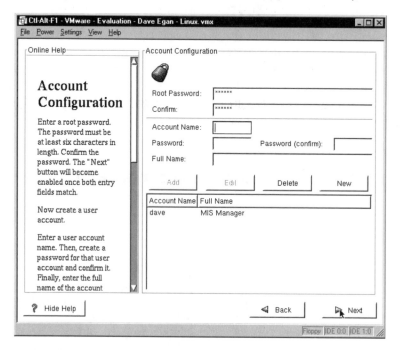

Authentication

The login on most any Linux or UNIX host can be validated locally or remotely with a centralized service like NIS or NIS+, as shown in Figure 2.12. With either authentication method, you can also include additional security settings like MD5 and the use of shadow passwords, both of which are *highly* recommended. The MD5 is a more secure and integrated form of password; the shadow password is actually an improved security scheme for UNIX and Linux password files. Normally UNIX and Linux keep each user-account setup information in a file that is readable by all users. With shadow passwords turned on, some of the more important aspects of this information is stored in a file that is not readable by the entire world, usually called **/etc/shadow**, but this is completely configurable.

Using NIS or NIS+

The standard UNIX- and Linux-based centralized *domain* login is provided by a service currently called Network Information Service (NIS), or the more current version from Sun Microsystems Inc. called NIS-PLUS (NIS+). Only Sun provides NIS+ servers. Linux has a compliant client.

NIS provides a centralized set of user management data files (analogous to the PDC in Microsoft Windows NT) to be duplicated to slave NIS servers (the BDC in NT) that validate logins from NIS-based clients (the NT LOGON through Netlogon). Figure 2.12 shows the NIS settings with no information provided (the default). You would need to know the NIS Domain name and you could use either a broadcast to find the nearest slave NIS server, or just enter the IP address if you know it.

Figure 2.12 Authentication configuration.

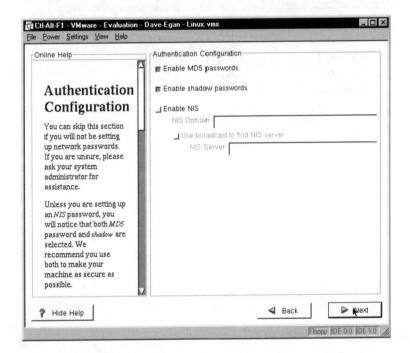

Package Selection

There are many packages from which to select. A package represents all the files associated with one product or a major component of a product. For example, the Apache Web server package contains all the programs and support files for this application. The packages are in the RPM (RPM Package Manager) format. This was developed by Red Hat and is available for all Linux versions to use.

The Basic Packages

The basic packages that represent the Linux operating system are pre-selected and not changeable when you get to your first installation screen. You can deselect any of the packages listed that are not needed, or add any you may want to include (see Figure 2.13). You do not necessarily need any other packages if you are planning on installing the database server; however, it would be a good idea to read the database installation documentation to see if certain packages are needed, like the language development services (C, C++, development libraries, etc.) for your database system to use at any time.

Figure 2.13 Package configuration.

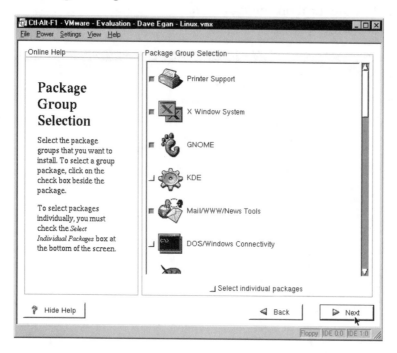

Optional Services to Install

There are many optional user, network, and productivity services to install. Table 2.1 contains the names of the packages that appear in the Package Configuration screen. Some of their basic contents are detailed along with an indicator for whether they are recommended (Yes), maybe recommended (M), or not recommended (n/N) for a real database server.

NOTE

The order presented in Table 2.1 matches the displayed order from the screen you will encounter, shown in Figure 2.13. Further grouping of these packages, suggested options to install, and basic details of the package sets are provided in Table 2.1.

Table 2.1 Red Hat Optional Installation Packages

Client/User Applications		
Printer Support	m	Local printer driver support
X Window System	m	Base system, needs Gnome or KDE too
Gnome	n	Desktop for X, needs base
KDS	n	Desktop for X, needs base
Mail/WWW/News Tools	n	Browsers
DOS/Windows Connectivity	n	Emulators and tools
Graphics Manipulation	n	Screen capture, manipulate, etc.
Games	N	Lots
Multimedia Support	N	Sound, video, etc.
Networked Workstation	Yes	Client network tools
Dialup Workstation	M1	Client tools
Network Server Services		
News Server	N	NNTPD
NFS Server	N	UNIX file and print sharing
SMB (Samba) Server	N	Win/NT file and print sharing
IPX/Netware Connectivity	N	Netware file and print services
Anonymous FTP Server	N	File transfer protocol (for Web)
Web Server	M2	Apache Web server
DNS Name Server	N	BIND 8 (for Internet/Intranet)
PostgreSQL Server	M3	Database server ** (free!)
Development Packages		
Network Management Station	Yes	SNMP and tools
TeX Document Formatting	N	Typesetting, publishing
Emacs	N	The ultimate editor environment
Development	M4	Compilers and libraries
Kernel Development	M5	To Rebuild kernel
Extra Documentation	Yes	HOWTOs, extra docs, info command
Utilities	Yes	More system stuff

The Optional Features

Here are some of the optional features and programs available that you may want to consider during your installation.

M1. Dialup networking may be useful for remote dial-in diagnostics and maintenance.

M2. With the Web server installed, you may be able to manage your system from a Web interface, but this is completely up to you or the application you install.

M3. If you do not want to purchase a SQL-compliant type database server application, you can use the free one called Postgres.

M4. You may be required to compile some aspects of your new database server application and you may need the development applications; check your documentation.

M5. The default kernel that most Linux installations use when you first install may not be optimized for your hardware.

TIP

To truly optimize many of the Linux versions, you need to run the kernel reconfiguration utilities to upgrade the kernel to support a more advanced-level CPU type (defaults to 386, change to 586, PII, PIII, Athlon, etc.) and to support SMP (Symmetric Multi-Processor hardware), RAID, SCSI, etc. You need to read up on this. Is it absolutely necessary? *No, but it is highly recommended.* It is not that hard once it has been explained. The extra documentation covers all the basics of rebuilding (recompiling) the kernel and then installing it. Any thick "Everything you want to know about..." book on Linux for your distribution will cover this topic in excruciating detail, and will be well worth the money spent.

Everything Option

There is always the option to install everything. If you have plenty of disk space available (about 1.5GB under the **/usr** partition), then this is often a desirable option to choose rather than go through each option to decide what is needed. A word to the wise, however; some of the packages installed will want to start daemons at system startup and will install files that may lead to security issues. Users and administrators alike should familiarize themselves with the packages and what they all do. For example, enabling NFS mounts on a server exposed to the Internet opens a significant security hole. There is wisdom in the thought that you should install only what you need on a mission-critical system. Linux makes it easy to add packages later if you find you need them; so, if in doubt, leave it out.

X Window Installation (Optional)

The X Window installation is probably the hardest part of the installation to understand for the average PC user. The X Window system is actually a user-level program, not kernel level, and wants to access the hardware of the video card directly. In a Windows environment, you get a driver for the video controller. Similarly, you get a driver configuration file, text-based in this case, that points to the video driver and sets some configuration options, notably the resolution settings.

You *do not* need to have X Windows to run Linux, and it is CPU intensive. On a real dedicated server, you would not install X Windows. As shown in Figure 2.14, you should select the **Skip X Configuration** option unless you have included the X Window package and at least one desktop, either Gnome or KDE.

Figure 2.14 Optional—X Window configuration, part 1.

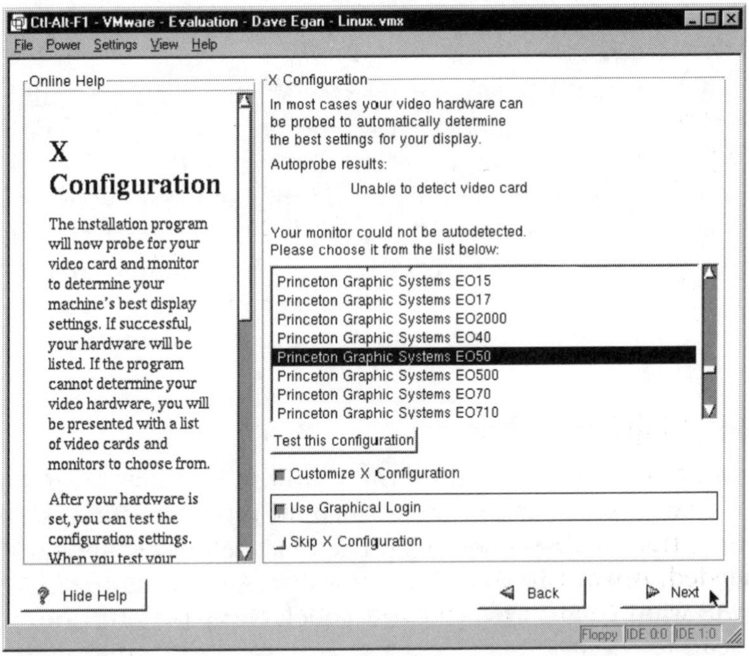

The following is a crude overview of how to install X Windows on a basic system. The system will probably be able to probe for the video card unless it is really new technology hardware, but in general, most of the known video chip sets will be discovered automatically, just like in Windows.

X Server Software

There is a different X Window server package for each type of hardware: generic VGA or SVGA; as well as for the well-known video chip sets S3 and ATI. If the probe is successful, the video card name and chip set will be shown. If it is not successful, you can select the hardware from a list provided. Generic video cards normally are based on one of the standard video chip sets like S3, ATI, etc. If it does not probe, especially true on laptops, you should select the generic SVGA driver and then select the Generic Multi-sync Monitor. This should work with most any basic hardware, but there are no guarantees. There is an entire site dedicated to configuration files for the various laptops that almost always have some proprietary hardware that may not probe properly. You can get more information from the following Web sites:

> www.XFree86.org
> for information about the X server.

> www.cs.utexas.edu/users/kharker/linux-laptop/
> for laptop support.

X Video Modes

After you have selected the video driver for X, you can optionally set the video modes, just like in Windows. You should be able to select various color depths—8,16, or 32 bits per pixel—and all of the various resolutions starting from 640x480 and going up to the highest level your card supports (see Figure 2.15). By default, it will pick the highest setting it can support with no other options. You can choose to change this so that you can switch between settings with the 3-key combination **Ctrl-Alt-+**. If you want more details, consult the installation guide or documentation for your version of Linux.

Actual Physical Installation

Basically, you have answered all of the required installation information and are now ready to start the actual formatting of the file systems and installation of the packages selected. The next screen to appear shows the Red Hat logo and prompts you either to go back and make changes (not recommended—start over instead) or to click **Next** to continue.

Figure 2.15 Optional—X Window configuration, part 2.

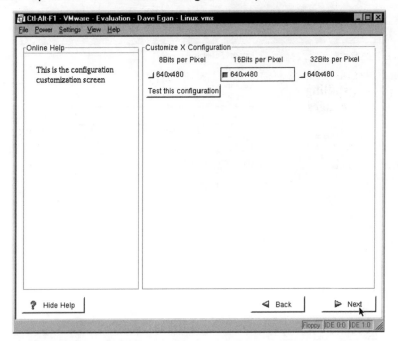

Figure 2.16 shows the formatting of the file systems (in Linux e2fs format, not DOS FAT or NTFS) as it appears on the installation screen before the actual installation starts. Figure 2.17 is a final screen that waits for you to press **Next** before the actual installation of files begins.

Package Installation

Figure 2.17 shows the installation as it is 90 percent through the fifth package. Note that the estimated time to install is over 289 hours! However, after more packages are completed, the installer settles down to a much more accurate estimate of the completion time. Typical install times are about 5 to 20 minutes on typical current hardware, depending also on how fast the disk I/O of the system is and how many packages are being installed.

Debian Install Plays Tetris

If you were installing using a Debian distribution, you would be given an option to play Tetris while the packages install. A nice touch, especially on older equipment when you may have a significant time requirement for installation of packages.

Figure 2.16 Formatting of the file system partitions before installation.

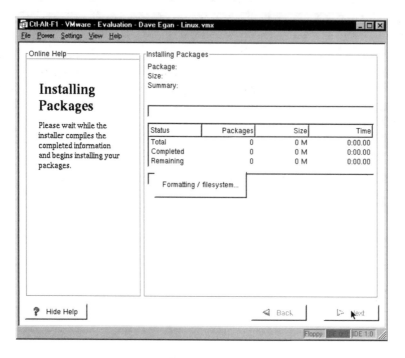

Figure 2.17 Package installation screen.

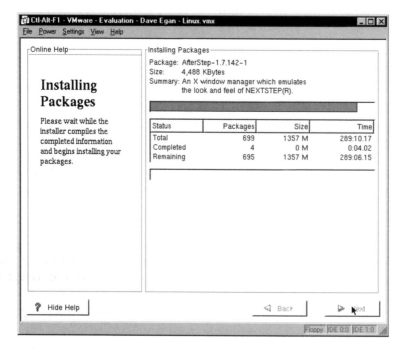

Linux Loader (LILO) and Boot Disk

The Linux loader and boot disk is highly recommended and requires only one diskette. This creates an alternate bootup to your system files, bypassing the current active partition. You can make this boot disk at any time using the **mkbootdisk** utility in Red Hat Linux (and the same or equivalents in the others; check your documentation). Figure 2.18 shows the screen you are presented with and waits for you to put a diskette into the drive or to cancel the action.

Figure 2.18 LILO configuration and boot disk creation (Do it!).

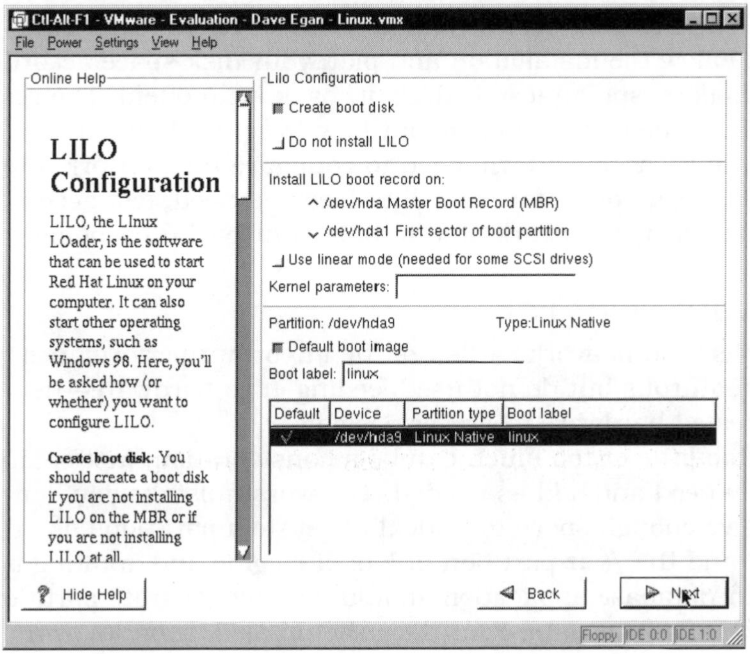

LILO Configuration

If you have installed Linux with a windows operating system already on the system, you could decide on which OS to boot by default. The Linux installation chooses the Linux boot partition by default in all cases.

Emergency Boot Disk

The emergency boot disk is highly recommended—make the boot disk. This is a *replacement* for the boot block only, a bypass of a corrupt boot partition (if your system loses its boot sector for any reason, stick this in and reboot the system). This boot disk is also used for emergency recovery, along with a second disk created with the **RESCUE.IMG** file as outlined earlier.

Installation Done!

You essentially are done! Reboot! The last screen congratulates you for your installation and prompts you to press **Enter** to reboot. Do not power down at this point; you want the system to do a proper shutdown. In fact, you should do an orderly shutdown *every* time you are going to power off your machine, or you take the risk of file corruption. Many databases also have their own procedures for an orderly shutdown which will save you considerable time and risk.

Configuring the Server to Run a Database

Find a good DBA and let him or her configure the server to run a database. Otherwise follow the installation and plan your disk space according to your needs (lots, spread it out, RAID it, back it up often). The rest of this book will provide more details about how to set up Linux as a database server. In essence, you will need to configure the network interface or interfaces, create or restore any data files you need, test access from any client across the network, and initiate your backup scheme.

Things to Watch Out For

Disks, RAM, CPUs, and network cards are the important performance features. Be adventurous but do not use bleeding-edge hardware—use tried and truly tested hardware wherever possible.

Partitioning too little or too much can be a consideration; just create what you initially need and add as needed. The worst mistake you can make is not to give enough space to critical file system partitions like the root partition, **/** and the **/var** partition (if lots of logging and auditing is being done). Your database application should be on a separate partition from the OS and from your data. Your data should also be on its own partition or on multiple separate partitions, depending on the design.

Additionally, if you keep each critical area on a separate partition, you easily can move it to a new, larger partition later. This makes management of growth much simpler. Separate partitions are easier to back up and restore, and much easier to manage in the areas of user quotas and security issues.

Other Flavors of Linux

This section has focused on a Red Hat installation, but obviously you can use any of the Linux distributions you want. Every one of them will be similar in performance, features, and stability. The only difference is in the installation, initially. Then there may be big differences in some of the system management utilities, but that will strictly be in their look and feel. Linux management does not change at the base level in any way. You still add users, network configurations, system configurations, and services the same way at the base level, although the interfaces may vary.

The other flavors of Linux were discussed in Chapter 1. A notable exception was one version, Stampede Linux, which you install via a network connection to be optimized for your specific hardware. The installation requires a network connection to the Internet and a UNIX sysadmin type who can decipher the typical UNIX installation requests. This installation style is not made to be an easy install; it downloads the source and then compiles it for your specific hardware settings so that it runs optimally on your hardware. For more information, see www.stampede.org.

Sample Database Scenarios

Here are a few examples of real-world scenarios implementing databases on Linux with the corresponding hardware resources recommended.

Scenario 1

Q: Assuming that you want to install an Oracle database server eventually, you first want to install a Linux Server for it. Your database will be 50MB with growth expected to enlarge it by 50MB a year. You will also be providing Web services from this server to 100 users. What do you need?

A: You want to have at least 256MB of RAM for this server and if possible, hardware RAID (or software RAID if not) on about 2GB of disk space for transactions and logging. You want a solid 10/100 network card; a single fast 500+ MHz CPU machine should be sufficient for the first year but most likely will be inadequate later on. Get a dual CPU machine for this if possible.

Scenario 2

Q: You are installing Informix, you have an 800MB database that will grow to 3GB this year, and *double* every six months after that with 500 users doing many short lookup requests most of the time and about 100 users adding data records constantly. What do you need?

A: You want at least 4GB of RAM, 4GB of swap, and at least two processors along with a large disk *farm* of at least 10–12 gigabytes to provide local live backups and lots of logging, transaction, and auditing space. You may want to go to an Alpha-based server to get the larger virtual memory size so you can keep the entire database in memory without need for swapping. If you exceed a 2GB user process size, you will need to go to the Alpha-based server for sure.

Summary

This section has provided you with a quick step-by-step GUI-based installation of a Red Hat system. Red Hat was used because it is the dominant Linux distribution on the market.

- The first thing you need to do is have a fully thought-out plan and design so you can match the hardware to your needs.
- You want to make sure you have compatible hardware, and hardware that is well-suited to the task of being a database server—preferably multiple CPUs, lots of RAM, and a fast underlying disk I/O subsystem with lots of disk space.
- It helps to understand the partitioning concepts of Intel PC motherboards, the limitation of 16 partitions on an IDE type drive, and 15 partitions on a SCSI drive.
- You need to be aware that partitioning your file system into smaller, easily managed parts is good and expected with most Linux and UNIX versions.
- Critical partitions for the system are **/**, **/usr**, **/var**, **/home**, **/usr**, **/opt**, and **swap**, to name just a few.
- The installation options you will be presented with may allow you to retain your current OS and dual boot with it, and some options may erase any other OS partitions. Production servers should generally be dedicated to Linux only, and should not use any non-Linux partitions.
- The packages to install are numerous, and only necessary packages should be installed.
- You should create the boot disk at the end of the installation.
- You should not use this database server as a user workstation as well; it should be dedicated to the purpose of database services only for best performance.
- System management tools vary considerably within Linux and UNIX in general; keep the supplied books handy.
- It is highly recommended that you find someone who has previous Linux or UNIX system administration skills since Windows system administration skills are not easily transferable.

If you have neither UNIX nor Linux experience, you have a whole new world to explore with hardware, software, and interfaces. Get in there and play, but use a test machine for that.

FAQs

Q: I have a really old disk, should I use that?

A: *No*, avoid it. In many cases, older disks do not use the advanced IO features of the motherboard and will slow down your machine considerably.

Q: I was told you can run Linux from Windows; is that true?

A: Yes, there is a very clever product called VMWare (www.vmware.com) that allows you to use almost any operating system (like NT or Linux) as the host OS, into which you can install one or more additional virtual OSs (like Win9x, NT, and Linux). The screen shots used in this manual were obtained during an installation of Linux onto a host NT 4.0 machine with all drives already FAT and NTFS formatted. VMWare created a virtual disk on one of the FAT volumes that just happened to have 1.8GB free. A full installation of Red Hat Linux in which six simulated partitions were created, as shown in the figures used earlier, used 1.3GB of the FAT partition (probably compressed format) for the virtual disk. Note: The recommended hardware is at least 266 MHz PC with 96MB RAM, and like all recommendations, this is low. Get lots more RAM and more horsepower if you can, or be prepared to go slowly through the molasses of installation (16 hours on a 166 MHz with 64MB RAM).

Q: Why choose Red Hat?

A Red Hat is a good choice because it is the most widely known, provides full support and training services, and is the market share leader.

Q: Is support important?

A: That depends. You can pay some support organization for their time or, if you have support staff, you can upgrade the skills of your staff for about the same fees.

Q: What if I have never seen UNIX?

A: The Internet is more than 90 percent UNIX-based, and it has not been a bad experience by not knowing at this point. The movie *Toy Story* was computer-generated entirely on UNIX machines. The movie *Titanic* used Linux on Alpha CPU servers to render all the special effects. UNIX is everywhere—it just does not mass market to the PC world like the competition does.

Q: I heard the installation is really ugggggly! Is this true?

A: For the average PC user who gets a machine with everything already set to go, yeah, you have to get under the hood a little. But with the current crop of GUI installations for Linux, you should be able to fumble your way through and get through a basic installation with little difficulty.

Chapter 3

Installing and Running Oracle on Linux

Solutions in this chapter:

- Concepts
- Installing Oracle8
- Installing Oracle8i
- Using Oracle8/8i

Introduction

Oracle has the world's largest market share in database management software. Oracle attained this lofty position by producing and maintaining one of the most powerful, scaleable, and versatile relational database management systems (RDBMS) in existence. Although the Oracle RDBMS is not open-source, it is a very stable and robust application once it is properly installed and configured. As with Linux and other powerful applications and platforms, Oracle is highly configurable and scaleable, which can make it seem complicated to the unfamiliar. Unlike some other SQL database server products, Oracle does not ship in a box-for-all-sizes.

Since Oracle8 is incredibly feature-rich, it would take volumes to explain each feature of the database. The goal of this chapter is to get you up and running with Oracle8 or Oracle8i on Linux, at which time you can seek out more advanced documentation. This chapter presents an overview of how to install, configure, and use the Oracle database running on a Linux server. Several Linux-specific issues are covered, but a more complete treatment of the Oracle database can be gained from any of the many publications on the software. At press time, there are two releases of the Oracle RDBMS available, Oracle8 and Oracle8i. Each release has two different editions, Standard and Enterprise. The Enterprise edition of Oracle8 provides more features and options than the Standard edition.

Oracle8 is currently version 8.0.5, and Oracle8i is currently version 8.1.5. One of the major features that differentiate Oracle8 from Oracle8i is that Oracle8i includes an optional Java runtime environment embedded within the server. This feature provides the ability to write Java-based procedures that can be run within the database server. Oracle8i also includes new Java-based applications including an installer, a database configuration assistant, and network configuration utilities. These programs generally make Oracle8i easier to install and use. Because the Java-based applications are new, they do not always run as expected under Linux. Some people experience difficulty getting the Java runtime environment correctly installed, or encounter an unexpected condition will cause the application to quit. Version 8.1.6 of Oracle 8i for Linux, called Oracle8i Release 2, is due out during the first quarter of 2000 and will include additional features and bug fixes.

It is well known that installing Oracle is no simple feat, but consider that once Oracle is installed, you will have one awesome database running on Linux. The installation instructions in this chapter include both Oracle8 and Oracle8i, which have many installation steps in common. Covering both versions adds complexity to the installation instructions, so read carefully. There are some major differences between installing the two versions, but generally they are similar. The installation instructions discuss Oracle8 Standard edition and Oracle8i Enterprise edition. The Standard edition is less expensive than the Enterprise edition, and includes fewer features and options. Which one should you install? Visit Oracle's Internet site (www.oracle.com) to compare the differences between the products. If you are interested in having a Java engine built into the database server, using XML, or using the friendly Java-based utilities, Oracle8i is the ticket. For a simple environment, using the least resources, Oracle8 will suit your needs. The Standard edition should include enough features to keep an Oracle beginner busy.

The following sections include a description of important concepts and terms that are necessary to become familiar with Oracle software, installation instructions for Oracle8 and Oracle8i, an overview of basic tools to use the database, and finally a brief introduction to a few third-party applications.

Concepts

Before diving into installation details, certain concepts need to be understood. Database usage is often divided into three categories: Online Transaction Processing (OLTP), Decision Support System (DSS), and Hybrid. OLTP is characterized by short database queries and updates, such as an airline reservation system. Decision Support Systems are characterized by long running queries, such as gathering information about weather patterns. A Hybrid system would include a mix of the two; for example a Web-based brokerage application might take orders (OLTP) and provide research information (DSS). The three classifications provide a basic understanding of how the database must be designed and configured.

There is an important distinction between an Oracle *database* and an Oracle *instance*. The database, identified by the database name (DB_NAME), is composed of the physical files used for storage. An instance, identified by the system identifier (SID), is composed of the memory structures and processes used to fulfill user requests. When an Oracle server is shutdown, the instance ceases to exist. The primary reason they are differentiated is because a single database can be serviced by multiple instances. The database and instance are composed of many components. Memory structures include the system global area, shared pool, database buffer cache, redo log buffer, and program global area. Logical structures include tablespaces, schemas, segments, extents, rollback segments, tables, and indexes. Physical components include data files, control files, redo logs, and parameter files.

System Global Area

The memory structures of an Oracle instance are contained in a memory region called the System Global Area (SGA). The SGA is allocated in virtual memory where the Oracle server process resides. The SGA comprises several memory structures including the shared pool, database buffer cache, and the redo log buffer. Many processes share the SGA.

Shared Pool

The shared pool contains two components, the library cache and the data dictionary cache. The library cache stores the most recently used SQL statements and their execution plans. The data dictionary cache stores the most recently used data dictionary information such as table definitions, usernames, and privileges. The size of the shared pool can affect performance of the database, especially in an OLTP environment.

Database Buffer Cache

When an SQL query is submitted by a user, the server process looks in the database buffer cache for data blocks to fulfill the request. If the blocks are not found in the database buffer cache, the server process must read the blocks from a physical device, and places a copy of the data in the buffer cache. Subsequent requests for the same blocks are likely to be found in memory, and may not require physical reads.

Redo Log Buffer

All changes made to data are stored in the redo log buffer, and are later copied to the physical redo log files.

Program Global Area

The program global area (PGA) is a memory region that contains data for a single server process. When used in a dedicated server configuration, the PGA contains a sort area, session information, cursor state, and stack space. PGA is allocated for a process when it is started and deallocated when the process is terminated.

Tablespace

A database is divided into logical storage units called tablespaces. A *tablespace* is used to group related logical structures together, and can be represented by one or more physical files. It is common practice to group certain types of objects within a tablespace. Examples might include temporary tables, rollback segments, or data dictionary tables.

Datafile

Each tablespace can have one or more *datafiles*, the actual physical files stored on the file system.

Extent

An extent is the smallest unit of storage in an Oracle database. An extent is made up of one or more file system blocks. For example, a Linux **ext2** file system is usually 2048 bytes per block, but can be set to 1024, 2048, or 4096 bytes per block. An extent can be configured to be one or more **ext2** blocks, depending on how the database will be used.

Segment

A segment is the physical representation of an object and is made up of one or more extents. A single table is an example of a segment.

Control Files

When the database starts up, it references a binary file called the *control file* to find the location of data files and the online redo logs. The control file is updated continuously while the database is running and must be available whenever the database is mounted or opened. The control file usually is mirrored across several devices. If any of the control files being used by the database becomes unavailable, then the database cannot function properly.

Redo Logs

Redo logs store all changes made to the database buffer cache, with a few exceptions. They are used to minimize the loss of data and for database reconstruction. Oracle requires at least two redo log files, and sets of files are often mirrored across multiple devices. Their configuration and size can impact performance. It is common to store redo logs on their own devices, separate from data files. The redo logs are written to sequentially, unlike rollback segments, which exist in data files similarly to database objects.

Rollback Segments

Rollback segments provide read-consistency by storing data that has been modified in the database, and are used to restore information after a rollback command. When a transaction begins to modify data in a table, the original data is copied to a rollback segment. If a second transaction needs the same data, and the first transaction has not committed the new data, Oracle will retrieve the data from the rollback segment.

Parameter Files

Parameter files specify how the instance is configured. The file is usually called the **INIT.ORA** or **INIT<SID>.ORA**. The instance name (SID) is attached to the file name.

SID

The system identifier represents a single instance. The **ORACLE_SID** environment variable represents the default Oracle instance. Throughout this document, the Oracle SID will be assumed to be **ORCL**. Since the SID is user-selected, and certain files utilize the SID identifier as part of the filename, you will see <SID> written in documentation. It is recommended that the instance name be four or less characters.

$ORACLE_HOME

The **ORACLE_HOME** environment variable is used to identify a particular installation of Oracle. (It is possible to have multiple versions of Oracle installed.) The **ORACLE_HOME** environmental variable can be changed to point at different versions. Throughout this document, **$ORACLE_HOME** will represent the actual directory structure where Oracle is installed. Oracle8 usually is installed under /u01/app/oracle/product/8.0.5, and Oracle8i is commonly installed under /u01/app/oracle/product/8.1.5.

$ORACLE_BASE

The **ORACLE_BASE** environment variable is used to identify the base of the Oracle installation tree.

Version Identifiers

Oracle has a five-number version identifier. The first number is the major release, the second number is the minor release, the third number is a code release by the engineering group, and the fourth and fifth numbers refer to a patch set. The first two or three numbers make up an individual product. For example, Oracle8i is version 8.1.5. A patch set might bring Oracle8i up to version 8.1.5.0.2. The farther a digit is to the right, the less significant the change.

PL/SQL

PL/SQL is an Oracle procedural language that extends SQL by adding application logic, including block structured procedural constructs. PL/SQL is used to write applications that can manipulate data in the database.

Schema

The schema represents all the objects owned by a particular account.

Installation

Installation of Oracle requires careful planning and attention to detail. This section includes instructions on installing both Oracle8 and Oracle8i. Although they are similar, there are some important differences. This section is divided into four components, pre-installation, installing Oracle8, installing Oracle8i, and post-installation. Oracle requires generous hardware resources. Generally, Oracle performs significantly better with more RAM, which makes sense considering that the more things it can store in memory, the fewer trips it will make to the physical drives. Oracle also performs significantly better with more drives, because there is less contention between files. The most important method of improving performance in Oracle is to add more RAM. The second most important method is to add more disks. Relational databases are usually IO bound.

Even though Oracle recommends 400MB of disk space and 32MB of RAM as a minimum for Oracle8 (see Table 3.1), realistically you should have 500MB of disk space and 128MB of RAM to do anything useful.

Table 3.1 Minimum Requirements for Oracle8

Hardware and Software	Requirements
Disk Space	400MB
Memory	32MB RAM
Swap Space	3 times the amount of RAM
Operating System	Linux kernel 2.0.34 or above
System Libraries	GNU C Library version 2.0.7

If you are installing Oracle8i (see Table 3.2), you really need at least 128MB of RAM to accommodate the Java Runtime Environment, and 198MB would be the minimum in a small production environment. You should have 1000MB of free disk space to accommodate the software and the database files.

Table 3.2 Minimum Requirements for Oracle8i

Hardware and Software	Requirements
Disk Space	693MB
Memory	128MB RAM
Swap Space	3 times the amount of RAM
Operating System	Linux kernel 2.2
System Libraries	GNU C Library version 2.1

Pre-Installation

Before installing the Oracle RDBMS, Linux must be prepared. Oracle is not an application you can install the instant you receive the CD-ROM or download the software. Installing Oracle takes time and patience. Documentation for Oracle software is located at http://technet.oracle.com/docs/index.htm. Before installing Oracle it is highly recommended that you read the *Oracle Release Note for LINUX* and the *Installation Guide for LINUX*. Pre-installation instructions for Oracle8 and Oracle8i are fairly similar, with the exception that Oracle8i requires Java and a different **$ORACLE_HOME**. You should take the following pre-installation steps:

1. Configure the file system
2. Configure swap space
3. Set Kernel parameters
4. Create user accounts and groups
5. Set up the Linux environment
6. Install the necessary Linux software packages
7. Install Java
8. Get the Oracle software and patches

Configure the File System

Mount points are the first issue to consider. Disk usage is often easier to determine when a server is being designed and built. The minimum for a production system should be six drives; the minimum for a development system should be four drives. Disks can always be added if necessary. The biggest concern is safety of the data. Data files and redo logs should reside on separate devices. If one of the drives containing data is lost, the redo logs can be used to restore the data. Generally, a larger number of smaller capacity drives are preferred over a smaller number of high capacity drives. If I were offered the choice between six 2GB drives and two 9GB drives, I would probably select the six-drive alternative. More drives provide increased performance with increased data protection. Another important issue to consider is drive contention between different applications. A 9GB drive that is partitioned into two 4.5GB partitions and shared between two different applications will be difficult to tune. When possible, dedicate drives to Oracle.

Oracle recommends using something called Optimal Flexible Architecture, or OFA. OFA is a particular method of file system layout that requires a minimum of four mount points at the same level of the directory structure. It is especially useful if you are running multiple database instances on the same server. Oracle documentation often refers to the OFA layout, so it is helpful if you are using it.

One Disk

You can install Oracle on a single hard drive, as long as you are not concerned with low performance and possible data loss. The layout I am about to describe may seem strange, and it is unnecessary, but it will get you in the habit of storing data across partitions, even if it is not across physical drives. Be aware that this is not recommended for a production environment, you may loose data, and you will get lower performance.

Locate a partition on your system with at least 600MB of free space using the **df –k** command. Let's say the **/usr/** partition has 1GB of available disk space. Create a directory under **/usr/local** called **oracle**, and then create four directories under **oracle** called **u01**, **u02, u03,** and **u04**.

```
$ df -k

Filesystem            1k-blocks      Used Available Use% Mounted on
/dev/sda3             3865709    2663841    1201868  69% /usr

mkdir /usr/local/oracle
mkdir /usr/local/oracle/u01
mkdir /usr/local/oracle/u02
mkdir /usr/local/oracle/u03
mkdir /usr/local/oracle/u04
```

Examples throughout the rest of the chapter will assume the mount points are located under the root/file system. Create symbolic links under the root file system.

```
ln -s /usr/local/oracle/u01 /u01
ln -s /usr/local/oracle/u02 /u02
ln -s /usr/local/oracle/u03 /u03
ln -s /usr/local/oracle/u04 /u04
```

Four Disks

A four-disk configuration provides significant data protection and a modest performance increase over a single-disk configuration. Create a partition on each physical drive to store Oracle data. Assign a partition to each Oracle directory, **/u01**, **/u02**, **/u03**, and **/u04**. If you have already installed Linux and you want to add three disks to your system for Oracle, use Disk Druid or **fdisk** to partition the disks, and use **mkfs** to format each partition. Create the **/u01**, **/u02**, **/u03**, and **/u04** directories under the root **/** file system and use the **mount** command to mount the partitions to the file system.

Configure Swap Space

Swap space should be three times the amount of RAM. Red Hat Linux 6.0 and the Linux kernel 2.2 now support swap partitions larger than 128MB. To create swap partitions or swap files larger than 128MB, you must specify the new style, **mkswap –v1**. If you do not have extra disk space to add a swap partition, you can add a swap file.

Kernel Parameters

The *Oracle Installation Guide for LINUX* recommends changing kernel parameters, which requires the kernel to be recompiled. It is usually not necessary to modify these parameters. The most important parameter is **SHMMAX**, which defines the maximum size of a shared memory segment. The default setting is 32MB on Red Hat Linux, which is generally sufficient for a basic database installation. If the SGA is sized to 128MB, it would require four segments of 32MB each. The kernel parameters are more of an issue on a server with a large SGA. In a production environment, **SHMMAX** should be configured to the same size as physical RAM. If you decide to make the changes, the files are located at /usr/src/linux/include/asm/shmparam.h and /usr/src/linux/include/linux/sem.h.

> **TIP**
>
> You can view the SHMMAX parameter with the following command as root: cat /proc/sys/kernel/shmmax.

OS Accounts and Groups

The Oracle server should not run under the root account. It is common to create an account called **oracle** that owns the Oracle server software and the background processes. Oracle defines a group within the Oracle server called OSDBA. Any account within Oracle that is a member of OSDBA receives DBA authority. Oracle uses a Linux group, **/etc/group**, to assign membership to the Oracle server OSDBA group. During installation, Oracle requests a Linux group to define OSDBA membership—the Linux group **dba** is often used. Oracle8i has a second group called **oinstall**, which can be used to assign authority to install software in the repository.

As root, use the **groupadd** command to add the **dba** group:

```
# groupadd dba
```

For Oracle8i, also add the **oinstall** group:

```
# groupadd oinstall
```

For Oracle8, create the Oracle account using the **dba** group as the default group:

```
# useradd -c DBA -g dba oracle
```

For Oracle8i, create the Oracle account using the **oinstall** group as the default group:

```
# useradd -c DBA -g oinstall -G dba oracle
```

Create a password for the oracle account:

```
# passwd oracle
```

File System Rights

In order for the **oracle** account to use the mount points during installation, it must have appropriate rights. Change the ownership of the mount points to the **oracle** account. Once the installation is completed, ownership of the top-most directories can be changed back to root.

```
# chown oracle.dba /u01
# chown oracle.dba /u02
# chown oracle.dba /u03
# chown oracle.dba /u04
# chmod 755 /u01
# chmod 755 /u02
# chmod 755 /u03
# chmod 755 /u04
```

Environment Settings

Certain environment variables need to be set before the Oracle server is installed. There are three places the environment variables can be placed.

If only the **oracle** account will be using the Oracle software, place the environment variables in the oracle account's **~/.bash_profile** file. If other accounts on the system will be using Oracle, the variables can be placed in the system-wide **/etc/profile** file. The downside to this location is that root will be required to make changes to the **/etc/profile** settings. If multiple databases will be installed on the server, it is best to place the variables in a separate executable script that can be run by the user. Oracle ships with a file called **oraenv** located under **$ORACLE_HOME/bin**.

Since the environment variables are required prior to installation, insert the following environment variables either in the **oracle** account's **~/.bash_profile** or in **/etc/profile**. You should then re-login to set up your environment or source the file. Notice that some of the directories in the environment settings do not yet exist. The instance **ORACLE_SID** is being set to **orcl** in the following example.

For the Oracle8 environment (8.0.5):

```
ORACLE_BASE=/u01/app/oracle

ORACLE_HOME=/u01/app/oracle/product/8.0.5

ORACLE_SID=orcl

ORACLE_TERM=vt100

PATH=$PATH:$ORACLE_HOME/bin

LD_LIBRARY_PATH=$LD_LIBRARY_PATH:$ORACLE_HOME/lib:$ORACLE_HOME/network/lib

export ORACLE_BASE ORACLE_HOME ORACLE_SID ORACLE_TERM LD_LIBRARY_PATH PATH
```

For the Oracle8i environment (8.1.5):

```
ORACLE_BASE=/u01/app/oracle

ORACLE_HOME=/u01/app/oracle/product/8.1.5

ORACLE_SID=orcl

ORACLE_TERM=vt100

PATH=$PATH:$ORACLE_HOME/bin

LD_LIBRARY_PATH=$LD_LIBRARY_PATH:$ORACLE_HOME/lib:$ORACLE_HOME/network/lib

export ORACLE_BASE ORACLE_HOME ORACLE_SID ORACLE_TERM LD_LIBRARY_PATH PATH
```

NOTE

The **LD_LIBRARY_PATH** environmental variable provides applications with the location of libraries. Some people have experienced problems with Oracle not finding libraries in the **LD_LIBRARY_PATH**. Directories containing libraries can also be added to the **/etc/ld.so.conf** file. The **ldconfig** command will reread the **ld.so.conf** file.

If you require a language other than the default, US7ASCII, check the Oracle installation documentation for the **NLS_LANG** and **ORA_NLS33** variables. Copy the following environmental variables to your shell start-up file.

You might find yourself regularly changing into the **$ORACLE_HOME** directory. A shortcut is to use **cd $ORACLE_HOME**. An easier method is to create an alias. Place the following command in the **/etc/bashrc**. Once the alias is defined, the **oh** alias command will bring you to **ORACLE_HOME**.

```
alias oh='cd $ORACLE_HOME'
```

Run the **umask** command to make sure the user file-creation mask (umask) is 022. If the umask is not 022, place **umask 022** in your shell startup file. This should not be necessary under most distributions of Linux, including Red Hat. The umask filters file system rights. A umask of 022 provides full rights to the owner, and removes the **write** right from group and other.

```
$ umask
```

```
022
```

Before you continue, run the **env** command to make sure that your environmental variables are configured properly.

X Windows Display

The X Windows server does not allow another user's process to access the screen by default. If you are installing Oracle8i, the Java GUI utilities require access to an X Windows server. As long as you are logged in as the **oracle** user and running the applications under the **oracle** account, the applications will have access to the X server. If you are logged in as root and you **su** to the **oracle** account and attempt to run an X window application as **oracle**, you might get an error. To prevent this, as the user you are logged in as, run **xhost +localhost**. The **xhost** command allows other accounts access to the X server. Next, as the other user, set the environment variable **DISPLAY** to **localhost**.

```
$ xhost +localhost
```

```
$ export DISPLAY=localhost:0.0
```

Linux Packages

The move from Red Hat Linux version 5.2 to version 6.0 resulted in a fundamental change to the core libraries. Red Hat 5.2 includes **glibc** 2.0 libraries and Red Hat Linux 6.0 includes new **glibc** 2.1 libraries.

Applications compiled under **glibc** 2.0 must be recompiled under the new libraries. Since Oracle8 was compiled for Red Hat Linux 5.2 using **glibc** 2.0, it requires backwards-compatible libraries to run on newer versions of Red Hat Linux. If you decide to install Oracle8 on Red Hat 6.0 or later, you must install compatibility libraries. Oracle8i was compiled with **glibc** 2.1 and therefore does not need the compatibility packages. Oracle8i should not run under versions of Red Hat Linux before 6.0 because the libraries are incompatible.

The compatibility packages are necessary only if you are installing Oracle 8.0.5. You do not need them if you are installing Oracle 8.1.5 on Red Hat Linux 6.0 or 6.1. The packages should be located on the Red Hat Linux installation CD-ROM, or they can be downloaded from an ftp site.

```
compat-binutils-5.2-2.9.1.0.23.1.i386.rpm
```

```
compat-egcs-5.2-1.0.3a.1.i386.rpm
```

```
compat-egcs-c++-5.2-1.0.3a.1.i386.rpm
```

```
compat-egcs-g77-5.2-1.0.3a.1.i386.rpm
```

```
compat-egcs-objc-5.2-1.0.3a.1.i386.rpm
```

```
compat-glibc-5.2-2.0.7.1.i386.rpm
```

```
compat-libs-5.2-2.i386.rpm
```

The C Development software must be installed. If you installed Red Hat 6.0 or 6.1 and selected GNOME Workstation, KDE Workstation, Server-Class, or Custom with the Development Package group during installation, the development software should be installed. TCL 7.5 needs to be installed if you want to use the Oracle Intelligent Agent. It is available from ftp://www.scriptics.com. If you do not know what it is, don't install it.

Java for Linux

If you choose to install Oracle8i, you must install a Java Runtime Environment. The **orainst** character mode tool for installing Oracle8 has been replaced in Oracle8i by a new GUI installer written in Java, called the Oracle Universal Installer (OUI). There have been complaints that the installer requires a machine running X Windows. If your system does not have X Windows installed, you can forward your X Windows session to another machine running an X Windows server.

You'll need to download the Java Runtime Environment (JRE) for Linux from Blackdown at http://www.blackdown.org. You should download JRE 1.1.6v5. When you download, select the **libc5** version for Red Hat 5.2, and the **glibc** version for Red Hat 6.0 and later. Copy the JRE to **/usr/local**. Uncompress the file and create a symbolic link to **/usr/local/jre**. The Universal Installer seems to expect the JRE to be installed under **/usr/local/jre**.

```
# cd /usr/local
# tar zxvf jre_1.1.6-v5-glibc-x86.tar.gz
# ln -s jre116_v5 jre
```

Place **/usr/local/jre/bin** into your PATH environment.

```
PATH=$PATH:/usr/local/jre/bin; export PATH
```

WARNING

There have been reported problems with versions of the JRE other than 1.1.6v5, such as the Installer failing to start, or certain installation steps failing to complete. Don't assume that a newer version will work better. Also, do not use the JDK for similar reasons. If you have a previous installation of Oracle that failed, you should delete previously installed files before re-installing.

Getting the Oracle Software

Oracle8 and Oracle8i can be purchased from the Oracle Store at http://oraclestore.oracle.com/ and downloaded from ftp://ftp.oracle.com/pub/www/otn/linux. You can also subscribe to the OTN Technology Track for Linux from the OTN site at http://technet.oracle.com. The subscription service provides 12 months of updates. Oracle has a site dedicated to Linux at http://platforms.oracle.com/linux/. If you decide to download the software, expect long download times. You can optionally download one large file or multiple smaller files.

Oracle Patches

Log in as the **oracle** user and create a directory called **patches**. You should download the newest patches available. For Oracle8, download the following files from ftp://oracle-ftp.oracle.com/server/patchsets/unix/LINUX/80patchsets/80510/, or from the Oracle Technology Network (OTN) at http://technet.oracle.com. The OTN requires you to open a free account. Patches for Oracle8i can be found at http://technet.oracle.com/support/tech/linux/support_index.htm. Place the downloaded patches into the patches directory: **glibcpatch.tgz**, **lnxpatch.tgz**, and **linux_80510patchset.tgz**. If you are installing Oracle8 on Red Hat 5.2, you do not need the **glibcpatch.tgz**. For Oracle8i, download the following patch: **linux_815patches.tgz**. Read the README for each patch. There should also be a Patch FAQ that will provide useful information. If you run into problems, these are the first things you should check.

Installing Oracle8

Oracle8 uses an installer called the Software Asset Manager, or **orainst**. The installer can be a little awkward to use. Use the **Tab** key to move between fields and buttons. Use the space bar to select an option. Use the **Enter** key to activate a button. If a field is too short to display its complete contents, move to the field using the **Tab** key, and use the right arrow key to see more of the field.

1. Log in as oracle.
2. Change to the directory containing the Oracle installation program.

```
cd /mnt/cdrom/orainst
```

3. Start the Oracle installer in text mode. (The Motif GUI mode will not work under Linux.) See Figure 3.1.

```
./orainst /c
```

TIP

If you are using a CD-ROM and **orainst** script will not run, make sure the CD-ROM is mounted with the exec parameter.

4. Select Custom Install. Press the **Tab** key to move to the installation type selection box, use the arrow key to select Custom, and press the **Enter** key to proceed.
5. Enter **OK** to get through the READMEs.
6. Select Install, Upgrade, or De-install software.
7. Select Install new product – Do Not Create DB objects.
8. Verify that your **Oracle_HOME** and **ORACLE_BASE** are correct.
9. Accept the defaults for log files.
10. Choose Install from CD-ROM.
11. Select a language.
12. The installer explains where the **root.sh** script will be placed for later use.

Figure 3.1 Oracle8 Installer.

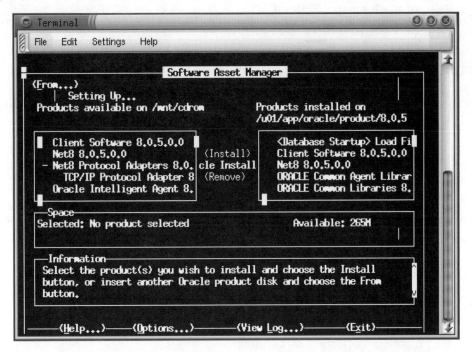

13. The Install Options screen appears. To see a complete description of an option, move your cursor to the option using the **Tab** key, and press the right-arrow key on your keyboard. Press the spacebar to select an option. Do not select the Oracle8 Server Documentation because there is a mistake in the directory structure that will cause the installation to fail. Do not select JDBC drivers or Intelligent agent at this time. The options you should select are Client Software, Net8, TCP/IP Protocol Adapter, Oracle Unix Installer, Oracle8 Standard or Enterprise (RDBMS), PL/SQL, Pro*C/C++, and SQL*Plus.

14. When you are finished with the selections, select the Install button and press **Enter**.

15. Enter **OK** for the **ulimit** message.

16. Select **dba** as your **dba** group.

17. Enter **OK** at the OSOPER prompt.

18. The installation begins. Once the installation completes, you should see a message that says, "The requested action has been performed for select products."

19. A message appears requesting the root account to run the **root.sh** script. Enter **OK**.

20. Exit the installer.

21. Open a new terminal window and **su** to the root account. As root, change directory to the **$ORACLE_HOME/orainst** directory and run the command **sh root.sh**. Check the environment variables for **ORACLE_OWNER**, **ORACLE_HOME**, and **ORACLE_SID**. If the variables are not correct, exit the script and set the environment variables provided previously in this chapter. The full pathname to the local bin directory should be **/usr/local/bin**. It is all right if **ORACLE_HOME** does not match the oracle account's home directory.

```
 [root@dbsvr orainst]# cd $ORACLE_HOME/orainst
[root@dbsvr orainst]# sh root.sh

Running Oracle8 root.sh script...

The following environment variables are set as:
     ORACLE_OWNER= oracle
     ORACLE_HOME=  /u01/app/oracle/product/8.0.5
     ORACLE_SID=   orcl
Are these settings correct (Y/N)? [Y]:

Enter the full pathname of the local bin directory [/usr/lbin]: /usr/local/bin

Checking for "oracle" user id...
ORACLE_HOME does not match the home directory for oracle.
Okay to continue? [N]: Y
Replacing existing entry for SID in /etc/oratab...
The previous entry is now in a comment.

Leaving common section of Oracle8 root.sh.
```

Installing the Patches

After Oracle8 has been installed, you need to install the patches. If you have not already downloaded the patches, they are located at ftp://oracle-ftp.oracle.com/server/patchsets/unix/LINUX/80patchsets/80510/. If you need the **glibcpatch.tgz** patch and it is not located at the previously mentioned site, you will need to get a free account at the Oracle Technology Network (http://technet.oracle.com) and locate the software section for Linux. Check for new patch releases. There are currently three

patches for Oracle8: **glibcpatch.tgz**, **lnxpatch.tgz**, and
linux_80510patchset.tgz. The **glibcpatch.tgz** file is necessary only if
you are installing Oracle 8.0.5 on a Red Hat Linux version 6.0 or later. It
may be necessary to re-install the **glibcpatch** after applying future patches. If you are installing on a Red Hat 5.2 machine, it is not necessary.
The **lnxpatch.tgz** includes patches specific to the Linux platform. The
linux_80510patchset.tgz has generic fixes for Oracle8. You should read
any documentation included with the patches.

lnxpatch

The **lnxpatch** is a shell script.

1. Change into the directory containing the patches.
2. Create a directory called **lnx**.
3. Move the **lnxpatch.tgz** file into the **lnx** directory.

```
mv lnxpatch.tgz lnx
```

4. Change to the **lnx** directory.

```
cd lnx
```

5. Extract the patch.

```
tar zxvf lnxpatch.tgz
```

6. Run the **lnxpatch.sh** script.

```
sh glibcpatch.sh
```

80510patchset

The 80510patchset is installed through the Oracle installer, **orainst**, that
you used to install the Oracle server.

1. Create a directory called **80510**.
2. Move the **80510patchset.tgz** file into the **80510** directory.

```
mv 80510patchset.tgz 80510
```

3. Change to the **glibc** directory.

```
cd 80510
```

4. Extract the patch.

```
tar zxvf 80510patchset.tgz
```

5. Start the Oracle installer.

```
orainst /c
```

6. Select Custom Install.

7. Enter **OK** to get through the READMEs.

8. Select Install, Upgrade, or De-Install Software.

9. Select Add/Upgrade Software.

10. Check the **ORACLE_HOME** directory.

11. Confirm the log file locations and enter **OK**.

12. Select Install from Staging Area.

13. Enter the full directory path where the **8051** patch is located; for example, **/home/oracle/patches/8.0.5/8051/**.

14. Select a language.

15. Create a new **root.sh** file.

16. Select **OK** to save your previous **root.sh** file.

17. Select **OK** at the post-installation step message.

18. Select the items listed in the left box, Oracle8 Standard and Precomp.

19. Select Install.

20. Enter **Yes** to upgrade each component.

21. Enter **OK** for the ulimit message.

22. Select **dba** as the group and enter **OK**.

23. Enter **OK** for the OSOPER group.

24. Once the installation is finished, exit the installer.

25. Run the **root.sh** script as root.

glibcpatch

The **glibcpatch** is a shell script.

1. Change into the directory containing the patches.

2. Create a directory called **glibc.**

3. Move the **glibcpatch.tgz** file into the **glibc** directory.

```
mv glibcpatch.tgz glibc
```

4. Change to the **glibc** directory.

```
cd glibc
```

5. Extract the patch.

```
tar zxvf glibcpatch.tgz
```

6. Run the **glibcpatch** script.

```
sh glibcpatch.sh
```

Creating the Database Objects

Follow these steps exactly to create the database objects.

1. Change to the directory containing the Oracle installation software.

```
cd /mnt/cdrom/orainst
```

2. Start the Oracle installer.

```
./orainst /c
```

3. Select Custom Install.
4. Enter **OK** at the README prompts.
5. Select Create/Upgrade Database objects.
6. Select Create Database Objects.
7. Verify the **ORACLE_HOME** and **ORACLE_BASE**.
8. Accept the defaults for the logfiles.
9. Verify that your **ORACLE_SID** is correct.
10. You might get a message indicating that the SID is already in use. This is because the **root.sh** script created an **/etc/oratab file**. Enter **Yes**.
11. At the Oracle Install screen, select the Oracle8 Standard RDBMS 8.0.5.0.0 for the database objects to be created.
12. Click the Install button.
13. Select Create Product DB Objects.
14. Choose Filesystem-based Database.
15. If you set up an OFA-compliant file system, select **Yes** at the distribute control files over multiple mount points.
16. Enter the mount points **/u02**, **/u03**, and **/u04** if you set up the OFA file system.
17. Select the character set.
18. Select the national character set.
19. Enter your password for the SYS account.
20. Enter your password for the SYSTEM account.
21. Optionally enter an internal password for dba and operator.
22. Enter a password for the TNS Listener.
23. Do not configure the MTS listener.
24. Accept the defaults for the control files.
25. Select **OK** at the next two screens.
26. Select **Yes** to accept the defaults.

27. The database build process begins, the Oracle server is started, and the objects are created.
28. Exit the installer.

Installing Oracle8i

The installation of Oracle8i is tricky because you must maneuver around bugs in the installation routine for version 8.1.5. The goal is to install the Oracle software first, install patches, create an actual database called **orcl**, and then start the instance.

The following installation instructions were performed on a system with a fresh copy of Red Hat Linux 6.1, including all available patches. Expect the Oracle Universal Installer (OUI) to gorge itself with memory. You should have at least 128MB of RAM and sufficient swap space before you begin the installation. To recap: Make sure the Java JRE is installed and the symbolic link **/usr/local/jre** exists. Make sure you have an **oracle** account, a **dba** group, and an **oinstaller** group. Oracle should be a member of both groups, **oinstall** being the primary group listed in **/etc/passwd**. Make sure the Oracle environmental variables exist using the **env** command.

> **WARNING**
>
> There have been problems running the installer over the default version of Enlightenment installed with Red Hat Linux 6.0. Enlightenment is the default window manager installed under Gnome. If you run into problems with the Oracle Universal Installer, you might want to upgrade Enlightenment or replace it with Sawmill. You can also switch to **fvwm** or KDE.

Login as the **oracle** user to perform the installation, and mount the CD-ROM containing the software. The assumed mount point for the CD-ROM is **/mnt/cdrom**. If you downloaded the software, replace **/mnt/cdrom** with the directory where the software is installed.

1. Change to the Oracle CD-ROM or installation directory.

```
$ cd /mnt/cdrom/
```

2. The *Oracle8i Installation Guide* for Linux says to run the **runInstaller** script. The **runInstaller** script doesn't function under Red Hat Linux 6.1, so you must use the **runIns.sh** script located under **/mnt/cdrom/install/linux**.

```
$ cd /mnt/cdrom/install/linux

$ ./runIns.sh
```

If you get a message from OUI about not being able to connect to X11 Windows server, you are probably logged into your window manager as another user, and you probably did a su (switch user) to the oracle account. Refer to the X-Windows section under Environment Settings. If you receive a strange Java error, make sure you have the correct version of the Java installed, have a /usr/local/jre directory, and have /usr/local/jre/bin in your $PATH. Use the 'which jre' command to make sure it is finding /usr/local/jre/bin/jre.

3. OUI presents a Welcome dialog box (see Figure 3.2). Take notice of the Help button located at the bottom of the OUI window. During the installation, you can get useful information by opening the Help window. Click **Next**.

Figure 3.2 Oracle Universal Installer.

4. The File Locations dialog box requests a source and a destination location for the software. The source should be your CD-ROM or the directory where you placed the Oracle software, **/mnt/cdrom/stage/products.jar**. The destination should be the OFA software directory, **/u01/app/oracle/product/8.1.5**. Change these directories to reflect your source and destination. The defaults should be sufficient if you have been following the directions in this chapter. Click **Next**.

5. The Unix Group Name dialog box requests a UNIX group to handle software installations. The entry can be left blank if you would prefer only the root account to install Oracle software. Enter the account **oinstall** that we created earlier. The idea is that anyone who is a member of the **oinstall** group can take care of Oracle software. This frees the person with the root account from administering Oracle. Click **Next**.

Figure 3.3 OUI orainstRootsh prompt.

6. The first time Oracle8i is installed on a system results in the dialog shown in Figure 3.3, requesting the root account to run a script called **/tmp/OraInstall/orainstRoot.sh**. The script creates a file in the **/etc** directory called **oraInst.loc** that contains the location of the **oraInventory** directory, and it changes the group ownership of the **oraInventory** directory to **oinstall**. If you do not get this prompt, either you have installed Oracle before, or the oracle account is not a member of the **dba** group. Open a new terminal window and **su** to the root account. As root, **cd** to the **/tmp/OraInstall** directory and type **./orainstRoot.sh**. When you are finished running the **orainstRoot.sh** script, select **Retry** on the dialog box.

```
# cd /tmp/orainstall

# ./orainstRoot.sh
```

7. The Available Products dialog box presents three options: server, client, and programmer. Since we are installing the server, make sure Orace8i Enterprise edition (or Standard edition) is selected and then select **Next**.

8. The Installation Types dialog box presents three options: Typical, Minimal, and Custom. Select **Custom** and then select **Next**. The Typical and Minimal options are not supposed to work under Red Hat 6.1.

9. The Available Product Components dialog box will appear. Make sure all of the Oracle Product Options are selected, except Intermedia. There is a bug in 8.1.5.0.1 and 8.1.5.0.2 that may cause problems if all the options are not installed, with the exception of Intermedia. Intermedia is not fully supported under 8.1.5. Product options are not actually used until you implement them. Select **Next**.

10. The Create Database dialog box will appear asking whether you want to create a new database using the Oracle Database Configuration Assistant. Select **No** and then select **Next**.

11. The Oracle Protocol Support dialog box will appear with an empty selection box. This is normal because Linux supports TCP/IP, which is installed by default. Select **Next**.

12. The Summary dialog box will appear; select **Install** to begin installation.

Figure 3.4 Setup privileges.

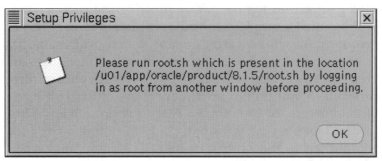

13. The Setup Privileges dialog will appear if this is the first time you have installed Oracle software on the machine (see Figure 3.4). During install, OUI checks to see if there is an **/etc/oratab** file that contains an entry for each database installed. If the file does not exist, a dialog box will appear that says, "Please run root.sh which is present in the location /u01/app/oracle/product/8.1.5/root.sh by logging in as root from another window before proceeding." Using another terminal window, **su** to root, and run the **root.sh** script. The script asks for the full pathname of the local bin directory. You should use the location **/usr/local/bin**. If you accidentally leave **/usr/bin** as the local bin directory, everything should work fine—it is just not considered proper. When you are finished, switch back to the dialog window and press **OK**.

```
$ su -
Password:
# cd /u01/app/oracle/product/8.1.5/
# sh root.sh
```

14. The Configuration Tools dialog box will appear, which includes Net8 Configuration Assistant and the Oracle Database Configuration Assistant entries. The Oracle Database Configuration Assistant might fail, which is fine. If the Database Configuration Assistant starts, simply press **Cancel** and then **Yes** at the exit dialog box. The database should not be created at this point because patches need to be installed. Close any error messages. You might get another error from the OUI; if so, select **OK**. At the Configuration Tools dialog box, press **Next**.

15. The End of Installation dialog box should appear. You can exit the OUI.

16. Run the **root.sh** script located under **$ORACLE_HOME/install/utl** to modify some file permissions.

```
$ cd $ORACLE_HOME/install/utl
```

```
$ sh linux.sh
```

Congratulations! You made it through the first step towards installing Oracle8i. You now have the software installed, but no database. Before the database is created, though, we need to install patches.

Installing the Patch

Download any current patches for Oracle8i. The current patch level is 8.1.5.0.2, which applies to both the Enterprise and Standard editions of Oracle8i. Make sure the **$ORACLE_HOME/bin** is in your path; otherwise the patch will fail. I am going to explain a few issues with previous patch files in case you run into problems. Previous patch releases for Oracle8 uncompressed the patch files directly into the current working directory, which could be messy. Most tar files create a subdirectory and then decompress the files into the subdirectory. With Oracle under Linux, it was necessary to create a subdirectory and move the patch into the directory before it was uncompressed. The 8.1.5.0.1 patch was even worse. It uncompressed into the current working directory, and then the patch would mysteriously fail because it would count the number of files in the directory, and it would find one file too many—the patch file itself. It was necessary to move the compressed patch file out of the directory before the patch would install. Oracle did a wonderful thing with the patch set for 8.1.5.0.2—the patch will uncompress into its own subdirectory. The reason I described issues with previous patches is because I can't be certain how future patches will be delivered, and you should be aware of previous problems. Read any documentation that ships with the patch. Always shut down the database server when you install patches that relate to the server.

1. Uncompress the patch.

```
$ cd /home/oracle/patches
```

```
$ tar zxvf linux_815patches.tgz
```

2. Make sure your **$ORACLE_HOME** environment variable is set:

```
$ echo $ORACLE_HOME
```

```
/u01/app/oracle/product/8.1.5
```

3. Change into the newly created patch directory:

```
$ cd linux_815patches
```

4. Read the README file:

```
$ more README
```

5. Run the shell script that's now in the current directory:

```
./linux_815patches.sh
```

Build the Database Creation Scripts

The Database Configuration Assistant utility (**dbassist**) is used to delete, create, or modify a database. There are two reasons why we will be creating database creation scripts rather than having the Oracle Database Configuration Assistant configure a basic database for us. The first is because you most likely will run into bugs during the installation process that will halt you in your tracks. The second is because it provides a great opportunity to see what components make up the database. Use the Help feature extensively during each of the steps to create the database scripts.

When you run **dbassist** you might get a warning that says "JNLS Exception:oracle.ntp.jnls.JNLSException Unable to find any National Character Sets. Please check installation." This is a known bug; ignore the warning and press **OK**.

1. Run **dbassist** (see Figure 3.5).
2. Select **Create database**.
3. Select **Custom** as the type of database to create. Typical is not supposed to work.
4. Select **Hybrid** as the type of environment in which the database will operate. If you know the database will be handling short transactions you can select Online Transaction Processing (OLTP). If you know you will be using your system for large reports, select Decision Support System (DSS). If you are not sure, Hybrid is the best choice.
5. When asked for the approximate number of users that will be connected concurrently to the database at any given time, keep the default.
6. Select **Dedicated Server Mode** when asked which mode you want your database to operate by default.

Figure 3.5 Oracle Database Configuration Assistant.

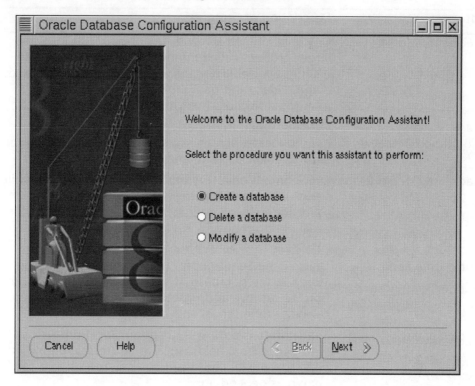

7. Select the options you would like to configure (see Table 3.3): Oracle interMedia, Oracle Visual Information Retrieval, Oracle interMedia Text, Oracle Time Series, Oracle Spatial, Oracle JServer, Advanced Replication, Enable interMedia demos, and SQL*Plus help tables. If you are simply going to test the database, it is not necessary to configure the options. The options will require additional disk space and use additional memory, especially JServer. The options can be configured later. I recommend not installing any of the options at this time. You will have more than enough features within the database itself to keep you busy learning.

Table 3.3 Oracle8i Options

Options	Description of Features
Oracle interMedia	Oracle combined a few different products into one larger product called interMedia. Oracle interMedia enables Oracle8i to manage text, documents, images, audio, video, and geographic information in an integrated fashion. (Not fully available under 8.1.5.)
Oracle Visual Information Retrieval	Oracle8i Visual Information Retrieval (VIR) makes it easy to locate visually similar images, based on criteria such as color, pattern, and texture.
Oracle interMedia Text	Oracle interMedia text provides text retrieval capabilities. It will index documents and provide text searches to locate archived documents. All search options are available from any PL/SQL or SQL tool. interMedia used to be called Oracle ConText.
Oracle Time Series	Oracle Time Series allows time-stamped data to be stored in the database. It supports a basic set of functions to retrieve and process data. Functions include calendar, time series, and time scaling.
Oracle Spatial	Spatial data is data with a specific location. Databases with geographic fields, such as addresses, phone numbers, and postal codes can be analyzed using a service known as geocoding.
Oracle JServer	JServer is Oracle's Java2-compliant Java virtual machine. Java code can be stored and executed from within the database.
Advanced Replication	Replication is the process of copying and maintaining database objects in multiple databases that make up a distributed database system.

8. The next dialog box (see Figure 3.6) requests a global database name and a SID. The global database name will default to **dbname**, and the SID will default to the value of the ORACLE_SID environment variable that should have been set previously, which may be **oracl**. The global database name refers to the database, whereas the SID refers to the instance servicing the database. The global database name can have two components, a database name and a domain name. This is similar to Internet host names. For example, using the address

www.oracle.com, the www is the hostname, and oracle.com is the domain. The idea is to allow every Oracle database in the world to have a unique qualified name. Oracle recommends that you use your current domain. For example, within Oracle, you might see global database names such as **db.oracle.com**. The database name is limited to eight characters and the domain is limited to 128 characters. The length of SID is operating-system-dependent, but should be kept to eight characters, although four is recommended. Usually the database name portion of the global database name is the same as the SID. A domain name is not necessary, so you can simply enter the same name in both fields, such as **orcl** and **orcl**. If the fields appear blank, press the button labeled **Next** and then at the next screen, press the **Back** button.

Figure 3.6 Database Configuration Assistant initialization parameters.

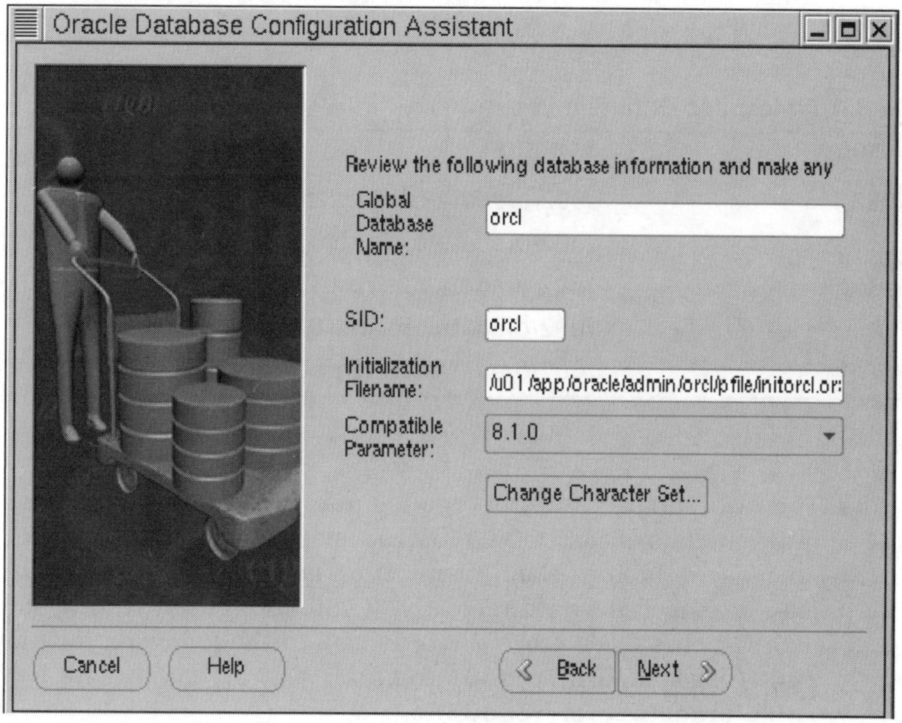

9. Review the control file parameter information. A control file is required to mount and access a database. For a basic test database, use the default parameters. If you set up your file system with Oracle's OFA, you can optionally change the directory path of the control files to **/u02/oradata/orcl/control01.ctl** and **/u03/oradata/orcl/control01.ctl**.

10. The next screen has tabs for SYSTEM, USER, ROLLBACK, INDEX, and TEMPORARY. These are tablespaces that serve specific purposes. The SYSTEM tablespace contains most of the administrative tables and the data dictionary, the USER tablespace stores user objects, the ROLLBACK tablespace stores rollback segments, the INDEX tablespace holds indexes, and the TEMPORARY tablespace stores temporary tables. Notice the initial size for each tablespace and the location. The defaults are fine for a test database. If you configured your file system with Oracle's OFA, reference Table 3.4 for directory locations.

Table 3.4 Tablespace Data File Locations

Tablespace	Location
SYSTEM	/u02/oradata/orcl/system01.dbf
USER	/u02/oradata/orcl/user01.dbf
ROLLBACK	/u02/oradata/orcl/rbs01.dbf
INDEX	/u02/oradata/orcl/indx01.dbf
TEMPORARY	/u02/oradata/orcl/temp01.dbf

11. The next screen contains redo log information. Increase the size of the redo logs to 5000KB (5MB). Redo logs are required to open the database. Each transaction gets recorded in a redo log—it is used for data recovery. If you configured your system with Oracle's OFA, store the redo logs in the following locations: **/u03/oradata/orcl/redo01.log** and **/u03/oradata/orcl/redo02.log**.

12. Review logging parameter information. The redo logs get switched under certain circumstances. The checkpoint interval guarantees they get switched at certain times.

13. The next screen displays System Global information that relates to memory usage. The SGA can dramatically affect database performance. A production database will require monitoring and modification of the SGA. The default parameters should be sufficient for a sample database.

NOTE

The database block size must be specified during database installation. It cannot be changed after the database has been created.

14. Review the debugging path into which debugging trace files for user and background processes get written.

15. Save information to a shell script rather than having the Oracle Database Assistant create the database for you. Select **Finished** when done. Save the script into the default path, which should be **/u01/app/oracle/product/8.1.5/install/sqlorcl.sh**.

Running the Database Creation Scripts

Take a look at the file **$ORACLE_HOME/install/sql<SID>.sh**. This file is used to call other files individually. Run the file to begin building the database.

```
$ cd $ORACLE_HOME/install

$ ./sqlorcl.sh
```

It's time to get a cup of coffee or tea, and patiently await your new database. A full instance with all options takes about 20 minutes to over an hour to build.

Post-Installation

Now that Oracle is installed, you must be chomping at the bit to start using it. Before you do, you need to take care of a few things, including changing a few critical passwords, setting a new date format, and configuring Linux to start and stop Oracle automatically.

SYS and SYSTEM Accounts

There are three special accounts created by default under Oracle: internal, SYS, and SYSTEM. The account internal is a special account, often used by scripts. The account SYS owns the administrative tables and the data dictionary. You should rarely use the SYS account. The SYSTEM account owns all administrative tables and views created after the database is installed, as well as those used by Oracle tools. The SYSTEM account is not directly related to the SYSTEM tablespace, even though they share the same name. The SYS and SYSTEM account passwords should be changed. Replace **newpassword** in the following example with a password of your own choosing.

To change the passwords, login using **svrmgrl**:

```
[oracle@dbsvr oracle]$ svrmgrl


Oracle Server Manager Release 3.0.5.0.0 - Production


(c) Copyright 1997, Oracle Corporation.   All Rights Reserved.


Oracle8 Release 8.0.5.1.0 - Production
PL/SQL Release 8.0.5.1.0 - Production


SVRMGR> connect internal
Connected.
SVRMGR> alter user sys identified by newpassword;
Statement processed.
SVRMGR> alter user system identified by newpassword;
Statement processed.
SVRMGR>
```

All of the base tables and views for the data dictionary are stored in the schema SYS. You should not modify any object in the SYS schema; this should be done only by Oracle. The SYSTEM account is granted all system privileges for the database and is used to create additional tables and views involved with database administration. The SYSTEM account is generally made the owner of tables and views used by Oracle tools.

Parameter File Configuration

Oracle uses a file called the *initialization parameter file* during startup. The file is named **initSID.ora**, and is simply referred to as **INIT.ORA**. Replace SID with your **$ORACLE_SID**. In Oracle8 the file is located under **/u01/admin/$ORACLE_SID/pfile**. In Oracle8i, the file is located under **/u01/app/oracle/admin/$ORACLE_SID/pfile**. The initialization file can include parameters to optimize database performance, set defaults, set limits, and specify filenames. The parameters that define the SGA memory structures are located in the **INIT.ORA** file. The default **INIT.ORA** file that is installed in a new database includes three basic settings labeled SMALL, MEDIUM, and LARGE. The medium and large settings are usually commented out. Depending on the amount of RAM installed, the parameters can be increased. It is beyond the scope of this chapter to describe the vast variety of initialization options. All that I can recommend is to start out with the default settings. One parameter that should be changed is the date format. The standard output for dates in the Oracle server appear with two-digit years; for example, 10-APR-99. To see four-digit years, the **nls_date_format** in the **INIT.ORA** file should be added. Edit the **INIT.ORA** file and add the following line:

```
nls_date_format = "YYYY-MM-DD"
```

Automatic Startup and Shutdown

It is helpful to have Oracle automatically start up and shut down with Linux. Oracle includes a script called **dbstart** that can be used in run-control scripts. The **dbstart** script consults the **/etc/oratab** file to see what instances should be started and stopped automatically.

```
# more /etc/oratab
# The last parameter tells dbstart whether it should start and stop Oracle
  (Y/N)
orcl:/u01/app/oracle/product/8.0.5:Y
```

A run-level is a logical state used to define a configuration. A system in run-level 3 might have different processes running than in run-level 4. A Red Hat system usually runs at run-level 3 or run-level 5. Run-level 3 is considered full multi-user mode, and run-level 5 provides an X Windows login screen. Under Red Hat Linux, run-control scripts are stored under **/etc/rc.d/init.d**. Symbolic links are created under **../rc0.d**, **../rc1.d**, **../rc2.d**, **../rc3.d**, **../rc4.d**, **../rc5.d**, and **../rc6.d**, depending on what run-level an action should take place. The symbolic links start with either S or K, depending on whether they should be started or killed, and are followed by a number depending on what order the scripts in the directory should run. The **telinit** command is used change Linux run-levels. Do a **man init** to find more information on run-levels.

You can use the following script as a starting point. Copy the contents to a file called **oracle** in the **/etc/rc.d/init.d** directory. You also need to make the script executable: **chmod u+x oracle**. Make sure to change the **ORA_HOME** environment variable to match your configuration.

```
#!/bin/bash
# Start and stop the Oracle Instance
#
# chkconfig: 345 91 19
# description: Starts the Oracle listener and instance

ORA_HOME="/u01/app/oracle/product/8.1.5"
ORA_OWNER="oracle"

if [ ! -f $ORA_HOME/bin/dbstart -o ! -d $ORA_HOME ]
then
        echo "Oracle startup: cannot start"
        exit 1
fi
case "$1" in
  start)
      # Startup the Oracle listener and instance
      echo -n "Oracle startup: "
      su - $ORA_OWNER -c "$ORA_HOME/bin/lsnrctl start"
      su - $ORA_OWNER -c $ORA_HOME/bin/dbstart
      touch /var/lock/subsys/oracle
      echo "Finished"
      ;;
  stop)
      # Shutdown the Oracle listener and instance
      echo -n "Oracle shutdown: "
      su - $ORA_OWNER -c "$ORA_HOME/bin/lsnrctl stop"
      su - $ORA_OWNER -c $ORA_HOME/bin/dbshut
      rm -f /var/lock/subsys/oracle
      echo "Finished"
      ;;
  reload|restart)
    $0 stop
    $0 start
      ;;
  *)
```

```
        echo "Usage: /etc/rc.d/init.d/oracle {start|stop|restart|reload}"
        exit 1
esac

exit 0
```

The line that says **# chkconfig: 345 91 19** is used by the **chkconfig** program. The **345** tells Linux in what run-levels the script should be run. The number **91** tells Linux in what order to start Oracle. The number **19** tells Linux in what order to stop Oracle. Running the **chkconfig** program will create symbolic links of the Oracle script into the various run-level directories. Do a **man chkconfig** to find more information about Red Hat's **chkconfig** utility.

```
#chkconfig -add oracle
```

Network Configuration

Networking under Oracle8/8i is called Net8. Oracle8 and Oracle8i use similar network configuration files. There is no utility to assist with network configuration in Oracle8; therefore, they must be modified by hand. Oracle8i provides a Java-based application called Network Assistant that configures the networking.

The Oracle server supports many network protocols. The two most popular methods of connecting to networked Oracle servers are TCP/IP hostnames and transport network substrate (TNS) service names. If you choose to install a single instance on your server, you can get by with using TCP hostnames to connect remotely. For example, if your Linux server had the hostname **fred**, you could use **fred** as the connect string for the service name to connect to the instance. A server running multiple Oracle instances cannot use TCP/IP hostnames. TNS maps service names to hosts running different protocols, including TCP/IP, and the instance name can be specified. TNS names are stored in the **$ORACLE_HOME/network/admin** directory in a file called **tnsnames.ora**.

Here is an example of the **tnsnames.ora** entry specifying the host 192.168.10.1, running on port 1521, with the instance name **orcl**.

```
orcl =
  (DESCRIPTION =
    (ADDRESS = (PROTOCOL= TCP)(Host= 192.168.10.1)(Port= 1521))
    (CONNECT_DATA = (SID = orcl))
  )
```

Oracle8i includes the Net8 Assistant, which can be used to configure networking (see Figure 3.7). If you only have one server, you can get away with using TCP Hostnames to access your server. Some organizations use Oracle Names Servers, which are centralized repositories of service names. Clients can use the Oracle Names Server as a resource to look up Oracle instances. Two Java applications—**netasst** and **netca**—are used to configure networking under Oracle8i.

Figure 3.7 Net8 Assistant.

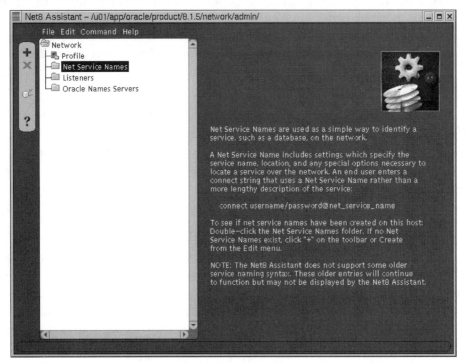

Using Oracle8/8i

Now that Oracle is installed, you are ready to start using it. This section describes how to start and stop the server, describes what processes are involved with the database, explains how to create an account, how to use SQL*Plus, provides an overview of the data dictionary, and gives a brief introduction on getting data into and out of the database.

Startup and Shutdown

The Oracle Server Manager, **svrmgrl**, or SQL*Plus can be used to start and stop the instance. The functionality of Server Manager is being integrated into SQL*Plus, and Oracle is planning to discontinue the utility at some point in the future. I prefer **svrmgrl** to SQL*Plus for performing basic database administration tasks, and therefore this section will briefly describe the Server Manager. The **l** in **svrmgrl** stands for line mode. Some platforms include a GUI version of the Server Manager; Linux does not. SQL*Plus will be described later in the chapter. Server Manager includes a group of commands to administer the database. The **STARTUP**, **SHUT-DOWN**, and **SHOW SGA** commands will be presented (see Table 3.5).

Table 3.5 Server Manager Startup and Shutdown Commands

Command	Description
STARTUP	Starts the instance, mounts the database to the instance, and opens the database.
STARTUP NOMOUNT	Starts the instance. Rarely used.
STARTUP MOUNT	Starts the instance and mounts the database to the instance. The database is not opened. Used for certain administrative tasks.
STARTUP OPEN RECOVER	Starts the instance, mounts the database to the instance, opens the database, and begins recovery. You will get an error if recovery is not necessary. Recovery usually begins automatically.
SHUTDOWN NORMAL	Oracle waits for all connections to disconnect.
SHUTDOWN TRANSACTIONAL	Oracle waits for all transactions to finish and then disconnects connections.
SHUTDOWN IMMEDIATE	Active transactions are rolled back, and connections are disconnected. Some SQL statements are allowed to finish.
SHUTDOWN ABORT	SQL statements being processed are terminated, uncommitted transactions are not rolled back, and all connections are disconnected.

An instance can be started with the **STARTUP** command and stopped with the **SHUTDOWN** command. The instance can be started without actually mounting the database using the **STARTUP NOMOUNT** command, which usually is performed only during database creation. The database can also be started and mounted, but not actually opened by using the **STARTUP MOUNT** command. This is useful if you want to rename files, enable or disable redo log archive log options, or perform a full database recovery. Use the **ALTER DATABASE OPEN** command to open a database. The **STARTUP RESTRICT** command is used to open the database in restricted mode, which allows database access to be restricted to only users with both the **CREATE SESSION** and **RESTRICTED SESSION** privileges. A parameter file can be selected by using the **STARTUP PFILE=initSID.ora** command. In most circumstances, the basic **STARTUP** command should be sufficient to start the database.

```
SVRMGR> help
The following are SIMPLIFIED syntax descriptions. For complete syntax
descriptions, please refer to the Oracle Server Manager User's Guide.


STARTUP      [DBA] [FORCE] [PFILE=filespec] [EXCLUSIVE | SHARED]
             [MOUNT dbname | OPEN dbname] [NOMOUNT]


SHUTDOWN     [NORMAL | IMMEDIATE | ABORT]


MONITOR      For graphical modes only, bring up a monitor


ARCHIVE LOG  [START] [STOP] [LIST] [NEXT] [<n>] [ALL] ['destination']


RECOVER      { [DATABASE [MANUAL] ] | [TABLESPACE ts-name [,tsname]] }


CONNECT      [username [/password] ] [INTERNAL] ['@'instance-spec]
DISCONNECT


SET          options: INSTANCE, ECHO, TERMOUT, TIMING, NUMWIDTH, CHARWIDTH
SHOW         LONGWIDTH, DATEWIDTH, AUTOPRINT and for SHOW: ALL, SPOOL


EXIT
REM
             SQL statements can also be executed.
```

The instance can be shutdown with the **SHUTDOWN** command. The biggest issue to deal with during shutdown is open transactions. If users are connected to the instance with open transactions, you must decide how to deal with the transactions. The **SHUTDOWN NORMAL** command waits for all currently connected users to disconnect from the database, in which case all transactions will be completed. The **SHUTDOWN IMMEDIATE** command will roll back any uncommitted transactions, and will disconnect connections to the instance. Despite the name of the command, it can take time to roll back uncommitted transactions. Certain processes are allowed to finish before disconnection. The **SHUTDOWN TRANSACTIONAL** command allows active transactions to complete. This command prevents users from losing work and will disconnect users from the instance once all transactions are finished. This option can take a long time if users leave uncommitted transactions open. The final, and last-ditch effort command is **SHUTDOWN ABORT**. This command shuts the instance down instantly. Client SQL statements are terminated, transactions are not rolled back, and all users are disconnected. This command will require a database recovery to be performed the next time the database is started, which should happen automatically. If it does not, use the **STARTUP OPEN RECOVER** command. Once any of the **SHUTDOWN** commands have been submitted, no further connections are permitted. For more information on the Server Manager, type **HELP** at the Server Manager prompt.

To see the System Global Area memory usage, use the **SHOW SGA** command from SQL*Plus or Server Manager. The command will list total system global area, fixed size, variable size, database buffers, and redo buffers.

```
SVRMGR> connect / as sysdba
Connected.
SVRMGR> show sga
Total System Global Area                    8154384 bytes
Fixed Size                                    48400 bytes
Variable Size                               6905856 bytes
Database Buffers                            1126400 bytes
Redo Buffers                                  73728 bytes
```

Background Processes

When Oracle is running, you will notice many different running processes. Here is a quick run-down of each process' responsibilities. A **ps** command will show that each process includes the instance SID as part of its process name.

```
[oracle@dbsvr oracle]$ ps aux|grep ora_
oracle    3798  0.0  4.4 114916 5656  ?      S    12:38   0:00 ora_pmon_orcl
oracle    3800  0.0  4.5 114884 5828  ?      S    12:38   0:00 ora_dbw0_orcl
oracle    3802  0.0  4.2 114368 5440  ?      S    12:38   0:00 ora_lgwr_orcl
oracle    3804  0.0  4.0 114348 5152  ?      S    12:38   0:00 ora_ckpt_orcl
oracle    3806  0.0  9.6 114388 12316 ?      S    12:38   0:02 ora_smon_orcl
oracle    3808  0.0  5.4 114396 7024  ?      S    12:38   0:00 ora_reco_orcl
oracle    3810  0.0  3.6 114300 4732  ?      S    12:38   0:00 ora_s000_orcl
oracle    3812  0.0  3.9 114416 5008  ?      S    12:38   0:00 ora_d000_orcl
oracle    3814  0.0  4.0 114468 5136  ?      S    12:38   0:00 ora_arc0_orcl
```

You may not have the same set of processes running on your machine. There are five Oracle processes you are almost guaranteed to have running: the database writer, log writer, system monitor, process monitor, and the checkpoint process. Notice that each process is preceded with **ora** and each ends with the instance name. The database writer (DBW0) is responsible for writing changed data to the physical data files. When data is changed, it is placed in the database buffer cache. During certain intervals the database writer writes dirty buffers from the database buffer cache to the database files. The database writer must ensure that sufficient numbers of free buffer are available in the database buffer cache. Database performance is improved since changes are made to a memory buffer rather than on disk. Multiple database writer processes can be started to improve performance, although one is usually sufficient. The log writer (LGWR) records changes registered in the redo log buffer to the redo log files. The log writer performs sequential writes to the redo log file under the following circumstances: when the redo log buffer is one-third full, when a timeout occurs (every three seconds), when a transaction commits, and before the database writer writes modified blocks in the database buffer cache to the data files. The system monitor (SMON) checks for database consistency and initiates recovery of the database when the database is opened. The process monitor (PMON) cleans up resources for failed processes. The checkpoint process (CKPT) is responsible for updating the database status information whenever changes in the buffer cache are permanently recorded in the database.

Optional processes include the archiver, recoverer, dispatcher, and the shared server process. The archiver (ARCn) copies the online redo logs to archival storage when they are full or when a switch occurs. Archiving redo logs is an important database protection strategy. If the database crashes and datafiles are lost, you can use the backups to restore the database to a certain point-in-time state, and then use the archived redo logs to bring the database further forward in history. If the database is in archive log mode and the archiver cannot find free space to archive a redo log, all database transactions will be halted. The recoverer (RECO) is used in a distributed database configuration to resolve pending transactions possibly caused by network or system failure. The dispatcher (Dnnn) is used in multithreaded server configurations. The dispatcher routes requests from each user process to shared server processes and back to the user process. There is at least one dispatcher for each communication protocol. The shared server process (Snnn) is used in a multithreaded server configuration to serve client requests. There are three additional processes you are unlikely to see right away, which include the lock process (LCK0), job queue (SNPn), and the queue monitor (QMNn). These processes are used for Oracle Parallel Server, refreshing table snapshots, and for Advanced Oracle Queuing, respectively.

Each process manages its own set of tasks. Sometimes one process will fight with another process over a resource. For example, the log writer and database writer might try to access a drive at the same time. Situations like these are important to consider in a robust production environment.

Creating an Account

There are three issues you need to consider when creating a user account. The first is to create the account itself, the second is to give rights to the account, and the third is to give the account a quota on one or more tablespaces. There are many issues to consider regarding Oracle security. The following instructions will help you create a basic login account with no thrills. You must be logged in with DBA rights to create user accounts. You should use the SYSTEM account to initially create an account for yourself. The following command creates a user named **pat** with the password **er34533**. The user has the default tablespace **users** and the temporary tablespace **temp**. It is important to specify a default tablespace for accounts. You do not want users creating objects in the SYSTEM tablespace. The final line provides the user unlimited space on the tablespace **users**. Rather than unlimited, you can limit the quota by specifying a size such as **50M** for 50 MB, or **500K** for 500 KB.

```
SQL> CREATE USER pat
  2   IDENTIFIED BY er34533
  3   DEFAULT TABLESPACE users
  4   TEMPORARY TABLESPACE temp
  5   QUOTA unlimited ON users;
```

Once the account has been created, it must be assigned rights to connect to the database. There are two types of privileges, system and object. System privileges enable users to perform actions in the database including creating, dropping, and altering tables, views, rollback segments, and procedures. Object privileges enable users to access and modify objects within the database such as tables, views, sequences, procedures, functions, or packages. There are 80 system privileges. The **GRANT** command grants a privilege to a user and the **REVOKE** command revokes a user's privilege. The **DBA_SYS_PRIVS** view lists the system privileges granted to users. A user can identify system privileges available to the current session by querying the **SESSION_PRIVS** view. Because there are so many individual privileges, it can be difficult maintaining multiple privileges on a large number of user accounts. Oracle helps the database administer with managing privileges through the use of *roles*. Privileges can be assigned to roles, which can themselves be granted to users. There are a variety of predefined roles in Oracle. The three most popular are CONNECT, RESOURCE, and DBA. The CONNECT role gives sufficient rights for most users to access and use the database. The RESOURCE role provides additional rights that might be useful to database programmers. The DBA role has all privileges. To assign users to a role, use the **GRANT** command. Users can be members of multiple roles.

```
SQL> GRANT CONNECT TO pat;
```

The DBA can change a user's password by using the **ALTER USER IDENTIFIED** command. An individual user can use the **PASSWORD** command to change the account password.

```
SQL> alter user pat identified by secret_pwd;


User altered.


SQL> password
Changing password for PAT
Old password:
New password:
Retype new password:
```

You can view connections with the following DBA command: **SELECT * from v$session**. To kill a session immediately, use the command **ALTER SYSTEM KILL SESSION sid,session**. Get the **sid** and the **session** from **v$session**. To disconnect a session after an active transaction has completed, use the command **ALTER SYSTEM DISCONNECT sid,session POST_TRANSACTION**. For example, after doing a **SELECT** query on **v$session**, a record exists for the user Pat with a SID of 7, and a SESSION of 15; you would use the command **ALTER SYSTEM KILL SESSION '7,15'**.

SQL*Plus

SQL*Plus is the primary interface to the Oracle server provided by Oracle for the Linux platform. It is a terminal-based application that supports SQL statements and PL/SQL blocks. It also has a variety of useful functions including the ability to format the output of SQL queries. SQL*Plus looks simple, but in reality it is chock-full of features. There are books dedicated to SQL*Plus. This section will briefly describe a few important features just to get you rolling. SQL*Plus should be installed in the

$ORACLE_HOME/bin directory. To start the application, you can either type **sqlplus** or you can append a connect string, **sqlplus pat/er34533**.

NOTE

The connect string is used to login to a database and is dependent on the network protocol. Two common protocols are TNS names and TPC/IP hostnames. Its standard form is user/password@net_service_name. Most applications will accept user@net_service_name and will prompt for the password. For example, an instance with the name **orcl** might be accessed by using the connect string scott/tiger@orcl. If only one instance is running on a server, the instance can often be accessed simply by using the TCP/IP hostname as the service name.

You will notice that SQL*Plus has the default prompt **SQL>**. You can change the prompt using the **SET** command: **SET SQLPROMPT *new-prompt>***. To exit SQL*Plus, simply type **EXIT**. SQL*Plus commands are case-insensitive. Once you are at the SQL> prompt, you can type SQL statements. A statement must end with a semicolon, a slash (/) on a line by itself, or a blank line. The blank line will end the SQL command input and store it in the buffer, but it will not submit the query.

All SQL commands are stored in the buffer. You can re-execute the buffer with a slash or the command **RUN**. You can view the buffer with the command **LIST**. To edit a command, type **LIST** to see the buffer. Each line will have a line number. Find the line you wish to change and type the line number in SQL*Plus. The line becomes active. Use the **CHANGE** command to modify text. For example, to change the word **all_objects** to **user_objects** use the command **change/all_/user_**.

The buffer is handy, but there is a better way to edit commands— using an editor. The SQL*Plus variable **_editor** contains the editor that will be opened by SQL*Plus. Use the **DEFINE** command to view and set the value of **_editor**. To view the value of **_editor**, simply type **define _editor**; to change the value, type **define _editor=vi**.

```
SQL>define _editor
DEFINE _EDITOR          = "ed" (CHAR)
SQL>define _editor=vi
SQL>define _editor
DEFINE _EDITOR          = "vi" (CHAR)
```

Use the **EDIT** command to place the contents of the buffer into the external editor. Oracle actually stores the contents of the buffer into a file called **afiedt.buf**, which is opened by the editor. Once you are finished making changes to the SQL statements, save the changes and exit the editor, and you will return to SQL*Plus. The buffer will now reflect the changes you made in the editor. Type the command **RUN** to execute the statement. It is common to end an SQL statement edited through an editor using a slash (/) on a line by itself.

```
SELECT user_name, city, state FROM customer_info
/
```

The contents of the buffer can be saved to a file by using the **SAVE** command. The extension **.sql** will be attached to the filename automatically. You can replace the buffer with the contents of a file by using the **GET** command. To execute a script immediately, rather than simply placing it into the buffer, use the @ command preceding the filename. The file must have the **.sql** extension to be recognized.

> SQL> SAVE *filename*
>
> SQL> GET *filename*
>
> SQL> @*filename*

The **HOST** command can be used to process Linux commands. For example, to see the contents of a directory within SQL*Plus, use the **HOST** command to run the **ls** command. A shortcut for **HOST** is an exclamation mark (**!**): SQL> **!ls**.

```
SQL> host ls
init.sql   loop.sql
SQL> !ls
init.sql   loop.sql
```

Preferences can be stored in a file called **login.sql** in the default directory from which SQL*Plus is launched. The **COMMIT** command must be used after changing data using an SQL statement. SQL*Plus can automatically commit transactions after each statement or after a certain number of statements using the **SET AUTOCOMMIT ON** or a number reflecting the number of statements between commits. To disable autocommit, use **SET AUTOCOMMIT OFF**. The **DESCRIBE** command, or **DESC**, is used to identify the structure of an object.

```
SQL> describe all_objects;
 Name                            Null?     Type
 ------------------------------- --------- -------------
 OWNER                           NOT NULL  VARCHAR2(30)
 OBJECT_NAME                     NOT NULL  VARCHAR2(30)
 SUBOBJECT_NAME                            VARCHAR2(30)
```

```
OBJECT_ID                  NOT NULL NUMBER
DATA_OBJECT_ID                      NUMBER
OBJECT_TYPE                         VARCHAR2(15)
CREATED                    NOT NULL DATE
LAST_DDL_TIME              NOT NULL DATE
TIMESTAMP                           VARCHAR2(19)
STATUS                              VARCHAR2(7)
TEMPORARY                           VARCHAR2(1)
GENERATED                           VARCHAR2(1)
```

SQL*Plus can also be used to start and shut down the instance. The statement, "Connect to Oracle as SYSDBA" has a special meaning. A user logged into the Oracle server as SYSDBA has special privileges. To login with SYSDBA authority, add the text **as sysdba** to the end of your connect string. For example, to have the account **pat** log in to the Oracle server with SYSDBA privileges, you would use the following connect string: **connect pat/mypasswd as sysdba**. As a shortcut, if you are logged into an account that is a member of the dba group, you can simply type **connect / as sysdba**. The user must be a member of the OSDBA group.

A popular user account in demonstrations is **scott** with the password **tiger**. If you create the account, it is not advisable to leave **tiger** as the password because it is widely known and published. Some utilities actually expect the account to exist, and fail if not found. Also popular is a set of tables including DEPT, EMP, BONUS, and SALGRADE. The tables can be created through the script **$ORACLE_HOME/rdbms/admin/utlsampl.sql**. A user with DBA privileges, besides SYSTEM, should run the script if you are interested creating the tables. The **$ORACLE_HOME/rdbms/admin** directory contains many optional scripts. Most of the scripts include comments that explain the purpose of the script. Certain scripts must be processed by a particular user such as SYS or SYSTEM.

Data Dictionary

Oracle's data dictionary is a central repository of read-only reference tables and views. Oracle uses the data dictionary to look up object definitions, space allocation, integrity constraints, privileges, auditing information, and other information. The underlying configuration of the data dictionary is a set of read-only, normalized tables that are difficult to read. User-accessible views are created to make the data easier for us humans to read. The data dictionary is owned by the SYS schema, and it should be altered only by Oracle Corporation. Changes to the SYS schema can damage the database, and thus the account should be kept secure. There are many public synonyms for data dictionary views, including three basic sets of views: ALL, USER, and DBA. There is also a set of dynamic performance tables that begin with **V\$**. The USER views include items in the user's schema. The ALL views include everything the user can access. The DBA views include what all users can see and are designed for the database administrator. The ALL_OBJECTS view is especially lengthy because it includes all the objects a user can access.

```
SELECT * from ALL_OBJECTS;
```

There are three other data dictionary objects that should be mentioned: DUAL, CAT, and DICT. DUAL is a special table composed of one column named DUMMY with the value **X**. The DUAL table is used to fulfill the requirement that all select statements include a FROM clause identifying a table.

```
SELECT sysdate FROM dual;
```

The CAT view is a synonym for USER_CATALOG. This view lists tables, views, synonyms, and sequences owned by the user.

```
SELECT * from CAT;
```

DICT is a synonym for DICTIONARY. This view contains descriptions of data dictionary tables and views.

```
SQL> COLUMN table_name FORMAT a15
SQL> COLUMN comments FORMAT a50
SQL> SELECT * FROM dict WHERE table_name='DICTIONARY';


TABLE_NAME       COMMENTS
---------------  --------------------------------------------------

DICTIONARY       Description of data dictionary tables and views
```

The dynamic performance views are updated by the Oracle server throughout its operation. These virtual tables are not accessible by most users and are used by the database administrator to get information about the database. It is used extensively in database performance tuning, the dynamic performance views being with V\$.

```
SQL> SELECT * from v$version;


BANNER
-------------------------------------------
Oracle8 Release 8.0.5.1.0 - Production
PL/SQL Release 8.0.5.1.0 - Production
CORE Version 4.0.5.0.0 - Production
TNS for Linux: Version 8.0.5.0.0 - Production
NLSRTL Version 3.3.2.0.0 - Production
```

Import/Export

There are three utilities used to get large amounts of data into and out of the Oracle database: Export, Import, and SQL*Loader. Each utility has a vast number of options and features. The Export utility, called **exp**, extracts the object definitions and data from an Oracle database and stores them in a binary file, often called a dump. The Import utility, **imp**, inserts the extracted data into either the same or another database. Export dump files can be read only by the Import utility. Export is not the typical method of backing up a database, but it can be used to create a permanent copy of a schema to be duplicated onto other servers, or to archive if a user leaves an organization. The primary use of Export and Import is to get data from one Oracle server to another. The script CATEXP.SQL or CATALOG.SQL, which runs CATEXP.SQL, must be run to configure Oracle for the Import utility. The script needs to be run only once.

SQL*Loader is used to import data from other databases. SQL*Loader can read an external file containing data stored in a variety of formats. For example, SQL*Loader can import a fixed-width file or a variable-width record using delimiters, such as a tab, to identify columns. SQL*Load requires a control file that describes the data and specifies the input data files. SQL*Plus produces a log file and a reject file containing rejected records.

For IT Professionals

WebDB

WebDB is an Oracle product that provides a Web-based interface to the Oracle database. WebDB is basically a Web-site construction kit written in PL/SQL. It is completely contained within the database and the user interacts solely through a standard Web browser. WebDB provides some database administration features such as account and object management. It also provides simple template-driven development tools that allow end-users to design their own Web pages, reports, and forms. The interface includes folders in which users can store reports, forms, and documents.

WebDB contains all the components for a complete site, including a PL/SQL and HTTP listener. When the HTTP listener receives a request, it forwards it to the PL/SQL gateway, which processes the request to the Oracle server and returns the results to the client. All Web-related files and data are stored within the server. WebDB uses standard Oracle security, which makes managing individual accounts easier.

Continued

Interfacing with WebDB is accomplished through standard Internet-based protocols. The client does not need special libraries or network software to connect to the WebDB server. WebDB builds on the skills that DBAs already possess. WebDB is suitable for an intranet site where users regularly interface with the database. It is useful to the DBA, end-user, and developers.

Third-Party Software

There are a number of third-party applications supporting Oracle for the Linux platform. Four applications will be mentioned in this section, including Orasoft SQLWork, Orasoft Object Manager, Orac, and Perl DBI.

Orasoft

Orasoft (www.orasoft.org) is an active open-source project working to bring high-quality, enterprise-level applications to the Linux platform. At press time, there are five applications including SQLWork, Procedit, Session Monitor, Table Browser, and ObjectManager. SQLWork is an SQL worksheet, Procedit is used to edit PL/SQL code, Session Monitor is used to monitor database connections, and Table Browser is used to browse Oracle tables. ObjectManager is the newest member of the application suite, and is designed for database administration. Session Monitor and Table Browser functionality are being rolled into ObjectManager.

SQLWork

Orasoft SQLWork is a graphical SQL worksheet, providing a friendly graphical interface to Oracle (see Figure 3.8). It is written using the GIMP Toolkit (GTK), preinstalled on most Linux distributions. There are many features available including history, bookmarks, printing, and exporting results to file. Results can be viewed free-form or using a grid layout, similar to a spreadsheet. The history feature provides a buffer to store previous commands. The bookmark feature allows you to save SQL statements for later use, similar to a Web browser. Query results can be saved to file or printed.

Figure 3.8 Orasoft SQLWork.

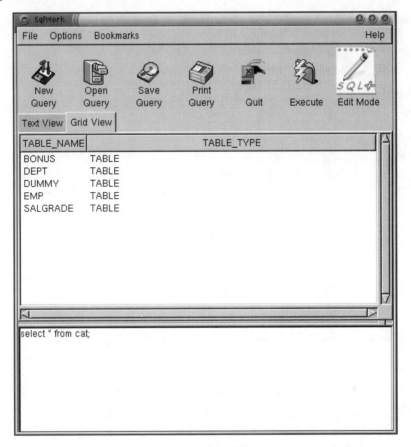

ObjectManager

Orasoft ObjectManager (OM) is designed for database administration. The OM screen is divided into two sections (see Figure 3.9). The leftmost side of the screen lists folders representing the different types of objects available within the Oracle RDBMS. Actually, more than just objects are represented. For example, there is a folder that contains items representing current connections to the database. OM can be used to view, delete, and create objects including tables, indexes, synonyms, and views. OM can also show information on db links, procedures, views, packages, triggers, synonyms, sequences, and types. The rightmost side of the window is used to display information about a selected object. Information is divided into topics accessible via tabs.

Figure 3.9 Orasoft Object Manager.

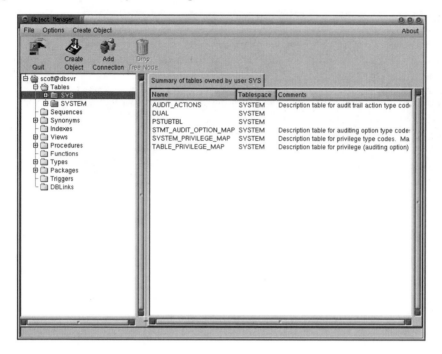

Orac

Orac (www.kkitts.com/orac-dba/) is a database administration tool designed for users with DBA privileges (see Figure 3.10). The application is open-source and written in Perl/Tk, a toolkit originally written to provide graphical functions to the Tcl scripting language. Tk is now available for Perl. Orac includes reporting, graphing, and table editing. It is chockfull of useful reports. For example, you can get a report complete with a bar chart of space utilization. There is also a menu on tuning. The interface takes a little getting used to, but once you get the hang of it, it is a time saver.

Perl/DBI

Perl has become a popular Web-based programming language. Oracle combined with Perl, the Apache Web server, and Linux, provides a powerful Internet platform. It is fairly easy to get Oracle running with Perl.

Connecting to Oracle with Perl requires two packages, DBI and DBD. DBI stands for database independent interface, and is a platform-neutral package of database functions. The second component is DBD, which

Figure 3.10 Orac.

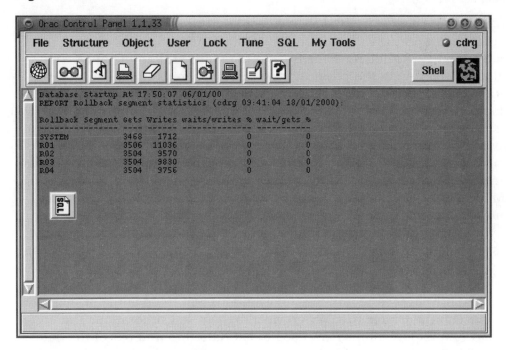

stands for database driver. Each database server requires a separate database driver—DBD::Oracle is the version used with Oracle. Both components can be downloaded from a Comprehensive Perl Archive Network (CPAN) site. A list of CPAN sites can be attained from http://www.perl.com/.

Here is a simple example of program that looks up a status code and prints the status message using Perl to connect to Oracle:

```perl
#!/usr/bin/perl
use DBI;
# Server name is Orcl, User is webuser, password is iluv8i
my $DBH = DBI->connect('orcl', 'webuser', 'iluvo8i') or warn("Cannot connect
to database ", $DBI::errstr);
my $sth = $DBH->prepare("select stat_msg from cust_table where
stat_code=1002");
$sth->execute;
my $hashref = $sth->fetchrow_hashref;
print "Status Message: $hashref->{STAT_MSG}\n";
$DBI->disconnect;
```

Summary

This chapter covered key Oracle concepts that are important to understand when working with the Oracle RDBMS. An important concept to understand is the difference between a database and an instance. The database represents the physical structures, whereas the instance represents the memory structures. A critical memory component is the System Global Area (SGA). The SGA is a key factor in performance tuning. Installation of both Oracle8 and Oracle8i require similar preinstallation steps. Oracle8 requires fewer hardware resources and has been around longer, but Oracle8i is geared toward Internet usage and includes a Java runtime environment built into the server, along with new security and XML features. Oracle8 was designed for Red Hat Linux 5.2 and requires compatibility libraries to run under Red Hat Linux 6.0 and 6.1.

Oracle8 and 8i provide many security features including system privileges, object privileges, and roles. The Data Dictionary is a central repository of read-only reference tables and views. Oracle uses the data dictionary to look up object definitions, space allocation, integrity constraints, privileges, and auditing information. SQL*Plus is the primary interface to the Oracle RDBMS provided by Oracle Corporation. The Import and Export utilities are used to get data into and out of the database. SQL*Loader is used to import data from other databases. Examples of third-party applications for Linux include SQLWork, Object Manager, and Orac. Perl is an excellent language to use in Web development and has excellent connectivity to Oracle.

FAQs

Q: Why can't I run any of the Oracle utilities?

A: Make sure **$ORACLE_HOME/bin** is located in your PATH.

Q: What is the password for the internal account? When I try to connect as the internal account in Server Manager, it requests a password.

A: You are probably logged into an account that is not a member of the dba group listed in the **/etc/group** file, such as root.

Q: The Oracle installer fails and complains about a missing program called **gmake**. Why?

A: Check to see if you have **gmake** installed under **/usr/bin**. If it is installed, make sure your PATH includes the **/usr/bin**. If **gmake** does not exist, as root you can create a symbolic link to **make**: **ln –s /usr/bin/make /usr/bin/gmake**.

Q: Where is the file **libclntsh.so.8.0**?

A: The **libclntsh.so.1.0** for Oracle8 and the **libclntsh.so.8.0** for Oracle8i can be generated by using the script **genclntsh** located in **$ORACLE_HOME/bin**, although it should have been created during installation. Run **genclntsh** if you have problems connecting between 8.1.5 and 8.0.5 machines.

Q: Where can I get more information about Oracle?

A: The Oracle Technology Network (http://technet.oracle.com) provides documentation on all of Oracle's products. Book publisher O'Reilly (http://www.oreilly.com/) has an excellent collection of well-written Oracle books. *Oracle: The Complete Reference* by George Koch and Kevin Loney is a large book that is a useful reference.

Q: Where can I find an Oracle user group?

A: The International Oracle User's Group (http://www.ioug.org/) maintains a list of Oracle user groups.

Chapter 4

An Informix Installation on Linux

Solutions in this chapter:

- Installation
- Space Considerations
- Configuration
- Other Tools
- Resources

Introduction

Informix, like Oracle, is a powerful commercial database. Informix, Oracle, and other enterprise-level databases like IBM's DB2 and Sybase all compete on a variety of platforms, but they are focused primarily on enterprise-level database management, where large volumes of database traffic and storage are required. These products are considered serious contenders for businesses looking for a production database server, one that meets certain load requirements usually found in mid-sized to large corporate business environments.

Informix was one of the first databases on UNIX. Informix had the first ISAM (Indexed Sequential Access Method) product for UNIX, called C-ISAM, which is still available today, and yes, you can get it for Linux. All current database products on the market use an ISAM methodology for their operation, without exception. Informix has many other firsts in the database world, and now can compete with much more expensive products.

All of these database products, including many others not mentioned here, meet a minimum requirement with ISO and the SQL standard as being *entry-level* database products. They all meet the minimum entry point for basic SQL compliance; in addition to the entry-level features that are allowed under the SQL specification, they also are allowed advanced-level features as optional features. No single vendor has implemented all the SQL specifications, but most vendors meet the minimums, and then choose to implement additional features when they have an opportunity to increase their competitive edge. For more information on the SQL standard, be sure to search the World Wide Web (WWW). Vendors also add additional features when endusers scream for more, or when the competition adds a feature that the endusers like and now simply cannot live without.

This chapter focuses on how to install and bring up an Informix engine in the Linux operating environment. The focus is not only on an enterprise-level database engine, but also on an engine that is scalable from Linux upward to the larger servers on the market, primarily in the UNIX operating systems market. Much of what you learn here can be applied to the other UNIX versions of Informix Dynamic Server in the rest of the UNIX world, and to some degree the NT world; however, for now you will find it easier not to worry about any comparisons to NT. Most of the enterprise engines on the market are on UNIX and NT, and in some cases, MVS (on mainframes). The only ones not found on UNIX are the database products from Microsoft, who choose NT as their banner platform from which to scale.

Microsoft is only now starting to take their database market seriously, building products for data warehousing, and data transformation to complement their SQL Server product line. Once a platform in the Intel x86 architecture is big enough for NT to enable it to run as fast as a UNIX or other platform, then SQL Server may have a chance in this arena. Until then you will notice significant performance differences between UNIX and NT, and of course, Linux. NT will tend to perform well using Informix in small workgroups, but better performance ratios are found in UNIX and Linux.

Preference usually follows lines of exposure. If a developer is exposed to Informix first, that developer most likely will continue to support Informix out of personal preference. This is especially true once you see how easy Informix is to manage compared to some of the other products on the market. The reason is simplicity: A typical Oracle instance takes approximately 600MB of disk space just for the software, not to mention the additional space needed for databases. A typical Oracle installation is far more complicated than Informix, not only in software layout, but also in configuration. Simply take a look at the Oracle software directory and you can see the difference once you've installed Informix next to it.

Oracle can take much longer to install and configure than Informix, not to mention the performance limitations when compared to Informix. If Oracle is your first engine, and Informix your second, you may be surprised at how simple it is. If Informix is your first engine, installing the Oracle software afterwards is a worthwhile learning experience.

Informix takes up considerably less space than Oracle—the engine and core developer SDK tools typically take up less than 150MB. However, this can vary depending on the additional components a developer can add to the Informix software directory, usually known in UNIX as the **$INFORMIXDIR**. We will go into detail describing the **$INFORMIXDIR** environment variable as well as everything else you need to get Informix up and running quickly, and professionally, in this chapter.

Typically, an Informix installation can be done in two hours or less; however, much of this depends on a little bit of advanced planning. The more you plan ahead, the faster the install can be. Although Informix engines are simple to install, they also require you to spend a little time understanding the ramifications of how you set things up. Bear in mind this is true for any software product, or any database product.

I will show you a good basic layout that you can expand on, which will work for almost any engine Informix sells, the only exception being their Standard Engine, which we are not covering in this chapter. Standard Engine (SE) is an engine that does not take advantage of the shared memory features of Informix Dynamic Server, nor many of the other features Dynamic Server has over Standard Engine.

Standard Engine has a few advantages for small shops and software deployments where the requirements of operation need little to no human intervention, or where the data requirements are very small or simple, and the features of the database are simple as well. SE was the engine of choice for a lot of vertical market VARs (value-added resellers) who found a simple, low-maintenance, low-cost engine for a variety of UNIX-based applications. Although SE has enjoyed the cost-sensitive space for most of the life of Informix, it can no longer be chosen simply on cost alone. There are too many things missing from SE to make it a serious choice compared to IDS in today's marketplace, unless you are only looking for very basic features in a database. Even more basic is C-ISAM, which is the lowest level of database products Informix offers.

C-ISAM is the basic foundation used by almost all database products on the market today, including the competition. However, C-ISAM is extremely limited and has a very narrow window of acceptable use, which for most situations makes it not an option at all. Keep in mind that Informix was the first company in the database market to offer an ISAM product in UNIX, and then went on to offer more sophisticated ISAM products in their Standard Engine, which allowed the use of Standard SQL to access the database. C-ISAM is available for Linux, and you may want to get a copy to learn how it works, and how other database products use it.

Informix Dynamic Server (IDS), originally called *Online Dynamic Server*, got its name from the way it works. IDS can adjust itself dynamically to the load put upon it, and offers several settings you can change without having to restart the engine. There are, of course, limitations to IDS, but for the most part this engine can take a lot of load and still deliver impressive performance. IDS is very reliable, and robust, and should be considered your minimal engine for the future if at all possible. It can be implemented with about the same simplicity as SE, without much more maintenance than was common with SE. IDS can be maintained simply, provided you take care of the full cycle of operations this engine entails. The benefits of IDS over SE are more noticeable in faster performance, but are noticeable also in the advanced data types available in IDS.

You will find IDS similar to SE in many respects, but you will also find IDS much more powerful, with much better performance than Standard Engine. The performance gains, as well as the advanced features, make it the preferred choice. If you are a developer who needs even more than performance you also should take advantage of IDS.2000, allowing you object-relational features not found in IDS 7.30. I would advise you to install IDS 7.30 first as a great exercise to get the feel of the basic engine, and then move up to IDS.2000. There are additional features in IDS.2000 that you may never need, but on the other hand, they may be essential. At any rate, it is better to learn the simpler of the two engines first, and then move to the more complicated.

For a complete product comparison of SE versus IDS versus IDS.2000, visit the Informix Web site. Because of SE's limitations, most serious shops will consider Dynamic Server as the minimum engine of choice for most, if not all, engine choices. This has become a serious choice only recently, as the cost of IDS has dropped significantly, mostly due to Linux and the competition in this space from SQL Server and other small-server products. Linux has had more to do with this in recent months as the kernel has improved to the point to where Linux can be taken seriously as a database server. The advantages Linux has over NT continue to be self-evident; however, even in Linux, care must be taken to configure your server properly for optimal performance. A good DBA will pay attention to the groundwork before the installation, not after.

The latest and greatest engine to come from Informix is not IDS 7.30, but rather IDS.2000, a complete, object-relational engine offering even more features for the discriminating shop requiring advanced object-orientated features from an SQL-compliant Relational Database Management System (RDBMS) that IDS cannot deliver. We will not cover IDS.2000 in this chapter, but keep in mind that much of IDS.2000 works the same way as IDS 7.30. What you learn about IDS 7.30 can be applied directly towards IDS.2000, because the engine is basically the same, but with sophisticated object-relational technology thrown in. As trivial as this sounds, it should be understood that although these two engines are significantly different, much of their basic behavior is the same. It is only when the Object Relational Database Management System (ORDBMS) features are used that the engines behave differently.

As a point of Linux history, Postgres, another popular database engine for Linux, has its roots in Ingres, and in Dr. Michael Stonebreaker, who invented Ingres. When Informix bought the commercial version of Postgres, called Illustra, they were essentially buying the brains behind Ingres (in object-relational form, now Postgres), and renamed it Universal Server.

Postgres continues to this day, and Universal Server, now absorbed by Informix, continues in IDS.2000. IDS 7.30 and the former Universal Server 9.x have combined to form the best of both worlds in IDS.2000. Architecturally the final result is similar enough to the past (i.e., IDS 7.30) to allow an upgrade from IDS 7.30 to IDS.2000 to occur with little to no modification of the environment. We will not be testing this case here, but Informix has published it as not only doable, but also part of a promotional upgrade offering.

Informix installations typically are divided into three parts:

- Extraction of software
- Installation branding
- Bringing software into operation

The first step, extraction of software, involves the acquisition and placement of the software. Much of this depends on the form in which the software is distributed, and what steps are necessary to place the software in a form suitable to getting to the installation branding. This first step is often the most difficult; the actual installation branding is the less painful part of your installation activities.

The second step, installation branding, has changed little in its original form, except in the Microsoft Windows world, where Install Shield has taken the place of the UNIX installation.

Informix has traditionally distributed their software under this three-step method, the distribution media usually being a CD with a tar file, or files, and in many cases, a CD with a CPIO file. There are, of course, exceptions and other formats. In recent months, some of the engine software has come with an option to install with an X Windows interface similar to the way WordPerfect is installed on UNIX, but this is not the norm.

The Linux distribution of Informix engines has been coming in Red Hat's RPM Package Manager and tar format, since the first Linux port was released. The latest 7.30 engine, IDS 7.30.UC10, is encased in an RPM file, which in turn is encased in a zip file. Other software components are coming in .tar.gz files, among other formats. For the purposes of this installation we will be working with RPM and zip files. The Linux compression tool **unzip** will be necessary—be sure to have this tool or some other tool that understands the zip compressed file format installed. This is not to be confused with gzip files.

The final step, making the software operational, depends a lot on the kind of hardware you have, and how much of the hardware you want to be used by the software. In most cases, we want to think of a database as being the primary occupant on a server-based platform.

Again, we are focusing on Linux-based servers for our installation. Linux servers are one of the most popular servers available, simply because of the versatility this operating environment affords, not to mention the extremely low cost of making additional computing resources available in small as well as large computing environments. There is an ever-widening segment of the computing population turning to Linux, so it will be a good part of your skill set for the future.

Installation

For our purposes, we will discuss installation in three parts: acquisition and server placement of the software, installation and branding, and disk setup and server operation.

Part I: Acquisition and Server Placement of the Software

Set up three environment variables in your root and informix logins. Yes, you will need an informix id, and an informix group. I discuss the reasons for this later, but it would be a good idea to take care of this first.

For now, set these environment variables in your environment; we'll talk about them as we go:

```
INFORMIXDIR=/opt/informix/ids ; export INFORMIXDIR

INFORMIXSERVER=rebel_shm ; export INFORMIXSERVER

ONCONFIG=rebel_shm.cfg; export ONCONFIG
```

Substitute the *rebel* name with your own; it will be referenced as we go. Make sure that you put these commands in your root and informix profiles, and that your profiles are bringing these values into your environment when you log in before proceeding with the installation. Until the **$INFORMIXDIR** variable is set, the installation cannot proceed correctly, or at all. Log out and then log in again and make sure these variables are set before proceeding.

Download the zip file from www.intraware.com. Inside this zip file will be an RPM file that contains tar files and an installation script. *Be sure to follow Informix's recommendations for installing their software.*

NOTE

The following steps should be done as root login. If you do not have root access, stop what you are doing and get root login permission for the duration of the install. Once the software has been installed, you will still need to be root to set up data directories. Do not use any other login unless the Informix installation documentation says to, or shows you that a nonroot login is okay. After the final installation and configuration, you can relinquish root login, and use the Informix login for day-to-day administration.

You can double-click the zip file for Karchiver to open it if Karchiver has been installed, and if you are using the HTML/Web file browser interface KDE uses for a file manager. This is easier than it sounds—simply double-click the zip file inside an Autostart window and Karchiver will pop up a listing of what's inside. At this point you should extract everything you see into a work directory, not where you will ultimately install the software. Under the File menu, select the **Extract to** menu option, pick a directory, and extract all the files (see Figure 4.1).

Figure 4.1 Karchiver view of a zip file from download.

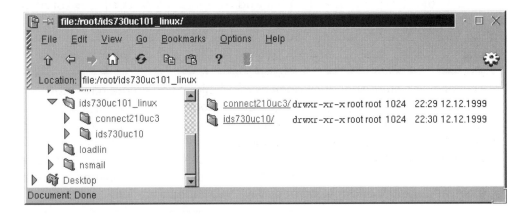

Once you have extracted all the files to a directory, you can also view the contents of the RPM file with **kpackage**; be sure to install this on your machine as well. As of this writing, **kpackage** is not yet part of the standard KDE installation package of programs, but a part of programs in the alpha/beta release of KDE programs (see Figure 4.2).

Figure 4.2 View of directories created after extracting files and an RPM of the Client SDK.

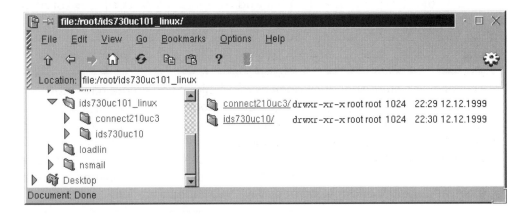

Notice in Figure 4.2 that I've extracted these files directly into my **/root** directory. Make sure you have enough room to hold the extracted files. The two RPM files you extract will contact approximately 60MB of software. They can go anywhere for now, because they are used only for installation; after that you can delete them or store them elsewhere to save some room on your hard drive. You might want to put them on a writable CD for the future.

You can either use **kpackage** to un-RPM the contents, or use the RPM commands stipulated in the Informix Installation documents. At this point, keep in mind that if you use **kpackage** to install the software, it will install it only in **/opt/informix**, so you need an **/opt** directory to do this, or the **kpackage** program will fail. The better way is to use **rpm** commands on the command line, because you can tell **rpm** where to put the software explicitly based on your $**INFORMIXDIR** setting. Right now is a great time to set this environment variable to where you want to put the Informix software. You should set it up in your root login, where you should already have created an Informix id and an Informix group.

Use whatever system administration commands you have to use to accomplish new user ids, and be sure to follow your Linux distributors' recommended method for adding users and groups. Most of the newer distributions come with some kind of program to add users and groups, and this should be used instead of editing the **/etc/passwd** and **/etc/group** files, even though this was the method used by the early UNIX and Linux distributions.

I would recommend you follow Informix's installation, and use command-line **rpm** commands to make it easier to install; allow them to support you if you run into trouble. The latest releases of Informix come with a limited amount of technical support when you purchase the software, so there is no reason not to follow the installation instructions they provide.

You can refer to http://www.informix.com/informix/resource/install/linux/0730x/01.fm.html on the WWW for online documentation, which gives you step-by-step instructions for installing the software. Keep in mind, at this stage we are still only finding a home for the software. Our next step will be the Installation and Branding phase. Once you have found a home for the software and extracted it out of the RPM file, you can brand it. Once you brand it, you can use it. Then we will configure the hard drive database spaces to hold databases and tables.

Part II: Installation and Branding

Create an **/opt/informix/ids** directory if you have an **/opt** directory. If you don't have an **/opt** directory, create an **informix** directory under the directory where you want to install software. I typically create an **/opt/informix/ids** directory under this one, so that when I install other engines I can create separate directories for these other software installs as well as keep the one I have now. So you should have a **/opt/informix/ids** directory to install to. You can call it whatever you want; the point will be to set your **INFORMIXDIR** directory to whatever this directory is called. I typically do the following:

```
INFORMIXDIR=/opt/informix/ids ; export INFORMIXDIR
```

This needs to be done before you use the command-line **rpm** commands so that you can extract the software based on your **$INFORMIXDIR**. The $ sign is merely a command-line prompt; do not use it in the commands shown (see Figure 4.3).

```
$ cd /root/ids730uc101_linux/connect210uc3
$ rpm -iv -prefix $INFORMIXDIR *.rpm
$ cd $INFORMIXDIR
$ ./installconn
```

Figure 4.3 Starting the Client SDK installation (Iconnect).

```
./ ../ connect210uc3.rpm
rebel:root # echo $INFORMIXDIR
/opt/informix/ids
rebel:root # rpm -iv --prefix $INFORMIXDIR *.rpm
iconn-2.10.UC3-1
++ Informix-Client SDK binary package installation has completed
++ successfully.  Please refer to the Installation Guide for further
++ installation instructions.
rebel:root # cd $INFORMIXDIR
rebel:root # lc
./ ../ conncontent.tar  installconn*
rebel:root # ./installconn
INFORMIX-Connect Version 2.10.UC3
Copyright (C) 1984-1999 Informix Software, Inc.
cat: /opt/informix/ids/etc/ClientSDK-cr: No such file or directory

Your existing INFORMIX shared libraries, if any, will be replaced and upgraded.
Are you sure? [yes/no]
yes

Is I-Connect being installed along with Informix Dynamic Server with
Universal Data Option (Release 9, requires to be run as user "informix")?
(yes or no)
no
Extracting files from conncontent file...


Installing I-Connect as user "root"...


Installation Script

Installation Script Requirements:
- A user "informix" and a group "informix" must be known to the system.
- The product source files must have been loaded by user root
- This installation procedure must be run by user root.

This script will change the owner, group, and mode of
many of the files of this package in this directory.


Press RETURN to continue,
or the interrupt key (usually CTRL-C or DEL) to abort.


Enter your serial number (for example, INF#X999999) >
AAC#A518469
Enter your serial number KEY (uppercase letters only) >
```

After you complete the installation script for the Client SDK, perform the same actions for the server installation:

```
cd /root/ids730uc101_linux/ids730uc10
```

```
rpm -iv -prefix $INFORMIXDIR *.rpm
cd $INFORMIXDIR

./installserver
```

You can do either the SDK or the engine first—it doesn't matter. Extract software from the **rpm**, brand the software, extract the second one from the second **rpm**, and then brand. This is the proper way, and will help you avoid problems. Once you have completed this phase of installation successfully, you are ready to set up the server for operation (see Figure 4.4).

Figure 4.4 Successful completion of IDS server installation.

It is important for you to rerun the installation script for each product if you anticipate moving the tree to another system or drive. Simply run the installation script for each product, making sure your **$INFORMIXDIR** is set beforehand, and the reinstallation can take place painlessly. You will notice that there are some tail-end linking operations that need to be done in order for the server to work properly. The reinstall performs this step last, so it is important for you to reinstall if you move the directory or tree. Keep in mind, Linux has no registry like NT or Windows 98, so the only things you need to worry about are the final links that are created at the end of the installation. You should also visit the Informix Web site for tips and techniques to recover disk space from some of the NLS files that are installed for languages you may not need.

A script is available to help you delete certain files, but bear in mind that a reinstall may fail if these files do not exist. You will have to re-extract the software, then basically reinstall from scratch.

One other final point to this part of installation: Do not remove the tar file for **iconnect** until you are certain that you will not need to reinstall. I personally wish that the SDK installation did not depend on this tar file to be placed in this directory; it requires you to allocate twice as much space for the SDK just to install it. In the future, Informix should allow you to keep the tar files and installation scripts elsewhere on the system for reinstallations, allowing you to reduce the allocation of space for software.

Part III: Disk Setup and Server Operation

We can now proceed with the operational aspects of IDS. What we are now discussing should be prepared for in advance, and you already should have reserved a certain amount of disk space for the dbspaces, where the actual database(s) and tables will reside. This chapter focuses on the installation aspects of an Informix server, so you should become familiar with some of the terminology of Informix before proceeding.

Please become very familiar with the *Administrator's Guide for IDS*, found at the Informix Web site, and available on CD-ROM. A physical printing of this manual is also available, usually at a significant cost. It is recommended that you obtain the latest CD-ROM of documentation known as the *Answers Online Documentation*, which contains documentation for all of the Informix database products. This CD-ROM is available directly from Informix and can be ordered from your regional sales office. The documentation is always available on the Informix Web site; take the time to download it and become familiar with the *Administrator's Guide*. It describes everything you need to know to make your installation a success. The advantages of raw versus cooked files are discussed here, so it is to your advantage to read it.

As of this writing, Linux still does not have a strong *raw disk* orientation like many of the existing UNIX platforms; however, this most likely will be available by the time this book goes into circulation. Some sites are using raw disks without incident, but as of this writing it is unsupported.

A *raw disk* installation, simply put, allows you to soft-link the Informix software directly to unformatted disks (hard drives that are unmounted file systems), and the Informix software takes over the formatting and disk operation. For raw disks, Informix is the disk operating system for drives set up as raw disks. The only thing for which Linux is responsible is an entry in the **/dev** directory pointing to the disk drive. A soft-link is created in a directory you choose, to point to the **/dev** directory, and the drive entry.

For example, you would create an **/opt/informix/links** directory, and then create soft-links in that directory to point to the **/dev** directory. If you had a disk in **/dev** called **/dev/rdisk1**, then you simply create a link to it:

```
$ cd /opt/informix/links

$ ln -s /dev/rdisk1 datadbs01
```

When you do an **ls –l**, you will see only the link, not the disk.

A cooked disk installation, simply put, allows you to create Linux files of a certain size that Linux will manage along with Informix. Cooked files are, and look like, regular Linux files.

Cooked files are created with a specific size in mind, and can be backed up with a standard backup, provided the Informix server is offline, and shut down. Cooked files must be closed just like regular Linux files in order to back them up. Benefits to cooked files are that they are simply Linux files, and backing them up is as simple as backing up any other Linux file.

When you perform an **ls –l** on the directory, the cooked files show up as regular Linux files (see Figure 4.5). When you look at raw disks, the directory listing usually shows a link to **/dev entries**, but no file sizes show up, as these disks are now under the control of Informix. To understand raw disks, use Informix **onstat** commands to see how much space they are using; this is the only way you can see what they contain. It is highly advisable for you to use cooked files until you become more familiar with how raw disks are set up.

Informix on Linux has very good performance using cooked files, but the preferred method in UNIX is to use raw disks, often giving a 15–20 percent performance advantage over cooked files. As of this writing, benchmarks were not available to compare the differences between raw disks and cooked files on Linux. Many x86 sites using the NT version of

Informix Dynamic Server are using cooked files exclusively, simply for the fact that raw disks on NT do not offer enough of a performance gain to make it worth the trouble to use them. The Administrator's Guide discusses this issue in more detail.

Cooked files are easier to manage in most situations, and I recommend you use cooked files in environments where you want a more simple administration, and you do not anticipate an extremely high load on the system. If you get into a situation where you need more performance, then you would most likely want to move to a raw disk installation for UNIX. Until raw disks are supported on Linux, stick with cooked files.

Figure 4.5 Sample directory listing of cooked file dbspaces that Informix software uses to store data.

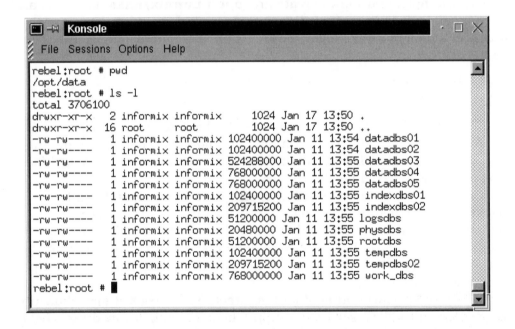

Setting Up Data Files for Informix

Create a second directory, **/opt/data**, or **/db/data**, or preferably, a separate hard drive called **/data**, and under it create a directory called **/data/informix**. I have a separate drive I call **/db**, and have created a **/db/data** directory for the home of all the data. For our install we will use **/opt/data**, but you should have a different directory. It is advisable to keep your data separate from your software if at all possible. As I describe later, you should allocate at least 500MB for the data, if not more. It makes no sense to scrimp on data space unless you cannot avoid it. When I talk about allocation of space, I'm referring to total space, not specific files. Your total aggregate space should be no less than 500MB, and we will create cooked files of different sizes within this space.

Informix uses *chunks* to describe the largest value for data space. All data resides inside chunks as pages, which are the smallest unit of measure for data space. Please refer to the *Administrator's Guide* for a complete description of chunks and pages. This chapter will use that terminology to finish the installation, so it is important for you to understand the concepts. You will find award-winning documentation with Informix software, so take advantage of it.

Once you are familiar with the concept of chunks and dbspaces, you are ready to configure your server for operation. We will set up a server that allows you to specify on your own how much data space to use, and the minimum operational space to set aside. This way you can grow the system with a minimum of aggravation.

There are several minimum dbspaces for which you will need to set aside disk space. These are the minimum; the rest are data spaces you decide to add as additional dbspaces. The following are operational spaces.

Rootdbs. dbspace containing the sysmaster database, the intelligence center for the database engine.

Physdbs. dbspace for buffering data before it is written to disk. This is contained in the rootdbs, but should be moved to its own dbspace for improved performance and administration. You can call this dbspace whatever you like; however, it is advisable to call it something consistent with what it is.

Logsdbs. dbspace for logical logs. Upon installation, it is contained in the rootdbs, but for better operation it should be placed in its own dbspace. You can call this dbspace whatever you like; however, it is advisable to call it something consistent with what it is.

Tempdbs01. dbspace for temp tables and sorting of queries. You can call this dbspace whatever you like; however, it is advisable to call it something consistent with what it is.

The following are data spaces. You may call these dbspaces whatever you like.

Dbs_dbs. dbspace for database creation, but not tables. A database entry is created, with a few basic system table entries, but user tables are referenced outside this space.

Datadbs01. dbspace for user tables.

Indexdbs01. dbspace for user indexes.

If you create this minimum set of dbspaces, you will have a minimum installation that can meet most of your needs as you learn about how the IDS engine works. It will also allow you to expand easily as your needs increase.

About Disks

You should set up an area on your system to accommodate Informix. There are three areas to consider: software, dbspaces, and a work area for backups, loading, and so on.

SCSI is recommended over IDE, for speed and flexibility. SCSI allows you to chain together drives more easily than IDE. However, if you are experienced enough with IDE, you could achieve a similar disk setup, but there are still limitations with IDE that do not allow you the same flexibility as SCSI. If at all possible, get a SCSI controller for your system, and use a SCSI drive.

Disks and Directories

Here are explanations of what the **/opt/informix/ids7.30** and **/opt/data** directories hold.

> **/opt/informix/ids7.30.** This directory holds software—everything software under this tree. Set aside, at a minimum, 500MB for the Informix software. No data is stored here. Using this convention for a directory name you can add other versions of the software under **/opt/informix**, and easily test switching or upgrading your software by simply changing the **$INFORMIXDIR** environment variable.

> **/opt/data.** This directory holds cooked-file dbspaces; if possible, this should be another disk. This directory is for data only.

Space Considerations

How much space should you set aside? You could take a 2GB disk and allocate space as follows.

For the operational spaces:

- 50MB for rootdbs
- 50MB for physdbs
- 100MB for logsdbs
- 300MB for tempdbs
- 500MB total

For the data spaces:

- 100MB for dbs_dbs—this will hold only database entries, and is not for tables.
- 250MB for datadbs01—this can be smaller if you are going to use it only for training, and it will hold tables.
- 250MB for indexdbs01—again, for training this can be smaller, but will hold only indexes.
- 600MB total.

If you have set aside a 2GB disk for example, you have now allocated a total of 1100MB to start with and there is still some room for growth. This is only a starting point, not necessarily hard and fast for all systems. These are also conservative resource settings, without a lot of wasted space for each dbspace. The only resource settings that are really firm are for rootdbs and physdbs, but even these are arbitrary: After properly configuring the system you will find these sizes might be adjusted for your site. Start with these, and change them later if you choose. The rootdbs space will have very little usage after we are done so you should not make it larger than 50MB; in most cases, even 20MB will be too much space. I make it 50MB as a safety precaution only.

/work is a mounted file system of your choosing for work. Set aside at least 1000MB for this disk. This is a Linux disk for preparing load files and managing data coming in and leaving the database. It's always a good idea to have a place to work on the system that is specific to different database projects. Under this directory you can create project directories or user-named directories, at your preference.

NOTE

Many BIOSs in PCs do not allow the use of large drives in Linux, even when the hardware is brand new. Most BIOSes do not support many of the larger drives—be careful when using IDE drives. This is one of the most important reasons to use SCSI, as you will not be limited by the on-board controller for your disk layout when configuring your drives for Linux.

This is not the only reason you should use SCSI drives; performance is another. Even with the advances in IDE drives, most shops will still configure and prefer SCSI drives. If you have already configured your drive, have an ample amount of room for the software and data. Then you are ready to install Informix.

Now that you can see how we are going to allocate space, you are ready to configure the server for its very first online operation.

Configuration

As I had originally pointed out in the beginning of this chapter, there were three environment variables you needed to set. We now are able to work with the second variable, the **INFORMIXSERVER**, and the third, the **ONCONFIG**.

Within the scope of this chapter, we are concerned only with getting the server up; performance considerations are outside the scope of this chapter, and should be noted as part of an ongoing learning process, trial and error, and operational documentation from Informix.

The **INFORMIXSERVER** variable directly corresponds to the **DBSERVERNAME** in the **$ONCONFIG** file. Use the same name for **DBSERVERNAME** as you have set up for **INFORMIXSERVER**. This is essential for networking connections between a client and the server. You will use the same name on a client for the **INFORMIXSERVER** variable on the clients you wish to connect to this server. **INFORMIXSERVER** also is used by utilities such as **onstat** to communicate with the right instance of the engine.

$INFORMIXDIR/etc/$ONCONFIG

Change the directory to the **$INFORMIXDIR**, and look at the tree of directories.

```
/opt/informix/ids
                        |__aaodir
                        |__bin
                        |__dbssodir
                        |__demo
                            |__dbaccess
                        |__etc
                        |__forms
                        |__gls
                            |__cm3
                            |__cv9
                            |__lc11
                                |__cs_cz
                                |__da_dk
                                |__de_at
                                |__de_ch
```

```
                              |__de_de
                              |__en_au
                              |__en_gb
                              |__en_us
                              |__es_es
                              |__fi_fi
                              |__fr_be
                              |__fr_ca
                              |__fr_ch
                              |__fr_fr
                              |__is_is
                              |__it_it
                              |__ja_jp
                              |__ko_kr
                              |__nl_be
                              |__nl_nl
                              |__no_no
                              |__os
                              |__pl_pl
                              |__pt_br
                              |__pt_pt
                              |__ru_ru
                              |__sk_sk
                              |__sv_se
                              |__th_th
                              |__zh_cn
                              |__zh_tw
                      |__incl
                          |__esql
                          |__hpl
                      |__lib
                          |__cli
                          |__dmi
                          |__esql
                      |__msg
                          |__en_us
                              |__0333
                      |__release
                          |__en_us
                              |__0333
```

We will be working in **$INFORMIXDIR** and in the regular Linux **/etc** directory. As you can see, Informix software has its own **/etc** directory, where we will find all the files necessary for configuration. The two most critical, **onconfig.std** and **sqlhosts**, will be our focus for the installation. You will make copies of these two files before the engine becomes operational. After the installation you will work with your **$ONCONFIG** again and make adjustments to make IDS fully operational.

You should check out the release notes for IDS for last-minute installation instructions regardless of what you read here or in the *Administrator's Guide*. You will find these release notes under the **$INFORMIXDIR/release/en_us/0333** directory. There are important notes concerning all aspects of the software you installed.

cd to **$INFORMIXDIR/etc** and **ls –CaF** this directory. You will see a variety of files—of particular note, **onconfig.std**. We need to make a copy of this file—the copy will be named whatever you set your **$ONCONFIG** variable to.

```
$ cd $INFORMIXDIR/etc

$ cp onconfig.std rebel_shm.cfg
```

In our case it is called **rebel_shm.cfg**. We put the **_shm** on the end as a matter of convention. You can have several different instances of Informix running on one server; the **_shm** simply means shared memory, and is more a matter of personal taste. Again, you can call the **ONCON-FIG** file whatever you want—just make sure you set it correctly, as we have shown you.

Once you have copied it, use your favorite text editor, and follow these instructions. It is important to save this file as ASCII text, so be sure your editor allows simple text editing. My personal preference is to use **vi**; however, in Linux there are several text editors resembling Notepad in Microsoft Windows. Substitute the following command with your favorite text editor, and the **ONCONFIG** can be edited.

```
$ vi rebel_shm.cfg


#**************************************************************************
#
#                         INFORMIX SOFTWARE, INC.
#
#  Title:         onconfig.std
#  Description: Informix Dynamic Server Configuration Parameters
#
#**************************************************************************


# Root Dbspace Configuration
```

```
ROOTNAME        rootdbs          # Root dbspace name
ROOTPATH        /dev/online_root # Path for device containing root dbspace
ROOTOFFSET      0                # Offset of root dbspace into device (Kbytes)
ROOTSIZE        20000            # Size of root dbspace (Kbytes)

# Disk Mirroring Configuration Parameters

MIRROR          0                # Mirroring flag (Yes = 1, No = 0)
MIRRORPATH                       # Path for device containing mirrored root
MIRROROFFSET    0                # Offset into mirrored device (Kbytes)

# Physical Log Configuration

PHYSDBS         rootdbs          # Location (dbspace) of physical log
PHYSFILE        1000             # Physical log file size (Kbytes)

# Logical Log Configuration

LOGFILES        6                # Number of logical log files
LOGSIZE         500              # Logical log size (Kbytes)

# Diagnostics

MSGPATH         /usr/informix/online.log         # System message log file
path
CONSOLE         /dev/console                     # System console message path
ALARMPROGRAM    /usr/informix/etc/log_full.sh    # Alarm program path
SYSALARMPROGRAM /usr/informix/etc/evidence.sh    # System Alarm program path
TBLSPACE_STATS  1

# System Archive Tape Device

TAPEDEV         /dev/tapedev    # Tape device path
TAPEBLK         16              # Tape block size (Kbytes)
TAPESIZE        10240           # Maximum amount of data to put on tape (Kbytes)

# Log Archive Tape Device

LTAPEDEV        /dev/tapedev    # Log tape device path
LTAPEBLK        16              # Log tape block size (Kbytes)
LTAPESIZE       10240           # Max amount of data to put on log tape (Kbytes)
```

```
# Optical

STAGEBLOB                          # Informix Dynamic Server/Optical staging area

# System Configuration

SERVERNUM           0              # Unique id corresponding to a Dynamic Server instance
DBSERVERNAME                       # Name of default database server
DBSERVERALIASES                    # List of alternate dbservernames
NETTYPE                            # Configure poll thread(s) for nettype
DEADLOCK_TIMEOUT 60                # Max time to wait of lock in distributed env.
RESIDENT            0              # Forced residency flag (Yes = 1, No = 0)

MULTIPROCESSOR   0                 # 0 for single-processor, 1 for multi-processor
NUMCPUVPS        1                 # Number of user (cpu) vps
SINGLE_CPU_VP    0                 # If non-zero, limit number of cpu vps to one

NOAGE               0              # Process aging
AFF_SPROC           0              # Affinity start processor
AFF_NPROCS          0              # Affinity number of processors

# Shared Memory Parameters

LOCKS            2000              # Maximum number of locks
BUFFERS          200               # Maximum number of shared buffers
NUMAIOVPS                          # Number of IO vps
PHYSBUFF         32                # Physical log buffer size (Kbytes)
LOGBUFF          32                # Logical log buffer size (Kbytes)
LOGSMAX          6                 # Maximum number of logical log files
CLEANERS         1                 # Number of buffer cleaner processes
SHMBASE          0x10000000L       # Shared memory base address
SHMVIRTSIZE      8000              # initial virtual shared memory segment size
SHMADD           8192              # Size of new shared memory segments (Kbytes)
SHMTOTAL         0                 # Total shared memory (Kbytes). 0=>unlimited
CKPTINTVL        300               # Check point interval (in sec)
LRUS             8                 # Number of LRU queues
LRU_MAX_DIRTY    60                # LRU percent dirty begin cleaning limit
LRU_MIN_DIRTY    50                # LRU percent dirty end cleaning limit
LTXHWM           50                # Long transaction high water mark percentage
LTXEHWM          60                # Long transaction high water mark
                                      (exclusive)
```

```
TXTIMEOUT                300           # Transaction timeout (in sec)
STACKSIZE                32            # Stack size (Kbytes)


# System Page Size
# BUFFSIZE - Dynamic Server no longer supports this configuration parameter.
#               To determine the page size used by Dynamic Server on your platform
#               see the last line of output from the command, 'onstat -b'.


# Recovery Variables
# OFF_RECVRY_THREADS:
# Number of parallel worker threads during fast recovery or an offline
# restore.
# ON_RECVRY_THREADS:
# Number of parallel worker threads during an online restore.

OFF_RECVRY_THREADS       10            # Default number of offline worker threads
ON_RECVRY_THREADS        1             # Default number of online worker threads


# Data Replication Variables
# DRAUTO: 0 manual, 1 retain type, 2 reverse type
DRAUTO                   0             # DR automatic switchover
DRINTERVAL               30            # DR max time between DR buffer flushes (in sec)
DRTIMEOUT                30            # DR network timeout (in sec)
DRLOSTFOUND        /usr/informix/etc/dr.lostfound  # DR lost+found file path


# CDR Variables
CDR_LOGBUFFERS           2048          # size of log reading buffer pool (Kbytes)
CDR_EVALTHREADS          1,2           # evaluator threads (per-cpu-vp,additional)
CDR_DSLOCKWAIT           5             # DS lockwait timeout (seconds)
CDR_QUEUEMEM             4096          # Maximum amount of memory for any CDR queue
                                         (Kbytes)


# Backup/Restore variables
BAR_ACT_LOG              /tmp/bar_act.log
BAR_MAX_BACKUP           0
BAR_RETRY                1
BAR_NB_XPORT_COUNT       10
BAR_XFER_BUF_SIZE        31
```

```
# Informix Storage Manager variables
ISM_DATA_POOL    ISMData        # If the data pool name is changed, be sure to
                                # update $INFORMIXDIR/bin/onbar.  Change to
                                # ism_catalog -create_bootstrap -pool <new name>
ISM_LOG_POOL     ISMLogs


# Read Ahead Variables
RA_PAGES                        # Number of pages to attempt to read ahead
RA_THRESHOLD                    # Number of pages left before next group


# DBSPACETEMP:
# Dynamic Server equivalent of DBTEMP for SE. This is the list of dbspaces
# that the Dynamic Server SQL Engine will use to create temp tables etc.
# If specified it must be a colon separated list of dbspaces that exist
# when the Dynamic Server system is brought online.  If not specified, or if
# all dbspaces specified are invalid, various ad hoc queries will create
# temporary files in /tmp instead.


DBSPACETEMP                     # Default temp dbspaces


# DUMP*:
# The following parameters control the type of diagnostics information which
# is preserved when an unanticipated error condition (assertion failure)
# occurs during Dynamic Server operations.
# For DUMPSHMEM, DUMPGCORE and DUMPCORE 1 means Yes, 0 means No.


DUMPDIR          /tmp           # Preserve diagnostics in this directory
DUMPSHMEM        1              # Dump a copy of shared memory
DUMPGCORE        0              # Dump a core image using 'gcore'
DUMPCORE         0              # Dump a core image (Warning:this aborts Dynamic
                                  Server)
DUMPCNT          1              # Number of shared memory or gcore dumps for
                                  a single user's session


FILLFACTOR       90             # Fill factor for building indexes
```

```
# method for Dynamic Server to use when determining current time
USEOSTIME        0        # 0: use internal time(fast), 1: get time from OS(slow)


# Parallel Database Queries (pdq)
MAX_PDQPRIORITY 100      # Maximum allowed pdqpriority
DS_MAX_QUERIES           # Maximum number of decision support queries
DS_TOTAL_MEMORY          # Decision support memory (Kbytes)
DS_MAX_SCANS    1048576  # Maximum number of decision support scans
DATASKIP                 # List of dbspaces to skip


# OPTCOMPIND
# 0 => Nested loop joins will be preferred (where
#       possible) over sortmerge joins and hash joins.
# 1 => If the transaction isolation mode is not
#       "repeatable read", optimizer behaves as in (2)
#       below.  Otherwise it behaves as in (0) above.
# 2 => Use costs regardless of the transaction isolation
#       mode.  Nested loop joins are not necessarily
#       preferred.  Optimizer bases its decision purely
#       on costs.
OPTCOMPIND       2       # To hint the optimizer


ONDBSPACEDOWN    2       # Dbspace down option: 0 = CONTINUE, 1 = ABORT, 2 = WAIT
LBU_PRESERVE     0       # Preserve last log for log backup
OPCACHEMAX       0       # Maximum optical cache size (Kbytes)


# HETERO_COMMIT (Gateway participation in distributed transactions)
# 1 => Heterogeneous Commit is enabled
# 0 (or any other value) => Heterogeneous Commit is disabled
HETERO_COMMIT    0


# Optimization goal: -1 = ALL_ROWS(Default), 0 = FIRST_ROWS
OPT_GOAL         -1


# Optimizer DIRECTIVES ON (1/Default) or OFF (0)
DIRECTIVES       1


# Status of restartable restore
RESTARTABLE_RESTORE OFF
```

The first section is extremely important, because you now have to change these settings to match where you will store the data. In our case, we will use **/opt/data** as our place to put the data, including the rootdbs.

```
# Root Dbspace Configuration - before

ROOTNAME          rootdbs          # Root dbspace name
ROOTPATH          /dev/online_root # Path for device containing root dbspace
ROOTOFFSET        0                # Offset of root dbspace into device
                                   #(Kbytes)
ROOTSIZE          20000            # Size of root dbspace (Kbytes)
```

Now we make our changes.

```
# Root Dbspace Configuration - after

ROOTNAME          rootdbs          # Root dbspace name
ROOTPATH          /opt/data/rootdbs # Path for device containing root dbspace
ROOTOFFSET        0                # Offset of root dbspace into device
                                     (Kbytes)
ROOTSIZE          20000            # Size of root dbspace (Kbytes)
```

Our system will be using a cooked file for rootdbs; we are done setting this variable. I mentioned that you might want the rootdbs to be 50MB instead of 20MB. You can change this to 50,000KB, which is roughly 50MB, setting it now if you wish, or you can leave it at the default of 20,000KB. This is only a precaution, and not necessary. I tend to give a little more room for rootdbs for the sake of safety, but after our configuration, it will have very little actual use except for the engine. There are several situations where a slightly larger rootdbs comes in handy, such as leaving the logical logs or the physical log inside the rootdbs.

NOTE

If you anticipate creating more than one instance on your server, please rename rootdbs to rootdbs01, physdbs to physdbs01, logsdbs to logsdbs01, and tempdbs to tempdbs01 when the reference is made in this installation to these dbspaces. This way the names are consistent with the instances and it makes managing them easier. Make the appropriate changes in your server's **$ONCONFIG** before performing **oninit –i**.
Do not change the **PHYSDBS** settings until after the first **oninit**, when you run **oninit –i**. *After* the engine is up and running, you can make changes.

When you install the engine, the physical log and the logical logs are inside the rootdbs, but we will be moving these logs out into their own spaces after the installation. This will leave very little use for the rootdbs; thus, to make the rootdbs very large can be a waste of disk space. The only reason you might want to change it now is due to the fact that you cannot change it later unless you re-initialize your instance. Now is the time to make this decision, or forever live with the 20MB default size. If you leave it at 20000, be sure to create a logsdbs and a physdbs for the logical logs and the physical log, and follow the instructions later in this chapter to move these logs into their own dbspaces.

After moving the logs out, you will have approximately 16MB of the 20MB of space that will probably never get used. I recommend you move these logs as a part of standard practice, which will allow you total flexibility later on when you want to adjust the size and the amount of the logical logs, and want to adjust the size of the physical log. We will perform this step last, after getting the engine running.

So, let's continue on our way towards configuring our server. We may or may not have a tape system for backups, but for now we want to disable tape backup until the server is completely operational.

```
# System Archive Tape Device - before


TAPEDEV          /dev/tapedev  # Tape device path
TAPEBLK          16            # Tape block size (Kbytes)
TAPESIZE         10240         # Maximum amount of data to put on tape (Kbytes)


# Log Archive Tape Device


LTAPEDEV         /dev/tapedev  # Log tape device path
LTAPEBLK         16            # Log tape block size (Kbytes)
LTAPESIZE        10240         # Max amount of data to put on log tape (Kbytes)
```

We make our changes as follows:

```
# System Archive Tape Device - after


# TAPEDEV        /dev/tapedev  # Tape device path
TAPEDEV          /dev/null     # Tape device path
TAPEBLK          16            # Tape block size (Kbytes)
TAPESIZE         10240         # Maximum amount of data to put on tape (Kbytes)
```

```
# Log Archive Tape Device

# LTAPEDEV        /dev/tapedev      # Log tape device path
LTAPEDEV          /dev/null         # Log tape device path
LTAPEBLK          16                # Log tape block size (Kbytes)
LTAPESIZE         10240             Max amount of data to put on log tape (Kbytes)
```

Notice I left the original values commented-out so that we can go back to these later and either change or keep them as a point of reference. It's always a good idea to comment out other values—copy and change the copy rather than just changing the original entry. This way you can keep track of changes.

We left our tape devices set to **/dev/null**, and this allows the IDS server to come up and work without worrying about where the backups will go—for now. Later on we will change this to a real tape backup if we have one, or leave it as is until we decide to have a real tape backup. Setting it to **/dev/null** is a standard way of telling the IDS server to ignore a physical device for backup, but still do the things necessary to tell the engine certain things are backed up, namely the logical logs. We will discuss the logical logs later on; for now we will only worry about bringing up the server.

Let's skip down now to the diagnostics section, and make a few changes here.

```
# Diagnostics   - before

MSGPATH            /usr/informix/online.log       # System message log file
path
CONSOLE            /dev/console                   # System console message path
ALARMPROGRAM       /usr/informix/etc/log_full.sh  # Alarm program path
SYSALARMPROGRAM /usr/informix/etc/evidence.sh     # System Alarm program path
TBLSPACE_STATS  1
```

I would recommend you create a separate logs directory for the messages that the engine will put out regarding its operation. The default values need to be changed, so it's a good idea simply to create a directory now, and allow the online.log and console messages to go in this new directory:

```
$ cd $INFORMIXDIR
$ mkdir logs
$ chown informix:informix logs
$ chmod 775 logs
```

```
# Diagnostics - after

MSGPATH            /opt/informix/ids/logs/online.log  # System message log file
                                                        path
# CONSOLE          /dev/null                           # System console message
                                                        path
CONSOLE            /opt/informix/ids/logs/console.log # For our initial
                                                        installation only!
ALARMPROGRAM       /opt/informix/ids/etc/log_full.sh   # Alarm program path
SYSALARMPROGRAM /opt/informix/ids/etc/evidence.sh      # System Alarm program
                                                        path
TBLSPACE_STATS  1
```

Notice that the CONSOLE messages are changed to **/dev/null** and **/opt/informix/ids/logs/console.log**. It is best for the initial installation routine to set it to **/opt/informix/ids/logs/console.log** so you can preserve the installation messages, but you can always change it later. Most of the messages for the console are not worth watching; again, this is a decision you can make for yourself. You might want to view them at first, then change them after you see if they are of value.

Skip down to the System Configuration section, and we will make a few more changes:

```
# System Configuration - before


SERVERNUM       0                  # Unique id corresponding to a Dynamic
                                   # Server instance
DBSERVERNAME                       # Name of default database server
DBSERVERALIASES                    # List of alternate dbservernames
NETTYPE                            # Configure poll thread(s) for nettype
DEADLOCK_TIMEOUT 60                # Max time to wait of lock in distributed env.
RESIDENT        0                  # Forced residency flag (Yes = 1, No = 0)
```

This is where we give our instance of the engine a name and tell it how to talk to the network:

```
# System Configuration - after


SERVERNUM       0                  # Unique id corresponding to a Dynamic Server
                                      instance
DBSERVERNAME    rebel_shm          # Name of default database server
DBSERVERALIASES rebel_net          # List of alternate dbservernames
```

```
NETTYPE             soctcp,1,1,NET    # Configure poll thread(s) for nettype
DEADLOCK_TIMEOUT 60                   # Max time to wait of lock in distributed env.
RESIDENT            0                 # Forced residency flag (Yes = 1, No = 0)
```

Keep track of these names; again, substitute the **rebel** part with your naming convention. We will reference these settings in our **$INFORMIXDIR/etc/sqlhosts** file, so remember what you set these to.

There is one setting that you *do* need to change for the logical logs before we bring up the server, so that you don't have to bounce the engine later. In keeping with understanding the process of moving the logical logs out of the rootdbs, you should change the **LOGSMAX** setting to something higher than the default, which starts at 6 (bolded for emphasis in the code example to follow). You will find this value in the Shared Memory section of the **$INFORMIXDIR/etc/$ONCONFIG**:

```
# Shared Memory Parameters


LOCKS           2000              # Maximum number of locks
BUFFERS         200               # Maximum number of shared buffers
NUMAIOVPS                         # Number of IO vps
PHYSBUFF        32                # Physical log buffer size (Kbytes)
LOGBUFF         32                # Logical log buffer size (Kbytes)
LOGSMAX         6                 # Maximum number of logical log files
CLEANERS        1                 # Number of buffer cleaner processes
SHMBASE         0x10000000L       # Shared memory base address
SHMVIRTSIZE     8000              # initial virtual shared memory segment size
SHMADD          8192              # Size of new shared memory segments
(Kbytes)
SHMTOTAL        0                 # Total shared memory (Kbytes). 0=>unlimited
CKPTINTVL       300               # Check point interval (in sec)
LRUS            8                 # Number of LRU queues
LRU_MAX_DIRTY   60                # LRU percent dirty begin cleaning limit
LRU_MIN_DIRTY   50                # LRU percent dirty end cleaning limit
LTXHWM          50                # Long transaction high water mark percentage
LTXEHWM         60                # Long transaction high water mark (exclusive)
TXTIMEOUT       300               # Transaction timeout (in sec)
STACKSIZE       32                # Stack size (Kbytes)
```

Change this to 50:

```
LOGSMAX         50                # Maximum number of logical log files
```

This will allow you to add logical logs later on without having to bounce the engine. We will be performing this step as we perform the installation, so change it now.

It is important for you to leave everything else at the default setting until after we get the engine up and running. By practicing step-wise refinement we can minimize our chances for a failed start-up. There are other changes we will be making, and in the future you can make these changes with a little experience; for now, leave the defaults alone.

There are settings for Data Replication, and although we are not concerned with these now, it *is* a good idea to change the path to reflect your installation:

```
# Data Replication Variables - before

# DRAUTO: 0 manual, 1 retain type, 2 reverse type

DRAUTO            0                    # DR automatic switchover

DRINTERVAL        30                     # DR max time between DR buffer flushes
                                          (in sec)

DRTIMEOUT         30                     # DR network timeout (in sec)

DRLOSTFOUND       /usr/informix/etc/dr.lostfound  # DR lost+found file path
```

After our changes (bolded for emphasis):

```
# Data Replication Variables - after

# DRAUTO: 0 manual, 1 retain type, 2 reverse type

DRAUTO            0                    # DR automatic switchover

DRINTERVAL        30                     # DR max time between DR buffer flushes (in sec)

DRTIMEOUT         30                     # DR network timeout (in sec)

DRLOSTFOUND       /opt/informix/ids/etc/dr.lostfound  # DR lost+found file path
```

Skip down a little further to the Backup section, and make another change:

```
# Backup/Restore variables  - before

BAR_ACT_LOG              /tmp/bar_act.log

BAR_MAX_BACKUP           0

BAR_RETRY                1

BAR_NB_XPORT_COUNT       10

BAR_XFER_BUF_SIZE        31
```

Here, we only need to change this to our **$INFORMIXDIR/logs** directory (bolded for emphasis):

```
# Backup/Restore variables - after

BAR_ACT_LOG              /opt/informix/ids/logs/bar_act.log

BAR_MAX_BACKUP           0
```

```
BAR_RETRY                    1
BAR_NB_XPORT_COUNT          10
BAR_XFER_BUF_SIZE           31
```

This file can grow quite large, and should be monitored as it grows. You can create a log file roll-off script, which we will cover at the end of this chapter. We will have a roll-off of not only this file but of the online.log as well. This will allow you to keep these log files small, and suitable for periodic analysis. You can archive them by the day, week, or month as you see fit.

This concludes the editing of the **ONCONFIG** file. Save this file with the changes you made, and get ready to edit another important file, the **$INFORMIXDIR/etc/sqlhosts** file. There are more changes we will be making to the **$ONCONFIG** later on, but for now these are all we need to make to get the engine to start.

The following are editing tasks on other ASCII files. Make sure these files are saved as text files just like your **ONCONFIG** was.

$INFORMIXDIR/etc/sqlhosts

Add these entries to your **$INFORMIXDIR/etc/sqlhosts** file:

```
rebel_shm      onipcshm      rebel      sv_rebel_shm
rebel_net      onsoctcp      rebel      sv_rebel_net
```

These are directly related to other entries in the **/etc/services** file, so make sure you keep track of them. A complete discussion of what these values mean can be found in the *Administrator's Guide*. As a matter of convention you can name the values in the far-right column whatever you want—here I have them prefixed with an **sv_** to indicate they refer to entries in the **/etc/services** file. For now, simply follow this convention for your first installation; after this you can change it to whatever you prefer.

/etc/services

Add these entries to your Linux /etc/services file (not **$INFORMIXDIR/etc/services**!):

```
sv_rebel_shm      60000/tcp   # Informix IDS 7.30 @ rebel
sv_rebel_net      60001/tcp   # Informix IDS 7.30 @ rebel
```

Make sure these port entries can be used; if they cannot be used, use other available port numbers. Any number between 0 and 65536 can be assigned a port number, including negative numbers. Many are preassigned as a matter of standards and conventions in the UNIX world, so you should take care not to use port numbers that are already assigned to other Ethernet channels.

Once you are done editing your **/etc/services** file, you need to restart your networking. In most cases restarting **inetd** will force **inetd** to reread the **/etc/services** file; however, a reboot may also be necessary for some of the Linux distributions. The various distributions have different run levels, which means that each distribution has unique procedures to restart networking. As a matter of tradition, many Linux system administrators do not want to cold-start their Linux servers to preserve the uptime, and strive only to restart what is necessary. For the sake of simplicity and reduced errors, reboot your Linux server if you can; otherwise, make absolutely sure that the networking layer of Linux is restarted, and that the **/etc/services** file is reread. If you don't, the Informix server will not be able to talk to clients on the network, or other problems may arise with the installation.

Notice that the entries in the **$INFORMIXDIR/etc/sqlhosts** file correspond to the entries in the **/etc/services** file. If these do not match, you won't be starting the engine.

/opt/data/rootdbs

To use a cooked file, we must create one in the **/opt/data** directory (see Figure 4.6):

```
$ mkdir /opt/data      # only if you do not have this directory!!!
$ chown informix:informix /opt/data
$ chmod 775 /opt/data
$ cd /opt/data
$ >rootdbs
$ chown informix:informix rootdbs
$ chmod 660 rootdbs
$ ls -l rootdbs
```

The rootdbs should now be zero bytes in size. It should be owned by Informix and have user and group permissions on it, but no public permissions. It should be **rw-rw——** when you run **ls -l** on the rootdbs file. The directory, in which the rootdbs lives, should be owned by Informix and the group id of Informix.

Starting Your Engine with oninit

If you have followed all the instructions up to now, you are ready to initialize your instance of Informix. Initialization is the process whereby the **sysmaster** database is created, and the rootdbs brought online. This will bring the engine up, and you will be able to start creating databases and tables.

Figure 4.6 Creating the /opt/data directory, and creating the rootdbs for initialization.

```
rebel:root # pwd
/opt
rebel:root # mkdir data
rebel:root # chmod 775 /opt/data
rebel:root # chown informix:informix /opt/data
rebel:root # cd /opt/data
rebel:root # >rootdbs
rebel:root # chown informix:informix /opt/data/rootdbs
rebel:root # chmod 660 /opt/data/rootdbs
rebel:root # ls -la
total 2
drwxrwxr-x   2 informix informix     1024 Jan 18 10:22 .
drwxr-xr-x  17 root     root         1024 Jan 18 10:22 ..
-rw-rw----   1 informix informix        0 Jan 18 10:22 rootdbs
rebel:root # ▮
```

You can now run the **oninit** program to initialize the rootdbs. Keep in mind that what we do now is only for the initial installation. After this you will not repeat this initialization start-up for everyday operations. The **oninit** program is the same program we use for starting and stopping the engine on a daily basis, but without the options for our initial installation. You need to be root for our install operation; hereafter, the only login for daily startup will be informix, and **oninit** is used without any options.

To initialize our engine, the following command is run from any directory:

```
$ oninit -ivy
```

Think of the **–ivy** command combination as poison ivy! Stay away from the **–i** option except to run this initialization. You want to use it only once—it will cause you pain if you use it again on the same instance.

- **-i** means initialize the instance—*do this only once*
- **-v** means verbose mode
- **-y** means answer yes to all prompts

Once you run the **oninit –ivy** command, the following dialog will appear:

```
rebel:root # oninit -ivy

Checking group membership to determine server run mode succeeded
Reading configuration file '/opt/informix/ids/etc/rebel_shm.cfg'...succeeded
```

```
Creating /INFORMIXTMP/.infxdirs ... succeeded
Creating infos file "/opt/informix/ids/etc/.infos.rebel_shm" ...
"/opt/informix/ids/etc/.conf.rebel_shm" ... succeeded
Writing to infos file ... succeeded
Checking config parameters...succeeded
Allocating and attaching to shared memory...succeeded
Creating resident pool 398 kbytes...succeeded
Creating buffer pool 402 kbytes...succeeded
Initializing rhead structure...succeeded
Initializing ASF ...succeeded
Initializing Dictionary Cache and Stored Procedure Cache...succeeded
Bringing up ADM VP...succeeded
Creating VP classes...succeeded
Onlining 0 additional cpu vps...succeeded
Onlining 2 IO vps...succeeded
Forking main_loop thread...succeeded
Initialzing DR structures...succeeded
Forking 1 'ipcshm' listener threads...succeeded
Forking 1 'soctcp' listener threads...succeeded
Starting tracing...succeeded
Initializing 1 flushers...succeeded
Initializing log/checkpoint information...succeeded
Opening primary chunks...succeeded
Opening mirror chunks...succeeded
Initializing dbspaces...succeeded
Validating chunks...succeeded
Creating database partition
Initialize Async Log Flusher...succeeded
Forking btree cleaner...succeeded
rebel:root # Initializing DBSPACETEMP list
Checking database partition index...succeeded
Checking location of physical log...succeeded
Initializing dataskip structure...succeeded
Checking for temporary tables to drop
Forking onmode_mon thread...succeeded
Verbose output complete: mode = 5
```

Immediately after this last message, you can press the **Return** or **Enter** key, and the command prompt will reappear. You can monitor the engine immediately, and check to see that it is running correctly.

You can check the status of your engine with the **onstat** command. As you can see in this example, our engine has been running for 26 minutes, 5 seconds:

```
rebel:root # onstat


Informix Dynamic Server Version 7.30.UC10 -- On-Line-Up 00:26:05 -- 8888 Kbytes


Userthreads
address    flags   sessid    user      tty       wait      tout locks   nreads   nwrites
10120014 ---P-D 1          root      -         0         0    0       54       2014
101204c8 ---P-F 0          root      -         0         0    0       0        1089
1012097c ---P--- 9          root      -         0          0   0       0        0
10120e30 ---P-B 10         root      -         0         0    0       6        0
10121798 ---P-D 12         root      -         0         0    0       0        0
 5 active, 128 total, 8 maximum concurrent


Profile
dskreads pagreads bufreads %cached dskwrits pagwrits bufwrits %cached
1764     1765     67300    97.38   1996     4570     19723    89.88


isamtot   open     start    read     write    rewrite  delete   commit   rollbk
56074     8740     9352     13263    6790     427      1161     772      0


gp_read   gp_write gp_rewrt gp_del   gp_alloc gp_free  gp_curs
0         0        0        0        0        0        0


ovlock    ovuserthread ovbuff    usercpu  syscpu   numckpts flushes
0         0            71        1.79     0.51     4        17


bufwaits lokwaits lockreqs deadlks  dltouts  ckpwaits compress seqscans
6        0        15805    0        0        1        90       411


ixda-RA  idx-RA   da-RA    RA-pgsused lchwaits
28       0        6        34         1
```

Hooray!! It's running!!

If the engine is *not* running, you will not see this dialogue, and will need to go back and recheck all the steps I have outlined to set your system up. Do the installation again if necessary, checking everything along the way. You can call Informix Technical Support for even more help on installing this software.

If you look at the size of **/opt/data/rootdbs** you will see it is the 20MB you set aside for it, as one big Linux file. The **oninit** program created the file to your specifications.

```
rebel:root # cd /opt/data
rebel:root # ls -l
total 20082
drwxrwxr-x   2 informix informix     1024  Jan 18 10:22 .
drwxr-xr-x  17 root     root         1024 Jan 18 10:22 ..
-rw-rw---    1 informix informix  20480000 Jan 18 13:00 rootdbs
rebel:root #
```

Logs can be checked with the additional **-l** option:

```
rebel:root # onstat -l


Informix Dynamic Server Version 7.30.UC10     -- On-Line-Up 00:26:08 -- 8888 Kbytes


Physical Logging
Buffer bufused   bufsize   numpages numwrits pages/io
  P-1  0            16       212      21        10.10%
      phybegin physize  phypos    phyused   %used
      10003f   500      212       0         0.00


Logical Logging
Buffer bufused   bufsize   numrecs   numpages numwrits recs/pages pages/io
  L-1  0            16       18630     1243     810      15.0        1.5
          Subsystem        numrecs   Log Space used
          OLDRSAM          18630     1304996


address   number   flags      uniqid   begin       size    used    %used
10039324 1         U-B----    1        100233      250     250     100.00%
10039340 2         U-B----    2        10032d      250     250     100.00%
1003935c 3         U-B----    3        100427      250     250     100.00%
10039378 4         U-B----    4        100521      250     250     100.00%
10039394 5         U---C-L    5        10061b      250     243     97.20%
100393b0 6         F------    0        100715      250     0       0.00%
```

Engine Messages stored in your **$INFORMIXDIR/logs/online.log** can be viewed using the **onstat –m** option:

```
rebel:root # onstat -m


Informix Dynamic Server Version 7.30.UC10     -- On-Line-Up 00:26:12 -- 8888 Kbytes
```

```
Message Log File: /opt/informix/ids/logs/online.log
Tue Jan 18 11:58:14 2000

11:58:14  Event alarms enabled.  ALARMPROG =
'/opt/informix/ids/etc/log_full.sh'
11:58:19  DR: DRAUTO is 0 (Off)
11:58:19  Requested shared memory segment size rounded from 588KB to 592KB
11:58:19  Informix Dynamic Server Version 7.30.UC10   Software Serial Number
          AAC#A518469
11:58:23  Informix Dynamic Server Initialized—Complete Disk Initialized.
11:58:23  Checkpoint Completed:  duration was 0 seconds.
11:58:23  Dataskip is now OFF for all dbspaces
11:58:23  On-Line Mode
11:58:23  Building 'sysmaster' database ...
11:58:27  Logical Log 1 Complete.
11:58:31  Logical Log 2 Complete.
11:58:31  Checkpoint Completed:  duration was 0 seconds.
11:58:33  Logical Log 3 Complete.
11:58:35  Logical Log 4 Complete.
11:58:41  'sysmaster' database built successfully.
11:58:41  'sysutils' database built successfully.
12:03:52  Checkpoint Completed:  duration was 0 seconds.
12:08:52  Checkpoint Completed:  duration was 0 seconds.
```

At this point, your engine is up, but not totally ready for prime time. There are some additional settings and configuration parameters we need to set up, such as the database spaces we talked about earlier in this chapter. Your engine is usable at this point only for the sake of the 20MB rootdbs dbspace, but this is hardly enough room to use as a database server. You need to complete the following steps, and make your system operational.

We also mentioned the **console.log** file; here is a sample of the output it saves:

```
rebel:root # cat $INFORMIXDIR/logs/console.log


        <<Informix Dynamic Server>>> Logical Log 1 Complete.


        <<Informix Dynamic Server>>> Logical Log 2 Complete.


        <<Informix Dynamic Server>>> Logical Log 3 Complete.


        <<Informix Dynamic Server>>> Logical Log 4 Complete.
```

As you can see, these kinds of messages may not need to be saved in a log file, and the **CONSOLE** setting in your **ONCONFIG** can be set to **/dev/null**. This will eliminate the need to monitor the size of this file.

To view memory allocation, use **onstat –g seg**:

```
rebel:root # onstat -g seg


Informix Dynamic Server Version 7.30.UC10     -- On-Line—Up 00:40:09 -- 8888
Kbytes


Segment Summary:
id          key         addr       size       ovhd       class   blkused   blkfree
769         1381386241  10000000   909312     872         R       104       7
770         1381386242  100de000   8192000    724         V       415       585
771         1381386243  108ae000   606208     608         M       67        7
Total:      -           -          9707520    -           -       586       599


    (* segment locked in memory)
```

This allows you to monitor memory usage and allocation that the IDS server has allocated for use by the engine. If the server needs more it will allocate memory usage based on settings in your **ONCONFIG**. We will cover this in the next part of our installation.

To view the disk usage of the engine, use **onstat –d**:

```
rebel:root # onstat -d


Informix Dynamic Server Version 7.30.UC10     -- On-Line—Up 00:00:20 -- 8888 Kbytes


Dbspaces
address   number   flags    fchunk    nchunks   flags    owner      name
1011e13c  1        1        1         1         N        informix   rootdbs
 1 active, 2047 maximum


Chunks
address   chk/dbs offset   size      free      bpages   flags   pathname
1011e1f8  1   1   0        10000     6971               PO-     /opt/data/rootdbs
 1 active, 2047 maximum
```

To continue our final configuration, you will need to make several final changes to your $**ONCONFIG** and then restart your engine.

> **NOTE**
>
> A complete listing of **onstat** options is available by using the `onstat –` command. Read the *Administrator's Guide* for a complete discussion of what all these options tell you. Included with this book are a couple of tools that provide much more comprehensive reporting about your engine.

Stopping Your Engine

Now that your engine is running, how do you turn it off? To stop the Informix engine, use the **onmode –ky** command.

```
$ onmode -ky
```

This will allow you to make changes to your **$ONCONFIG** and restart the engine.

A whole series of additional features are contained in the **onmode** command. Be sure to read your *Administrator's Guide* for more information on how and for what the other options are used.

Final Configuration

What's next? Your engine is running, but really not operational. The next phase will allow our server to be useful, especially for endusers.

We will set up our engine for our final configuration, one that you can change to suit your needs from here. You need to make sure you have the disk space for the following actions. If you have done your space allocations for your disks as outlined in the beginning of this chapter, you are now ready to complete the following steps.

Review

Let's quickly review some of the key dbspaces we covered.

rootdbs. Created during our installation and initialization of the database.

physdbs. Will contain the physical log; must be moved out of the rootdbs into its own dbspace.

logsdbs. Will contain the logical logs; must be moved out of the rootdbs into their own dbspace.

tempdbs. Defaults to the rootdbs, will point to its own dbspace, and is used for sorts, queries, and temp tables.

dbs_dbs. Will contain database entries, but no table entries.

datadbs01. Will contain tables.

indexdbs01. Will contain indexes.

Physdbs

For performance considerations, it is a standard practice to relocate the physical log to its own dbspace. The physical log is a buffer, or cache, of database activity that has yet to be written to the database. Relocating it to its own dbspace allows you to expand or decrease its size as your needs allow, without impacting the rootdbs, and allows you to increase performance.

As previously discussed, the rootdbs contains the brains behind every database you create on this server, for this instance. You can have multiple instances of Informix; each instance has its own rootdbs and dbspaces separate from other instances. It is important to minimize the risk to the rootdbs. Relocating the physical log is one of the first steps we will take to make sure the rootdbs is left for only the minimum of activity—keeping track of where everything is in your databases—and managing the engine.

Make sure your Informix engine is up and running.

```
$ onstat
```

If the engine is not running, start it now with the **oninit** program, with *no* options, or at a minimum using only the **–v** option (the verbose flag):

```
$ oninit -v
```

You do not use the **–i** option to run **oninit** after you create the rootdbs. Doing so is the equivalent of reformatting your hard drive. The one exception you can use is **oninit –v**, which shows verbose output as the engine starts. Using the **–i** option on a production server would only serve to expedite work on your resumé.

Once the engine is up and running, you can create the physdbs first with UNIX/Linux commands, and then with Informix commands, as you did with the rootdbs.

Create a physdbs File

UNIX and Linux allow you to create a zero-length file when you issue the
>filename command.

```
$ cd /opt/data
$ >physdbs
$ chown informix:informix physdbs
$ chmod 660 physdbs
```

This creates the file, but with absolutely nothing in it.

We will need to do most of the following steps in single-user, or *quiescent* mode, as it is referred to. We will also take advantage of two utilities—**onspaces** and **onparams**—programs you only use as a DBA.

Onspaces can be used in multi-user mode, but **onparams** must be run when the engine is in single-user mode. To get to single-user mode, run the **onmode** command **onmode –s**. Adding an **s** to this command removes the following question:

```
rebel:root # onmode –s


This will perform a GRACEFUL SHUTDOWN -
Do you wish to continue (y/n)? y


rebel:root # onstat


Informix Dynamic Server Version 7.30.UC10   -- Quiescent–Up 00:22:36 -- 8888 Kbytes


Userthreads
address    flags    sessid    user      tty    wait    tout    locks    nreads    nwrites
10120014  ---P–D 1            informix -         0       0       0        11        5
101204c8  ---P–F 0            informix -         0       0       0        0         2
1012097c  ---P--- 9           informix -         0       0       0        0         0
10120e30  ---P–B 10           informix -         0       0       0        0         0
10121c4c  ---P–D 13           informix -         0       0       0        0         0
 5 active, 128 total, 18 maximum concurrent


Profile
dskreads pagreads bufreads %cached dskwrits pagwrits bufwrits %cached
20       38       36       44.44   7        7        2        0.00


isamtot  open    start    read    write    rewrite   delete    commit    rollbk
16       4       5        3       0        0         0         0         0
```

```
gp_read   gp_write  gp_rewrt  gp_del    gp_alloc  gp_free   gp_curs
0         0         0         0         0         0         0


ovlock    ovuserthread ovbuff   usercpu   syscpu    numckpts  flushes
0         0            0        2.95      0.09      1         10


bufwaits  lokwaits  lockreqs  deadlks   dltouts   ckpwaits  compress  seqscans
0         0         10        0         0         0         0         0


ixda-RA   idx-RA    da-RA     RA-pgsused  lchwaits
0         0         0         0           0
```

If you look at the top line, you'll see Informix IDS is now quiescent, or in *single-user mode*. This is the only mode in which you can run **onparams** to perform some of the more critical commands, such as rolling out the physical log into another dbspace. At other times and on other platforms, **onparams** must be run with the engine totally off.

Let's now create a physdbs. To do this we first must create a 20MB physdbs dbspace with the **onspaces** command, and then roll out the physical log using the **onparams** command. The commands throughout the remainder of the chapter are bolded within the code examples to allow you to more easily discern what happens.

```
rebel:root # onspaces -c -d physdbs -p /opt/data/physdbs -o 0 -s 20480
Verifying physical disk space, please wait ...
Space successfully added.

** WARNING **  A level 0 archive of Root DBSpace will need to be done.
rebel:root # ontape -s -L 0
Archive to tape device '/dev/null' is complete.

Program over.
rebel:root # onstat -l


Informix Dynamic Server Version 7.30.UC10  -- Quiescent—Up 00:46:17 -- 8888
Kbytes


Physical Logging
Buffer bufused  bufsize  numpages numwrits pages/io
  P-1  4          16        4        0         0.00%
```

```
       phybegin physize   phypos    phyused   %used
        10003f    500       223        4       0.80


Logical Logging
Buffer  bufused  bufsize  numrecs  numpages numwrits  recs/pages pages/io
  L-3   0          16        21       5        5         4.2        1.0
           Subsystem       numrecs   Log Space used
           OLDRSAM           21         1092


address   number    flags     uniqid    begin      size     used     %used
10039324 1          U-B----   1         100233      250      250    100.00%
10039340 2          U-B----   2         10032d      250      250    100.00%
1003935c 3          U-B----   3         100427      250      250    100.00%
10039378 4          U-B----   4         100521      250      250    100.00%
10039394 5          U-B----   5         10061b      250      250    100.00%
100393b0 6          U---C-L   6         100715      250        7      2.80%
```

You'll notice we also performed an **ontape** command after creating the physdbs dbspace. This is essential to allow the physdbs dbspace to be usable. Running **onstat –l** shows that the logical log file output has also changed because we did a backup command with **ontape**. Run the **onstat –d** command now, and run it again after we roll out the physical log.

```
rebel:root # onstat -d


Informix Dynamic Server Version 7.30.UC10  -- Quiescent–Up 00:52:05 -- 8888
Kbytes


Dbspaces
address   number    flags     fchunk   nchunks  flags    owner     name
1011e13c 1          1         1         1        N       informix rootdbs
1011efa8 2          1         2         1        N       informix physdbs
  2 active, 2047 maximum


Chunks
address    chk/dbs offset    size      free     bpages   flags pathname
1011e1f8 1    1     0        10000     6921              PO- /opt/data/rootdbs
1011f064 2    2     0        10240     10187             PO- /opt/data/physdbs
  2 active, 2047 maximum
```

Now you can see that the physdbs space is present. The output unfortunately shows the size incorrectly, but you simply multiply this roughly by two, and it will be the 20480KB we allocated, or 20MB.

Run **onparams** without options to see what options are available.

```
$ onparams
```

```
Usage:   onparams  { -a -d DBspace [-s size]        |
                     -d -l logid [-y]               |
                     -p -s size [-d DBspace] [-y] }


    -a  - Add a logical log
    -d  - Drop a logical log
    -p  - Change physical log size and location
    -y  - Automatically responds "yes" to all prompts
```

We will be using the **-p** option to create a physdbs of 20MB. Remember, we originally allocated 50MB for the physical log, but we're only using 20MB. This will allow us some room to grow.

To create the physdbs, use the following **onparams** command:

```
$ onparams -p -s 50000 -d physdbs -y
```

Watch what happens when you run the command:

```
rebel:root # onparams -p -s 20000 -d physdbs -y
Shutting down, please wait ...
Initializing, please wait ...
Recovering, please wait ...
rebel:root # onstat -d


Informix Dynamic Server Version 7.30.UC10  -- Quiescent-Up 00:00:31 -- 8888
Kbytes


Dbspaces
address   number  flags   fchunk   nchunks  flags   owner     name
1011e13c  1       1       1        1        N       informix  rootdbs
1011e428  2       1       2        1        N       informix  physdbs
 2 active, 2047 maximum


Chunks
address   chk/dbs offset   size     free     bpages  flags  pathname
1011e1f8  1   1   0        10000    7421             PO-    /opt/data/rootdbs
1011e348  2   2   0        10240    187              PO-    /opt/data/physdbs
 2 active, 2047 maximum
```

The physical log was originally only 1MB in size, this being the default at the engine install. Now we can see it has used up all but a few bytes in our new 20MB physdbs. You'll see that rootdbs gained 1MB in available free space. After we roll out our logical logs, rootdbs will gain even more space. If you look in your **/opt/data** directory you will see the new physical log dbspace you created, as another cooked file:

```
rebel:root # ls -l
total 40643
drwxrwxr-x    2 informix  informix      1024 Jan 24 11:14 .
drwxr-xr-x   17 root      root          1024 Jan 18 10:22 ..
-rw-rw----    1 informix informix  20971520 Jan 24 12:25 physdbs
-rw-rw----    1 informix informix  20480000 Jan 24 12:25 rootdbs
```

Physdbs is also slightly larger physically than rootdbs—this is because all our commands refer to KB sizes rather than MB sizes. 20000KB equates to 20480MB, the install size we gave to the rootdbs. 20480KB equates to 20971520 bytes, the actual size of physdbs, which we created when we used the **onspaces** command using KB sizes, not MB sizes.

In most cases, almost without exception, Informix commands are going to refer to information in KB, not MB. It is important for you to pay attention to this characteristic of Informix commands so that you are using them in the right context; that is, you think first in KB, not MB. You can think in MB but only in terms of converting the KB to MB.

Logsdbs

Now let's create a logsdbs as a home for our logical logs, currently residing in rootdbs. Make sure your engine is in quiescent mode, and then follow along to create the logsdbs.

We are going to create 20 new logical logs, 1MB each, so we need a logical log dbspace of at least 26MB if not more, and it's a great idea to make it a little larger so you can add more logs as you need them. Our first logsdbs is going to be 50MB, to allow us some room for growth. We have six logical logs in the rootdbs and we want 26, so we will create 20 new ones.

First we want to create our logsdbs:

```
rebel:root # onspaces -c -d logsdbs -p /opt/data/logsdbs -o 0 -s 50000
Verifying physical disk space, please wait ...
Space successfully added.

** WARNING **  A level 0 archive of Root DBSpace will need to be done.
rebel:root # ontape -s -L 0
```

```
onstat
Archive to tape device '/dev/null' is complete.

Program over.
rebel:root # onstat -d


Informix Dynamic Server Version 7.30.UC10   -- Quiescent—Up 02:52:04 -- 8888
Kbytes


Dbspaces
address   number    flags     fchunk    nchunks   flags     owner     name
1011e13c 1          1         1         1         N         informix rootdbs
1011e428 2          1         2         1         N         informix physdbs
1011f00c 3          1         3         1         N         informix logsdbs
 3 active, 2047 maximum


Chunks
address   chk/dbs offset    size      free      bpages    flags pathname
1011e1f8 1    1   0         10000     7421                PO-   /opt/data/rootdbs
1011e348 2    2   0         10240     187                 PO-   /opt/data/physdbs
1011f0c8 3    3   0         25000     24947               PO-   /opt/data/logsdbs
 3 active, 2047 maximum
```

Now that the logsdbs dbspace exists, you can roll the logical logs out of the rootdbs, into the logsdbs. When the installation started, it created six logical logs, so we will add 20 logical logs for a total of 26. Why 26? Adding 20 logs is a great exercise, and will give you a good idea of how the engine works. It is a good idea to have many small logical logs; the guidelines are covered in the *Administrator's Guide.*

To move the logical logs out of rootdbs you must have new logs in place already available for use by the engine, which will take the place of the existing logical logs. The bare minimum of logical logs is three, so in order to do this we have to tell the engine which logs are the good ones, and which can be deleted. We also cannot delete or remove any logical logs that are in use, so we need to tell the engine to use the new ones so the old ones can then be removed.

Create logsdbs

Make sure you have created the new logsdbs dbspace with the **onspaces** command we discussed at the beginning of this section, and then proceed.

Make sure the engine is in single-user mode by running the **onmode -sy** command:

```
rebel:root # onmode -sy
```

Perform a level-zero backup to clean up any outstanding log entries.

```
rebel:root # ontape -s -L 0
Archive to tape device '/dev/null' is complete.


Program over.
rebel:root # onstat -ld


Informix Dynamic Server Version 7.30.UC10    -- On-Line -- Up 00:19:33 -- 8888
Kbytes


Dbspaces
address   number  flags     fchunk   nchunks  flags   owner     name
1011e13c  1       1         1        1        N       informix  rootdbs
1011e508  2       1         2        1        N       informix  physdbs
1011e5c4  3       1         3        1        N       informix  logsdbs
 3 active, 2047 maximum


Chunks
address   chk/dbs offset    size     free      bpages   flags pathname
1011e1f8  1   1   0         10000    7421               PO-   /opt/data/rootdbs
1011e348  2   2   0         10240    187                PO-   /opt/data/physdbs
1011e428  3   3   0         25000    24947              PO-   /opt/data/logsdbs
 3 active, 2047 maximum


Physical Logging
Buffer bufused  bufsize   numpages numwrits pages/io
  P-1   4       16        4        0        0.00%
        phybegin physize  phypos   phyused  %used
        200035   10000    3        4        0.04


Logical Logging
Buffer bufused  bufsize   numrecs  numpages numwrits recs/pages pages/io
  L-1   0       16        17       3        3        5.7        1.0
        Subsystem      numrecs   Log Space used
        OLDRSAM        17        772


address   number  flags     uniqid   begin     size     used     %used
10039324  1       U-B----   1        100233    250      250      100.00%
```

10039340	2	U-B----	2	10032d	250	250	100.00%
1003935c	3	U-B----	3	100427	250	250	100.00%
10039378	4	U-B----	4	100521	250	250	100.00%-
10039394	5	U-B----	5	10061b	250	250	100.00%
100393b0	6	U---C-L	6	100715	250	17	6.80%

Create New Logical Logs

Run the **onparams** command multiple times to create logical logs:

```
rebel:root # onparams -a -d logsdbs -s 1024
Logical log successfully added.
rebel:root # onstat -l


Informix Dynamic Server Version 7.30.UC10    -- Quiescent -- Up 00:23:25 -- 8888
Kbytes


Physical Logging
Buffer bufused  bufsize  numpages numwrits pages/io
  P-1  5        16       5        0        0.00%
      phybegin physize  phypos   phyused  %used
       200035  10000    3        5        0.05


Logical Logging
Buffer bufused  bufsize  numrecs   numpages numwrits recs/pages pages/io
  L-2  0        16       21        4        4        5.2        1.0
          Subsystem     numrecs  Log Space used
          OLDRSAM       21       940


address   number  flags    uniqid   begin       size   used   %used
10039324 1        U-B----  1        100233      250    250    100.00%
10039340 2        U-B----  2        10032d      250    250    100.00%
1003935c 3        U-B----  3        100427      250    250    100.00%
10039378 4        U-B----  4        100521      250    250    100.00%
10039394 5        U-B----  5        10061b      250    250    100.00%
100393b0 6        U---C-L  6        100715      250    18     7.20%
100393cc 7        A------  0        300035      512    0      0.00%
```

Each time you add a log without running a level-zero backup using the **ontape** command, you can see the new logical log when you run **onstat -l** marked with an **A**. This new log is created but unusable until you run a level-zero backup. Even though we are backing up to **/dev/null**, this tells the engine to use the new logical log.

We are going to create 20 new logical logs 1MB in size, for a total of 20MB of logical log space usage. You can do this in a for-loop, or repeat the command 20 times as shown earlier:

```
for log in 1 2 3 4 5 6 7 8 9 10 11 12 13 14 15 16 17 18 19 20
do
        LOG_COUNT='expr $LOG_COUNT + 1'
        echo $LOG_COUNT
        onparams  -a -d logsdbs -s 1024
done
```

However you decide to add them, perform this operation and then run **onstat** to see your new logical logs:

```
rebel:root # onstat -l
```

```
Informix Dynamic Server Version 7.30.UC10    -- Quiescent -- Up 00:27:36 -- 8888
Kbytes


Physical Logging
Buffer bufused  bufsize   numpages numwrits pages/io
   P-1   1        16         6        1        6.00%
         phybegin physize   phypos   phyused  %used
         200035   10000     8        1        0.01


Logical Logging
Buffer bufused  bufsize   numrecs   numpages numwrits recs/pages pages/io
   L-1   0        16         98        24       24       4.1        1.0
         Subsystem      numrecs   Log Space used
         OLDRSAM          98        4164


address   number   flags    uniqid   begin        size     used    %used
10039324  1        U-B----  1        100233       250      250     100.00%
10039340  2        U-B----  2        10032d       250      250     100.00%
1003935c  3        U-B----  3        100427       250      250     100.00%
10039378  4        U-B----  4        100521       250      250     100.00%
10039394  5        U-B----  5        10061b       250      250     100.00%
100393b0  6        U---C-L  6        100715       250      38      15.20%
100393cc  7        A------  0        300035       512      0       0.00%
100393e8  8        A------  0        300235       512      0       0.00%
10039404  9        A------  0        300435       512      0       0.00%
10039420  10       A------  0        300635       512      0       0.00%
1003943c  11       A------  0        300835       512      0       0.00%
10039458  12       A------  0        300a35       512      0       0.00%
```

10039474	13	A------	0	300c35	512	0	0.00%
10039490	14	A------	0	300e35	512	0	0.00%
100394ac	15	A------	0	301035	512	0	0.00%
100394c8	16	A------	0	301235	512	0	0.00%
100394e4	17	A------	0	301435	512	0	0.00%
10039500	18	A------	0	301635	512	0	0.00%
1003951c	19	A------	0	301835	512	0	0.00%
10039538	20	A------	0	301a35	512	0	0.00%
10039554	21	A------	0	301c35	512	0	0.00%
10039570	22	A------	0	301e35	512	0	0.00%
1003958c	23	A------	0	302035	512	0	0.00%
100395a8	24	A------	0	302235	512	0	0.00%
100395c4	25	A------	0	302435	512	0	0.00%
100395e0	26	A------	0	302635	512	0	0.00%

```
rebel:root # onstat -d


Informix Dynamic Server Version 7.30.UC10    -- Quiescent -- Up 00:27:41 -- 8888
Kbytes


Dbspaces
address    number   flags    fchunk   nchunks   flags   owner     name
1011e13c 1          1        1        1         N       informix rootdbs
1011e508 2          1        2        1         N       informix physdbs
1011e5c4 3          1        3        1         N       informix logsdbs
 3 active, 2047 maximum


Chunks
address    chk/dbs offset   size     free      bpages   flags pathname
1011e1f8 1   1    0         10000    7421               PO-   /opt/data/rootdbs
1011e348 2   2    0         10240    187                PO-   /opt/data/physdbs
1011e428 3   3    0         25000    14707              PO-   /opt/data/logsdbs
 3 active, 2047 maximum
```

As you can see, logsdbs is indeed being used and the rootdbs remains the same. We now need to make our new logs available. Perform a level-zero backup, and run **onstat –l** again:

```
rebel:root # ontape -s -L 0
Archive to tape device '/dev/null' is complete.
```

```
Program over.
rebel:root # onstat -l

Informix Dynamic Server Version 7.30.UC10 -- Quiescent -- Up 00:30:20 -- 8888
Kbytes

Physical Logging
Buffer bufused  bufsize   numpages numwrits pages/io
  P-1   4        16         10       2        5.00%
        phybegin physize  phypos   phyused  %used
        200035   10000    9        4        0.04

Logical Logging
Buffer bufused  bufsize   numrecs   numpages numwrits recs/pages pages/io
  L-1   0        16         115       27       27       4.3        1.0
        Subsystem      numrecs   Log Space used
        OLDRSAM         115       4936
```

address	number	flags	uniqid	begin	size	used	%used
10039324	1	U-B----	1	100233	250	250	100.00%
10039340	2	U-B----	2	10032d	250	250	100.00%
1003935c	3	U-B----	3	100427	250	250	100.00%
10039378	4	U-B----	4	100521	250	250	100.00%
10039394	5	U-B----	5	10061b	250	250	100.00%
100393b0	6	U---C-L	6	100715	250	41	16.40%
100393cc	7	F------	0	300035	512	0	0.00%
100393e8	8	F------	0	300235	512	0	0.00%
10039404	9	F------	0	300435	512	0	0.00%
10039420	10	F------	0	300635	512	0	0.00%
1003943c	11	F------	0	300835	512	0	0.00%
10039458	12	F------	0	300a35	512	0	0.00%
10039474	13	F------	0	300c35	512	0	0.00%
10039490	14	F------	0	300e35	512	0	0.00%
100394ac	15	F------	0	301035	512	0	0.00%
100394c8	16	F------	0	301235	512	0	0.00%
100394e4	17	F------	0	301435	512	0	0.00%
10039500	18	F------	0	301635	512	0	0.00%
1003951c	19	F------	0	301835	512	0	0.00%
10039538	20	F------	0	301a35	512	0	0.00%
10039554	21	F------	0	301c35	512	0	0.00%
10039570	22	F------	0	301e35	512	0	0.00%
1003958c	23	F------	0	302035	512	0	0.00%

```
100395a8 24        F------  0          302235      512         0     0.00%
100395c4 25        F------  0          302435      512         0     0.00%
100395e0 26        F------  0          302635      512         0     0.00%
```

Now we have new logical logs that can be used, and we can delete the ones in the rootdbs. To do this we need to tell the engine which logs are the ones to point to as current logs. This is accomplished with the **onmode** command:

```
rebel:root # onmode

usage:   onmode -abcDdFklMmnOpQRrSsuyZz
         -a <kbytes>      Increase shared memory segment size.
         -b <version>     Revert Dynamic Server disk structures.
         -c [block | unblock]    Do Checkpoint. Block or unblock server.
         -D   <max PDQ priority allowed>
         -d   {standard|{primary|secondary <servername>}} set DR server type
         -F   Free unused memory segments
         -k   Shutdown completely
         -l   Force to next logical log
         -M   <decision support memory in kbytes>
         -m   Go to multi-user on-line
         -n   Set shared memory buffer cache to non-resident
         -O   Override space down blocking a checkpoint
         -p <+-#> <class>    Start up or remove virtual processors of
              a specific class
         -Q   <max # decision support queries>
         -R   Rebuild the /INFORMIXDIR/etc/.infos.DBSERVERNAME file
         -r   Set shared memory buffer cache to resident
         -S   <max # decision support scans>
         -s   Shutdown to single user
         -u   Shutdown and kill all attached sessions
         -y   Do not require confirmation
         -Z <address> heuristically complete specified transaction
         -z <sid    Kill specified session id
```

The three options we are interested in are the **–l**, **–c**, and **–m** options. The two options **–l** and **–c** manage the logical logs. The **–l** option forces the engine to use the next logical log and the **–c** option tells the engine to perform a checkpoint. Checkpoints are covered in the *Administrator's Guide*, and essentially are a mark that the engine puts on logical log activity with which to allow the logs to be backed up, and how much to recover when doing a database restore. The **–m** option allows us to bring the server back up into multi-user mode.

We need to not only move the current log activity to the new logical logs, but also perform a checkpoint to free up the old logs so they can be deleted. The engine should be totally on the new logs before we can delete the old ones. So you simply perform the following commands on the old logs until **onstat** shows you that the engine is using the new logs. In our particular case, we need to do this six times. The following output shows our logs after running **onmode –l** three times:

address	number	flags	uniqid	begin	size	used	%used
10039324	1	U-B----	1	100233	250	250	100.00%
10039340	2	U-B----	2	10032d	250	250	100.00%
1003935c	3	U-B----	3	100427	250	250	100.00%
10039378	4	U-B----	4	100521	250	250	100.00%
10039394	5	U-B----	5	10061b	250	250	100.00%
100393b0	6	U-B---L	6	100715	250	43	17.20%
100393cc	7	U-B----	7	300035	512	1	0.20%
100393e8	8	U-B----	8	300235	512	1	0.20%
10039404	9	U---C--	9	300435	512	0	0.00%
10039420	10	F------	0	300635	512	0	0.00%

As you can see in this example, the checkpoint log is now **log 9** in the new logs, but the last log backed up is **log 6**. Run **onmode –c** now, which will have the last log backed up as log number 9:

address	number	flags	uniqid	begin	size	used	%used
10039324	1	U-B----	1	100233	250	250	100.00%
10039340	2	U-B----	2	10032d	250	250	100.00%
1003935c	3	U-B----	3	100427	250	250	100.00%
10039378	4	U-B----	4	100521	250	250	100.00%
10039394	5	U-B----	5	10061b	250	250	100.00%
100393b0	6	U-B----	6	100715	250	43	17.20%
100393cc	7	U-B----	7	300035	512	1	0.20%
100393e8	8	U-B----	8	300235	512	1	0.20%
10039404	9	U---C-L	9	300435	512	1	0.20%
10039420	10	F------	0	300635	512	0	0.00%

Now that the current logs are the new ones and not the old ones, you can delete the old ones:

```
$ onparams –d –l 1 –y
$ onparams –d –l 2 –y
$ onparams –d –l 3 –y
$ onparams –d –l 4 –y
$ onparams –d –l 5 –y
$ onparams –d –l 6 –y
```

The preceding command is repeated for logs 1 through 6.

Here we see the **onparams** command on the last logical log deleted, number 6, and our **onstat –l** command shows those logs as missing:

```
rebel:root # onparams -d -l 6 -y
Logical log 6 successfully dropped.
** WARNING ** A level 0 archive will need to be done of the rootdbs before
level 1 or 2 archive is attempted after dropping the logical log (see Dynamic
Server Administrator's manual)
rebel:root #
rebel:root # onstat -l


Informix Dynamic Server Version 7.30.UC10    -- Quiescent -- Up 00:47:29 -- 8888
Kbytes


Physical Logging
Buffer bufused  bufsize   numpages numwrits pages/io
  P-1  0        16        16       9        1.78%
       phybegin physize   phypos   phyused  %used
       200035   10000     19       0        0.00


Logical Logging
Buffer bufused  bufsize   numrecs   numpages numwrits recs/pages pages/io
  L-3  0        16        147       44       44       3.3        1.0
       Subsystem      numrecs  Log Space used
       OLDRSAM        147      6344


address   number  flags     uniqid   begin      size    used    %used
100393cc  7       U-B----   7        300035     512     1       0.20%
100393e8  8       U-B----   8        300235     512     1       0.20%
10039404  9       U---C-L   9        300435     512     13      2.54%
10039420  10      F------   0        300635     512     0       0.00%
1003943c  11      F------   0        300835     512     0       0.00
10039458  12      F------   0        300a35     512     0       0.00%
10039474  13      F------   0        300c35     512     0       0.00%
10039490  14      F------   0        300e35     512     0       0.00%
100394ac  15      F------   0        301035     512     0       0.00%
100394c8  16      F------   0        301235     512     0       0.00%
100394e4  17      F------   0        301435     512     0       0.00%
10039500  18      F------   0        301635     512     0       0.00%
1003951c  19      F------   0        301835     512     0       0.00%
10039538  20      F------   0        301a35     512     0       0.00%
10039554  21      F------   0        301c35     512     0       0.00%
```

```
10039570 22        F------  0        301e35        512        0        0.00%
1003958c 23        F------  0        302035        512        0        0.00%
100395a8 24        F------  0        302235        512        0        0.00%
100395c4 25        F------  0        302435        512        0        0.00%
100395e0 26        F------  0        302635        512        0        0.00%
```

You can also see that the rootdbs reclaimed some space when you run
the **onstat –d** command:

```
rebel:root # onstat -d


Informix Dynamic Server Version 7.30.UC10 -- Quiescent -- Up 00:49:54 -- 8888
Kbytes


Dbspaces
address   number   flags    fchunk   nchunks   flags   owner      name
1011e13c 1         1        1        1         N       informix   rootdbs
1011e508 2         1        2        1         N       informix   physdbs
1011e5c4 3         1        3        1         N       informix   logsdbs
 3 active, 2047 maximum


Chunks
address   chk/dbs offset   size     free      bpages  flags pathname
1011e1f8 1   1   0        10000    8921              PO-   /opt/data/rootdbs
1011e348 2   2   0        10240    187               PO-   /opt/data/physdbs
1011e428 3   3   0        25000    14707             PO-   /opt/data/logsdbs
 3 active, 2047 maximum
```

Now you need to recreate logs 1 through 6 in the new logsdbs:

```
rebel:root # onparams  -a -d logsdbs -s 1024
```

Perform this six times, and then run the **onstat** command:

```
rebel:root # onstat -l


Informix Dynamic Server Version 7.30.UC10 -- Quiescent -- Up 00:52:57 -- 8888
Kbytes


Physical Logging
Buffer bufused  bufsize   numpages numwrits pages/io
  P-1  1        16        18       10       1.80%
      phybegin physize   phypos   phyused  %used
      200035   10000     20       1        0.01
```

```
Logical Logging
Buffer bufused  bufsize  numrecs   numpages numwrits recs/pages pages/io
   L-1  0        16       172       51       51       3.4        1.0
         Subsystem     numrecs   Log Space used
         OLDRSAM       172       7384


address   number   flags   uniqid    begin       size      used    %used
10039324 1         A------  0         302835      512       0       0.00%
10039340 2         A------  0         302a35      512       0       0.00%
1003935c 3         A------  0         302c35      512       0       0.00%
10039378 4         A------  0         302e35      512       0       0.00%
10039394 5         A------  0         303035      512       0       0.00%
100393b0 6         A------  0         303235      512       0       0.00%
100393cc 7         U-B----  7         300035      512       1       0.20%
100393e8 8         U-B----  8         300235      512       1       0.20%
10039404 9         U---C-L  9         300435      512       20      3.91%
10039420 10        F------  0         300635      512       0       0.00%
1003943c 11        F------  0         300835      512       0       0.00%
10039458 12        F------  0         300a35      512       0       0.00%
10039474 13        F------  0         300c35      512       0       0.00%
10039490 14        F------  0         300e35      512       0       0.00%
100394ac 15        F------  0         301035      512       0       0.00%
100394c8 16        F------  0         301235      512       0       0.00%
100394e4 17        F------  0         301435      512       0       0.00%
10039500 18        F------  0         301635      512       0       0.00%
1003951c 19        F------  0         301835      512       0       0.00%
10039538 20        F------  0         301a35      512       0       0.00%
10039554 21        F------  0         301c35      512       0       0.00%
10039570 22        F------  0         301e35      512       0       0.00%
1003958c 23        F------  0         302035      512       0       0.00%
100395a8 24        F------  0         302235      512       0       0.00%
100395c4 25        F------  0         302435      512       0       0.00%
100395e0 26        F------  0         302635      512       0       0.00%
```

Perform a level zero backup and you are finished!

```
rebel:root # ontape -s -L 0
Archive to tape device '/dev/null' is complete.

Program over.
rebel:root # onstat -l
```

Informix Dynamic Server Version 7.30.UC10   -- Quiescent -- Up 01:03:37 -- 8888
Kbytes

Physical Logging

Buffer bufused bufsize   numpages numwrits pages/io
  P-1   4   16   22   11   2.00%
       phybegin physize phypos   phyused %used
       200035   10000   21   4   0.04

Logical Logging

Buffer bufused bufsize numrecs   numpages numwrits recs/pages pages/io
  L-1   0   16   189   54   54   3.5   1.0
         Subsystem   numrecs Log Space used
         OLDRSAM   189   8156

address	number	flags	uniqid	begin	size	used	%used
10039324	1	F------	0	302835	512	0	0.00%
10039340	2	F------	0	302a35	512	0	0.00%
1003935c	3	F------	0	302c35	512	0	0.00%
10039378	4	F------	0	302e35	512	0	0.00%
10039394	5	F------	0	303035	512	0	0.00%
100393b0	6	F------	0	303235	512	0	0.00%
100393cc	7	U-B----	7	300035	512	1	0.20%
100393e8	8	U-B----	8	300235	512	1	0.20%
10039404	9	U---C-L	9	300435	512	23	4.49%
10039420	10	F------	0	300635	512	0	0.00%
1003943c	11	F------	0	300835	512	0	0.00%
10039458	12	F------	0	300a35	512	0	0.00%
10039474	13	F------	0	300c35	512	0	0.00%
10039490	14	F------	0	300e35	512	0	0.00%
100394ac	15	F------	0	301035	512	0	0.00%
100394c8	16	F------	0	301235	512	0	0.00%
100394e4	17	F------	0	301435	512	0	0.00%
10039500	18	F------	0	301635	512	0	0.00%
1003951c	19	F------	0	301835	512	0	0.00%
10039538	20	F------	0	301a35	512	0	0.00%
10039554	21	F------	0	301c35	512	0	0.00%
10039570	22	F------	0	301e35	512	0	0.00%
1003958c	23	F------	0	302035	512	0	0.00%
100395a8	24	F------	0	302235	512	0	0.00%
100395c4	25	F------	0	302435	512	0	0.00%
100395e0	26	F------	0	302635	512	0	0.00%

You can now see the disk usage with **onstat –d**:

```
rebel:root # onstat -d


Informix Dynamic Server Version 7.30.UC10    -- Quiescent -- Up 01:05:27 -- 8888
Kbytes


Dbspaces
address  number   flags    fchunk   nchunks  flags    owner     name
1011e13c 1        1        1        1        N        informix rootdbs
1011e508 2        1        2        1        N        informix physdbs
1011e5c4 3        1        3        1        N        informix logsdbs
 3 active, 2047 maximum


Chunks
address  chk/dbs offset   size     free     bpages   flags pathname
1011e1f8 1   1   0        10000    8921              PO-   /opt/data/rootdbs
1011e348 2   2   0        10240    187               PO-   /opt/data/physdbs
1011e428 3   3   0        25000    11635             PO-   /opt/data/logsdbs
 3 active, 2047 maximum
```

As you can see, rootdbs gained some space. It now has almost 17MB free, more than enough to handle the engine, made up of the sysmaster database and the sysutils database, which is used to manage Informix backups.

From here we have a couple more steps, and your system will be operational.

Tempdbs

Informix engines must have a workspace for sorting queries, and a place to put temporary tables. If you do not specify a place for this to occur, the engine will use /tmp, and its own space, called **INFORMIXTEMP**, usually placed in the **/** directory. This is not good: We need to create a tempdbs to allow our system to control where temp tables and sorts will occur.

Creating this dbspace is a little different. We must tell the engine to use this as a temporary dbspace; otherwise it will treat it as a regular dbspace. We add the **–t** option to do this:

```
$ onspaces -c -t -d tempdbs    -p /opt/data/tempdbs  -o 0 -s 102400


rebel:root # onspaces -c -t -d tempdbs -p /opt/data/tempdbs -o 0 -s 300000
Verifying physical disk space, please wait ...
Space successfully added.
rebel:root # ls -l
```

```
total 392018
drwxrwxr-x   2 informix informix    1024 Jan 24 17:41 .
drwxr-xr-x  17 root     root         1024 Jan 24 17:41 ..
-rw-rw----   1 informix informix 51200000 Jan 24 17:52 logsdbs
-rw-rw----   1 informix informix 20971520 Jan 24 17:52 physdbs
-rw-rw----   1 informix informix 20480000 Jan 24 17:52 rootdbs
-rw-rw----   1 informix informix 307200000 Jan 24 17:52 tempdbs
```

As you can see, a tempdbs has now been created, and will be usable once we make some final changes in the **$INFORMIXDIR/etc/$ONCON-FIG** file.

We will repeat these steps for the **dbs_dbs** space and the **datadbs01** dbspace. This will complete our dbspace creation; the final steps will be in the **$INFORMIXDIR/etc/$ONCONFIG**. After that, you can start making databases!

I put the following in one script, and watched it run:

```
onspaces -c -d dbs_dbs     -p /opt/data/dbs_dbs     -o 0 -s 100000
onspaces -c -d datadbs01   -p /opt/data/datadbs01   -o 0 -s 250000
onspaces -c -d indexdbs01  -p /opt/data/indexdbs01  -o 0 -s 250000
ontape -s -L 0
```

```
onspaces -c -d dbs_dbs -p /opt/data/dbs_dbs -o 0 -s 100000
Verifying physical disk space, please wait ...
Space successfully added.

** WARNING **  A level 0 archive of Root DBSpace will need to be done.
onspaces -c -d datadbs01 -p /opt/data/datadbs01 -o 0 -s 250000
Verifying physical disk space, please wait ...
Space successfully added.

** WARNING **  A level 0 archive of Root DBSpace will need to be done.
onspaces -c -d indexdbs01 -p /opt/data/indexdbs01 -o 0 -s 250000
Verifying physical disk space, please wait ...
Space successfully added.

** WARNING **  A level 0 archive of Root DBSpace will need to be done.
```

Then run the ontape command again:

```
rebel:root # ontape -s -L 0
Archive to tape device '/dev/null' is complete.

Program over.
```

```
rebel:root # onstat -d
```

```
Informix Dynamic Server Version 7.30.UC10 -- Quiescent -- Up 01:36:42 -- 8888
Kbytes
```

```
Dbspaces
address   number   flags    fchunk   nchunks   flags    owner     name
1011e13c  1        1        1        1         N        informix  rootdbs
1011e508  2        1        2        1         N        informix  physdbs
1011e5c4  3        1        3        1         N        informix  logsdbs
1039738c  4        2001     4        1         N T      informix  tempdbs
103977ec  5        1        5        1         N        informix  dbs_dbs
10397ca8  6        1        6        1         N        informix  datadbs01
1039b21c  7        1        7        1         N        informix  indexdbs01
 7 active, 2047 maximum
```

```
Chunks
address   chk/dbs offset   size     free     bpages   flags pathname
1011e1f8  1    1   0        10000    8921              PO-   /opt/data/rootdbs
1011e348  2    2   0        10240    187               PO-   /opt/data/physdbs
1011e428  3    3   0        25000    11635             PO-   /opt/data/logsdbs
10397448  4    4   0        150000   149947            PO-   /opt/data/tempdbs
103978a8  5    5   0        50000    49947             PO-   /opt/data/dbs_dbs
10397d64  6    6   0        125000   124947            PO-   /opt/data/datadbs01
1039b2d8  7    7   0        125000   124947            PO-   /opt/data/indexdbs01
 7 active, 2047 maximum
```

As you can now see, all the essential database spaces are created, and are available for use. There is only one small problem: You need to finish a few final settings in your **$INFORMIXDIR/etc/$ONCONFIG** before your system is ready. For example, the tempdbs space won't be used until you activate it in the **$ONCONFIG**.

Shut the engine down with the **onmode –ky** command:

```
$ onmode -ky
```

Final $ONCONFIG Configuration Settings

Edit your **$INFORMIXDIR/etc/$ONCONFIG**, and make the final settings as follows.

Physical Log

You'll notice that the physdbs settings have been changed for you:

```
# Physical Log Configuration


PHYSDBS         physdbs            # Location (dbspace) of physical log
PHYSFILE        20000              # Physical log file size (Kbytes)
```

Logical Log

The number of **LOGFILES** changed for you, but **LOGSIZE** didn't change, so it's a good idea to set it to whatever your system should have.

Default Values

```
# Logical Log Configuration


LOGFILES        26                 # Number of logical log files
LOGSIZE         500                # Logical log size (Kbytes)
```

New Values

```
# Logical Log Configuration


LOGFILES        26                 # Number of logical log files
LOGSIZE         1024                # Logical log size (Kbytes)
```

In our case we set it to 1024, which is basically 1MB in size. See the *Administrator's Guide* for details on what your system's logical log size should be.

Memory Usage

The default size of 8MB is pretty conservative. It's probably a good idea to increase this—you should try different increments to see what works best for you:

Default Size

```
SHMVIRTSIZE     8000               # initial virtual shared memory segment size
```

New Size

```
SHMVIRTSIZE     24000              # initial virtual shared memory segment size
```

You can leave this alone, test all the other settings first, and then enlarge memory usage last. In our examples at the end of this section, the output from restarting the engine will show this instead of changing it now. Change memory usage last in case it gives you problems.

LRU Settings

Please see your *Administrator's Guide* and other Informix documentation for the reasoning behind these new settings. Remember, the focus here is on installation, so I'm giving you a few settings for now that will help your performance—the rest is up to you to learn why.

Default Values

```
LRUS              8               # Number of LRU queues

LRU_MAX_DIRTY    60               # LRU percent dirty begin cleaning limit

LRU_MIN_DIRTY    50               # LRU percent dirty end cleaning limit
```

These settings are covered in several books dedicated solely to Informix, and will help you tremendously. There is also an ongoing discussion in the USENET newsgroup comp.databases.informix about where many of these settings belong. These shown here are based on experience, and on good performance improvements on Linux.

New Values

```
LRUS              4               # Number of LRU queues

LRU_MAX_DIRTY     5               # LRU percent dirty begin cleaning limit

LRU_MIN_DIRTY     1               # LRU percent dirty end cleaning limit
```

DBSPACETEMP Settings

You need to change this so that your new tempdbs dbspace can be used for temp tables, and sorts for queries.

Default Value

```
# DBSPACETEMP                     # Default temp dbspaces
```

New Value

```
DBSPACETEMP   tempdbs
```

Restart Your Engine

Restart your Informix engine with the **oninit** command **$ oninit –v** and watch the output.

Once it is up, you can see the changes using the **onstat –m** command:

```
rebel:root # oninit -v
Checking group membership to determine server run modesucceeded
Reading configuration file '/opt/informix/ids/etc/rebel_shm.cfg'...succeeded
Creating /INFORMIXTMP/.infxdirs ... succeeded
Creating infos file "/opt/informix/ids/etc/.infos.rebel_shm" ...
"/opt/informix/ids/etc/.conf.rebel_shm" ... succeeded
Writing to infos file ... succeeded
Checking config parameters...succeeded
Allocating and attaching to shared memory...succeeded
Creating resident pool 398 kbytes...succeeded
Creating buffer pool 402 kbytes...succeeded
Initializing rhead structure...succeeded
Initializing ASF ...succeeded
Initializing Dictionary Cache and Stored Procedure Cache...succeeded
Bringing up ADM VP...succeeded
Creating VP classes...succeeded
Onlining 0 additional cpu vps...succeeded
Onlining 2 IO vps...succeeded
Forking main_loop thread...succeeded
Initialzing DR structures...succeeded
Forking 1 'ipcshm' listener threads...succeeded
Forking 1 'soctcp' listener threads...succeeded
Starting tracing...succeeded
Initializing 1 flushers...succeeded
Initializing log/checkpoint information...succeeded
Opening primary chunks...succeeded
Opening mirror chunks...succeeded
Initializing dbspaces...succeeded
Validating chunks...succeeded
Initialize Async Log Flusher...succeeded
Forking btree cleaner...succeeded
Initializing DBSPACETEMP list
rebel:root # Checking database partition index...succeeded
Checking location of physical log...succeeded
Initializing dataskip structure...succeeded
Checking for temporary tables to drop
Forking onmode_mon thread...succeeded
Verbose output complete: mode = 5

rebel:root # onstat -m
```

```
Informix Dynamic Server Version 7.30.UC10    -- On-Line -- Up 00:01:11 -- 8888
Kbytes


Message Log File: /opt/informix/ids/logs/online.log


Mon Jan 24 18:25:43 2000


18:25:43  Event alarms enabled.  ALARMPROG = '/opt/informix/ids/etc/log_full.sh'
18:25:48  DR: DRAUTO is 0 (Off)
18:25:48  Requested shared memory segment size rounded from 588KB to 592KB
18:25:49  Informix Dynamic Server Version 7.30.UC10    Software Serial Number
            AAC#A518469
18:25:50  Informix Dynamic Server Initialized — Shared Memory Initialized.
18:25:50  Physical Recovery Started.
18:25:50  Physical Recovery Complete: 0 Pages Restored.
18:25:50  Logical Recovery Started.
18:25:53  Logical Recovery Complete.
            0 Committed, 0 Rolled Back, 0 Open, 0 Bad Locks


18:25:53  Onconfig parameter LOGFILES modified from 6 to 26.
18:25:53  Onconfig parameter LOGSIZE modified from 500 to 1024.
18:25:53  Onconfig parameter DBSPACETEMP modified from <blank> to tempdbs.
18:25:53  Dataskip is now OFF for all dbspaces
18:25:53  On-Line Mode
18:25:53  Checkpoint Completed:  duration was 0 seconds.
```

Everything works fine, except I want to increase memory usage, so I make the change in the **$ONCONFIG** file, and then restart the engine. The **onstat –m** output shows the change, as well as the top line of the onstat report:

```
rebel:root # onmode -ky
rebel:root # oninit -v
rebel:root # onstat -m


Informix Dynamic Server Version 7.30.UC10   -- On-Line -- Up 00:00:14 -- 24888
Kbytes


Message Log File: /opt/informix/ids/logs/online.log
18:25:53  Checkpoint Completed:  duration was 0 seconds.
18:27:12  Informix Dynamic Server Stopped.
```

```
Mon Jan 24 18:27:33 2000

18:27:33  Event alarms enabled.  ALARMPROG = '/opt/informix/ids/etc/log_full.sh'
18:27:39  DR: DRAUTO is 0 (Off)
18:27:39  Requested shared memory segment size rounded from 588KB to 592KB
18:27:39  Informix Dynamic Server Version 7.30.UC10   Software Serial Number
            AAC#A518469
18:27:40  Informix Dynamic Server Initialized — Shared Memory Initialized.
18:27:41  Physical Recovery Started.
18:27:41  Physical Recovery Complete: 0 Pages Restored.
18:27:41  Logical Recovery Started.
18:27:44  Logical Recovery Complete.
            0 Committed, 0 Rolled Back, 0 Open, 0 Bad Locks


18:27:44  Onconfig parameter SHMVIRTSIZE modified from 8000 to 24000.
18:27:44  Dataskip is now OFF for all dbspaces
18:27:44  On-Line Mode
18:27:44  Checkpoint Completed:  duration was 0 seconds.



rebel:root # onstat -g seg


Informix Dynamic Server Version 7.30.UC10   -- On-Line -- Up 00:09:24 -- 24888
Kbytes

Segment Summary:
id      key         addr      size       ovhd    class blkused  blkfree
1537    1381386241 10000000 909312       872      R      104      7
1538    1381386242 100de000 24576000     972      V      504      2496
1539    1381386243 1184e000 606208       608      M      67       7
Total:  -          -         26091520    -        -      675      2510


    (* segment locked in memory)
```

Your system is now operational, and suitable for use by your endusers!

When you create a database, create it in the **dbs_dbs** dbspace. When you create a table, create it in **datadbs01**. When you create an index, create it in **indexdbs01**. Complete instructions on how to do this are in the Informix documentation, using standard SQL and SQL commands specific to Informix engines. The setup that I've shown you here can allow you the best flexibility, and room for growth.

Other Tools

The following are a few of the tools that come with the Informix database engine.

onlog. A logical log browser that allows you to view the contents of your logical logs. You simply run **onlogs**, and the display will show you the contents of the logical logs.

dbschema. A report-writer for the DBA, allowing you to produce SQL statements that can be used to create databases and tables.

dbexport /dbimport /dbload. Tools that allow you to back up your database completely in one convenient file, and that can be used to restore a database with very little work.

finderr. A program that produces detailed documentation about an Informix error message. You run **finderr** with an error number you provide it, and it produces a small page of information about the nature of the problem.

SMI Tables. You should become familiar with the sysmaster database located in the rootdbs dbspace. It contains a wealth of information about your engine. For example, you can produce reports about disk usage that are a little easier to read.

The following report, called **IDSspaces**, shows you a nice report about disk usage. Instead of this:

```
rebel:root # onstat -d


Informix Dynamic Server Version 7.30.UC10   -- On-Line -- Up 00:38:51 -- 24888
Kbytes


Dbspaces
address   number   flags   fchunk   nchunks   flags   owner     name
1011e13c  1        1       1        1         N       informix  rootdbs
1011e888  2        1       2        1         N       informix  physdbs
1011e944  3        1       3        1         N       informix  logsdbs
1011ea00  4        2001    4        1         N T     informix  tempdbs
1011eabc  5        1       5        1         N       informix  dbs_dbs
1011eb78  6        1       6        1         N       informix  datadbs01
1011ec34  7        1       7        1         N       informix  indexdbs01
 7 active, 2047 maximum


Chunks
address   chk/dbs offset   size     free      bpages   flags pathname
```

```
1011e1f8 1    1    0        10000    8921          PO-    /opt/data/rootdbs
1011e348 2    2    0        10240    187           PO-    /opt/data/physdbs
1011e428 3    3    0        25000    11635         PO-    /opt/data/logsdbs
1011e508 4    4    0        150000   149947        PO-    /opt/data/tempdbs
1011e5e8 5    5    0        50000    49947         PO-    /opt/data/dbs_dbs
1011e6c8 6    6    0        125000   124947        PO-    /opt/data/datadbs01
1011e7a8 7    7    0        125000   124947        PO-    /opt/data/indexdbs01

7 active, 2047 maximum
```

you could see this:

```
rebel:root # IDSspaces
```

Informix DB Space Report Mon Jan 24 18:39:14 EST 2000

datadbs01

DB No	Chk No	DB Space Name	Total	Free	Used	Pct Full	Total	Free	Used
			-------	Pages---------		Pct	-------Kilobytes-------		
6	6	datadbs01	125000	124947	53	0.04	256000	255891	108
		datadbs01	125000	124947	53	0.04	256000	255891	108

dbs_dbs

DB No	Chk No	DB Space Name	Total	Free	Used	Pct Full	Total	Free	Used
			-------	Pages---------		Pct	-------Kilobytes-------		
5	5	dbs_dbs	50000	49947	53	0.11	102400	102291	108
		dbs_dbs	50000	49947	53	0.11	102400	102291	108

indexdbs01

DB No	Chk No	DB Space Name	Total	Free	Used	Pct Full	Total	Free	Used
			-------	Pages---------		Pct	-------Kilobytes-------		
7	7	indexdbs01	125000	124947	53	0.04	256000	255891	108
		indexdbs01	125000	124947	53	0.04	256000	255891	108

logsdbs

DB No	Chk No	DB Space Name	Total	Free	Used	Pct Full	Total	Free	Used
			-------	Pages---------		Pct	-------Kilobytes-------		
3	3	logsdbs	25000	11635	13365	53.46	51200	23828	27371
		logsdbs	25000	11635	13365	53.46	51200	23828	27371

```
physdbs

  DB Chk DB            ---------  Pages-----------   Pct   -------Kilobytes-------
  No  No Space Name      Total    Free     Used     Full   Total      Free    Used
   2   2 physdbs          10240    187    10053    98.17    20971       382   20588
         physdbs          10240    187    10053    98.17    20971       382   20588


rootdbs

  DB Chk DB            ----------  Pages-----------   Pct   -------Kilobytes-------
  No  No Space Name      Total    Free     Used     Full   Total      Free    Used
   1   1 rootdbs          10000   8921     1079    10.79    20480     18270    2209
         rootdbs          10000   8921     1079    10.79    20480     18270    2209


tempdbs

  DB Chk DB            ---------  Pages --------   Pct   -------Kilobytes-------
  No  No Space Name      Total    Free     Used   Full   Total      Free    Used
   4   4 tempdbs         150000 149939       61   0.04  307200    307075     124
         tempdbs         150000 149939       61   0.04  307200    307075     124
```

Following is another view using another program called **IDSchunks**:

```
rebel:informix $ IDSchunks 3

Linux rebel 2.2.13 #1 Mon Nov 8 15:51:29 CET 1999 i686 unknown

/opt/informix/ids/etc/rebel_shm.cfg

Report 3: Order By Data Space Name, Database, Chunk, File


datadbs01

  Dbs Chk Filesystem                    Total Pages   Free Pages   % Free
    6   6 /opt/data/datadbs01               125000       124947  %  99.96


datadbs02

  Dbs Chk Filesystem                    Total Pages   Free Pages   % Free
    8   8 /opt/data/datadbs02                25000        24947  %  99.79
    8   9 /opt/data/datadbs02.02             25000        24997  %  99.99
    8  10 /opt/data/datadbs02.03             25000        24997  %  99.99
                                            75000        74941  %  99.92

dbs_dbs

  Dbs Chk Filesystem                    Total Pages   Free Pages   % Free
    5   5 /opt/data/dbs_dbs                  50000        49947  %  99.89


indexdbs01

  Dbs Chk Filesystem                    Total Pages   Free Pages   % Free
    7   7 /opt/data/indexdbs01             125000       124947  %  99.96
```

```
logsdbs
    Dbs Chk Filesystem                 Total Pages   Free Pages   % Free
     3   3 /opt/data/logsdbs                25000        11635   %  46.54

physdbs
    Dbs Chk Filesystem                 Total Pages   Free Pages   % Free
     2   2 /opt/data/physdbs                10240          187   %   1.83

rootdbs
    Dbs Chk Filesystem                 Total Pages   Free Pages   % Free
     1   1 /opt/data/rootdbs                10000         8577   %  85.77

tempdbs
    Dbs Chk Filesystem                 Total Pages   Free Pages   % Free
     4   4 /opt/data/tempdbs               150000       149947   %  99.96


            Total All Chunks              570240       545128   %  95.60
```

You'll notice in this report that I've added a couple of chunks to the **datadbs02** dbspace, to illustrate the output of this report.

This report and other DBA tools are available at http://www.inxutil.com. **IDSspaces** was created as a shell script that makes a query to the database engine, and formats the information in a more usable form than onstat. If you download **IDSspaces**, you get the source code with it!

Dbaccess

One of the most important tools that comes with the engine is **dbaccess**. This is a character-based application that allows you to take a peek at the engine, database, and tables. It allows you to do queries against tables and to perform database maintenance on all the databases for a particular instance. Please read the documentation available for dbaccess in the *Dbaccess Users' Guide*. When you run **dbaccess**, you get the following display:

```
DBACCESS:   Query-language  Connection  Database  Table  Session  Exit
Use SQL query language.


--------------- Press CTRL-W for Help---------------
```

Dbaccess is easy to use, and runs nicely in a VT-100 window. It offers you an excellent scratch pad to work with your database. There are also GUI-based tools that Informix is developing and eventually will offer as part of the engine distribution.

Onmonitor

One of the tools we didn't use for the installation was **onmonitor**. **Onmonitor** is available for engine monitoring and maintenance, but does not offer you a lot of flexibility or hand-holding.

You can run **onmonitor** and change or view many of your settings for the engine; however, most Informix DBAs opt for command-line control. In a production environment, the more control you have, the better off you are, simply because one wrong command can erase company data. Simply run **onmonitor** and the following output will appear as a character-based user interface along the same lines as dbaccess:

```
Dynamic Server:    Status  Parameters  Dbspaces  Mode  Force-Ckpt  ...
Status menu to view Dynamic Server.


----------------On-Line---------- Press CTRL-W for Help. ----------
```

For example, you can view the same basic information with **onmonitor** as you can with the **onstat** command:

```
STATUS:   Profile  Userthreads  Spaces  Databases  Logs  Archive  ...
Display system profile information.


---------------On-Line---------- Press CTRL-W for Help.----------
        Boot Time   Mon Jan 24 18:27:33 2000
     Current Time   Mon Jan 24 18:56:48 2000
```

Disk Reads	Buff. Reads	%Cached	Disk Writes	Buff. Writes	%Cached
108	1167	90.75	22	22	0.00

Over Lock	Over Userthread	User Time	Sys. Time	Checkpoints
0	0	3	0	3

ixda-RA	idx-RA	da-RA	RA-pgsused	Latch Waits
5	0	0	5	0

Buff. Waits	Lock Waits	Lock Req.	Deadlocks	DLTimeouts	Check Waits
2	0	356	0	0	0

CALLS:	Open	Start	Read	Write	
	168	211	354	7	
					Total Calls
	Rewrite	Delete	Commit	Rollback	1051
	0	0	0	0	

This is a program you will rarely need to use if you learn to use the **onstat** command and the **$ONCONFIG** settings. It is much easier and safer (less risky) to edit the **$ONCONFIG** by hand, and restart the engine. There are also things you can do with the **onmode** command to save you from restarting the engine, thus eliminating the need for **onmonitor**. It is important to review all the commands and programs that are available to you in the **$INFORMIXDIR/bin** directory. A Web-based system administration tool is also now available for people wanting to manage the server with a Web browser.

Resources

Several avenues of help and resources are available to you if and when you need help with Informix products. Some of the contacts are with Informix in the way of customer support; others are contacts with other Informix professionals and customers.

Informix Technical Support

You can call Informix Tech Support at 1-800-331-1763 to get a live customer support engineer to help you with your particular problem. Informix technical support has won awards over the years for their outstanding response times and solutions.

Informix Web Site

You can visit the Informix Web site at http://www.informix.com, and take advantage of other methods of customer support. There is an Informix Developer's Network at the Informix Web site with many topics covered, and in many cases a limited-access discussion group for each of the product areas. There is also TechInfo Center, a great way for you to get information on bug fixes and other technical information.

Usenet News Group comp.databases.informix

This is a news group accessible on the Internet via a news server, e-mail mailing list, or Web-based news servers such as DejaNews. You can find out more about accessing this newsgroup by visiting the IIUG Web site, home of the International Informix User Group, at http://www.iiug.org, or by visiting a Web-based news server.

International Informix User Group (IIUG)

The IIUG at http://www.iiug.org is known as a great resource for people using Informix products. Not only can you find several e-mail lists to subscribe to here, you can also find a wealth of tools to augment your Informix world. There are also links to local user groups, probably one close to you, and the instructions for starting your own user group.

Informix Press

Several books exist for Informix users. Most books are written by top professionals in the Informix world with many years of experience using Informix products. You can find new titles at the Informix Web site as well as titles available through most of the major book stores and Web-based book distributors. Informix also produces most of their documentation on CD sets available at a significant cost savings over the printed materials. You can contact your nearest sales office and order the documents on CD.

Informix Training

Informix has some of the best, award-winning training available. I have seen people with little or no experience with Informix products trained quickly and thoroughly in using the products by going through the recommended courses that Informix offers. Several of the courses on databases are generic enough to apply to other database products, and offer a very sound foundation on which to build your database wisdom. If you are serious about performance tuning and learning more about the database engine, then you should take the training applicable to your work. Informix also offers certification programs as well to make sure your hard work and skills are recognized in the business community as a standard business managers can use to gauge your proficiency. The more you know, the more you should be recognized for it.

Summary

Now that you've installed IDS for Linux, what can you do with it? Well, for starters you can connect almost any ODBC-compliant user interface to the server, and begin immediately to develop and connect applications to the database engine. You can create and connect Web applications and clients directly to the engine with either ODBC, JDBC, and I-connect network connections. The range of applications is limited only by your imagination.

Informix IDS 7.3x is a very powerful SQL database engine, with everything you need for an enterprise-level database server. This server is capable of being highly reliable and robust for a variety of data storage and retrieval operations involving low- and high-volume access rates. Some of the fastest database servers in use today are Informix database servers on UNIX. Informix has outperformed competitive servers from other vendors and continues to lead the pack. The Linux version of IDS is no different internally than the other UNIX platforms; the only limitation you will face is the current Linux kernel and your hardware platform.

IDS 7.3 can scale from one to N users, the only limitation is, of course, your hardware. You can learn everything for the UNIX version in the Linux version, with the exception being the high-performance loader, and raw disks, both not available as of this writing. IDS is compatible to a certain degree with the Standard Engine, but only in its core features. The Standard Engine has more limitations and fewer data type choices than the shared memory engine in IDS. Standard Engine is a passive, ISAM-based engine. SE is highly reliable, but not as capable of some of the more advanced features of the IDS engine. You will find SE compares to IDS the way propeller-driven airplanes compare to jets. Both are valid flight machines and each have their appropriate uses.

The total installation time can be as fast as two hours, if you have prepared your environment, or longer depending on what you didn't prepare for. It is extremely important for you to read the Administrator's Guide, to become familiar with the various settings and controls you can place on the engine.

FAQ

Q: Can I use Microsoft products with an Informix database on Linux?

A: Of course you can! Any Microsoft product or Microsoft-based software product that can connect to an ODBC database can connect to an Informix database on Linux. You simply set up the networking connection between the Linux server and the Microsoft client, and you can be connected.

Q: Can I connect an Informix database on Linux to an Informix database on another UNIX platform?

A: Yes. You need to configure the networking parameters in the appropriate configuration files, and you can network two different database servers together. You can also connect these servers using data replication.

Q: How much hardware do I need to set up an Informix database?

A: The whole installation can take up approximately 500MB for a small system, and more for a larger database. Informix can run in as little as 8MB of memory.

Q: Where is the best place to go to find out more information on Informix?

A: The Informix FAQ is located at http://www.iiug.org, which is the home of the International Informix User's Group. A FAQ, as well as a plethora of free tools are available at the IIUG Web site for you to use with the Informix family of products. Much of the history of Informix engines is covered in the FAQ. You will find a rich resource of tools, routines, 4GL programs, ESQLC programs, as well as tips and techniques to help you run one of the best database engines available. You can download or upload your own tools at the IIUG site, and develop your own open source projects with other developers.

   The FAQ will also point you to other Informix resources like the Informix Developer's Network at http://www.informix.com/idn/. This is a Web site for the serious Informix developer, complete with discussion groups to talk about various topics with other developers, DBAs and others. You will need to register to gain access, but this is a worthwhile Web site to visit often to stay abreast of changes and upgrades to software.

## Chapter 5

Installing and Utilizing Sybase on Linux

Solutions in this chapter:

- Installation

- Configuration

- Testing the Database

- Database Design

- Issues

Introduction

In the middle of 1998, I was commissioned to develop a Web-administered database of digitized and cataloged fine art for a nonprofit organization. This organization was operating on a shoestring budget (as all nonprofits do) and could not afford to invest large sums of money into a large database solution, so Linux became the obvious choice. After spending a few weeks experimenting with some test cases on many of the open-source and freeware databases for Linux, we became heavily discouraged with speed when we reached the tens of thousands of records in the test sets. Since the full set was to start at 200,000 records and then grow to millions, these solutions were not feasible, and so were eliminated.

Discouraged with the performance of the open-source databases, we were forced to use NT as our database platform running Microsoft SQL Server 6.5. We still wanted to leverage the fast and reliable Web server (Apache) and Perl on Linux, so we started using Sybase's Open Client software with the Perl library, written by Michael Peppler. Luckily Microsoft appears to have gotten SQL Server from Sybase originally, and the Open Client was still able to connect. We were not pleased with the performance of SQL Server on NT, but we couldn't afford a better solution at the time.

After about a month of development, we heard rumors that Sybase was planning on releasing their SQL Server version 11.0.3 for Linux. Best of all, they were releasing it for free, and none of our month of development was wasted since we were already using their client libraries. When Sybase released the SQL Server, we downloaded and installed it. With absolutely no tuning, the exact same development database we were using on NT SQL Server performed easily 10 times faster under Sybase on Linux. We were extremely pleased and proceeded to develop the product completely on no-cost software. Since the time of the deployment of that product, Sybase has released Adaptive Server Enterprise (ASE) 11.9.2 for Linux, as well as many other products. ASE 11.9.2 was released free for development purposes, but requires a license fee for deployment. Sybase has continued to offer free use and deployment of SQL Server 11.0.3.

In this chapter, we will cover how to install Sybase SQL Server running on the Linux platform, and further provide some minimal tuning for it. Since there are already many good books published with much more room to devote to the running and tuning of Sybase SQL Server, this chapter focuses specifically on those things that must be done to get SQL Server running and running well on Linux.

Installation

As was mentioned in the introduction, Sybase currently is providing two versions of their database server for the Linux platform. Sybase SQL

Server 11.0.3.3 is available for free download from Sybase's Web site (http://www.sybase.com/products/databaseservers/linux/) and is free for both development and deployment. Sybase Adaptive Server Enterprise (ASE) 11.9.2 is also available for free download from Sybase's Web site, but the license allows use only for one machine and only for development. To deploy ASE 11.9.2 on Linux, a license fee is required. This chapter concentrates on the 11.0.3.3 version, which fits well with the nature of Linux because it is free, but much of what is said here should also apply to 11.9.2.

Sybase has done a good job at making their Linux database servers quite easy to install on Red Hat Linux by distributing them as RPM Package Manager files. Sybase should run on other versions of Linux that are running kernel 2.0.36 or higher and glibc2, but the user of these systems may have to download and install RPM Package Manager utilities from http://www.rpm.org/.

Installing SQL Server 11.0.3

To install SQL Server 11.0.3.3, first either download the RPMs from Sybase's Web site or obtain them from the Red Hat 5.2 supplemental CD. The following two RPMs are needed:

- **sybase-11.0.3.3-1.rpm** This contains the Sybase SQL Server program files.
- **sybase-docs-11.0.3.3-1.rpm** This contains the documentation for Sybase SQL Server.

These documents are available only in Postscript format, and are quite long. If you obtain the RPMs from the Red Hat 5.2 CD, the version number will be 11.0.3-2.

NOTE

There was quite a bit of confusion with the release of Red Hat Linux 5.2, as Sybase 11.0.3 was included on the supplemental CD distributed with the purchased copy of Red Hat 5.2. The RPM on Sybase's Web server was sybase-11.0.3-1.rpm and the RPM on the CD was sybase-11.0.3-2.rpm, so people who were looking on the Web were afraid they were not getting the newest version. The only difference between these two RPMs was that the second did not automatically spawn the setup script upon installation of the RPM. Red Hat had asked Sybase to repackage because their graphical RPM tool did not support this automatically spawned setup script. The version available on Sybase's Web site at the time of this writing was 11.0.3.3, and should probably be used since it probably contains bug fixes.

Setting Up the Target Machine

Before actually installing these RPMs, it is important to discuss the partitioning of your target machine's hard drives. There was quite a bit of arguing in the sybase-linux discussion group on the Internet about what was the best way to partition and use your machine's hard-drive space. The general consensus about what was right is what I will describe here, but if you are interested in reading the entire discussion, you can see archived messages from the list at http://forum.swarthmore.edu/epigone/ase-linux-list.

Sybase on Linux (like many programs on UNIX machines) accesses its database devices through the file system. Thus Sybase's SQL Server doesn't really care whether your database device is a file in some file system or a device like a partition of a hard drive (e.g., **/dev/sda1**). There are advantages and disadvantages to each.

Using a file in the file system gives you the advantage of having control over the database device file as you would any other file on the file system. This includes moving it around, creating symbolic links to it, and copying it to another machine. Before Sybase released their replication software for Linux, this was the one of the easy ways to replicate a database. Unfortunately, under the second extended file system (which is the most common file system used on Linux), files are limited to two gigabytes in size. Thus, a database device that exists as a file on the file system is limited to two gigabytes.

Using a disk partition like **/dev/sda1** under Linux does not really supply the database with any substantial speedup as you might expect because of Linux's extensive use of caching. Access to the disk partition and to the file system are both cached in the Linux cache system. Using a dedicated disk partition allows for devices larger than two gigabytes, which is important for large databases. On the other hand, a partition dedicated to the database can only be accessed through the corresponding block device, and must be allocated by partitioning the disk.

One of the large arguments among those on the Sybase-Linux group was whether usage of these two types of database devices was good at all. Many DBAs from other UNIX platforms would argue that the only way to have a database device was to have it on a "raw" disk partition. This type of disk partition is a device in the system that the operating system does not cache at all, and all writes are written directly to disk before control is returned to the writing program. Linux kernels through the 2.2 series do not support true "raw" devices, though some form of raw devices are expected to be supported in later kernel releases. The DBAs who believe that these devices are required say that since Sybase maintains its own cache and expects all things written to disk to be really written, when it regains control after a write some inconsistencies may appear in the event of a power outage. Understandably, if Sybase thought something was written to disk but Linux was really just caching it in memory to be written to disk at some future time and the power failed before Linux actually wrote it, then the system could be left in an inconsistent state. The best argument that I have heard against this stated that any database server would have an uninterruptible power supply (UPS) on it. If the UPS told the machine the power failed, it could ensure that the database and the rest of the processes were shut down in the event of a power outage before the UPS battery failed.

With the discussion of possible data devices out of the way, I can make some recommendations. If you can afford it, dedicate the entire machine to just the database and give the machine lots of physical memory (as much as you can afford). Sybase may be able to get by with 32MB of memory (nothing else running on the machine), but there will be a lot of disk accesses, as it cannot maintain enough information in cache. I don't recommend using less than 128MB of memory in a database server, and obviously the more you use the better your performance will be. If you plan on having the machine run multiple queries at one time, you may want to consider multiple processors. I do not recommend running a Web server and the database server on the same machine. You can do it, but you will have a much faster and more responsive database if the machine isn't busy doing other things as well.

For any nontrivial database, you need to devote at least three SCSI hard drives to the system. You should not use IDE devices for a database server. For a more robust system, I would recommend at least six SCSI hard drives in a RAID configuration to allow for data survival in case of physical media failure. The first hard drive can be reasonably small (less than 4GB), as it should contain the Linux operating system, the database application, and little else. The second hard drive (or RAID volume) should be entirely devoted to the database transaction logs. The third hard drive or volume can then be devoted entirely to database devices. If you plan on running multiple databases on this one machine you may consider placing each database on a separate device on a separate disk so queries are not forcing the disk to seek between the two devices on one disk.

Partition the first SCSI disk with at least five Linux native partitions and probably a Linux swap partition. The first native partition should be your root file system and should be kept reasonably small (approximately 200–300MB). The second native partition should be your **/usr** file system and should contain about 2GB of space. The third partition should be your **/opt** file system, where Sybase will install itself from the RPMs. This partition should be at least large enough to hold the installed Sybase distribution (approximately 300MB). The final two Linux native partitions should be left without a file system and should each be about 50MB in size. This partition will hold the master and sybsystemprocs devices for Sybase. Partition the second and third SCSI hard drive as one large partition Linux native (the entire size of the disk), but don't create a file system on them.

Install your Linux distribution on the first SCSI hard drive.

Installing Sybase

After setting up the machine and installing Linux as we just described, we will gather some information that we will need to install Sybase. First, we need to know what devices correspond to the partitions on the hard drives that we just set up. The **fdisk** program can be used to display all partition information on a hard drive. Following is a typical usage case for the fdisk program to obtain the partitions:

```
# fdisk /dev/sda


The number of cylinders for this disk is set to 1247.
There is nothing wrong with that, but this is larger than 1024,
and could in certain setups cause problems with:
1) software that runs at boot time (e.g., LILO)
2) booting and partitioning software from other OSs
    (e.g., DOS FDISK, OS/2 FDISK)


Command (m for help): p


Disk /dev/sda: 255 heads, 63 sectors, 1247 cylinders
Units = cylinders of 16065 * 512 bytes


    Device Boot   Start      End     Blocks   Id  System
/dev/sda1    *        1       33     265041   83  Linux      ←mounted /
/dev/sda2            34      295    2100483   83  Linux      ←mounted /usr
/dev/sda3           296      336     321300   83  Linux      ←mounted /opt
/dev/sda4           337     1247    7309575    5  Extended
/dev/sda5           337      436     803250   83  Linux      ←master device
/dev/sda6           437      536     803250   83  Linux      ← sybsysprocs device
/dev/sda7           537      554     144585   82  Linux Swap ←linux swap
/dev/sda8           555     1247    5558490   83  Linux      ←mounted /home


Command (m for help): q
```

We need to know what partition was set aside for the master partition and **sybsystemprocs** partition. For this discussion, we will assume that it is partition 5 and 6 on the first SCSI disk. This partition corresponds to the device special file **/dev/sda5** and **/dev/sda6**, respectively. Also, we need to know the other two disks partitions we set aside on the second and third hard drive. For this discussion, we will assume they are **/dev/sdb1** and **/dev/sdc1**, respectively.

Login on the Linux console as root and install the RPM package with the following command:

```
rpm -ivh sybase-11.0.3.3-1.rpm
```

This command will install the Sybase SQL Server in the directory **/opt/sybase**. After installing the files, it will return to the command prompt. To continue with installation, execute the shell script located at **/opt/sybase/install/sybinstall.sh**. This shell script first will show the license agreement, which you must agree to, then continue to prompt you through the installation and setup of the database server. Figure 5.1 is a transcript of the questions asked followed by a discussion of the options.

The first question that the script asks is if it should create a user account for the Sybase database server. You should probably let the script do this so the server can run as the Sybase user and group accounts. It will then prompt for the group and user creation. Answer yes to both of these questions. The script will prompt for a password for the Sybase user account. Choose a password for this user account and enter it twice. The script then updates the ownership of the files in the **/opt/sybase** directory appropriately so that the newly created user and group own them.

The script indicates that the **/opt/sybase/install/sybinit** file should be executed as the Sybase user to continue the installation procedure. Before doing this, we have to update the ownership of a couple of other files. Specifically, we must allow the Sybase user and Sybase group to write to the partitions that we set aside for Sybase devices. To do this, as root, execute the follow commands (replacing **/dev/sdxx** with the actual disk devices that you wish to use for the database devices):

```
[root@wanderer install]# cd /dev
[root@wanderer /dev]# chown sybase:sybase /dev/sda5
[root@wanderer /dev]# chown sybase:sybase /dev/sda6
[root@wanderer /dev]# chown sybase:sybase /dev/sdb1
[root@wanderer /dev]# chown sybase:sybase /dev/sdc1
```

Now that we have given the Sybase user ownership of the device files that it will use as database devices, it is probably a good idea to ensure that no other users have read rights to the database partitions. If other

Figure 5.1 sybinstall.sh prompts.

```
DO YOU AGREE WITH THE LISTED LICENSE CONDITIONS? [Yes/No/List]: yes


Do you want this script to proceed by installing an account? [y/n]: y


Group sybase not found. Create it now? [y/n]: y


    Group and permissions for /opt/sybase are set !


User sybase not found. Create it now? [y/n]: y

Changing password for user sybase

New UNIX password:

Retype new UNIX password:

passwd: all authentication tokens updated successfully


    User sybase is available, release user id is set !


This completes your Sybase Adaptive Server Enterprise (ASE) package

installation.  To run Sybase ASE, you may like configuring your master

and sybsystemprocs databases by continuing the installation procedure

after logging in as sybase and executing /opt/sybase/install/sybinit.


This action is the default when you login for the first time.

Re-running this configuration procedure can be initiated by removing

the .readme and .sybinit files from the 'sybase' installation

directory.
```

users had access to the device files, they could potentially read the data out of the device files that is maintained in the data and reconstruct your database without going through Sybase's permission structure. The

following commands will ensure only the Sybase user and Sybase group
have any access to these files:

```
[root@wanderer /dev]# chmod o-rwx /dev/sda5
[root@wanderer /dev]# chmod o-rwx /dev/sda6
[root@wanderer /dev]# chmod o-rwx /dev/sdb1
[root@wanderer /dev]# chmod o-rwx /dev/sdc1
```

Installing Optional Client Software

There are several client software packages that can be used to make
administering and developing for the Sybase platform considerably easier.

SQSH

The first package is a command line and X11 application called *sqsh* (pro-
nounced *squish*). This application is available from
http://www.voicenet.com/~gray/sqsh.html and is available under the
GNU General Public License (GPL). This is an application that provides a
much nicer command-line interface to SQL statement execution than the
isql program included with Sybase — making it almost a must for server
administration through an SQL shell. You can download both the source
and binary packages from this URL.

I recommend getting the binary package and installing it somewhere
in your path. Once installed, you can use this to connect to the database
from the command line instead of isql. This program provides many feature improvements over isql, including:

- Command completion and command line editing
- Variables
- Redirection
- Backgrounding
- Job control
- History

Development Libraries

The other client software packages that I recommend are development
libraries. They provide the "glue" that connects software that you develop
to the Sybase server. Sybase 11.0.3.3 ships with a copy of the Open
Client Library for C, but if you are not developing in C, you will need
these alternative libraries.

Perl development provides quick and powerful scripts to be written to
alter items in the database. There are currently two interfaces to Sybase

through Perl. The first and older interface is the *sybperl package*. This package provides a near mirror of the C API provided by the Open Client Library to Perl applications. The second package is a DBI driver that fits into the Perl DBI interface. There are advantages and disadvantages to using each package. The DBI package allows you to develop Perl code that can connect to any database for which there is a DBI driver (very much like ODBC or JDBC, respectively). However, as DBI is a database generic, there are some things that it cannot do. The **sybperl** package provides the power to do all of the things to the Sybase server that you would be able to do through the Open Client Library of Sybase, but is specifically for connecting to a Sybase server. Both of these packages are available through CPAN. Try http://www.cpan.org/ or a local mirror.

If you prefer to develop in the Java language, Sybase provides a pure Java JDBC driver called **jConnect** from their Web site at http://www.sybase.com/products/internet/jconnect/. This driver can be run on any platform that has a Java virtual machine.

Configuration

We are now ready to continue with configuration as the installation shell script specifies. We will change to or log in as the Sybase user and then execute the **/opt/sybase/install/sybinit** application. It will provide us with several screens of console menus to progress through installation.

I noticed that on my Red Hat 6.1 machine, **sybinit** complained about loading localization files. I had been using Red Hat 5.2 prior to this, so this appeared to have been a new problem introduced by Red Hat 6.1. I looked into it a little bit and came to the conclusion that the environment variables **$LANG** and **$LC_ALL** were causing this problem. It appears that Sybase does not understand the **en_US** locality that is set in these variables. Unsetting these variables will cause Sybase to revert to using the default locale, which is **us_english**.

A better solution to this may be to edit the text file at **/opt/sybase/locales/locales.dat**. This file defines the method of mapping these locale strings in LANG and LC_ALL to Sybase's understanding of these locales. Currently, it appears that Sybase maps the strings **ENGLISH**, **FRENCH**, **GERMAN**, and **JAPANESE** to its locale definitions for the Linux platform. If this file is edited to change these lines:

```
[linux]

        locale = ENGLISH, us_english, iso_1
        locale = FRENCH, french, iso_1
        locale = GERMAN, german, iso_1
        locale = JAPANESE, japanese, eucjis
```

```
        locale = default, us_english, iso_1
```

to

```
[linux]
        locale = en_US, us_english, iso_1
        locale = ENGLISH, us_english, iso_1
        locale = fr_FR, french, iso_1
        locale = FRENCH, french, iso_1
        locale = de_DE, german, iso_1
        locale = GERMAN, german, iso_1
        locale = ja_JP, japan, eucjis
        locale = JAPANESE, japanese, eucjis
        locale = C, us_english, iso_1
        locale = default, us_english, iso_1
```

then the $LANG and $LC_ALL environment variables should be able to be left alone. Obviously, if you have your $LANG and $LC_ALL variables set to some language other than those specified in the changed file, you will have to add that entry to the file with the proper language mapping. Sybase 11.0.3.3 appears to come with language mappings only for the Chinese, French, German, Japanese, Spanish, and US_English locales, but interestingly enough, the **locales.dat** file includes mappings only for US_English, French, German, and Japanese. The other mappings should be added easily.

Configuring Sybase Database Server

From the screen shown in Figure 5.2, first select **3. Configure a Server product** by pressing the **3** key.

Figure 5.2 Initial screen of the sybinit application.

```
SYBINIT


1.   Release directory:   /opt/sybase


2.   Edit / View Interfaces File


3.   Configure a Server product

4.   Configure an Open Client/Server product
```

Continued

Figure 5.2 Continued

```
Ctrl-a Accept and Continue, Ctrl-x Exit Screen, ? Help.


Enter the number of your choice and press return:
```

Both the SQL Server and Backup Server should be configured in order for the Sybase database server to function properly. Configure the SQL Server first by pressing **1**, then configure the Backup Server by pressing **2** from the screen shown in Figure 5.3.

Figure 5.3 Server Product screen of the sybinit application.

```
CONFIGURE SERVER PRODUCTS


Products:



    Product             Date Installed    Date Configured

1.  SQL Server          10 Sep 1998 15:47

2.  Backup Server       10 Sep 1998 15:47



Ctrl-a Accept and Continue, Ctrl-x Exit Screen, ? Help.


Enter the number of your choice and press return:
```

Since this is a new SQL Server installation, you should choose **1. Configure a new SQL Server** from the screen shown in Figure 5.4. This same application (sybinit) can be used in the future to alter any of the settings that we are now setting by choosing **2. Configure an existing SQL Server**.

Figure 5.4 SQL Server Configuration screen of the sybinit application.

```
NEW OR EXISTING SQL SERVER


1.   Configure a new SQL Server

2.   Configure an existing SQL Server

3.   Upgrade an existing SQL Server



Ctrl-a Accept and Continue, Ctrl-x Exit Screen, ? Help.



Enter the number of your choice and press return:
```

At this step of installation we have to choose a name for this SQL Server (Figure 5.5). This name is simply a logical name to indicate to clients on this machine to which physical SQL Server (IP address and port number) to actually connect. If you are going to run multiple SQL Server instances on a single machine (or if you are sharing the interfaces configuration file across multiple servers and clients), then each server must have a different name. Many clients use **SYBASE** as the default SQL Server to connect to if a name isn't specified, so you may want to leave this set as SYBASE. If you wish to change the name, choose **1** and enter the new name. When you have decided upon a final name for the server, press **Ctrl-A** to continue to the next screen.

Figure 5.5 Add New SQL Server screen of the sybinit application.

```
ADD NEW SQL SERVER


1.   SQL Server name:   SYBASE



Ctrl-a Accept and Continue, Ctrl-x Exit Screen, ? Help.



Enter the number of your choice and press return:
```

Each of the actions shown in Figure 5.6 should be completed in the order they are listed. The first step is to add an entry to the interfaces file. Sybase uses this file (which is just a plain text file at

/opt/sybase/interfaces) to specify to both clients and the server which IP address and port to use. It maps logical names to these parameters so that clients can connect to servers.

Figure 5.6 SQL Server Configuration screen of the sybinit application.

```
SQL SERVER CONFIGURATION


1.   CONFIGURE SERVER'S INTERFACES FILE ENTRY              Incomplete


2.   MASTER DEVICE CONFIGURATION                           Incomplete

3.   SYBSYSTEMPROCS DATABASE CONFIGURATION                 Incomplete

4.   SET ERRORLOG LOCATION                                 Incomplete

5.   CONFIGURE DEFAULT BACKUP SERVER                       Incomplete


6.   CONFIGURE LANGUAGES                                   Incomplete

7.   CONFIGURE CHARACTER SETS                              Incomplete

8.   CONFIGURE SORT ORDER                                  Incomplete


9.   ACTIVATE AUDITING                                     Incomplete


Ctrl-a Accept and Continue, Ctrl-x Exit Screen, ? Help.


Enter the number of your choice and press return:
```

The first two settings on this screen specify how many times a client should try to reconnect if it can't connect initially, and how long between connection attempts, respectively. These can safely be left set at 0. By selecting **3. Add a new listener service** on the screen shown in Figure 5.7, you can specify what port and hostname the server should be bound to as well as specifying another logical name alias for the server.

Figure 5.7 SQL Server Interfaces File Entry screen of the sybinit application.

```
SERVER INTERFACES FILE ENTRY SCREEN


        Server name:  SYBASE


1.   Retry Count:  0

2.   Retry Delay:  0


3.   Add a new listener service


Ctrl-a Accept and Continue, Ctrl-x Exit Screen, ? Help.


Enter the number of your choice and press return:
```

A port number for the Sybase server to listen on should be specified in the screen shown in Figure 5.8. This server port should be higher than 1024, since the server runs as a regular user and not as root. I recommend using port 1433, because this is the default port that Microsoft SQL Server uses. This makes it easier for Microsoft SQL Server clients on Windows platforms to access the Sybase SQL Server (there are some limitations to using these clients, as the development of Sybase and Microsoft SQL Server deviated after Microsoft initially licensed the code from Sybase).

The hostname/address field should be set to the hostname or IP address of the interface on which you want SQL Server to listen. Sybase SQL Server will listen only on this interface, not on all interfaces.

The name alias field allows you to specify another logical name for this SQL Server. This logical name will specify to this particular interface entry.

When these settings are as desired, press **Ctrl-A** to return to the SQL Server Interfaces File Entry screen. You can add another listener entry to the interfaces file if you want the same SQL Server to listen on another interface or port. When you have entered all of the listener interfaces you want, press **Ctrl-A** and answer yes to the prompt to save the changes to the interfaces file.

Figure 5.8 SQL Server TCP Service Listener Interfaces File Entry screen of sybinit.

```
EDIT TCP SERVICE


1.   Hostname/Address: wanderer.deftech.com

2.   Port:

3.   Name Alias:


4.   Delete this service from the interfaces entry


Ctrl-a Accept and Continue, Ctrl-x Exit Screen, ? Help.


Enter the number of your choice and press return:
```

Figure 5.9 shows my interfaces file created through the sybinit application with two listener interfaces. As you can see, one interface is on the **wanderer.deftech.com** interface at port 1433 and the other is on the localhost interface also at port 1433. The two interfaces have different logical names—WANDERER and LOCALSERVER. Changes can be made to this file from outside of sybinit, because it is just a regular text file.

After finishing with the server's interface file, continue on to menu item **2. Master Device Configuration** to choose the location of the master device from the screen shown in Figure 5.6. Specify the file to contain the master device (**/dev/sda5** in our example's case) and the size of the device. The device should be at least 21MB, but must be the exact size of the partition created earlier if using a device. When you are finished choosing these parameters, press **Ctrl-A** to continue. The sybinit application will give you a warning that the file or device that you have chosen is not recommended for a server device. This is because of the raw versus block devices issue discussed in the earlier section on setting up the target machine. Just press **Return** to continue.

Next, set up the sybsystemprocs database device as you did for the master device. The only difference for this setup is to choose **/dev/sda6** as the device's file location.

Step 4 specifies where Sybase SQL Server should write error messages. You should indicate a file to which the messages are appended. This can be any file on the file system to which the Sybase user has write

Figure 5.9 Interfaces file created by the sybintit application.

```
## WANDERER on wanderer.deftech.com
##      Services:
##              query   tcp     (1433)


WANDERER
        query tcp ether wanderer.deftech.com 1433


## LOCALSERVER on localhost
##      Services:
##              query   tcp     (1433)


LOCALSERVER
        query tcp ether localhost 1433


## SYBASE on wanderer.deftech.com
##      Services:
##              query   tcp     (1433)
##              query   tcp     (1433)
##              master  tcp     (1433)
##              master  tcp     (1433)


SYBASE
        query tcp ether wanderer.deftech.com 1433

        query tcp ether localhost 1433

        master tcp ether wanderer.deftech.com 1433

        master tcp ether localhost 1433
```

access. This file should be checked periodically, as any errors encountered in the SQL Server will be logged here.

Step 5 specifies the logical name of the Sybase Backup Server that this server should use for backups. This can be any existing Sybase Backup Server known in the interface file or a name you will use to create a new backup server in Backup Server Configuration. If this is a stand-alone server, just create a name and remember it to put in the Backup Server Configuration, later. **SYB_BACKUP** is the default name.

Step 6 chooses the language encodings and the default language that you wish to have installed for this database.

Step 7 chooses the character sets installed and the default character set that you wish to have installed for this database.

Step 8 chooses the ordering method that applies to this database. Be careful when choosing this character ordering as it applies to both SORT BY statements and to the = operator. Thus, if you choose case-insensitive character ordering, *ABC* = *Abc* = *abc* in all comparison SQL statements.

Step 9 chooses whether auditing is enabled for this database. A discussion of this is beyond the scope of this chapter, but the sybase-docs.11.0.3.3.rpm package contains sufficient information about setting up auditing. For our example, we will just leave auditing off (the default).

After completing all nine steps so that the menu items say complete, press **Ctrl-A** to continue. sybinit will ask if you want to execute the SQL Server Configuration now. Answer yes to this and sybinit will set up the master and **sybsystemprocs** database devices and start the database server. It will give you the same warning about the block device for the master device. Once again, just press **Return** to ignore this warning. Assuming all goes well, your Sybase database server should be up and running at the end of this process. Figure 5.10 shows the results of running this process on my machine. Note that I am not using **/dev/sda5** for the master device, but a regular file at **/opt/sybase/master.dat** instead. This is because this is only a development and demonstration machine, not a release database.

Figure 5.10 Process of installing and running Sybase database server.

```
Execute the SQL Server Configuration now? y


WARNING: '/opt/sybase/master.dat' is a regular file which is not recommended for a
Server

device.

Press <return> to continue.

Running task: create the master device.

Building the master device
```

Continued

Figure 5.10 Continued

```
.Done

Task succeeded: create the master device.

Running task: update the SQL Server runserver file.

Task succeeded: update the SQL Server runserver file.

Running task: boot the SQL Server.

waiting for server 'SYBASE' to boot...

Task succeeded: boot the SQL Server.

Running task: create the sybsystemprocs database.

sybsystemprocs database created.

Task succeeded: create the sybsystemprocs database.

Running task: install system stored procedures.

........................................................................
........................................................................
..............Done

Task succeeded: install system stored procedures.

Running task: set permissions for the 'model' database.

Done

Task succeeded: set permissions for the 'model' database.

Running task: set the default character set and/or default sort order for the SQL
Server.

Setting the default character set to iso_1

Sort order 'binary' has already been installed.

Character set 'iso_1' is already the default.

Sort order 'binary' is already the default.

Task succeeded: set the default character set and/or default sort order for the SQL
Server.

Running task: set the default language.

Setting the default language to us_english

Language 'us_english' is already the default.

Task succeeded: set the default language.
```

Continued

Figure 5.10 Continued

Configuration completed successfully.

Press <return> to continue.

Configuring Sybase Backup Server

After the database server comes up successfully, continue by choosing to configure the backup server from the screen shown in Figure 5.3. If you are setting up a server farm, you typically will want only a single backup server to which all of the database servers will talk. In order for each of the machines to talk to it, you must add the logical name for the backup server to the interfaces file on each of the database servers and set up the default backup server that the database servers point to from the screen shown in Figure 5.6, Step 5. If this is to be a stand-alone server or the backup server for the farm, then you will need to create a new backup server to run on this machine.

Choose to create a new backup server from the menu, and then give it a logical name. You should use the same name that you specified to be the default backup server for the database server on the screen shown in Figure 5.3. After choosing a name and pressing **Ctrl-A**, the sybinit program will display the screen shown in Figure 5.11.

Step 1 chooses the file to which messages from the backup server should be appended. Any file in the file system can be specified.

Step 2 creates an entry in the interfaces file for the backup server. This interface entry is very similar to the entries for the database server. You can specify the retry count, retry delay, and listener services for this

Figure 5.11 Backup Server Configuration screen of sybinit application.

BACKUP SERVER CONFIGURATION

1.   Backup Server errorlog: /opt/sybase/install/backup.log

2.   Enter / Modify Backup Server interfaces file information

3.   Backup Server language: us_english

4.   Backup Server character set: iso_1

5.   Backup Server tape configuration file: /opt/sybase/backup_tape.cfg

Continued

Figure 5.11 Continued

```
Ctrl-a Accept and Continue, Ctrl-x Exit Screen, ? Help.


Enter the number of your choice and press return:
```

backup server. You must specify at least one listener service, which can be any port and interface that you want.

Steps 3 and 4 specify the language and the character set that you want the backup server to use for its encodings.

Step 5 specifies the configuration file that contains information about backup server's tapes. A discussion of this is beyond the scope of this chapter, but is covered in the System Administrator's Guide in the docs RPM package as well as on Sybase's docs online Web site at http://sybooks.sybase.com.

After completing all five steps, press **Ctrl-A** and sybinit will prompt you to start the backup server now. Answer yes, and it will attempt to start the backup server. Assuming all goes well, the backup server will now be running. Figure 5.12 shows the results of starting the backup server through sybinit on my machine.

Figure 5.12 Process of initial backup server startup.

```
Execute the Backup Server configuration now? y

Running task: update the Backup Server runserver file.

Task succeeded: update the Backup Server runserver file.

Running task: boot the Backup Server.

waiting for server 'SYB_BACKUP' to boot...

Task succeeded: boot the Backup Server.


Configuration completed successfully.

Press <return> to continue.
```

Configuring Sybase Client/Server Libraries

After configuring both the server products, the client library products must be configured. This step is essentially just a process of going through the menu selections, since there are no parameters to set. There are three client products to configure under the menu item **4. Configure an Open Client/Server product** from the screen shown in Figure 5.2.

Choose each one and allow them to be configured. When finished, press **Ctrl-A** several times to exit the sybinit application.

Many client applications expect the $SYBASE environment variable to be set to the root of the Sybase installation tree so that they can find the interfaces file and some of the other data files. If many users on your machine are likely to be executing client software from this or other Linux machines, make sure that you put the following line in **/etc/profile** so this variable gets set for everyone:

```
export SYBASE=/opt/sybase
```

Also be aware that some scripts and servers that will be accessing this server through the client libraries in C or in Perl will be looking for this environment variable. If odd behavior is happening from your CGI sybperl scripts or from open client applications that they can't connect to the server, check that they have the $SYBASE variable in their environment.

Starting the Database Server and Backup Server on Boot

At this point both your database server and your backup server should be up and running successfully. For an independent database server, however, you would want these servers to start at boot time. Sybase's installation did create a file at **/etc/rc.d/init.d/sybase**, which is an **rc** startup script compatible with Red Hat's standard method of starting and stopping services at boot and shutdown. To make Sybase start at boot time and properly terminate at shutdown, you would need to create symbolic links to this file in **/etc/rc.d/rc0.d**, **/etc/rc.d/rc3.d**, **/etc/rc.d/rc5.d**, and **/etc/rc.d/rc6.d**, respectively. The meaning of these directories is beyond the scope of this chapter, but the following set of commands will ensure that Sybase starts on boot and terminates on shutdown properly. These commands must be executed as root.

```
#cd /etc/rc.d/rc0.d
#ln -s ../init.d/sybase K05sybase
#cd /etc/rc.d/rc3.d
#ln -s ../init.d/sybase S95sybase
#cd /etc/rc.d/rc5.d
#ln -s ../init.d/sybase S95sybase
#cd /etc/rc.d/rc6.d
#ln -s ../init.d/sybase K05sybase
```

After successfully executing these commands, all Sybase Database and Backup Servers on this machine will be started at the next boot time.

Setting the System Administrator's Password

At this stage we have an operating Sybase Database Server running. We can connect to this server from the local machine by the logical names we gave it in the interfaces file. Sybase provides an application called isql that provides an interactive SQL shell to send SQL statements to the database server and retrieve the results sets to be displayed to screen. (Optionally, you can download sqsh, which is a much nicer tool that provides similar functionality. See the description of it, earlier.)

Sybase initially installs the database server with the System Administrator (**sa**) password set to an empty string. This is highly insecure; therefore, you should change it as soon as possible. To change the sa password, we need to log on to the server with the isql tool and execute the **sp_password** stored procedure, as follows.

```
[brad@wanderer bard]$ /opt/sybase/bin/isql -U sa -S WANDERER
Password:
1> sp_password @new_password="INOTELL"
2> go
Password correctly set.
(return status = 0)
```

Normally, if you are setting a password for a user, you must also specify the **caller_password**, **new_password**, and **loginame** parameters to the **sp_password** stored procedure.

Configuring Database Devices and Databases

The next step to configuring our server is to create the database devices for the user databases tables. In our example case we will have only one user database on this machine, but we very easily could have multiple databases on each device and multiple devices on this machine, as well as a single database that spans multiple devices. All of these possibilities are supported by Sybase and are logical extensions of our example.

To create a new database device, use the **disk init** command. The syntax of the disk init command is:

```
DISK INIT NAME="<name>", PHYSNAME="<device>", VDEVNO=<devnumber>,

SIZE=<size> [,CNTRLTYPE=<controller>] [,VSTART=<offset>] [,CONTIGUOUS]
```

To create a device as a file on the file system we would just specify PHYSNAME as the full path to the file to create. To create a device on a Linux device (like a hard drive partition) we just specify **PHYSNAME** as the full path to the device special file. The **NAME** parameter to disk init is a unique string name to reference this database device on this server.

VDEVNO is an integer device number for the new device. This should be one higher than the max device currently known to the server. You can find out what devices are currently known and what device numbers they have with the **sp_helpdevice** stored procedure. **SIZE** is the size of the new device as an integral number of 2048 byte blocks. When setting the size of a database device that is going to occupy a disk partition, be sure to specify it as large as the partition itself. You can have only one database device on a disk partition.

So, for our example, we would execute the following two commands in isql:

```
1> disk init name="xact", physname="/dev/sdb1",
2> VDEVNO=2, SIZE=<SIZE OF PARTITION in 2KB blocks>
3> go
1> disk init name="data1", physname="/dev/sdc1",
2> VDEVNO=3, SIZE=<SIZE OF PARTITION in 2KB blocks>
3> go
```

Now we have two new devices available to put user databases on in our SQL Server. The first device, called **xact**, will hold our transaction logs. (It is always a good idea to have your transaction logs on a separate physical device than your database so if one of the physical devices fails, you can retrieve the database from the other device.) The second device, called **data1**, will hold the data tables for the database. We named it **data1** so that we could add more data devices (more hard drives) as our database grows.

The next step is to actually create some user databases to reside on the new devices, using the create database SQL command. This command must be executed while you are in the master database (type use master). The syntax for this command is:

```
create database database_name
[on {default | database_device} [= size]
    [, database_device [= size]...]
[log on database_device [ = size ]
    [, database_device [= size]]...]
[with override]
[for load]
```

The on clause specifies on which device the database should be put, and the **=size** clause specifies the database size in megabytes. The log on clause indicates where the SQL Server should put the transaction log. In our example we have only one database, which we will call **user_data**, and will create it to occupy fully both the **data1** and the **xact** database devices. The command for doing this is as follows:

```
1> create database user_data on data1=<SIZE OF PARTITION in MB>
2> log on xact=<SIZE OF PARTITION in MB>
3> go
CREATE DATABASE: allocating 51200 pages on disk 'data1'
CREATE DATABASE: allocating 14336 pages on disk 'xact'
```

We now have a very large user database called **user_data** that we can use. To use this database, switch to it with the use **user_data** command. Then you can create tables, view, stored procedures, etc.

Creating User Logins and Permissions

It is probably not a good idea to use the **sa** user for all of your database connections from clients. You can create new user logins, users, and groups for particular databases and specify what permissions different users or groups have.

Logins are not the same as users. Login names apply only to the actual login process to the database. After logging in, the actual user name may change depending on which database the user is currently in. Some logins may have the same user name and some may be aliased to other users in different databases. Some logins may not have any access to a database at all. New logins can be created while in the master database with the **sp_addlogin** stored procedure. This procedure requires two parameters, the login name and the password. We will create two logins for our example **user_data** database:

```
1> sp_addlogin brad, <password>
2> go
Password correctly set.
Account unlocked.
New login created.
(return status = 0)
1> sp_addlogin mary, <password>
2> go
Password correctly set.
Account unlocked.
New login created.
(return status = 0)
```

Once you have created logins, you should also specify the default database for the login. If no default database is specified, then the login user will be placed in the master database. This is usually not what you want to happen, since no regular users should be able to change anything in the master database. Therefore, use the **sp_defaultdb** stored procedure in the master database to specify in which database these users should be put immediately upon logging in. In our example database the logins created earlier should be placed in **user_data**, so we will execute the following commands in isql:

```
1> use master
2> go
1> sp_defaultdb brad, user_data
2> go
Default database changed.
(return status = 0)
1> sp_defaultdb mary, user_data
2> go
Default database changed.
(return status = 0)
```

For IT Professionals

Users and Groups

In large database situations where you can separate users into a quantifiable number of groups where each group has a like set of permissions for objects in the database, it is a good idea to set up these groups and give the permissions to the groups. This lets you easily add and remove users to the system without having to remember and update each of the objects to which a particular user needs permissions.

Especially in the current economy where employee loyalty is often almost unheard of, adding and removing users to a database would become a full time job for an IT person in a large company. There would also be the invariable new employee that needs access to something to get a critical project done, but does not have access due to an oversight in permission setting. If this person is known to be of a particular type of user (perhaps 'sales') when he or she was created, this person would simply have been specified as being a part of the sales group, and thus all the permissions applicable to the sales group applies to him or her.

Groups are collections of users who have like permissions. With the use of groups, you can specify permissions based on types of users, and then as your user base grows, you can add new users to the groups without having to change permissions on all the objects in the database. To create a new group in a particular database, first use the database and then execute the **sp_addgroup** stored procedure. This procedure takes one parameter, the new group name, and creates this group. We will create one group named editors for our example database:

```
1> use user_data
2> go
1> sp_addgroup editors
2> go
```

A user in a database can, but need not, have the same name as a particular login. The owner of the database is a special user named **dbo**, but the **sa** login is the dbo of any database, for example. To add another login that should be dbo for a particular database, first add the login as described earlier and then create an alias from this login to the user dbo. This is accomplished through the sp_addalias stored procedure. This procedure sets the specified login to mean the specified user in the current database. This same stored procedure can provide any login alias for any user. So to specify the login we created to be the dbo for the **user_data** database in our example, we would execute the following commands as sa in isql:

```
1> use user_data
2> go
1> sp_addalias brad, dbo
2> go
Alias user added.
(return status = 0)
```

Other users of the database can be added through the **sp_adduser** stored procedure. This stored procedure indicates the login name, the new user name in this database, and the group to which this user belongs. In our example, **mary** is a new user to be added to the **user_data** database. Mary is an editor, so we will make her a member of the editors group to inherit all the permissions that all editors have.

```
1> use user_data
2> go
1> sp_adduser mary, mary, editors
2> go
New user added.
(return status = 0)
```

At the outset, only the dbo has permission to anything in a database. Each object (table, view, stored procedure, or column) in the database has a set of permissions associated with it for each user or group. The dbo has the ability to grant permission to other users of the database for certain actions on certain objects. The process of granting permissions to a user or group allows them that permission (select, update, insert, delete, references, or execute) on a particular object. The syntax for the grant and revoke commands are:

```
grant {all [privileges]| permission_list}
on { table_name [(column_list)]
    | view_name[(column_list)]
    | stored_procedure_name}
to {public | name_list | role_name}
[with grant option]
```

```
revoke [grant option for]
{all [privileges] | permission_list}
on { table_name [(column_list)]
    | view_name [(column_list)]
    | stored_procedure_name}
from {public | name_list | role_name}
[cascade]
```

So for our example, will grant the group editors the ability to select data (read) from the authors, chapters, and books tables. (We must create these tables first.) These commands will do the trick:

```
1> grant select on authors to editors
2> grant select on chapters to editors
3> grant select on books to editors
4> go
```

Testing the Database

At this stage you should have a fully functioning database with a user database setup called **user_data**, and two logins: **brad** and **mary**. Currently, both of these logins should default to starting in the **user_data** database, but **mary** (and the whole editors group) doesn't have any permissions (unless you set up the authors, chapters, and books tables and granted editors permission to these). We will now go through some basic steps to test your database setup.

First of all, execute the following command to verify that your database server is running:

```
# /etc/rc.d/init.d/sybase status

USER          PID %CPU %MEM   VSZ   RSS TTY       STAT START   TIME COMMAND
sybase        648  0.0  8.5 21764 10904 pts/0     S    18:26   0:02
/opt/sybase/bin/dataserver -d/opt/sybase/master.dat -sSYBASE -
e/opt/sybase/install/errorlog -i/opt/sybase
sybase        649  0.0  3.1  6720  4088 pts/0     S    18:26   0:00
/opt/sybase/bin/backupserver -SSYB_BACKUP -e/opt/sybase/install/backup.log -
I/opt/sybase/interfaces -M/opt/sybase/bin/sybmultbuf -Lus_english -Jiso_1 -
c/opt/sybase/backup_tape.cfg
```

You should see one line for each database server for each CPU that you have. The preceding output shows the status of my machine running both a database server called **SYBASE** and a backup server called **SYB_BACKU**P. If only the first line appears (USER PID ...), then your Sybase database server is not running. Execute the following:

```
/etc/rc.d/init.d/sybase start
```

to start the database server. After doing so, execute the **sybase status** command again to ensure that it is running. If the server is not running, then check the error log in the file that you specified to sybinit. This file defaults to **/opt/sybase/install/errorlog.** Any error messages that it indicates there should be remedied, and then restart the server with the earlier **sybase start** command.

Once you have verified that your database server is actually running, you should be able to connect to it as any of the three users that we have set up. To connect to the server from the command line, execute the following command:

```
# /opt/sybase/bin/isql -U <username> -S <servername>
```

and enter your password. You should then get a prompt that looks like 1>. This indicates that you are entering a new query to send to the database and are on the first line of the query. You can enter the query in SQL with as many carriage returns in it as you need. Each time you press **Return**, you will see the prompt's number increment by one. When you are happy with the command as typed, type **go** on a line by itself and press **Return**. This will instruct isql to send the query to the server and display the results on the screen. (sqsh provides much nicer features including allowing you to edit the command after typing it.)

NOTE

Many Sybase commands produce output wider than 80 columns. If you run them in an xterm or console that is at least 120 columns wide, the output will be much easier to read. Some of the code to follow has been modified slightly *only* to maintain the columnular format for ease in readability.

Let's try out some simple commands to get the hang of the SQL shell. First of all, let us find out what objects are in the database that we can use. Sybase provides a very helpful stored procedure to find out exactly this. It is **sp_help**, and given no parameters it will list all the objects (tables, views, stored procedures, etc.) in the current database. Given the parameter of a particular object, it will display information about that object. For example, if we are in the **user_data** database (log in as **brad** or log in as **sa** then execute use **user_data** command) and execute **sp_help**, we will get a listing something like this:

```
1> sp_help
2> go
Name                     Owner                Object_type
----------------         ------------------   -----------

sysalternates    dbo            system table
sysattributes    dbo            system table
syscolumns       dbo            system table
syscomments      dbo            system table
sysconstraints   dbo            system table
sysdepends       dbo            system table
sysgams          dbo            system table
sysindexes       dbo            system table
syskeys          dbo            system table
syslogs          dbo            system table
sysobjects       dbo            system table
syspartitions    dbo            system table
sysprocedures    dbo            system table
sysprotects      dbo            system table
sysreferences    dbo            system table
sysroles         dbo            system table
syssegments      dbo            system table
systhresholds    dbo            system table
systypes         dbo            system table
sysusermessages  dbo            system table
```

sysusers	dbo			system table	

User_type	Storage_type	Length	Nulls	Default_name	Rule_name
---------------	-----------------	------	------	---------------	-----------

(return status = 0)

This shows all the objects (which right now are just system tables) in the database as well as who owns them. We can then execute **sp_help** with one of these tables as a parameter and we get the columns in this table. For example, if we execute **sp_help sysusers** we get a listing something like this:

```
1> sp_help sysusers
2> go
```

Name	Owner	Type
---------------------------	-----------------------------------	------------
sysusers	dbo	system table

Data_located_on_segment	When_created
---------------------------------	-----------------------------
system	Jan 1 1900 12:00AM

Column_name	Type	Length	Prec	Scale	Nulls	Default_name	Rule_name	Identity
---------------	--------	-------	----	----	-----	---------------	------------	-------
suid	smallint	2	NULL	NULL	0	NULL	NULL	0
uid	smallint	2	NULL	NULL	0	NULL	NULL	0
gid	smallint	2	NULL	NULL	0	NULL	NULL	0
name	sysname	30	NULL	NULL	0	NULL	NULL	0
environ	varchar	255	NULL	NULL	1	NULL	NULL	0

index_name	index_description	index_keys	index_max_rows_per_page
-----------	-----------------------------	----------------	-----------------------
sysusers	clustered, unique located on system	suid	0
ncsysusers1	nonclustered, unique located on system	name	0
ncsysusers2	nonclustered, unique located on system	uid	0

(3 rows affected)

keytype	object	related_object	object_keys	related_keys
-------	-----------	---------------	--------------------	--------------------
foreign	sysalternates	sysusers	suid, *, *, *, *, *, *, *	suid, *, *, *, *, *, *, *
common	sysobjects	sysusers	uid, *, *, *, *, *, *, *	uid, *, *, *, *, *, *, *
common	sysprotects	sysusers	uid, *, *, *, *, *, *, *	uid, *, *, *, *, *, *, *

```
common    systypes    sysusers    uid, *, *, *, *, *, *, *    uid, *, *, *, *, *, *, *
primary   sysusers    -- none --  suid, *, *, *, *, *, *, *    *, *, *, *, *, *, *, *
Object is not partitioned.
```

```
(return status = 0)
```

This gives us all kinds of information that we don't necessarily need, but does tell us what columns are in the table and what type they are. It also tells us which indexes are on the table, and on which columns.

Let's start creating our own objects by creating a new table. Say, for example, that we are interested in creating a user-based Web site that will allow users to log in with a username and a password. We will obviously need a way of knowing what users we know about and what passwords they have. We are probably also interested in some personal information like their name and e-mail address as well. Therefore, to store all of this information so we can easily extract it, we will create the following table:

```
1> CREATE TABLE user_logins (
2>      username VARCHAR(20) PRIMARY KEY,
3>      password VARCHAR(20),
4>      fname    VARCHAR(30),
5>      lname    VARCHAR(50),
6>      email    VARCHAR(100)
7> )
8> go
```

After executing this code in isql in the **user_data** database, we will now have a new object called **user_logins**. If you are curious, try **sp_help** to display all objects again and see what it says about **user_logins**. We can now add some data to this table:

```
INSERT INTO user_logins (username, password, fname, lname, email) VALUES
('brad', 'let me in', 'Brad', 'Dietrich', 'brad@deftech.com')
INSERT INTO user_logins VALUES ('mary', 'let me in', 'Mary', 'Poppins',
'mary@somewhere.net')
INSERT INTO user_logins VALUES ('brad', 'password', 'Brad', 'Poppins',
'brad@somewhere.net')
```

Notice that we get an error when we tried to add another user with the same username. This is because we called username a **PRIMARY KEY**, indicating that the username field must be unique. Sybase will not let us insert the same key into this field twice.

We now have to extract some information from the database. We are interested in a complete list of all of our users sorted by last name. We will execute the following command to find this out:

```
SELECT username, lname, fname, email FROM user_logins SORT BY lname
```

The sort operation on this table would take quite a long time if this table were longer, because we never declared an index on this column. An index on a column makes sorts and references to the column incredibly faster than the same sort or reference without an index. Good database design requires deciding which columns must be indexed and which do not. Indexing every column is self-defeating because it increases the overhead on the database both in size (to maintain the index trees) and in speed (to update the index trees when the table changes). To create an index on the **lname** and **fname** columns so that this previous report will run better, we must execute:

```
CREATE INDEX user_logins_lname_fname ON user_logins(lname, fname)
```

Finally, we should delete this table, because we are not interested in keeping it around since it is only a test. We will delete it with the following command:

```
DROP TABLE user_logins
```

If all of these commands worked for both the **sa** user and the brad user then your database is fully configured and running correctly. If any errors occurred during this simple database test, you should go back through this chapter, ensuring that you completed all the configuration and installation tasks as described. Keeping your database running top-notch is often a full-time job for a trained DBA; small databases should also be able to be maintained and run through the commands we discussed in this chapter.

Database Design

Database design is a very important step in any database development project. It is usually the first step in the development, and can be one of the most critical. A poor database design usually is doomed to remain in place because the cost of changing it means completely redeveloping all of the applications that rely on it.

When setting out to develop a new database, a lot of thought needs to be put into not only what type of data needs to be stored in the database, but also what all the interdependencies and use cases are that may exist now or in the future. Designing a database becomes almost like trying to predict the future, since any nontrivial database is likely to be around for quite some time. Therefore, we must consider what questions are likely to be asked of the database and how the responses are likely to be structured.

To try and portray some of the considerations that go into developing a good database, let us consider, as an example, the company publishing this book. They may want to create a database of information about all the books that they publish, which chapters are in which books, and which authors wrote which chapters. As a first attempt at designing this database, let's consider the pieces of data that are likely to be referenced from others.

Obviously, the books that they publish will contain chapters. We will represent this by including the book's primary key in the chapter column. This will allow us easily to know which chapters belong to which book.

The next set of data to relate is the author to the chapter. It is possible (and is the case in this book) that different people write different chapters in a book. Thus, our data model has to be able to allow each chapter to have a different author. One way of doing this would be to include the primary key of the author table in the chapter table. This will work so long as there is not more than one author for each chapter. Because it is certainly foreseeable that multiple authors may be writing a chapter, this data model would be a poor choice. Likewise, we cannot include the primary key of the chapter in the author table, because it is certainly possible for the same author to write multiple chapters.

This many-to-many relationship comes up quite a lot in data modeling. To model this many-to-many relationship properly, we could take the naive approach and create multiple author key columns in the chapter table, but we would invariably run into the problem that the number of key columns that we created was not enough. Also, trying to write an SQL statement to handle the case of multiple foreign key columns would be cumbersome at best.

The best way to model this many-to-many relationship is to create another linking table that will contain a key to both the chapter table and to the author table. Thus for every chapter that an author wrote, there would be one row in the linking table, and for every chapter that had multiple authors, there would be one row in the linking table for each author.

In the hopes of clarifying this example, the following SQL script will create the four tables, populate them with some example data, and query them. In our example, we will say that there is only one book title "The Wild Database Model." This one book has only two chapters titled "Chapter 1" and "Chapter 2." Chapter 1 was written exclusively by **Joe User** and Chapter 2 was written by both **Joe User** and **Sally User**.

```
CREATE TABLE books (
    book_id NUMERIC(10,0) PRIMARY KEY,
    book_title VARCHAR(100)
)


CREATE TABLE chapters (
    chapter_num NUMERIC(10,0) PRIMARY KEY,
    book_id NUMERIC(10,0) REFERENCES books(book_id),
    chapter_title VARCHAR(100)
)


CREATE TABLE authors (
    author_id NUMERIC(10,0) PRIMARY KEY,
    fname VARCHAR(30),
    lname VARCHAR(30)
)


CREATE TABLE chapter_author_link (
    link_id NUMERIC(10,0) IDENTITY PRIMARY KEY,
    chapter_num NUMERIC(10,0) REFERENCES chapters(chapter_num),
    author_id NUMERIC(10,0) REFERENCES authors(author_id)
)


INSERT INTO books VALUES (1, 'The Wild Database Model')
INSERT INTO chapters VALUES (1, 1, 'Chapter 1')
INSERT INTO chapters VALUES (2, 1, 'Chapter 2')
INSERT INTO authors VALUES (1, 'Joe', 'User')
```

```
INSERT INTO authors VALUES (2, 'Sally', 'User')
INSERT INTO chapter_author_link (chapter_num, author_id)
VALUES (1, 1)
INSERT INTO chapter_author_link (chapter_num, author_id)
VALUES (2, 1)
INSERT INTO chapter_author_link (chapter_num, author_id)
VALUES (2, 2)

SELECT book_title, chapter_num, chapter_title, lname, fname
FROM books, chapters, authors, chapter_author_link
WHERE books.book_id=chapters.book_id
AND chapters.chapter_num=chapter_author_link.chapter_num
AND authors.author_id=chatper_author_link.author_id
```

```
Results:
book_title                    chapter_num chapter_title lname fname
-----------------------       ---------- ------------ ----- -----
The Wild Database Model            1     Chapter 1     User  Joe
The Wild Database Model            2     Chapter 2     User  Joe
The Wild Database Model            2     Chapter 2     User  Sally
```

Issues

This section will discuss some issues that arise when using Sybase. Some of these issues are generic Sybase issues that affect all platforms of Sybase, and some of these are specific to the Linux port of Sybase.

Identity Columns (Auto Increment)

Sybase provides the ability to create integer columns that automatically increment whenever there is an insert operation on the table. These columns can be very nice when used to generate primary keys for columns in the table that do not inherently have any particularly unique data, or when used to reference a particular column from another table without using a longer string primary key.

An identity column must be of the NUMERIC data type and will always be an integer. The size of the data type is not critical, but there are some implications of using too large a NUMERIC. To create an identity column, do so when you create the table with a syntax like this:

```
CREATE TABLE <tablename> (
    table_id NUMERIC(<size>,0) IDENTITY PRIMARY KEY,
    ...
)
```

If you decide to use identity columns, then there are a few things to be aware of. First of all, Sybase will not let you insert your own value into the identity column of a table unless you tell it you are going to beforehand. To tell Sybase you are going to enter your own value into an identity column, execute the following command:

```
set identity_insert <table_name> on
```

After executing this command, you can insert values into the identity column as if it were any normal NUMERIC column. Be sure to set the **identity_insert** back off for the table when you are done with the set command. After setting **identity_insert** to off, Sybase will start producing values for identity columns with the next value generated being one higher than the maximum value in the column currently.

If you use identity columns in Sybase for any amount of time, you may notice that at some point your identity column starts producing some really large numbers with a large gap from the last number it produced. This occurs because of an optimization Sybase uses called the *identity burning set*. When you insert the first row into a table with an identity column, Sybase actually reserves a set of numbers to issue them quickly to future inserts—the identity burning set. If the database is shut down with nowait specified or through a catastrophic failure, then Sybase won't know which of these numbers in this set has been issued yet. Therefore, it just starts by allocating another set of numbers, thus the large gap in numbers assigned. This can be limited by editing the **SYBASE.cfg** file in **/opt/sybase** and setting the identity burning set factor to a small number, but the only way to eliminate it from occurring is to ensure the database is always shut down properly. (See the following discussion about Sybase **rc** scripts.)

The last important thing to know about identity columns is the special global variable **@@IDENTITY**. This variable is a global per-session variable that always contains the last assigned identity value in the last insert statement. With the use of this variable, you can find out what number was assigned to the most recent insert into a table with an identity column. An example of using this is displayed in Figure 5.13.

SQL Conformance

One very large problem with Sybase 11.0.3.3 is its failure to directly support the JOIN syntax in the FROM clause of SQL statements. Many new databases allow for two tables that are related through a primary/foreign key relationship to be directly joined with the JOIN clause. Sybase does provide the same functionality as a join clause, but provides it through

Figure 5.13 Example isql session displays the usage of the @@IDENTITY variable.

```
1> CREATE TABLE table_a (
2>     table_a_id NUMERIC(10,0) IDENTITY PRIMARY KEY,
3>     value_a VARCHAR(30)
4> )
5> go
1> CREATE TABLE table_b (
2>     table_b_id NUMERIC(10,0) IDENTITY PRIMARY KEY,
3>     table_a_id NUMERIC(10,0) REFERENCES table_a(table_a_id),
4>     value_b VARCHAR(30)
5> )
6> go
1> INSERT INTO table_a (value_a) VALUES ('value_a')
2> INSERT INTO table_b (table_a_id, value_b) VALUES (@@IDENTITY, 'value_b')
3> go
(1 row affected)
(1 row affected)
1> SELECT * FROM table_a, table_b WHERE table_a.table_a_id=table_b.table_a_id
2> go
table_a_id    value_a              table_b_id    table_a_id            value_b
------------  -------------------  ------------  --------------------  -------
           1 value_a                         1                     1  value_b
```

the *=, =, and =* operators in the WHERE clause. This limitation is more of an inconvenience in porting from one database platform to another than a flaw. All of the SQL statements that need to be ported will need to be converted to using the operator syntax rather than the JOIN syntax.

Figure 5.14 shows a hypothetical database that might be created for keeping track of who is writing which chapters of this book. As you can see, there are only two tables, one called **authors** and one called **chapters**. The chapters table defines a referential link to the authors table so that each chapter must have a defined author in the authors table.

Figure 5.14 SQL Code to create two interdependent tables.

```
CREATE TABLE authors (

    lname VARCHAR(30) PRIMARY KEY,

    fname VARCHAR(30),

    initial CHAR(1)

)


CREATE TABLE chapters (

    chapter_number NUMERIC(10,0) PRIMARY KEY,

    author_lname VARCHAR(30) REFERENCES authors(lname),

    title VARCHAR(100)

)
```

As Figure 5.15 shows, we will populate this table with authors' names, like the author of this chapter, and the chapters table with the chapter title and who wrote the chapter. If we don't use a value for **author_lname** for which we have already created a row in the authors table, Sybase will give us an error. This is the desired effect, because we indicated that we wanted this column to reference the other column in the authors table.

Figure 5.15 SQL Code to populate tables.

```
INSERT INTO authors (fname, lname, initial) VALUES ('Brad', 'Dietrich', 'W')
INSERT INTO chapters (chapter_number, author_lname, title)
VALUES (6, 'Dietrich', 'Sybase')
```

Most modern relation databases use the **JOIN** syntax in the **FROM** clause of the **SELECT** statement to retrieve the information from these two tables. The statement in Figure 5.16 is the statement that most databases would use in this example. Unfortunately, Sybase does not support this in version 11.0.3.3. Figure 5.17 shows how this statement would have to be phrased to have the same effect in Sybase.

Figure 5.16 SQL Code to retrieve title and author for a chapter using JOIN syntax.

```
SELECT chapter_number, title, lname, fname
FROM chapters INNER JOIN authors ON chapters.author_lname=authors.lname
WHERE chapter_number=6
```

As you can see, the phase in Figure 5.17 has exactly the same meaning, but is simply reworded. The JOIN syntax appears to have been adopted to keep all table relationships together in the FROM clause so that it is easier for people reading the SQL statement to understand what is happening. Table 5.1 shows the mappings between Sybase's operators and the JOIN syntax used in other RDBMs.

Figure 5.17 SQL Code to retrieve title and author for a chapter using Sybase syntax.

```
SELECT chapter_number, title, lname, fname
FROM chapters, authors
WHERE chapters.author_lname=authors.lname AND chapter_number=6
```

Table 5.1 Mapping from JOIN Syntax to Sybase's Operators

Join Syntax	Sybase's Operator
INNER JOIN	=
LEFT JOIN	*=
RIGHT JOIN	=*

Run Environment

There is a really in-depth description of tuning Sybase SQL Server included in the docs RPM package as well as on Sybase's document Web site http://sybooks.sybase.com/. There are a couple of topics that I feel absolutely must be addressed in this chapter, however, which will drastically improve your performance and reduce your headaches with Sybase SQL Server on Linux.

Sybase Memory Usage

You must tell Sybase how much of the system memory that it should use. By default, it uses only about 16MB of memory for its internal caches and data. You will get far better performance if you make this number quite a bit larger. The basic rule is to subtract the amount of physical memory that you need to run the other processes that are going to be running on this machine (hopefully few) from your total physical memory. This amount is the amount that you should give to Sybase. Be careful that you do not use too much memory for Sybase, otherwise Linux will be forced to drop something out to disk swap when it runs out of physical memory. This will absolutely kill the performance of a database server.

You can specify the amount of memory that Sybase should try and get with the 'total memory' line in the **SYBASE.cfg** file in the /opt/sybase directory. The number you set here is the number of 2KB blocks that Sybase should use for its shared memory.

There is one slightly sticky problem with setting this value. Sybase was developed to run on SMP machines, and thus it always allocates this large chunk of memory as shared memory so that all of its individual processes (on each processor) can access its memory. Linux, in its default configuration, does not allow for shared memory segments to be larger than about 32MB in size. Fortunately with the advent of the Linux 2.2.x kernel, this default can be changed at boot type through the **/proc/sys** file system. To specify the largest shared memory segment that Linux will allow, execute the following command:

```
echo 134217728 > /proc/sys/kernel/shmmax
```

This will increase the maximum shared-memory segment size to 128MB. The theoretical maximum that Linux allows is 1GB.

NOTE

Setting shared memory this high takes away precious address space on servers with more than 2GB of RAM; use of true 64-bit hardware is recommended.

You will have to add this to your **rc scripts** somewhere so that this will happen on boot so before the sybase server is started. I recommend adding it to your **/etc/rc.d/init.d/sybase** script so that it reads something like this:

```
start)
      echo -n "Setting Shared Memory Max to 128MB ... "
      echo 134217728 > /proc/sys/kernel/shmmax
      echo "done"
      echo -n "Starting Sybase ASE ... "
      ( cd ${SYBASE}/install ; \
        unset LANG ; unset LC_ALL ; \

        for run_server in RUN_* ; do \
          su -c "startserver -f ${run_server}" sybase > /dev/null 2>&1 ; \
            echo -n "${run_server} " ; \
        done )
      echo
      ;;
```

Sybase rc Scripts

Unfortunately, the rc script that is provided with Sybase (**/etc/rc.d/init.d/sybase**) causes the Sybase SQL Server to shut down with **nowait** when they are requested to stop. If you are using IDENTITY columns (Sybase's auto-increment integer column), this can cause a very annoying behavior that causes large jumps in the numbers that these columns produce. The solution to this problem is to change the **rc script** to shut down the Sybase SQL Server with **wait**, rather than **nowait**. Here is what you need to change:

```
stop)
  echo -n "Shuting down Sybase ASE configured servers: "
  killproc dataserver
  killproc backupserver

  # Add your own openserver applications.
  echo
  ;;
```

to

```
stop)
  echo -n "Stopping Sybase SQL Server"
  /opt/sybase/bin/isql -Usa -P******* -S$DSQUERY <<EOSQL
shutdown SYB_BACKUP with nowait
go
shutdown
go
exit
EOSQL
    echo
  ;;
```

This is potentially a security threat, since your sa password must be stored in this file. Be sure to protect this file from prying eyes (**chmod 700 /etc/rc.d/init.d/sybase**). Only the root user should ever be executing this file, so no other users should be able to read, write, or execute it.

tempdb

Sybase uses a database called **tempdb** for all of the temporary tables that it uses to produce complex queries such as group by, order by, and joins. This database is in the default configuration of Sybase SQL Server, a 2MB database on the master device. I have found this database to be too small (have gotten out of space errors) and too slow. Many people recommend putting this database on a RAM disk so that it is very fast and can be larger than 2MB.

Red Hat 6.1's default kernel has the RAM disk max size set as 4MB. If you wish to have a tempdb on a RAM disk larger than 4MB, then you will have to edit your **/etc/lilo.conf** file and add the following line to the section under your booting kernel, and then execute the **lilo** command to reinstall LILO.

```
append="ramdisk_size=<size in KB>"
```

Assuming that you have specified the size of the RAM disk that you want to use as the tempdb database in **/etc/lilo.conf**, you can continue by adding this device to the Sybase database. Therefore, if you want **/dev/ram** (the RAM disk) to be a device for your database, execute the following command in isql as sa.

```
1> disk init name="tempdbdev", physname="/dev/ram", vdevno=XX,
size=<size of partition in 2k blocks>
(replace XX with correct vdevno!)
2> go
```

You should now have created a new database device that uses **/dev/ram** as its storage. You must use this device only for the **tempdb** database. This device (since it only exists in RAM) will not contain anything useful upon machine reboots. Since tempdb is intended to contain nothing useful upon database startup (Sybase creates tempdb from the model database every time it starts up), it can easily use RAM as its storage medium. Therefore, we must now move tempdb to using this new **tempdbdev** device. The following set of commands will create a 20MB disk device and move tempdb from the master device to this device.

```
# /opt/sybase/bin/isql -U sa
Password:
1> disk init name="tempdbdev", physname="/dev/ram", vdevno=4, size=10000
(Note: replace =10000 with the number of 2k blocks that you
specified for your ramdisk_size in /etc/lilo.conf file)
2> go
1> alter database tempdb on tempdbdev=20
(Note: replace =20 with the number of megabytes that you
specified for your tempdbdev in disk init)
2> go
Extending database by 9984 pages on disk tempdbdev
1> use tempdb
2> go
1> sp_helpdb tempdb
(Note: this only displays the usage of the database)
2> go
```

name	db_size	owner	dbid	created	status
tempdb	21.5 MB	sa	2	Jan 12, 2000	select into/bulkcopy

device_fragments	size	usage	free kbytes
master	2.0 MB	data and log	1184
tempdbdev	19.5 MB	data and log	19968

device	segment
master	default
master	logsegment
master	system
tempdbdev	default

```
    tempdbdev                               logsegment
    tempdbdev                               system


(return status = 0)
1> sp_dropsegment "default", tempdb, master
2> go
DBCC execution completed. If DBCC printed error messages, contact a user with
System Administrator (SA) role.
Segment reference to device dropped.
(return status = 0)
1> sp_dropsegment "logsegment", tempdb, master
2> go
DBCC execution completed. If DBCC printed error messages, contact a user with
System Administrator (SA) role.
DBCC execution completed. If DBCC printed error messages, contact a user with
System Administrator (SA) role.
Could not update the last-chance threshold for database tempdb
Segment reference to device dropped.
(return status = 0)
1> sp_dropsegment "system", tempdb, master
2> go
DBCC execution completed. If DBCC printed error messages, contact a user with
System Administrator (SA) role.
Segment reference to device dropped.
WARNING: There are no longer any segments referencing device 'master'.  This
device will no longer be used for space allocation.
(return status = 0)
1> sp_helpdb
2> testdb
3> go
The specified database does not exist.
(return status = 1)
1> sp_helpdb
2> tempdb
3> go
 name          db_size       owner      dbid     created          status
 ------------- ----------    ---------  -------  ---------------  --------------------
 tempdb           21.5 MB    sa            2     Jan 12, 2000     select into/bulkcopy

 device_fragments           size          usage                free kbytes
 ------------------------   -----------   --------------------  ----------------------
 master                        2.0 MB     data only                    1232
 tempdbdev                    19.5 MB     data and log                19888

 device                                   segment
 --------------------------------         ---------------------------------------------
 master                                      -- unused by any segments --
 tempdbdev                                default
 tempdbdev                                logsegment
 tempdbdev                                system


(return status = 0)
```

Notice the warning that the final **sp_dropsegment** message gave us. This is exactly what we want (none of the tempdb databases use the master device anymore) so don't be afraid of it. One final note about setting tempdb on a RAM disk—remember that the amount of RAM that you specify to tempdb must be subtracted from your total RAM before determining how much RAM that Sybase should grab for its internal cache (see the preceding section on memory usage).

Summary

This chapter discussed installing and configuring Sybase SQL Server on Red Hat Linux 6.1. Sybase has been very devoted to the Linux community by providing this older server for free and providing their current server for a similar licensing scheme as their NT products. Sybase SQL Server 11.0.3.3 is an older product and is missing some features of the more recent products like Oracle 8i, but for the price and performance, it has provided many previous projects that I have worked on with successful results. As I said at the beginning of this chapter, I was working with a fairly large database for a company with no money, and Sybase fit the bill perfectly.

Admittedly, I owe much of my success to the tremendous amount of support and help that I obtained from many of the online sources I have mentioned in this chapter. The Sybase on Linux mailing list has many good devoted Sybase DBAs, and developers who are more than willing to answer questions, and who have answered some for me. This list is available for subscription at http://www.isug.com/ISUG2/ase_linux_form.html, or a searchable archive is available at http://forum.swarthmore.edu/epigone/ ase-linux-list. There is also an International Sybase User Group (ISUG) that provides many services to Sybase DBAs and developers. Check out their Web site at http://www.isug.com/.

FAQs

Q: How do you make a numeric column in Sybase that automatically increments?

A: Sybase uses IDENTITY columns for this purpose. The syntax for creating an identity column is: CREATE TABLE <tablename> (table_id NUMERIC(<size>,0) IDENTITY). These columns usually are used to ensure that there is a primary key on the table, so this column can also be specified as being the primary key. See the earlier section "Issues," about Identity Columns to see some of the issues surrounding use of Identity columns.

Q: I just want a small database—do I really need to devote two entire hard drives to it?

A: No. It is recommended from a recovery standpoint that your transaction logs and data actually exist on different physical media in the event that one of the physical media devices fails. If you have a small database and are willing to take the risk of device failure, then you can certainly put both your transaction log and data on the same device. In fact, you can specify your database devices to be files in your files system if you don't want to devote entire unformatted partitions to them.

Q: My indexes on my tables don't appear to be working anymore. What happened?

A: Sybase does not rebuild indexes every time that you insert new data into a table. The query optimizer for Sybase has the tough job of deciding whether or not a table's index is sufficiently up to date or whether a table scan would be faster. If you have tables for which the data is changing or being added quite often, then you should have Sybase periodically rebuild the indexes on those tables. This can be accomplished by running the update statistics <table> command in **isql**.

Q: My transaction log fills up my entire database device and then my inserts fail. How can I stop this from happening?

A: Sybase writes an entry in the transaction log for every transaction that you execute on the database. In the case of large data changes using **INSERT**, **UPDATE**, or **DELETE**, you may fill up the transaction log device, causing the actual command to wait in the background until enough transaction log room is free to continue the command. To continue this command, log into the database as the **sa** user and dump the transaction log for the offending database (you may have to specify the with **no_log** setting if the log is really full). This will not dump any currently running transactions, so if these changes are one large transaction (e.g., **DELETE FROM <table>** on a long table) it is possible that this action will never be completed because there is not enough room in the transaction log to write this entire transaction entry. If this is the case, break the transaction down into smaller chunks and execute each chunk, then dump the transaction log.

Q: But isn't there a way just to dump the transaction log automatically?

A: Yes. Sybase provides the ability to truncate the log whenever it does a checkpoint. A checkpoint is Sybase's period check to see if the data in the data device is consistent with what it should be. This happens every couple of seconds. You can indicate that Sybase should dump the transaction log when this happens by executing the following command as **sa** in the master database:

```
sp_dboption <dbname>, trunc, true
```

Installing DB2 Universal Database Version 6.1 on Red Hat Linux

Solutions in this chapter:

- **Preparing your Red Hat Workstation for a DB2 Installation**

- **Installing DB2**

- **Configuring the Control Center**

- **Installing a DB2 Client**

- **Configuring a DB2 Client to Communicate with a DB2 Server**

Introduction

In a world that seems to grow smaller every day, it's important to have a database that can embrace as much of that world as possible. A "universal" database ought to be just that: *universal*. DB2 Universal Database (DB2) version 6.1 is truly a universal database! Consider these DB2 benefits:

Universally applicable. To data warehousing, decision support, data mining, online transaction processing (OLTP), and online analytical processing (OLAP).

Universally scalable. DB2 is the industry's only database capable of scaling from desktop to high-end parallel processing systems, which is vital for enterprise customers engaged in large-scale transaction processing, data warehousing, and data mining activities. All this, plus the reliability and industrial strength you expect from IBM, and a dramatic ease of use and installation, led *PCWeek* to call DB2 "the most technically advanced database server on the market."

Universally accessible. In today's wired world, a database needs to be universally accessible, so that users of every system in a diverse network may enjoy the benefits of database access. Not only does DB2 run on the most popular operating systems—Linux, Windows NT, Windows 9x, OS/2, AIX, PTX, HP-UX, and Sun Solaris—a DB2 database may be accessed by an even wider array of client applications. But it's DB2's Java and JDBC support that truly makes database access universal. Using JDBC (Java database connectivity), you can provide client access to DB2 via a "thin" Java applet. Thin-client JDBC applications will run in any Java-enabled Web browser, enabling any knowledge worker in an organization to access a database through a workstation running a supported Web browser (Netscape Navigator is included with DB2). And keep this in mind: Both the development cycle and the learning curve for thin-client JDBC applications is very quick, so it's easy to keep up with changing business conditions, and keep programming and training costs down. Alternatively, complete, highly sophisticated client applications can still be built in Java and DB2 data can be accessed through JDBC.

Universally manageable. Apart from putting businesses on the Web, managing large amounts of information, and handling data mining and data warehousing, DB2 actually makes it all seem easy with its first-class management tool, the Control Center. The Control Center makes both local and remote system management simple, thereby lowering the total cost of ownership of your DB2 solution.

These are just a few of the key features that make DB2 truly one of the world's leading databases. Now you can combine the power of Linux with the world's most trusted database for e-business, IBM's DB2. DB2 Universal Database for Linux offers unmatched Internet functionality. The DB2 Control Center offers administrators an easy-to-use interface for maintaining databases that can be run from any Java-enabled Web browser. For Java developers, DB2 for Linux offers support for JDBC and SQLJ, and Net.Data allows for the creation of dynamic data-driven Web applications. Perl developers can also take advantage of DB2's Perl driver for the Perl Database Interface.

DB2 for Linux is a great choice for e-business. As the foundation for e-business, DB2 is one of the industry's most noted multimedia, Web-ready relational database management systems, strong enough to meet the demands of large corporations and flexible enough to serve medium-sized and small businesses. With version 6.1, DB2 for Linux provides significant enhancements to ease the development of e-business applications. Some of the features included in the new DB2 for Linux are as follows:

Ease of Administration Enhancements. Includes the new Index Smart Guide and Performance Monitor.

Application Development Enhancements. Includes enhanced UNICODE support, and increased table/column limits.

OLE DB Container Support. Provides access to OLE DB-enabled data sources such as Microsoft Access and Lotus Approach.

DB2 Connect Support. Allows you to protect and leverage your current investment in your host and AS/400-based DB2 data sources; with over 70 percent of the world's data managed by DB2, the DB2 Connect feature allows you to put efforts into mining and using your data, instead of porting it.

With more than 6500 business partners now enrolled, the number of partners committed to IBM's data management solutions grew by 50 percent in 1999. Over 50,000 programmers participated in the DB2 version 6.1 beta program, and now you can try the real thing.

This chapter will take you through the steps involved to install a DB2 server, create a sample database, configure the graphical administration tools, install a DB2 client, and configure a connection between a DB2 server and a DB2 client.

Preparing Your Red Hat Workstation for a DB2 Installation

Before you begin to install a DB2 product on your Red Hat workstation, you have to prepare your workstation for DB2. The tasks involved in

For IT Professionals

DB2 Personal Developer's Edition

Did you know that you can download a non–time-limited version of DB2 Personal Developer's Edition for Linux? All other evaluation copies of DB2 are time-limited. DB2 Personal Developer's Edition provides all the tools for one software developer to develop desktop business tools and applications for DB2 Universal Database Personal Edition. This product is provided at no charge when downloaded, and may be used for the evaluation, demonstration, testing, and development of application programs. If you want to use it in a production environment, you have to get the correct licensing. Support is available for a fee.

Included in DB2 Personal Developer's Edition are the following:

- DB2 Universal Database Personal Edition, which is a single-user, full-function DB2 database. This version of DB2 can connect to remote DB2 databases, but cannot service inbound client requests for data.
- DB2 Connect Personal Edition for connecting workstation applications to host and AS/400 databases. With this product, your workstation can access DB2 data that resides on a host or AS/400-based system.

Included in the download files for both DB2 Universal Database Personal Edition and DB2 Connect Personal Edition are the following features:

- DB2 administration tools, including the Control Center.
- DB2 Software Developers Kit, including APIs, tools, and documentation for developers.

The DB2 and DB2 Connect Personal Edition products are available for Linux, OS/2, Windows 9x, and Windows NT.

Want more information? Visit IBM's DB2 for Linux page at http://www4.ibm.com/software/data/db2/linux/.

enabling your workstation for a DB2 product depend on what version of Red Hat Linux you are running. As the Linux operating system evolves, and relationships strengthen between IBM and the Linux vendors, you should expect to see these types of preparation steps disappear. Until then, follow these instructions carefully to ensure that your installation runs smoothly and is configured in the least amount of time.

Before you can install a DB2 product on a Linux-based workstation, you must ensure that your Linux workstation meets the following requirements:

1. Linux kernel 2.0.35 or higher
2. **RPM** (Red Hat package manager)
3. **pdksh** package (public domain Korn shell)
4. **glibc** version 2.0.7 or higher
5. **libstdc++** version 2.8.0 or higher

NOTE

If you use the rpm −qa command to list the installed packages on Red Hat version 6.0 or version 6.1, only the libstdc++ 2.9.0 library is shown; however, DB2 requires libstdc++ 2.8.0. The libstdc++ 2.8.0 library is included with the base installation. You can verify this by checking the contents of the /usr/lib directory.

Preparing Red Hat Version 5.2 and Version 6.0 for a DB2 Installation

A default Red Hat version 5.2 and version 6.0 installation is relatively easy to prepare for DB2. Simply add the missing **pdksh** package that is required to run DB2 Installer if it isn't already installed. This package is available on the Red Hat version 5.2 and version 6.0 CD-ROMs, in the **/Red Hat/RPMS** directory, and can be installed using the **rpm −i** command.

TIP

If you are using the Gnome or KDE environment, you could use a graphic tool to add this package.

For example, if you wanted to install the **pdksh-5.2.13-3** package on either version of Red Hat, enter the following command:

```
rpm -i pdksh-5.2.13-3
```

You are now ready to install DB2 on a workstation that is running Red Hat version 5.2 or version 6.0. Go to the section, *Installing DB2 Universal Database Version 6.1 on Red Hat Linux*, later in this chapter.

Preparing Red Hat Version 6.1 for a DB2 Installation

Recently, Red Hat version 6.1 became generally available. This version of Red Hat has a problem with its dynamic loader library and causes DB2 to crash when it tries to start the database manager for an instance. The database manager, started by entering the **db2start** command, is required to start an instance, create a database, and access data within a database. Essentially, if you do not have a started database manager, you cannot use DB2. Since DB2 Installer will perform most of the configuration steps required to setup a DB2 server, it will have to create and start an instance. This will cause the installation to hang.

IBM is working with Red Hat to fix this problem; in the meantime, there are some steps you have to perform to avoid this problem and to install DB2 successfully. In order for your Red Hat version 6.1 workstation to install a DB2 product, you have to download a patch file from the Web. To make things a little more confusing, the patch that you download depends on where the DB2 code that you want to install came from. Your DB2 code could come from one of two sources: the IBM-distributed version of DB2 that became generally available in the fall of 1999 or the version of DB2 that is bundled in the Red Hat version 6.1 box.

TIP

> I recommend that you maintain your version of DB2 at the most recent FixPack level. At the time this book was written, this was FixPack 2. The version of DB2 that is shipped with Red Hat version 6.1 is DB2 with FixPack 1. DB2 FixPacks are available for download at ftp://ftp.software.ibm.com/ps/products/db2/fixes/english-us/db2linuxv61. Each FixPack's name starts with FP and then the number of the FixPack. For example, the name for FixPack 2 would start with FP2. If you have the resources when you finish your DB2 installation, upgrade your version of DB2 to the latest FixPack.

To ensure that you download the correct patch file and implement this patch correctly, perform the following steps:

1. Log on to your workstation as a user with *root* authority.
2. Connect to IBM's support ftp site at
   ftp://ftp.software.ibm.com/ps/products/db2/tools.
3. Download the appropriate path file.

   If you want to install the copy of DB2 that came in your Red Hat version 6.1 box, download the **db2rh61fix.tgz** patch. If you are going to install any other copy of DB2, download the **db2rh61gafix.tgx** patch.

You must ensure that the copy of the DB2 that you are going to install *did not* come in your Red Hat version 6.1 box if you download the **db2rh61gafix.tgx** patch. You cannot share these fixes.

4. Unzip and untar the patch file by entering the following command:

```
tar xvf patch_name
```

where **patch_name** is the name of the appropriate patch file that you downloaded for your copy of DB2.

5. Implement the patch. When you have finished unzipping and untarring the patch, you will be left with three files in your directory. One of these files is called **readme.txt**. This file gives complete instructions on how to implement this fix.

After you have addressed the problem associated with dynamic loader library in version 6.1, you need to ensure that you add the missing **pdksh** package that is required to run DB2 Installer. This package is available on the Red Hat version 6.1 CD-ROM, in the **/Red Hat/RPMS** directory, and can be installed using the **rpm –i** command.

TIP

If you are using the Gnome or KDE environment, you could use a graphic tool to add this package.

For example, if you wanted to install the **pdksh-5.2.14-1** package on Red Hat version 6.1, enter the following command:

```
rpm -i pdksh-5.2.14-1
```

You are now ready to install a DB2 product on a workstation that is running Red Hat version 6.1.

Installing DB2

This section will take you through the setup and installation of a DB2 server, as well as the creation of a sample database that will be used to verify the installation. Before performing the tasks in this section, be sure that you have completed all the steps to enable your workstation for a DB2 installation as discussed in the preceding section. Once the installation is complete, verify it by locally connecting to the sample database that you created and by accessing data from it.

The instructions in this section assume that you install and configure your DB2 server using the defaults provided by the DB2 Installer installation tool. The DB2 Installer is a menu-based installation program that assists you in accomplishing time-consuming installation and configuration tasks for DB2. The instructions in this section also assume that you do not maintain previous versions of a DB2 product on your workstation, or any of the default users (**db2inst1**, **db2fenc1**, and **db2as**). If you have any of these users on your system, remove them using the **userdel** command. I recommend that you follow the instructions in this chapter on a workstation that has never had a DB2 product installation performed on it.

You could install DB2 using the **rpm** command; however, it would require some effort to configure your server correctly after the installation completes. I recommend that you use the DB2 Installer to install and maintain any DB2 products.

Performing the Installation

Now that your Red Hat workstation is DB2-enabled, you are ready to install DB2 Universal Database version 6.1. The instructions in this section assume that you are going to install DB2 Universal Database Workgroup Edition on a DB2-enabled Red Hat workstation that has never had a copy of DB2 installed on it before.

TIP

Sometimes display problems can occur when running DB2 Installer. If your display encounters these problems, you can press CTRL-L at any time to refresh your current screen.

To avoid most of the potential display problems, I recommend that you install DB2 in a virtual console session. A virtual console session is a terminal window outside of the standard graphical interface that is installed with most Red Hat workstations. To change to a virtual console, press CTRL-ALT-F1. To change back to the graphical interface, press CTRL-ALT-F7.

To install DB2, perform the following steps:

1. Log on to the Red Hat workstation as a user with *root* authority.
2. Insert the DB2 Universal Database Version 6.1 CD-ROM into the CD-ROM drive.

3. Even if you are installing DB2 on a workstation that is running Red Hat version 6.1 and are using the image created by the patch file you downloaded, you still need to use the DB2 CD-ROM. The patch file uses the files that it creates, along with the files on the DB2 CD-ROM, to install DB2. For more information, see the **readme.txt** file that was included with the patch.

4. Mount the CD-ROM by entering the following command:

```
mount -t iso9660 -o ro /dev/cdrom /mnt/cdrom
```

5. Change focus to the mounted CD-ROM directory by entering the following command:

```
cd /mnt/cdrom
```

6. If you are installing DB2 on a workstation that is running Red Hat version 6.1, don't forget to change focus to the directory that you created when you implemented the patch file. For more information, refer to the **readme.txt** file that was provided with the patch.

7. Enter the **./db2setup** command to start the DB2 Installer. The Install DB2 V6 window opens as shown in Figure 6.1.

Figure 6.1 The Install DB2 v6.1 window.

```
+----------------------------- Install DB2 V6.1 -----------------------------+
|                                                                            |
|  Select the products you are licensed to install.  Your Proof of           |
|  Entitlement and License Information booklet identify the products for      |
|  which you are licensed.                                                    |
|                                                                            |
|  To see the preselected components or customize the selection, select       |
|  Customize for the product.                                                 |
|    [ ] DB2 Administration Client                        : Customize... :   |
|    [ ] DB2 UDB Workgroup Edition                        : Customize... :   |
|    [ ] DB2 Software Developer's Kit                     : Customize... :   |
|                                                                            |
|  To choose a language for the following components, select Customize for    |
|  the product.                                                               |
|      DB2 Product Messages                               [ Customize... ]   |
|      DB2 Product Library                                [ Customize... ]   |
|                                                                            |
|                                                                            |
|                                                                            |
|                                                                            |
|  [  OK   ]                        [ Cancel ]                 [ Help ]       |
+----------------------------------------------------------------------------+
```

8. From the product list, select the DB2 product that you want to install. For our example, select **DB2 UDB Workgroup Edition**. Press the **TAB** key to change the highlighted option and the **ENTER** key to select or deselect an option. For more information or assistance during the installation of DB2, select **Help**.

9. If you want to customize the installation of your DB2 product, select **Customize** to the right of the DB2 product that you selected to install. The options that you can select during a DB2 installation are shown in Figure 6.2.

Figure 6.2 Customization window for DB2 Workgroup Edition.

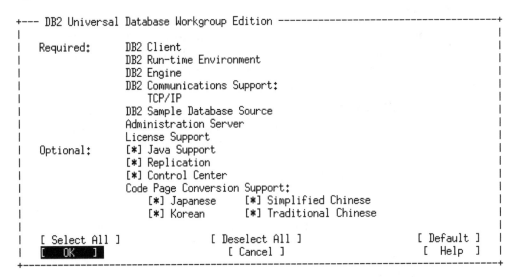

Select All will select all of the optional components for this DB2 installation. For our example, you can customize this list; however, ensure that you have selected at least the **Java Support** and the **Control Center** components, and select **OK**.

10. To customize the DB2 Product Messages, select the appropriate **Customize** option. The DB2 Product Messages window opens as shown in Figure 6.3. For our example, the default settings are fine. Select **OK**.

11. To customize the DB2 Product Library, select the appropriate **Customize** option. The DB2 Product Messages window opens as shown in Figure 6.4. The default is to install the DB2 documentation and Control Center help in English. For our example, the default settings are fine. Select **OK**.

Figure 6.3 Customizing the DB2 Product Messages.

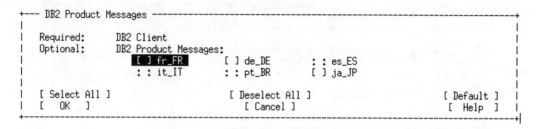

```
+--- DB2 Product Messages ---------------------------------------------------+
|                                                                            |
|  Required:      DB2 Client                                                 |
|  Optional:      DB2 Product Messages:                                      |
|                 [ ] fr_FR        [ ] de_DE        : : es_ES                |
|                 : : it_IT        : : pt_BR        [ ] ja_JP                |
|                                                                            |
|  [ Select All ]                  [ Deselect All ]              [ Default ] |
|  [  OK   ]                          [ Cancel ]                 [ Help   ]  |
+----------------------------------------------------------------------------+
```

Figure 6.4 Customizing the DB2 Product Library.

```
+--- DB2 Product Library ----------------------------------------------------+
|                                                                            |
|  Required:      DB2 Client                                                 |
|  Optional:      DB2 Product Library (HTML):                                |
|                 [*] en_US        [ ] fr_FR        [ ] de_DE                |
|                 : : es_ES        : : it_IT        : : pt_BR                |
|                 [ ] ja_JP                                                  |
|                 Control Center Help (HTML):                                |
|                 [ ] fr_FR        [ ] de_DE        : : es_ES                |
|                 : : it_IT        : : pt_BR        [ ] ja_JP.ujis           |
|                                                                            |
|  [ Select All ]                  [ Deselect All ]              [ Default ] |
|  [  OK   ]                          [ Cancel ]                 [ Help   ]  |
+----------------------------------------------------------------------------+
```

12. Select **OK**. The Create DB2 Services window opens as shown in Figure 6.5.

13. Select **Create a DB2 Instance** to create an instance. This instance will be used to store the sample database that you will create. When you select this option, the DB2 Instance window opens as shown in Figure 6.6.

    The DB2 Installer will generate a default user that will be known as the *instance-owner*. This user will have System Administrative (SYSADM) authority over the instance. A user that has SYSADM authority on an instance has complete control and authority over all of the objects in the instance.

Figure 6.5 The Create DB2 Services window.

```
+----------------------------- Create DB2 Services ----------------------------+
|                                                                              |
|   Select the items you want to create, and select OK when finished.          |
|                                                                              |
|   A DB2 Instance is an environment where you store data and run              |
|   applications.  An instance can contain multiple databases.                 |
|                                                                              |
|   ( ) Create a DB2 Instance.                                 : Customize... : |
|   (*) Do not create a DB2 Instance.                                          |
|                                                                              |
|   An Administration Server provides services to support client tools that    |
|   automate the configuration of connections to DB2 databases.                |
|                                                                              |
|   ( ) Create the Administration Server.                      : Customize... : |
|   (*) Do not create the Administration Server.                               |
|                                                                              |
|                                                                              |
|                                                                              |
|                                                                              |
|                                                                              |
|                                                                              |
|                                                                              |
|                                                                              |
|                                                                              |
|   [   OK   ]                     [ Cancel ]                      [  Help  ]   |
+------------------------------------------------------------------------------+
```

Figure 6.6 The DB2 Instance window.

```
+--- DB2 Instance -------------------------------------------------------------+
|   applications.  An instance can contain multiple databases.                 |
|   Authentication:                                                            |
|       Enter User ID, Group ID, Home Directory and Password that will be      |
|       used for the DB2 Instance.                                             |
|       User Name          [db2inst1]                                          |
|       User ID            [501    ]                     [ ] Use default UID   |
|       Group Name         [db2iadm1]                                          |
|       Group ID           [103    ]                     [ ] Use default GID   |
|       Home Directory     [/home/db2inst1 ]                                   |
|       Password           [               ]                                   |
|       Verify Password    [               ]                                   |
|                                                                              |
|   Select Properties to view or change more                  [ Properties... ] |
|   options.                                                                   |
|                                                                              |
|   Select Default to restore all default                        [ Default ]   |
|   settings.                                                                  |
|   [  OK  ]                       [ Cancel ]                     [  Help  ]    |
+------------------------------------------------------------------------------+
```

For our example, accept the default values. Enter a password in the **Password** field and verify it in the **Verify Password field**. If you fail to specify a password, the default password **ibmdb2** will be used. I recommend that you do not use the default password. Since this password is used for any DB2 product installation and is therefore well known, it could pose a security risk to your network.

For more information on SYSADM authority, see the *DB2 Administration Guide*.

14. Select the **Properties** option. Figure 6.7 shows the properties that you can specify.

Figure 6.7 Properties of an instance.

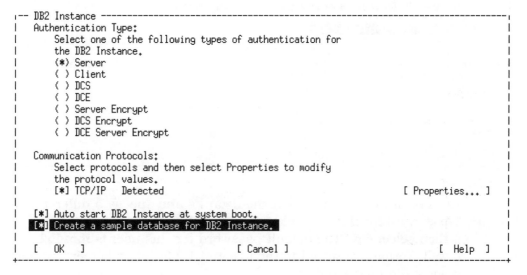

For our example, select the **Auto start DB2 Instance at system boot** and the **Create a sample database for DB2 Instance** options. Selecting these options will have the instance that the DB2 Installer creates auto-start each time the system is rebooted, and creates a sample database called **SAMPLE**. The auto-start option eliminates the need for a SYSADM user to start the instance each time the workstation is rebooted.

The default selections for Authentication Type and
Communication Protocols are fine for our example.

15. Select **OK.**

16. You will be asked to create a user that will be used to execute
user-defined functions (UDFs) and stored procedures. This is
shown in Figure 6.8.

Figure 6.8 The Fenced User window.

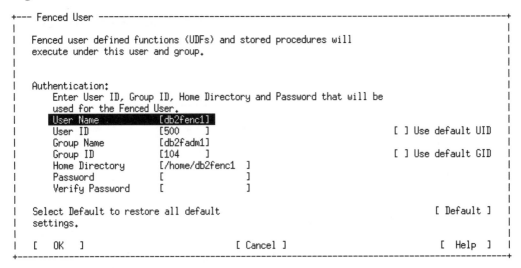

```
+--- Fenced User ---------------------------------------------------------+
|                                                                         |
|   Fenced user defined functions (UDFs) and stored procedures will       |
|   execute under this user and group.                                    |
|                                                                         |
|                                                                         |
|   Authentication:                                                       |
|       Enter User ID, Group ID, Home Directory and Password that will be  |
|       used for the Fenced User.                                         |
|       User Name        [db2fenc1]                                       |
|       User ID          [500    ]                    [ ] Use default UID  |
|       Group Name       [db2fadm1]                                       |
|       Group ID         [104    ]                    [ ] Use default GID  |
|       Home Directory   [/home/db2fenc1 ]                               |
|       Password         [         ]                                     |
|       Verify Password  [         ]                                     |
|                                                                         |
|   Select Default to restore all default                   [ Default ]   |
|   settings.                                                             |
|                                                                         |
|   [  OK  ]                      [ Cancel ]                [ Help ]  |
+-------------------------------------------------------------------------+
```

For our example, accept the defaults and specify a different
password for this user like you did with instance-owner user,
then select **OK**. The default password for this user is **ibmdb2** as
well. You are returned to the Create DB2 Services screen, as was
shown in Figure 6.5.

You will not need to use this user for our example. For more
information on UDFs and stored procedures, refer to the
Administration Guide.

17. Select **Create the Administration Server** to create the
Administration Server. The Administration Server, often referred
to as the DAS, is a special instance reserved for administration
tasks. This instance is used by the Control Center to perform
remote administrative tasks. For more information on the
Administration Server, refer to the *Administration Guide*. When
you select this option, the Administration Server window opens
as shown in Figure 6.9.

Figure 6.9 The Administration Server window.

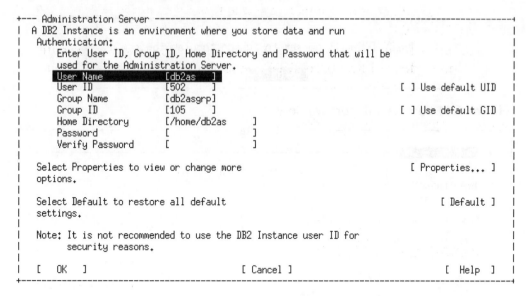

The DB2 Installer program will generate a default user that will be known as the instance-owner of the Administration Server. This user will have System Administrative (SYSADM) authority over the Administration Server instance.

For our example, accept the default values. Enter a password in the **Password** field, verify it in the **Verify Password** field, and select **OK**. If you fail to specify a password, the default password **ibmdb2** will be used. I recommend that you do not use the default password. Since this password is used for any DB2 product installation and is therefore well known, it could pose a security risk to your network.

A pop-up window will appear informing you of your DB2 System Name, as shown in Figure 6.10.

Make note of this name, and press **OK**. You are returned to the Create DB2 Services window as was shown in Figure 6.5.

18. Select **OK** to begin the installation of DB2. The Summary Report window opens as shown in Figure 6.11. The Summary Report lists all of the components that the DB2 Installer will attempt to install and configure. To review the list of components, select **More** and use the cursor keys to scroll the report. When you have finished reviewing this list, select **Continue**.

Figure 6.10 DB2SYSTEM name window

Figure 6.11 Summary Report window.

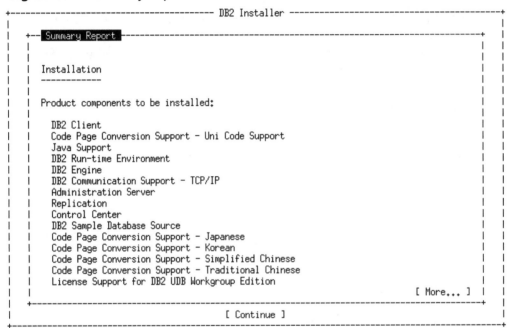

TIP

If the Summary Report does not contain the components you want to install, or if it contains components that you do not want to install, you still have to select Continue. You will have the option to go back and edit these selections in the next step.

---

19. After you select **Continue**, a pop-up window will appear, which warns you that the installation is about to begin. This is shown in Figure 6.12. If you are satisfied with your selections and you want to begin installing DB2, select **OK**. If you want to edit your selections, select **Cancel**.

Figure 6.12 Warning pop-up window.

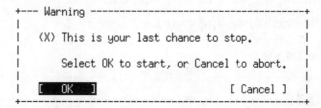

20. When the installation completes, the Status Report window opens. This window, as shown in Figure 6.13, lists all of the actions performed by the DB2 Installer and notes whether each task was successful or not.

Figure 6.13 Status Report window.

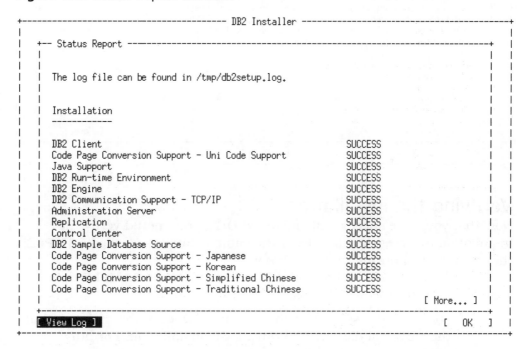

To review the entire list, use the cursor keys to scroll the contents of the report.

If you received any errors after the installation completes, you can review a log of the installation by selecting **View Log**. A sample log file that contains errors as a result of installation tasks is shown in Figure 6.14.

When you are finished, select **OK**, then **Close**, and dismiss any remaining windows by selecting **OK**.

You have finished installing your DB2 server!

Figure 6.14 The log file.

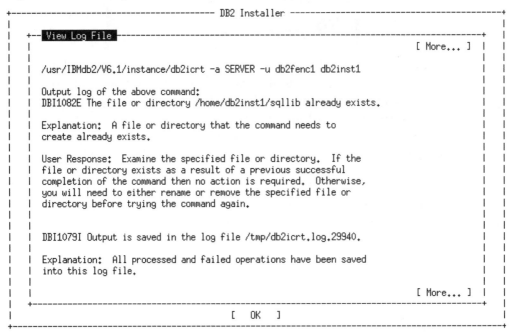

Verifying the Installation

Now that you have successfully installed DB2, you should verify the installation by accessing data from the sample database (called **SAMPLE**) that was created during the installation.

To verify your installation and access data from the **SAMPLE** database, perform the following steps.

1. Log on to the system as the instance-owner of the instance that the DB2 Installer created during the installation. For our example, enter the following command:

```
su - db2inst1
```

TIP

If you use this method to log on to the system to verify the installation, you must enter this command with the – parameter, as shown in the preceding example. If you enter this command as su db2inst1, you will receive an error because DB2 will not correctly read the DB2 profile.

2. Start the database manager with the **db2start** command. To access a database that resides in an instance, the instance must be started and running. If you recall, we selected to have this instance auto-start; you should receive the following message after entering this command:

```
SQL1026N  The database manager is already active.
```

TIP

If you receive an **SQL10007N Message "-1393" could not be retrieved. Reason Code: "1"** error, fear not! DB2 isn't aware what the default instance is. This would happen if your DB2 profile file was not executed at login. For this example, if you receive this error, enter the export DB2INSTANCE=db2inst1 command.

3. Enter the following command to connect to the **SAMPLE** database:

```
db2 connect to sample
```

You should receive the following output:

```
Database Connection Information

Database server    = DB2/LINUX 6.1.0
SQL authorization ID   = DB2INST1
Local database alias   = SAMPLE
```

4. Enter the follow command to select a list of all employees who belong to department 20 in the staff table:

```
db2 "select * from staff where dept = 20"
```

NOTE

You must enter this command with the double quotes ("") to ensure that Linux does not misinterpret the asterisk as an operating system command. If you ever issue a DB2 command with a character that may have special meaning on the operating system, you should enclose the contents of the command in quotation marks, as shown here.

You should receive the following output:

ID	NAME	DEPT	JOB	YEARS	SALARY	COMM
10	Sanders	20	Mgr	7	18357.50	-
20	Pernal	20	Sales	8	18171.25	612.45
80	James	20	Clerk		13504.60	128.20
190	Sneider	20	Clerk	8	14252.75	126.50

       4 record(s) selected.

5. Enter the following command to reset the database connection:

```
db2  connect reset
```

Congratulations! You have successfully installed and configured a DB2 Workgroup Edition server and are ready to start using one of the world's leading databases on the world's most popular platform for e-commerce.

If you want to use the Control Center, first you need to configure it for use. For more information, see the next section. If you want to install a DB2 client, see the section *Installing a DB2 Client*, later in this chapter.

Configuring the Control Center

If you want to use the Control Center to manage remote workstations and schedule scripts to run on your DB2 server, you have to set up the Java Run-Time Environment (JRE). You can run the Control Center either as a Java application or as a Java applet through a Web server. I recommend that you run the Control Center as a Java application. For more information, refer to the Control Center README file, called **readme.htm**, located in the **/usr/IBMdb2/V6.1/cc/prime** directory. The instructions in this section will assume that you are setting up the Control Center to run as a Java application. If you do not want to use the Control Center, you can skip this section and proceed to the section *Installing a DB2 Client*, later in this chapter.

To set up the Control Center on your DB2 server, perform the following steps.

1. Log on to your workstation as a user with *root* authority.

2. Download an appropriate JRE. For all the latest information on supported JREs and browsers, go to http://www.software.ibm.com/data/db2/.

   To run the Control Center you need to be running at least Java 1.1.7 v3 or later.

   A JRE for Red Hat is available from the Blackdown Web site at http://www.blackdown.org/java-linux/mirrors.html.

   For this example, I visited the mirror site at ftp://metalab.unc.edu/pub/linux/devel/lang/java/blackdown.org/JDK-1.1.7/i386/glibc/v3/ and downloaded the **jre_1.1.7-v3-glibc-x86-native.tar.gz** file and placed it in the **/tmp** directory.

NOTE

There are two types of threads associated with a JRE—native and green. Threads affect the way the Java code is run on your work station. You must download the native threads version of the JRE that you want to use. The DB2 Control Center does not support green threads.

3. Change focus to the directory where you downloaded the JRE. For our example, this would be the **/tmp** directory. Enter the following command to change to this directory:

   ```
   cd /tmp
   ```

4. Once you have downloaded the appropriate JRE, you need to **unzip** and **untar** it by entering the following command:

   ```
   tar xvfz  jre_1.1.7-v3-glibc-x86-native.tar.gz
   ```

5. Log on to your workstation as the instance owner. For our example, log on to the workstation as the **db2inst1** user.

TIP

You can use the su – db2inst1 command to log on as this user; however, ensure that you enter this command with the – parameter so that the DB2 profile gets read correctly.

6. Update your **PATH** so that your workstation knows the location of the JRE's binary files that you just installed. Assuming that you are following the example, enter the following command:

```
for Bash or Bourne shells -> export PATH=/tmp/jre117_v3/bin:$PATH
for C shell                -> setenv PATH /tmp/jre117_v7/bin:${PATH}
```

where **/tmp/jre117_v7/bin** is the path to JRE binary files that you downloaded.

NOTE

This will only set the path for the current session and will suffice for our example. If you want this change to be permanent, you need to add this setting to your profile.

7. Start the Control Center JDBC Applet Server by entering the following command:

```
db2jstrt 6790
```

The port number 6790 is an arbitrary number; any four-digit port number can be used, as long as it is not in use by another application.

8. Start the Control Center by entering the following command:

```
db2cc 6790
```

This command will start the Control Center using the port you specify. For our example, we specified port 6790. If you specified a different port number when you started the JDBC Applet Server, you must use this number when you enter this command.

9. After you enter the **db2cc 6790** command, the Control Center Sign On window opens, as shown in Figure 6.15. Enter a user ID and password that is defined on the local workstation with the correct authorities. For our example, use the **db2inst1** user ID and whatever password you specified for this user when you installed the DB2 server, then click **OK**.

Figure 6.15 The Control Center Sign On window.

10. The Control Center opens as shown in Figure 6.16. You can now start to use the Control Center to manage your local and remote DB2 workstations. For more information on the Control Center, refer to the Control Center's online help or the *DB2 Administration Guide.*

Figure 6.16 The Control Center.

Installing a DB2 Client

This section will take you through the setup and installation of a DB2 client. Before performing the steps in this section, be sure that you have completed all the tasks to enable your workstation for a DB2 product installation as discussed in the section *Preparing Your Red Hat Workstation for a DB2 Installation*, at the beginning of this chapter.

The instructions in this section assume that you install and configure your DB2 client using the defaults provided by the DB2 Installer installation tool. The DB2 Installer is a menu-based installation program that assists you in accomplishing time-consuming installation and configuration tasks for your DB2 products. The instructions in this section also assume that you do not maintain previous versions of a DB2 product on your workstation, or the default **db2inst** user. If you have this user on your system, remove it using the **userdel** command. I recommend that you follow the instructions in this chapter on a workstation that has never had a DB2 product installation performed on it.

> **TIP**
>
> Sometimes display problems can occur when running DB2 Installer. If your display encounters these problems, you can press **CTRL-L** at any time to refresh your current screen.
>
> To avoid most of the potential display problems, I recommend that you install DB2 in a virtual console session. A virtual console session is a terminal window outside of the standard graphical interface that is installed with most Red Hat workstations. To change to a virtual console, press **CTRL-ALT-F1**. To change back to the graphical interface, press **CTRL-ALT-F7**.

You can use the instructions in this section to install a DB2 Run-Time Client or a DB2 Administration Client. For our example, we will install a DB2 Administration Client since it is available on the DB2 Universal Database version 6.1 CD-ROM that you used to install your DB2 server. DB2 Administration Clients are also available on the DB2 Administration Client CD-ROMs; DB2 Run-Time clients are available only on the DB2 Run-Time Client CD-ROMs. For more information, see the *DB2 and DB2 Connect Installation and Configuration Supplement*.

To install a DB2 Client, perform the following steps.

1. Log on to the Red Hat workstation as a user with *root* authority.

2. Insert the DB2 Universal Database version 6.1 CD-ROM into the CD-ROM drive.

 Even if you are installing a DB2 client on a workstation that is running Red Hat version 6.1 and are using the image created by the patch file you downloaded, you still need to use the DB2 CD-ROM. The patch file uses the files that it creates, along with the files on the DB2 CD-ROM, to install a DB2 client. For more information, see the **readme.txt** file that was included with the patch.

3. Mount the CD-ROM by entering the following command:

```
mount -t iso9660 -o ro /dev/cdrom /mnt/cdrom
```

4. Change focus to the mounted CD-ROM directory by entering the following command:

```
cd /mnt/cdrom
```

If you are installing a DB2 client on a workstation that is running Red Hat version 6.1, don't forget to change focus to the directory that you created when you implemented the patch file. For more information, refer to the **readme.txt** file that was provided with the patch.

5. Enter the **./db2setup** command to start the DB2 Installer. The Install DB2 V6 window opens as shown in Figure 6.17.

Figure 6.17 The Install DB2 v6.1 window.

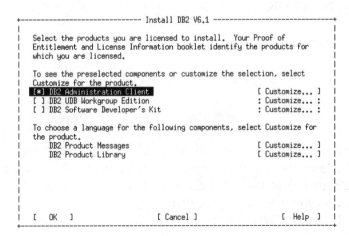

6. From the product list, select the DB2 product that you want to install. For our example, select **DB2 Administration Client**.

   Press the **TAB** key to change the highlighted option and the **ENTER** key to select or deselect an option. For more information or assistance during the installation of a DB2 client, select Help.

7. If you want to customize the installation of your DB2 client, select **Customize** to the right of the DB2 product that you selected to install. The options that you can select during a DB2 Administration Client installation are shown in Figure 6.18.

Figure 6.18 Customization window for a DB2 Administration Client.

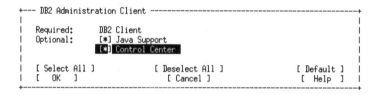

8. **Select All** will select all of the optional components for this DB2 Client installation. For our example, customize this list so that you install the **Java Support** and the **Control Center** components, and then select **OK**.

9. To customize the DB2 Product Messages, select the appropriate **Customize** option. The DB2 Product Messages window opens as shown in Figure 6.19. For our example, the default settings are fine. Select **OK**.

Figure 6.19 Customizing the DB2 Product Messages.

```
+--- DB2 Product Messages ------------------------------------------+
| [*] DB2 Administration Client                                     |
| Required:    DB2 Client                                           |
| Optional:    DB2 Product Messages:                                |
|                  [ ] fr_FR      [ ] de_DE      : : es_ES          |
|                  : : it_IT      : : pt_BR      [ ] ja_JP.ujis     |
|                                                                   |
| [ Select All ]           [ Deselect All ]         [ Default ]     |
| [   OK   ]                 [ Cancel ]             [  Help  ]       |
+-------------------------------------------------------------------+
```

10. To customize the DB2 Product Library, select the appropriate
    Customize option. The DB2 Product Messages window opens as
    shown in Figure 6.20. The default is not to install the DB2
    documentation, but to install the Control Center's help for
    English. For our example, the default settings are fine. Select
    OK.

Figure 6.20 Customizing the DB2 Product Library.

```
+--- DB2 Product Library ----------------------------------------------+
| To see the preselected components or customize the selection, select |
|  Required:     DB2 Client                                            |
|  Optional:     DB2 Product Library (HTML):                           |
|                  [ ] en_US        [ ] fr_FR        [ ] de_DE          |
|                  : : es_ES        : : it_IT        : : pt_BR          |
|                  [ ] ja_JP.ujis                                      |
|                Control Center Help (HTML):                           |
|                  [ ] fr_FR        [ ] de_DE        : : es_ES          |
|                  : : it_IT        : : pt_BR        [ ] ja_JP.ujis     |
|                                                                      |
|   [ Select All ]        [ Deselect All ]          [ Default ]        |
|   [  OK   ]                 [ Cancel ]              [ Help ]          |
+----------------------------------------------------------------------+
```

11. The Create DB2 Services window opens as shown in Figure
    6.21. Did you notice that it is a little different from the window
    that appeared when you installed a DB2 server? It is missing the
    DB2 Administration Server. You cannot create a DB2
    Administration Server on a client.

Figure 6.21 The Create DB2 Services window for a DB2 client.

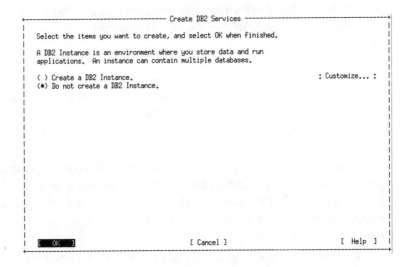

12. Select **Create a DB2 Instance** to create an instance. This instance will be used to store the information required to connect to a remote DB2 server and configure performance on the DB2 client workstation. You cannot physically store a database in a client's instance, only catalog information that tells the client where the database that you want to access is located. When you select this option, the DB2 Instance window opens as shown in Figure 6.22.

Figure 6.22 The DB2 Instance window for a DB2 client.

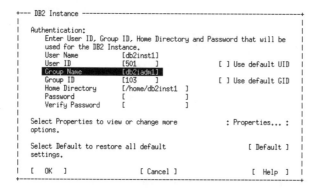

The DB2 Installer will generate a default user that will be known as the instance-owner. This user will have System Administrative (SYSADM) authority over the instance. A user that has SYSADM authority on an instance has complete control and authority over all of the objects in the instance.

For our example, accept the default values. Enter the *same* password in the **Password** field as you did for the DB2 server installation, verify it in the **Verify Password** field, and select **OK**.

TIP

We are going to use the same user ID and password on the DB2 server and the DB2 client to simplify our example scenario.

If you fail to specify a password, the default password **ibmdb2** will be used. I recommend that you do not use the default password. Since this password is used for any DB2 product installation and is therefore well known, it could pose a security risk to your network.

For more information on SYSADM authority, see the *DB2 Administration Guide*.

13. Select **OK** to begin the installation of the DB2 client. The Summary Report window opens as shown in Figure 6.23. The Summary Report lists all of the components that the DB2 Installer will attempt to install and configure. To review the list of components, select **More** and use the cursor keys to scroll the report. When you have finished reviewing this list, select **Continue**.

Figure 6.23 Summary Report window.

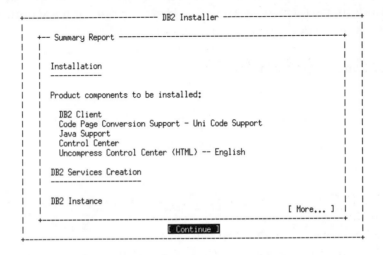

```
+------------------------------ DB2 Installer ------------------------------+
|                                                                          |
|   +-- Summary Report ---------------------------------------------+      |
|   |                                                               |      |
|   |  Installation                                                 |      |
|   |  ------------                                                 |      |
|   |                                                               |      |
|   |  Product components to be installed:                          |      |
|   |                                                               |      |
|   |    DB2 Client                                                 |      |
|   |    Code Page Conversion Support - Uni Code Support            |      |
|   |    Java Support                                               |      |
|   |    Control Center                                             |      |
|   |    Uncompress Control Center (HTML) -- English                |      |
|   |                                                               |      |
|   |  DB2 Services Creation                                        |      |
|   |  ----------------------                                       |      |
|   |                                                               |      |
|   |  DB2 Instance                                      [ More... ] |      |
|   +---------------------------------------------------------------+      |
|                            [ Continue ]                                  |
+--------------------------------------------------------------------------+
```

> **TIP**
>
> If the Summary Report does not contain the components that you want to install, or if it contains components that you do not want to install, you still have to select Continue. You will have the option to go back and edit these selections in the next step.

14. After you select **Continue**, a pop-up window will appear to warn you that the installation is about to begin. This is shown in Figure 6.24. If you are satisfied with your selections and you want to begin installing your DB2 client, select **OK**. If you want to edit your selections, select **Cancel**.

Figure 6.24 Warning pop-up window.

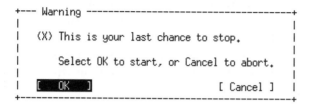

15. When the installation completes, the Status Report window opens. This window, as shown in Figure 6.25, lists all of the actions performed by the DB2 Installer and notes whether each task was successful or not.

Figure 6.25 Status Report window.

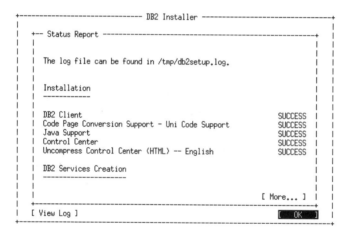

To review the entire list, use the cursor keys to scroll the contents of the report.

If you received any errors after the installation completes, you can review a log of the installation by selecting **View Log**. A sample log file is shown in Figure 6.26.

When you are finished, select **OK**, then **Close**, and dismiss any remaining windows by selecting **OK.**

Congratulations! You have successfully installed and configured a DB2 client and are ready to configure it to communicate with a remote

Figure 6.26 The log file.

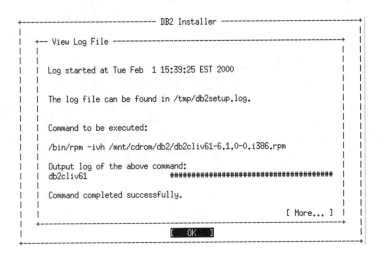

DB2 server. Remember, if you want to use the Control Center on this workstation, you will have to perform some steps before using it. For our example this is not necessary, as we will not be using the Control Center on the DB2 client workstation. If you plan to use to Control Center on this workstation in the future, be sure to complete the steps in the section *Configuring the Control Center*, earlier in the chapter. If you want to connect a DB2 client to a database that resides on a remote DB2 server, see the next section.

Configuring a DB2 Client to Communicate with a DB2 Server

This section describes how to configure a DB2 client to communicate with a DB2 server using the command-line processor. This section also assumes that TCP/IP is functional on the client and server workstations and was functional before you installed your DB2 server or DB2 client.

Before a DB2 client can be configured to communicate with a DB2 server, the DB2 server must have been configured to accept inbound client requests. By default, the DB2 Installer will autoconfigure your DB2 server for TCP/IP communications. If you did not use the DB2 Installer to install your DB2 server, you would have to configure inbound client communications manually using the command-line processor. For information on how to configure your DB2 server manually for inbound client communications, refer to the *DB2 and DB2 Connect Installation and Configuration Supplement.*

TIP

Due to the characteristics of the TCP/IP protocol, TCP/IP may not be immediately notified of the failure of another workstation. As a result, a DB2 client application accessing a remote DB2 server using TCP/IP, or the corresponding agent at the server, may sometimes appear to be hung. DB2 uses the TCP/IP SO_KEEPALIVE socket option to detect when there has been a failure and the TCP/IP connection has been broken.

If you are experiencing problems with your TCP/IP connection, refer to the *DB2 Troubleshooting Guide* for information on how to adjust this parameter, and for information about other common TCP/IP problems.

To configure a DB2 client to communicate with a DB2 server using TCP/IP, perform the following steps.

1. Identify and record the required TCP/IP parameters. These parameters are presented in Table 6.1.

Table 6.1 Required TCP/IP Parameters for DB2 Client-to-Server Communications

Parameter	Description	Sample Value	Your Value
Hostname (hostname) or **IP address (ip_address)**	Use the hostname or IP address of the remote DB2 server.	db2server or 9.21.125.124	
	To resolve this parameter:		
	■ Enter the **hostname** command at the DB2 server to obtain the hostname.		
	■ Enter the **ping hostname** command to obtain the IP address, or contact your system administrator.		

Continued

Table 6.1 Continued

Parameter	Description	Sample Value	Your Value
Service Name (svcename) **or** **Port number/Protocol (port_number/tcp)**	Values required in the **/etc/services** file. The Service Name is an arbitrary local name that represents the connection port number on a DB2 client. The port number for a DB2 client must be the same as the port number that the svcename name maps to in the **/etc/services** file on the DB2 server. (The svcename parameter is defined in the database manager configuration file on the DB2 server.) This port number must not be in use by any other applications, and must be unique within the **/etc/services** file. To determine the **svcename** parameter, log on to the DB2 server as a user with SYSADM authority and enter the **db2 get dbm cfg** command. The default **svcename** parameter for a default DB2 server installation is **db2cdb2inst1**, which	`db2cdb2inst1` maps to the port `50000/tcp`.	

Continued

Table 6.1 Continued

Parameter	Description	Sample Value	Your Value
	maps to the default port number **50000**. If you are following the instructions in this chapter, you can use these default values.		
Node name (node_name)	A local nickname for the remote DB2 server to which you are trying to connect. A computer is often referred to as a node. You can choose any name you want; however, all node name values within your local node directory must be unique. I recommend that you use the hostname of the remote DB2 server so that you always know to which workstation this node is referring.	db2server	

2. Ensure that the remote DB2 server's TCP/IP address can be resolved. If you are planning to specify the IP address of the remote DB2 server directly, or you have a name server on your network, you can skip this step. You can verify this by pinging your DB2 server using the **ping hostname** command.

The DB2 client must be able to resolve the address of the DB2 server to which it is attempting to establish communications. If a name server does not exist on your network, you must directly specify a hostname that maps to the IP address of the server in the local **/etc/hosts** file.

TIP

If you are planning on supporting any UNIX-based DB2 client that is using Network Information Services (NIS), and you are not using a name server on your network, you must update the /etc/hosts file located on your NIS master server.

As a user with *root* authority, edit the client's local **/etc/hosts** file and add an entry for the DB2 server's hostname. For example:

```
9.21.125.124     db2server   # host address for the computer db2server
```

where:

- 9.21.125.124 is the IP address of the remote DB2 server.
- db2server is the hostname of the remote DB2 server.
- # denotes the start of a comment describing this entry.

TIP

If the server is not in the same domain as the client, you must provide a fully qualified domain name such as db2server.vnet.com, where vnet.com is the domain name.

3. Update the local **/etc/services** file. If you are planning to set up communications between a DB2 client and a DB2 server using only the port number of the remote DB2 server, you can skip this step.

Using a local text editor, as a user with *root* authority, add an arbitrary Service Name and the port number that matches the remote DB2 server's port number to the DB2 client's services file for TCP/IP support. For example:

```
db2cdb2inst1  50000/tcp # DB2 client service name & matching DB2 server port
```

where:

- **db2cdb2inst1** is an arbitrary local name that represents the port number on the DB2 client.

- **50000** is the port number to which the **svcename** parameter in the database manager configuration file on the remote DB2 server maps, in the remote DB2 server's **/etc/services** file. The port number used on the DB2 client must match the port number used on the DB2 server.
- **tcp** is the communication protocol that you are using.
- # denotes the start of a comment describing this entry.

TIP

If you plan to support a UNIX-based DB2 client that uses Network Information Services (NIS), you must update the /etc/services file located on your NIS master server.

4. Catalog a TCP/IP node. You must add an entry to the DB2 client's node directory to describe the remote DB2 server. This entry specifies the chosen nickname (**node_name**), the **hostname** or IP address, and the **svcename** or port number that the DB2 client will use to access the remote DB2 server. To catalog a TCP/IP node, perform the following steps:

a. Log on to the system as a user with SYSADM or SYSCTRL authority. For our example, you can use the instance owner user ID **db2inst1**.

TIP

If you use this **su** command to log on to the system, you must enter this command with the – parameter; for example, **su – db2inst1**. If you do not use this parameter, you will receive an error, because DB2 will not read the DB2 profile correctly.

b. Catalog the TCP/IP node by entering the following commands with any variation of the parameters within the square brackets:

```
db2 "catalog tcpip node node_name remote [hostname or ip_address]
         server [svcename or port_number]"
db2 terminate
```

For example, to catalog the remote server db2server on the node called db2server, using the service name db2cdb2inst1, enter the following commands:

```
db2 "catalog tcpip node db2server remote db2server server db2cdb2inst1"

    db2 terminate
```

To catalog a remote server with the IP address **9.21.125.124** on the node called **db2server** using the port number **50000**, enter the following commands:

```
db2 "catalog tcpip node db2node remote 9.21.125.124 server 50000"

db2 terminate
```

5. Catalog the database. Before a client application can access a remote database, the database must be cataloged on the DB2 server and on any DB2 clients that will connect to it. When you create a database on a DB2 server, it is cataloged automatically on the DB2 server with the same database alias name as the database name. The information in the database directory, along with the information in the node directory, is used on the DB2 client to establish a connection to the remote database. To catalog a database, perform the following steps:

a. Identify and record the required database parameters. These parameters are presented in Table 6.2.

Table 6.2 Required Database Parameters for Client-to-Server Communications

Parameter	Description	Sample Value	Your Value
Database name (database_name)	The database alias (database_alias) of the remote DB2 database. When DB2 Installer created the SAMPLE database, it was automatically cataloged on the DB2 server with the database alias the same as the database name.	SAMPLE	

Continued

Table 6.2 Continued

Parameter	Description	Sample Value	Your Value
Database alias (database_alias)	A local nickname for the remote database, on the DB2 client. If you do not provide one, the default is the same as the database name parameter in this table. This name must be unique on the DB2 client. I recommend that you use the same name as the database name (the database alias name of the remote database) to avoid confusion. This is the name that you use when connecting to a database from the DB2 client.	**SAMPLE**	
Node name (node_name)	A local nickname for the remote DB2 server to which you are trying to connect. A computer is often referred to as a node. Use the same name that you used when you cataloged the node in the previous step.	db2server	

    b. Log on to the system as a user with SYSADM or SYSCTRL
      authority. For our example, you can use the instance owner
      user ID **db2inst1**.

TIP

If you use this su command to log on to the system, you must enter this command with the – parameter; for example, su – db2inst1. If you do not use this parameter, you will receive an error, because DB2 will not read the DB2 profile correctly.

c. Catalog the database by entering the following commands:

```
db2 "catalog database database_name as database_alias at node
node_name"
```

```
db2 terminate
```

For example, to catalog a remote database that was cataloged with the database alias **SAMPLE** so that it has the local database alias SAMPLE, on the node **db2server**, enter the following commands:

```
db2 "catalog database sample as sample at node db2server"
```

```
db2 terminate
```

6. You have finished configuring the client for communications! To connect the DB2 client to the DB2 server, perform the following steps.

NOTE

You must have the database manager on the remote DB2 server started before you can connect to the remote database. In our example, the instance that you created was set to autostart by default. If you have stopped this instance, you must enter the db2start command, as the db2inst1 user, on the remote DB2 server before completing these steps.

a. Log on to the system as the **db2inst1** user ID.

TIP

If you use this su command to log on to the system, you *must* enter this command with the – parameter; for example, su – db2inst1. If you do not use this parameter, you will receive an error, because DB2 will not read the DB2 profile correctly.

b. Enter the following command to connect to the remote database:

```
db2 connect to database_alias user userid using password
```

where:

- **database_alias** is the DB2 client's alias for the remote DB2 database.
- **userid** is a user ID that is defined on the remote DB2 server. For our example, use the **db2inst1** user.
- **password** is the password for the **userid** that you specified.

If you have been following our example, and you created the same user ID with the same passwords on both the DB2 server and the DB2 client, you do not have to specify the userid and password parameters with this command. By default, the DB2 client will pass the current user's user ID and password to the DB2 sever for authentication. Since they are the same, this will not be an issue for this example.

For example, to connect to a remote DB2 database with the database alias name SAMPLE, which was cataloged on the DB2 client with the local database alias name SAMPLE, as the user db2inst1, enter the following command:

```
db2 connect to sample
```

NOTE

You do not have to use the **userid** and **password** parameters when you connect to the remote DB2 database. When you installed the DB2 client, you created a user with the same user ID (**db2inst1**) and password as you did on the client. You did this to simplify the example. If you were logged on to the DB2 client with a user ID that was not defined on the remote DB2 server, you would have to use the **userid** and **password** parameters to specify a valid user.

You should receive the following output:

```
Database Connection Information

Database server        = DB2/LINUX 6.1.0
SQL authorization ID   = DB2INST1
Local database alias   = SAMPLE
```

c. Enter the following command to select a list of all employees that belong to department 20 in the staff table:

```
db2 "select * from staff where dept = 20"
```

NOTE

You must enter this command with the quotes ("") to ensure that Linux does not misinterpret the asterisk as an operating system command. If you ever issue a DB2 command with a character that may have special meaning on the operating system, you should enclose the contents of the command in quotation marks, as previously shown.

You should receive the following output:

```
ID      NAME    DEPT   JOB    YEARS   SALARY    COMM

10      Sanders 20     Mgr     7      18357.50    -
20      Pernal  20     Sales   8      18171.25   612.45
80      James   20     Clerk          13504.60   128.20
190     Sneider 20     Clerk   8      14252.75   126.50

       4 record(s) selected.
```

d. Enter the following command to reset the database connection:

```
db2  connect reset
```

Congratulations! You have successfully installed and connected a DB2 client to a remote DB2 server. This completes the typical client-to-server business model that you set out to install and configure.

Troubleshooting the Connection

If you are having problems connecting the DB2 client to the DB2 server, check the following items:

1. If used, the **/etc/services** and the **/etc/hosts** files were updated correctly.
2. The node was cataloged with the correct hostname or IP address and the correct service name or port number. Remember, the port number must match, or the service name must map to, the port number used on the DB2 server. To verify these settings, enter the following command as the **db2inst1** user:

   ```
   db2 list node directory
   ```

3. The node name that you specified when you cataloged the database points to the correct entry in the node directory. You can verify this by entering the following command as the **db2inst1** user:

   ```
   db2 list database directory
   ```

   Ensure that the **Node** name field matches the name you used when you create the node entry for the remote DB2 server.
4. The database on the DB2 client was cataloged properly, using the DB2 server's database alias name that was cataloged when the database was created on the DB2 server, as the database on the DB2 client. By default, the DB2 server's database alias name for the database name SAMPLE is SAMPLE.

If the connection still fails after you verify these items, see the *Troubleshooting Guide.*

Summary

So what have you accomplished? Well, believe it or not, companies around the world are scrambling to perform the very tasks that you just did! You installed a DB2 server, configured it for the graphical tools and communications, and then created a sample database. Then you installed a DB2 client and retrieved data from the DB2 server over a LAN connection using TCP/IP.

It's not too hard to see how far Linux has come in these last few years. Linux offers users stability, functionality and value that rivals any platform in the industry. Millions of users world-wide have chosen Linux for applications from Web and e-mail servers to departmental and enterprise vertical applications. Linux is no longer a pet project that IT professionals use behind closed doors, far from the watchful eyes of senior management. It's out there, and that senior management team had better be aware of it. Take a look at the plans of any major software or hardware distributor or manufacturer and you are going to find a business plan that includes Linux. Take a look at the recent turns in the stock markets, too. The recent flurry of Linux-related IPOs and the run-up of their stock is hard to miss.

Yes, there is truly a Linux craze out there, right in the middle of a database era. Now you have the building blocks to take advantage of what some consider to be the best in their fields, Red Hat and DB2.

FAQs

Q: I had started the DB2 Installer, but had to exit it abnormally. When I try to start the DB2 Installer again, I receive the error shown in Figure 6.27.

Figure 6.27 Error received when a previous instance of DB2 Installer was not stopped correctly.

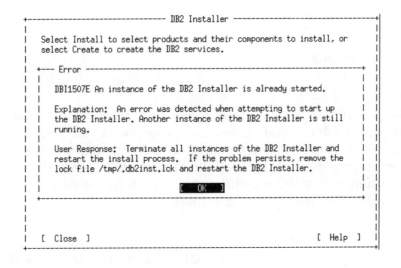

A: Because you did not exit the DB2 Installer correctly, the **/tmp/.db2inst.lck** file was not removed. To start the DB2 Installer program, you have to remove this file by entering the following command:

```
rm /tmp/.db2inst.lck
```

Once you remove this file, you can start DB2 Installer again.

Q: I did *not* choose to follow your instructions directly. During the installation of a DB2 server, I chose not to create the Administration Server. When I did this, I received the warning shown in Figure 6.28. So?

Figure 6.28 Warning shown when you select not to create the Administration Server on a server product.

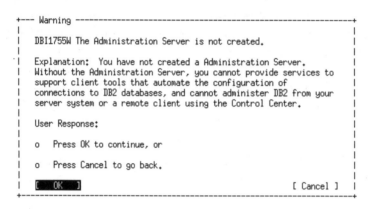

```
+--- Warning -------------------------------------------------------------+
|                                                                         |
|   DBI1755W The Administration Server is not created.                     |
|                                                                         |
|   Explanation:  You have not created a Administration Server.           |
|   Without the Administration Server, you cannot provide services to      |
|   support client tools that automate the configuration of               |
|   connections to DB2 databases, and cannot administer DB2 from your      |
|   server system or a remote client using the Control Center.            |
|                                                                         |
|   User Response:                                                        |
|                                                                         |
|   o    Press OK to continue, or                                         |
|                                                                         |
|   o    Press Cancel to go back.                                         |
|                                                                         |
|   [   OK   ]                                          [ Cancel ]  |
+-------------------------------------------------------------------------+
```

A: This is a standard warning that is displayed whenever you choose not to create the Administration Server. I *recommend* that you always select to create the Administration Server. Without the Administration Server, your system will not be able to administer other DB2 workstations remotely, schedule local jobs to run at different times, or be available for remote administration.

Q: When I entered the **db2start** command to start my instance's database manager, I received an **SQL10007N Message "-1393" could not be retrieved. Reason Code: "1"** error.

A: DB2 isn't aware what the default instance is. When you enter the **db2start** command, DB2 will attempt to start the default instance. The default instance is determined by the **DB2INSTANCE** environment variable, which is set by the DB2 Installer program during installation. The most common occurrence of this error is when you log on to your system using the **su** command without the – parameter, as discussed previously in this chapter. If you receive this error, enter the **export DB2INSTANCE=db2inst1** command (of course, if you wanted the default instance to be something other than the **db2inst1** instance, you would specify that instance instead).

Q: I used the default values (**db2cdb2inst1** and **50000**) that you said I could use when I configured the DB2 client to communicate with the DB2 server. The connection failed! I went through the *Troubleshooting the Client-to-Server* section, and I entered all of the commands correctly. What happened?

A: It could be a number of reasons; however, it probably has something to do with **svcename** and the **port number**. Have you ever had a previous installation of DB2 on this machine? The instructions in this chapter assumed that a previous version of DB2 has not been installed on this machine and the default service name and port number were available for use. If DB2 was installed on this machine, and removed, check the **/etc/services** file and see if **db2cdb2inst1** maps to **50000**. Perhaps when you removed DB2, you forgot to clean up the **/etc/services** file and this service name or port number was not available to the DB2 Installer. Did you change any of the default settings during the installation?

Q: I started the DB2 Installer after I had already installed a DB2 product. Why does the window look like Figure 6.29 all of a sudden?

Figure 6.29 DB2 Installer window after you have installed a DB2 product.

```
+--------------------------------------- DB2 Installer ----------------------------------------+
|                                                                                              |
|   Select Install to select products and their components to install, or                      |
|   select Create to create the DB2 services.                                                  |
|                                                                                              |
|                                                                                              |
|   To select products and their components, select                        [ Install... ]      |
|   Install.                                                                                    |
|                                                                                              |
|                                                                                              |
|   To create a DB2 Instance, or the Administration                        [ Create... ]       |
|   Server, select Create.                                                                      |
|                                                                                              |
|                                                                                              |
|                                                                                              |
|                                                                                              |
|                                                                                              |
|                                                                                              |
|                                                                                              |
|                                                                                              |
|                                                                                              |
|                                                                                              |
|                                                                                              |
|   [ Close ]                                                              [ Help ]             |
+----------------------------------------------------------------------------------------------+
```

A: After you have a DB2 product installed, the DB2 Installer main window will always appear different. This is because you are given more options. You can install an additional DB2 product by selecting **Install**. Or you can use the DB2 Installer creation feature to create any additional DB2 instances or the Administration Server, by selecting **Create**. If you use the DB2 Installer to create an instance or the **Administration** Server, it will be configured automatically for inbound DB2 client communications; otherwise, you will have to configure each one manually. I recommend that you use the DB2 Installer to create any instances on your workstation, or the Administration Server.

Q: Now that I have a DB2 client-to-server business model, where do I go from here?

A: Great question! The answer is that it depends on what you want to do. Here is a roadmap:

If you want to	Go and see
Install multiple DB2 clients without having to run the DB2 Installer program at each and every target DB2 client workstation	DB2 and DB2 Connect Installation and Configuration Supplement
Learn more about the functions of DB2 and how it works (for example, creating databases, table spaces, instances, backup and recovery schemes, etc.)	DB2 Administration Guide
Load data into your databases or export data from an existing DB2 database	DB2 Data Movement and Utilities Guide
Find out more of what IBM is doing with Linux, DB2, or other IBM products	http://www-4.ibm.com/software/data/db2/ or http://www-4.ibm.com/software/is/ mp/linux/
Find answers to problems with DB2	DB2 Troubleshooting Guide
Access data that resides on a host or AS/400 DB2 database	DB2 Connect Quick Beginnings
Learn more about DB2's SQL	DB2 SQL Getting Started Guide or the SQL Reference
Uninstall DB2	DB2 and DB2 Connect Installation and Configuration Supplement or DB2 Quick Beginnings for UNIX

MySQL on Linux

Solutions in this chapter:

- **Installation**
- **Configuration**
- **Issues**
- **Troubleshooting**

Introduction

MySQL is a complex database, yet the installation is not nearly as complex as you might think. By making a few decisions before you start your installation, you can make it a very smooth process. Before you begin, however, you should have a Linux machine available, and plenty of disk space. The machine should have roughly 30–40 MB of free space for the installation and database files. Memory is also a key factor—the more memory available in the machine for the database, the better. Generally, 64 megabytes or more will suffice.

MySQL comes in a variety of distributions, each with their respective positive and negative aspects. There are binary distributions, RPM (Red Hat Package Manager for Red Hat Linux) installations, and source distributions. Binary distributions and RPM distributions are the easiest to set up and can get you up and running in minutes. These distributions set up and configure most of the installation for you. Source distributions take more time to install and set up, but are the most powerful distributions, allowing users to configure and tweak their distributions to the fullest potential. Source distributions also free you from having to have a binary distribution created for you. Source distributions can be highly optimized for a specific type of platform, allowing you to generate a database that will run as fast as possible on your platform.

Each distribution also has a different level of development; some of them are bleeding-edge distributions, only for those who want to check out the new features even if there are more frequent crashes. The stable versions, which are recommended for first-time users, contain all the major features and are completely robust and well tested. The latter versions are for those upgrading from past versions and are behind the stable versions. These are for historical purposes only. For any type of database that will be supporting an application, you should use the stable versions. Most likely, unless you need a new feature that is being developed in the new versions, a stable version will provide all the necessary features.

Installation of these distributions, especially for the binary and RPM distributions, are covered next, and should not take very long to complete. These are very easy to install and will get you on your way to leveraging the power of MySQL in your application. The source distribution takes a few more steps, but the steps are not very complex and are fully explained. Once you have completed one source distribution, you can tackle most other open-source distributions. Power users can use the source distribution to optimize their speed and how they want the database to perform. Even if you do not install the other types of distributions, it is good to review them and get a feel for how they are set up, in case your platform changes or you want to move to a different type of distribution.

Once installed, the next steps are to secure the database. Making sure that only authorized users can access the database is a very important step. Depending on your application, database security should be taken seriously, especially in e-commerce applications where data is very sensitive, such as credit card numbers. Each user should be required to have a password. The users will also be granted certain privileges based on what type of usage they expect from the database. If a user only needs to read from the tables, this can be accomplished without giving the user the power to execute any command on the database. Users and privileges are important ways to prevent unauthorized access and usage of your database.

A database should always be available. Installing custom scripts to your server to make sure the database is always running will keep the database up. The scripts that start the database also make sure the database is constantly running, keeping downtime to a minimum. There are other tools that will give vital information about the database and how much work it is doing, and tools to make sure the administration of the database is an easy task, allowing an administrator to perform all the common tasks of a DBA. There are also some ways to increase the performance of your MySQL installation, by using performance attributes of the MySQL database, compiling your distribution for more optimization, and using different hardware setups. All of these steps will allow you to set up a powerful database for your application.

Installation

Before installing MySQL, you must first decide on one of three versions. The recommended one is the stable version, labeled *3.22.X*. This version is very well tested, does not have any untested features, is ready for production, and is recommended for first-time users. The development version, *3.23.X*, is targeted mainly towards developers contributing to the improvement of MySQL, and has many untested new features. This version is not recommended in a production environment. The last version, *3.21.X*, is a deprecated version. This mainly provides a way for previous users to upgrade to this version without any major changes in functionality. This is also more of a historical version and not intended to be used.

After choosing the version, a decision between binary, RPM, and source distributions must be made. A binary distribution is already compiled for you. All you need to do is install it and decide on the location of the files. The drawback is you must find the appropriate binary for your platform.

Not all platforms are kept up to date for each version. The RPM distribution is for those with a Red Hat Linux distribution. It is similar to a binary in that it is already compiled and it even sets up the system environment for you. The last option is the source distribution. This distribution allows the most customization, comes with more documentation and examples, and can be optimized for speed. Binaries may require root privileges, and RPM distributions must be installed as the root user. Both binaries and RPMs are platform-specific. The source distribution is highly customizable, not platform-specific, can be run by any user, and is recommended over the other two distributions for these reasons.

For the next part of the installation, you need to locate a MySQL distribution. It is best to get the distribution from a *mirror*, a site that copies the latest files from the official site to its own location. You can find a mirror site that is close to you, which will probably decrease your download time depending on how close the mirror site is. Mirrors also help drive traffic away from the official site, helping to preserve bandwidth. The list of mirror sites can be found at http://www.mysql.com/mirrors.html.

Of course you can always download the distribution from the official site if you cannot find an appropriate mirror site. The official location is http://www.mysql.com/download.html.

Naming Conventions

The MySQL distributions are in the **Downloads** directory. As of this writing, the latest development distribution is 3.22.32. The examples that follow show the different types of formatting for each one. The X denotes the minor version.

For binaries, you will see the following:

mysql-3.22.X-PLATFORM.tar.gz

For RPMs:

MySQL-3.22.X-1.PLATFORM.rpm (the server)
MySQL-bench-3.22.X-1.PLATFORM.rpm (tests and benchmarks)
MySQL-client-3.22.X-1.PLATFORM.rpm (client)
MySQL-devel-3.22.X-1.PLATFORM.rpm (for custom clients)

For source:

mysql-3.22.X.tar.gz

These are the files you need for each respective distribution.

You might also notice that some files have an extra tag on them—either *alpha*, *beta*, or *gamma*. These specify how mature the distribution is. *Alpha* denotes that there are new features that have been implemented but not tested. This is not a well-tested distribution, and should be used only to experiment. *Beta* is a distribution that has new features with some testing, but generally needs more broad testing, which the users

For Managers

MySQL Versions, Licensing, and Support

MySQL is an open-source package, which means that the source code to the database and relevant tools are freely available. This is immensely powerful for many reasons. One is that if there are any problems with the database, they may be able to be fixed if competent developers are on hand. Open source software is also being updated constantly. This brings the user the latest and greatest features of the database, but it can also add an extra burden of management. Keeping up with the latest version and relevant versions of libraries and tools in the support environment can be a bit much at times. Even though versions are constantly changing, you do not have to constantly upgrade. Once you have a distribution in a server environment up and running, you do not have to upgrade as soon as the next version appears, especially if all the functionality necessary in your application exists. It is better to wait for a few revisions after the next major release. Keep up-to-date on the latest features being added; if the feature is something that is necessary for the application, it might be worth upgrading right away. Also, if a feature you are currently using has a bug or related problem, upgrading sooner to alleviate the problem is advised.

MySQL requires no license for usage, even in commercial applications. If you sell the server along with other services, charge for installation of MySQL, or include MySQL in a distribution that charges for usage, you will require a license. The license is required per CPU; in the case of multiple CPUs, it still counts as a single CPU. The latest prices can be found at http://www.mysql.com/Manual_chapter/manual_Licensing_and_Support.html#Cost. As of this writing, One CPU was $200, with discounts of $10 up to $50.

If you benefit from using MySQL either in commerce or other applications, they ask that you buy a support license to help further the development. The support is separated into four different types: basic e-mail, extended e-mail, login support, and extended login support. The basic starts at EURO 170, extended e-mail at EURO 1000, login support at EURO 2000, and extended login support at EURO 5000.

Continued

> If you decide to use binary distributions with MySQL, it is best to stick with the same platform throughout. The binary distributions are not updated as frequently, and new versions might not be available to you for a while after their release. If you use a Linux-based machine on the Intel platform, you should have access to the latest binaries. Other platforms might not be as up-to-date with their binary distributions.

can help with. *Gamma* usually indicates that it is a stable release and is available for full-time use. Again, unless the new features are needed, the gamma releases will have all the features you will need.

To unpack these distributions, you will need a few GNU tools, such as **tar** and **gunzip**. You can determine if you have these tools with the following commands:

```
shell$ which tar
/bin/tar
shell$ which gunzip
/usr/bin/gunzip
```

If a pathname shows up below, the tool is installed in that directory. If these tools do not exist, refer to the documentation of your Linux distribution to determine how to add them. The location of these files is also determined by your PATH environment variable settings. If nothing shows up, you can also try looking in these directories for the files. You can also query RPM for Red Hat Linux:

```
shell$ rpm -q make
gzip-1.2.4-14

shell$ rpm -q gzip
make-3.77-6
```

These tools can be installed from your distribution or from GNU distributions. More information can be found at the GNU Web site: http://www.gnu.org/software/software.html.

Installation of Binary Distribution

After you download the file, move it to the directory where you want to install the files, such as **/usr/local** (this may require root privileges). To unpack the distribution, execute the following command in the same directory where you moved the file.

```
shell$ gunzip -c mysql-3.22.X-PLATFORM.tar.gz | tar -xvf -
```

This will create a directory of the same name: **mysql-3.22.X-PLATFORM**. We can create a link to this directory to make it easier to reference:

```
shell$ ln -s mysql-3.22.X-PLATFORM mysql
```

The next step will install and set up the database and relevant tables. Change into the new **mysql** directory and run the following:

```
shell$ scripts/mysql_install_db
Creating db table
Creating host table
Creating user table
Creating func table
Creating tables_priv table
Creating columns_priv table

To start mysqld at boot time you have to copy support-files/mysql.server
to the right place for your system

PLEASE REMEMBER TO SET A PASSWORD FOR THE MySQL root USER !
This is done with:
./bin/mysqladmin -u root password 'new-password'
See the manual for more instructions.

Please report any problems with the ./bin/mysqlbug script!

The latest information about MySQL is available on the Web at
http://www.mysql.com
Support MySQL by buying support/licenses at http://www.tcx.se/license.htmy.
```

The database can then be started in the same directory:

```
shell$ /bin/safe_mysqld &
```

You are now ready to configure your database.

Installation of RPM Distribution

This type of installation requires root privileges, but will perform the entire configuration and setup for you. Make sure you download at least the client and server RPMs listed earlier, and make sure they are the same version. For minimal installation without custom clients all you need are the following:

```
MySQL-3.22.X-1.PLATFORM.rpm
MySQL-client-3.22.X-1.PLATFORM.rpm
```

You will also need the latest **rpm** tool, which comes with the Red Hat Linux distribution. If your installation does not have this installed, refer to your Red Hat documentation for installation of this tool. The database files can then be all installed together as follows:

```
shell# rpm -vi MySQL-3.22.X-1.PLATFORM.rpm MySQL-client-3.22.X-x.PLATFORM.rpm
```

You can verify that is installed:

```
shell$ rpm -q MySQL
```

```
MySQL-3.22.X-1
```

This will install all the necessary files and start the database. It will also set up the necessary scripts in the **/etc** that will start the database each time the machine is booted. This distribution will also create a user named **mysql** for the database to run as. The files will also be owned by this user, to prevent tampering. The database will even be started for you. The next step is configuring your database.

Installation of Source Distribution

In addition to these tools, you will also need the GNU tools **gcc** and **make**. You can determine if you have these tools with the following commands:

```
shell$ which gcc
/usr/bin/gcc
shell$ which make
/usr/bin/make
```

The **gcc** that is installed must be version 2.81 or later. You can determine your version with the following:

```
shell$ gcc -v
Reading specs from /usr/lib/gcc-lib/i386-redhat-linux/egcs-2.91.66/specs
gcc version egcs-2.91.66 19990314/Linux (egcs-1.1.2 release)
```

If this is not the correct version, refer to your Linux distribution documentation to find out how to upgrade. Also, visit the GNU Web site listed earlier for help in the installation of these tools.

To unpack the distribution, execute the following command in the same directory where you moved the file.

```
shell$ gunzip -c mysql-3.22.X.tar.gz | tar -xvf -
```

This will create the directory **mysql-3.22.X**. Change into that directory and run **configure** to determine your environment information and prepare for compilation. There are a few options you can pass to **configure** in order to include other system variables to override the default (**/usr/local/mysql**):

- prefix=/path (where files are installed)
- localstatedir=/path (where database files are installed)
- with-charset=CHARSET (which language to install)

You can refer to many more options in the documentation:

```
shell$ ./configure --prefix=/my/home/
```

Now compile everything using **make**:

```
shell$ ./make
```

Install all files into the prefix directory:

```
shell$ ./make install
```

Change into the directory where you installed the files and set up the necessary tables:

```
shell$ ./scripts/mysql_install_db
Creating db table
Creating host table
Creating user table
Creating func table
Creating tables_priv table
Creating columns_priv table

To start mysqld at boot time you have to copy support-files/mysql.server
to the right place for your system

PLEASE REMEMBER TO SET A PASSWORD FOR THE MySQL root USER !
This is done with:
/usr/local/mysql/bin/mysqladmin -u root password 'new-password'
See the manual for more instructions.

Please report any problems with the /usr/local/mysql/bin/mysqlbug script!

The latest information about MySQL is available on the Web at
http://www.mysql.com
Support MySQL by buying support/licenses at http://www.tcx.se/license.htmy.
```

You can now start the database server:

```
shell$ /my/home/mysql/bin/safe_mysqld &
```

You can check and see if the database is running as follows:

```
shell$ ps -aux | grep mysql | grep -v grep
mysql     1877  0.1  0.7 10636 1004 ttya2  SN  17:14    0:00 /usr/sbin/mysqld
mysql     1879  0.0  0.7 10636 1004 ttya2  SN  17:14    0:00 /usr/sbin/mysqld
mysql     1880  0.0  0.7 10636 1004 ttya2  SN  17:14    0:00 /usr/sbin/mysqld
```

These lines show the database running, at which user it is running, and system information about the process. If these lines do not show up the database is not running. Please check your earlier steps and make sure you are able to start the database. For most of the configuration, operations such as adding users and privileges can be done only when the database is running.

Configuration

The basic layout of the MySQL directory is set up in two different ways, depending on which distribution you have installed. For binaries, it looks like this:

bin	main and support programs
data	the databases themselves and log files
include	header files
lib	libraries
scripts	scripts used for installation
share/mysql	error messages
sql-bench	benchmarks

For source distributions, it looks like this:

bin	main and support programs
include/mysql	include files
info	documentation
lib/mysql	libraries
libexec	the server istelf
share/mysql	log files for errors
sql-bench	benchmarks and test suites
var	the database files and log files

Security

Restricting user access to the database and only letting them perform certain actions will help improve your application. This is an important step that cannot be stressed enough. If this database is merely being set up for evaluation, this is not needed. Any service or application that will use this database to store live data should be secured.

Let's start by changing the password for the root user in the database. This is done as follows:

```
shell$ /my/path/mysql/bin/mysqladmin -u root password 'new-password'
```

Also, make sure that any new users that are created in the database have passwords.

Another easy way to set up MySQL to be secure is to run it as its own user. Running the daemon as a new user and setting all the file permissions to that user will prevent tampering by other users and make it more secure. Also, not running the daemon as root will prevent attempts by crackers to attack the daemon to get root privileges.

If you installed the Red Hat RPM, then this part of the configuration is done for you. If you installed the binary or source distribution, you need to complete some further steps.

A user should be created for the database to run as, such as **mysql**. This can be added to the password file using **adduser**.

```
shell$ /usr/sbin/adduser mysql
```

Once an entry has been made in **/etc/passwd** for this user, it can be edited to point to the correct database directory (**/my/path/mysql/var**) along with the appropriate shell (default is fine).

This user should own all of the files. You can do this with **chmod**:

```
shell$ chmod -R mysql /my/path/mysql
```

You can also make sure that only this new user has write permission:

```
shell$ chmod -R go-w /my/path/mysql
```

which will set all the files in **/my/path/mysql** to be owned by this user. Make sure that only this user **mysql** has the privilege to write to these files.

MySQL also has runtime options to make it run more securely:

- **secure** Does a reverse lookup on the IP addresses and makes sure they are not forged. This will add an extra layer of protection from requests coming from the outside that are trying to change their remote address to bypass any restrictions.
- **skip-networking** Allows only connections on the local machine and not over the network. This is another good option if the machine on which the database runs is not protected by a firewall.

Please see the MySQL documentation for further security enhancements to the MySQL daemon for protection.

Privileges

MySQL allows different users to perform different actions on, and with, the database based on their privileges. These privileges are stored in a table and checked when the user tries to execute an action. The following privileges are set up in MySQL:

select. Reads from a row in a table.

insert. Creates a row in a table.

update. Updates a row in a table.

delete. Removes a row in a table.

index. Adds/removes indexes on a table.

alter. Allows ALTER TABLE **sql** command.

create. Creates a database/table.

drop. Removes a database/table.

grant. Gives users privileges.

file. Reads and writes external files to the database.

reload. Reloads or flushes tables.

shutdown. Shuts down the database properly.

process. Displays or removes processes.

These privileges will determine what actions you can perform on the database. Not all users should be able to use the more powerful features, such as **grant**, **alter**, **file**, **process**, and **shutdown**. Those should be reserved for the administrator.

After the root password is changed, let's add some new users. There are two main ways to add new users to the database: using the **grant** option or using SQL to insert new rows into the user tables.

For **grant**, first make sure the database is up, and use **mysql** to make a connection.

```
./mysql -p —user=root mysql
Enter password:
Reading table information for completion of table and column names
You can turn off this feature to get a quicker startup with -A

Welcome to the MySQL monitor.  Commands end with ; or \g.
Your MySQL connection id is 3 to server version: 3.22.30

Type 'help' for help.


mysql>
```

The user table looks as follows:

```
mysql> describe user;
```

Field	Type	Null	Key	Default	Extra
Host	char(60)		PRI		
User	char(16)		PRI		
Password	char(16)				
Select_priv	enum('N','Y')			N	
Insert_priv	enum('N','Y')			N	
Update_priv	enum('N','Y')			N	
Delete_priv	enum('N','Y')			N	
Create_priv	enum('N','Y')			N	
Drop_priv	enum('N','Y')			N	
Reload_priv	enum('N','Y')			N	
Shutdown_priv	enum('N','Y')			N	
Process_priv	enum('N','Y')			N	
File_priv	enum('N','Y')			N	
Grant_priv	enum('N','Y')			N	
References_priv	enum('N','Y')			N	
Index_priv	enum('N','Y')			N	
Alter_priv	enum('N','Y')			N	

```
17 rows in set (0.01 sec)
```

The host field is the location from which the user is connecting. The database will let you connect based on your username and the IP address or hostname from which you are connecting. This information is matched with this list, which compares hostname, username, and password to see if the connection should be granted. The hostname maybe be a full hostname or an IP address, such as **test.machine.com** or **1.2.3.4**. Wildcards can also be used, symbolized by **%**, to allow a broader range and allowing you to be less specific when specifying a whole LAN or domain; for example, **%.machine.com** or **1.2.3.%**.

Once you have the **mysql** prompt, you are at the database command level and can now execute SQL commands. Here we will execute **GRANT** statements and create an administrator and a user account:

```
mysql> GRANT ALL PRIVILEGES ON *.* TO dba@localhost
            IDENTIFIED BY 'dbapassword' WITH GRANT OPTION;
mysql> GRANT ALL PRIVILEGES ON *.* TO dba@"%"
            IDENTIFIED BY 'dbapassword' WITH GRANT OPTION;
```

This will allow our new user **dba** to connect both locally or from anywhere remotely, and use all the privileges of the database. The new user's password is now **dbapassword**. We can now use the **GRANT** command to add another local user with less privileges:

```
Mysql> GRANT SELECT,INSERT ON *.* TO testuser@localhost
                IDENTIFIED BY 'testuserpassword'
```

This user can now connect from the local machine, with a password of **testuserpassword**, and can run **SELECT** and **INSERT** on tables.

If you know SQL well, you can bypass **GRANT** and insert the data into the user table yourself. We now can manipulate this table directly with the **INSERT** command, with the preceding dba account example as follows:

```
mysql> INSERT INTO user VALUES('localhost','dba',PASSWORD('dbapassword'),
                  'Y','Y','Y','Y','Y','Y','Y','Y','Y','Y','Y','Y','Y','Y')
mysql> INSERT INTO user VALUES('%','dba',PASSWORD('dbapassword'),
                  'Y','Y','Y','Y','Y','Y','Y','Y','Y','Y','Y','Y','Y','Y')
```

The

```
mysql> INSERT INTO user
VALUES('localhost','testuser',PASSWORD('tsetuserpassword'),
                  'Y','Y','N','N','N','N','N','N','N','N','N','N','N','N')
mysql> FLUSH PRIVILEGES;
```

There are two more tables that can be used to grant access. The **db** table states the users that can access which databases, from which hosts they can connect, and the allowed privileges.

The **db** table looks like this:

```
mysql> describe db;
```

Field	Type	Null	Key	Default	Extra
Host	char(60)		PRI		
Db	char(32)		PRI		
User	char(16)		PRI		
Select_priv	enum('N','Y')			N	
Insert_priv	enum('N','Y')			N	
Update_priv	enum('N','Y')			N	
Delete_priv	enum('N','Y')			N	
Create_priv	enum('N','Y')			N	
Drop_priv	enum('N','Y')			N	
Grant_priv	enum('N','Y')			N	

References_priv	enum('N','Y')			N	
Index_priv	enum('N','Y')			N	
Alter_priv	enum('N','Y')			N	

13 rows in set (0.00 sec)

Another table, the *host* table, determines which hosts are allowed to connect to which database. The host table looks like this:

```
mysql> describe host;
```

Field	Type	Null	Key	Default	Extra
Host	char(60)		PRI		
Db	char(32)		PRI		
Select_priv	enum('N','Y')			N	
Insert_priv	enum('N','Y')			N	
Update_priv	enum('N','Y')			N	
Delete_priv	enum('N','Y')			N	
Create_priv	enum('N','Y')			N	
Drop_priv	enum('N','Y')			N	
Grant_priv	enum('N','Y')			N	
References_priv	enum('N','Y')			N	
Index_priv	enum('N','Y')			N	
Alter_priv	enum('N','Y')			N	

12 rows in set (0.01 sec)

Access Control

Once you have configured the privileges and the user- and hostnames of where you want to grant access, each connection will be evaluated to determine if it should be allowed. MySQL will look at the username and host first. When the connection is made, all the parameters are matched against the entries in this list. It will keep comparing them from the beginning until the end until the first one is matched. If it is not matched, the request is denied. Make sure the list is sorted correctly; the database does not match all cases, just the first one it comes to that works.

If the connection is allowed, the database will then verify that you have access to the database(s) you are trying to access. It will then consult the db and host tables and match up your host with the database you are trying to access. Unlike for the previous check, the database will consult the tables based on the type of access that is requested.

Administrative requests check only the user table, because it is the only table where administrative privileges are located. If the user has this privilege, the action will be granted or otherwise denied. Database-related ones used to manipulate rows in a table are first checked in the user table. If the user does not have these privileges, the database will then go to the db and host tables and verify that this request should be granted. If the user is not listed in the db table, the request is denied. If the user's host field is blank, it will cross-reference it with the host table and determine if the access should be granted.

By setting up a simple access control list, you easily can specify which users can connect to your database, and from which host. This is extremely powerful. You can exclude everyone from outside your domain and allow only people in the local network or allow only specific users from specified IP addresses.

System Setup

To keep the database running all the time, you must set up your system to start the database automatically when it boots up. This is set up in the **/etc/rc.d** directory on your machine. If you set up the RPM distribution, this is already done for you. A file can be created that will set up the environment and the pathnames, and then load the database daemon. Here we will set up by creating an **rc** script to accomplish this. Creating **rc** scripts requires root privileges and can be done only by the administrator.

First, let's create a new script in the **rc** directory called **mysql**. Change into **/etc/rc.d/init.d** and create the **mysql** file. Here we will set up the environment for the database. All scripts start by telling the system which shell to perform **execute** with the following:

```
#!/bin/sh
```

Next, we set up the path and directory names:

```
PATH=/sbin:/usr/sbin:/bin:/usr/bin
basedir=/my/path/mysql
pid_file=/my/path/mysql/var/mysqld.pid
mysql_daemon_user=mysql
export PATH
```

Then we set up the startup part of the script. This will change into the **mysql** directory specified previously; make sure the **safe_mysqld** program exists, and then executes it, specifying the user and **pid_file** to use as defined earlier. The **pid** file contains the process id, which can be used to stop the process in the later half of the script.

```
mode=$1
```

```
cd $basedir

case "$mode" in
  'start')
    # Start daemon
    if test -x bin/safe_mysqld
    then
      # Startup database
      bin/safe_mysqld —user=$mysql_daemon_user —pid-file=$pid_file &
    else
      echo "Can't execute $basedir/bin/safe_mysqld"
    fi
    ;;
```

The last part will stop the database using the **pid** file generated earlier.

```
  'stop')
    # Stop daemon using the pid file
    if test -f "$pid_file"
    then
      mysqld_pid='cat $pid_file'
      echo "Stopping database with pid $mysqld_pid"
      kill $mysqld_pid
    else
      echo "Cannot find $pid_file."
    fi
    ;;
```

Finally, we provide some syntax specifications and exit:

```
  *)
    # usage
    echo "usage: $0 start|stop"
    exit 1
    ;;
esac
```

Again, this should be placed in **/etc/rc.d/init.d/mysql**. To make sure this gets executed upon bootup, make a symbolic link in each of the run-level directories to start and stop it.

Execute this in the **rc0.d**, **rc1.d**, and **rc6.d** directories:

```
shell$ ln -s ../init.d/mysql K90mysql
```

Execute this in the **rc2.d**, **rc3.d**, **rc4.d**, and **rc5.d** directories:

```
shell$ ln -s ../init.d/mysql S90mysql
```

This should start the database server upon boot and shut it down during the reboot/shutdown phase of the server. This occurs in different run-levels; this is why a script has to be linked in each level's directory, depending on the run level. Knowing run levels is important for administrative purposes; for more information on run levels, see your Linux distribution documentation. Other important applications related to the database can be started here as well.

Performance

A few optimizations can be done to improve the performance of MySQL with the compiler. By using the **-static** flag you will get the fastest database possible. Also, by using UNIX sockets and not using network connections will improve performance as well.

Different hardware configurations also help. By storing the database across multiple disks, the wait for head movements and seek times goes down because more disks are doing the work instead of one being the bottleneck. This is also known as *striping*. For striping on a larger scale, using a Redundant Array of Independent Disks (RAID) will give you the best results.

Using symbolic links also helps by making links to directories in the distributions that are on other drives. Removing the swap file also helps too, for the operating system could be slowing down the database access by using the drive heads to swap out programs from memory.

The MySQL daemon itself also can be tuned. There are a variety of variables that can be tuned to increase performance. These can be set with the **mysqladmin** tool.

```
shell$ ./mysqladmin variables
```

Variable_name	Value
back_log	5
connect_timeout	5
basedir	/home/bschwab/mysql/
datadir	/home/bschwab/mysql/var/
delayed_insert_limit	100
delayed_insert_timeout	300
delayed_queue_size	1000
join_buffer	131072
flush_time	0

```
| key_buffer                | 8388600                                    |
| language                  | /home/bschwab/mysql/share/mysql/english/   |
| log                       | OFF                                        |
| log_update                | OFF                                        |
| long_query_time           | 10                                         |
| low_priority_updates      | OFF                                        |
| max_allowed_packet        | 1048576                                    |
| max_connections           | 100                                        |
| max_connect_errors        | 10                                         |
| max_delayed_insert_threads| 20                                         |
| max_join_size             | 4294967295                                 |
| max_sort_length           | 1024                                       |
| max_write_lock_count      | 4294967295                                 |
| net_buffer_length         | 16384                                      |
| pid_file                  | /home/bschwab/mysql/var/obsidian.pid       |
| port                      | 3306                                       |
| protocol_version          | 10                                         |
| record_buffer             | 131072                                     |
| skip_locking              | ON                                         |
| skip_networking           | OFF                                        |
| socket                    | /tmp/mysql.sock                            |
| sort_buffer               | 2097144                                    |
| table_cache               | 64                                         |
| thread_stack              | 65536                                      |
| tmp_table_size            | 1048576                                    |
| tmpdir                    | /tmp/                                      |
| version                   | 3.22.30                                    |
| wait_timeout              | 28800                                      |
+---------------------------+--------------------------------------------+
```

The variables are as follows:

backlog. Amount of requests waiting to be filled. This is the listen queue for incoming TCP/IP connections and is very operating-system specific.

concurrent_inserts. ON (default) allows INSERTS on MyISAM (disk-based) tables while SELECTS are occurring.

connect_timeout. Number of seconds to timeout on network connection.

delayed_insert_timeout. Time to wait for INSERT DELAYED before dropping request.

delayed_insert_limit. How long to wait for SELECTS after INSERT DELAYED.

delay_key_write. The default allows **delay_key_write** on CREATE TABLE, which speeds up writing on keys.

delayed_queue_size. Queue size in rows for INSERT DELAYED.

flush_time. Flushes all tables after this many seconds.

init_file. Loads an initialization file on startup.

interactive_timeout. How long in seconds the database will leave an inactive connection open before it is closed.

join_buffer_size. Buffer size for table joins, allocated only at join; used for faster joins.

key_buffer_size. Size of buffer for index blocks; increasing gives better index handling.

long_query_time. Sets the **slow_queries** counter when the query takes longer than this.

max_allowed_packet. Maximum size of a packet; used to protect the database from bogus connections. Might need to be increased for BLOB columns.

max_connections. Number of connections allowed at one time.

max_connect_errors. After this many errors, a connection from this host will be disallowed.

max_delayed_threads. Number of threads for INSERT DELAYED.

max_join_size. Maximum size of a join.

max_sort_length. Sorting size when using BLOB or TEXT values.

max_tmp_tables. Not yet implemented.

net_buffer_length. Buffer size is always reset to this for requests between queries.

net_retry_count. Number of retries before aborting connection.

record_buffer. Buffer size of sequential table scan per thread.

skip_show_databases. Prevent users from seeing the database table for security reasons.

sort_buffer. Thread sort buffer size.

table_cache. How many open tables are available for threads. This will consume more file descriptors.

tmp_table_size. Size of temporary tables.

thread_concurrency. Number of threads being run at the same time.

> **thread_stack.** Size of the stack per thread.
>
> **wait_timeout.** Same as **interactive_timeout**.

Issues

Depending on your Linux distribution, MySQL might have some problems running. MySQL works best with the latest version of **glibc**. This is the C library on which the database is based. MySQL requires at least version 2.0.7 of **glibc**. Most problems are related to not having the latest version of this library. You can find out which version is installed on your system with the following:

```
shell$ rpm -q glibc
```

If you use a binary distribution instead, you do not have to worry about the library version you are using. Older distributions have **libc**, the predecessor to **glibc**. As long as **libc** is at least 5.4.46, it will work. For Red Hat 4.X, there is a problem with resolving hostnames with older **libc**. This can be fixed by updating to at least **libc**, 5.4.46. For Red Hat 5.X, installing the latest **glibc** should work with the following RPMs:

```
glibc-2.0.7-19
```

```
glibc-devel-2.0.7-19
```

Updating libraries requires root privileges. If you do not have root privileges, ask your system administrator to install or upgrade these libraries to the latest versions.

Threads

MySQL also uses threads under Linux. Threads are smaller pieces of a program that can allow more work to get done by the machine than with a single process. As long as the latest **glibc** is in place, this should work without having to install any new programs. This can be downloaded at http://www.mysql.com/Downloads/Linux.

Also, with **glibc** versions that are 2.1.1 or below, a problem occurs with **INSERT DELAYED** commands. This can be fixed with a patch at http://www.mysql.com/Downloads/Patches/glibc-pthread_cond_timed-wait.patch.

MySQL development version 3.23.7 contains a temporary work-around for this problem.

Run Environment

Once MySQL is installed, there are a variety of tools to gather information about your database. The first tool, **mysqladmin**, performs most of the administrative duties that you will need including creating and deleting databases, flush tables, change passwords for users, reload, shutdown, and find out the status of the database.

First, go into the bin directory of your MySQL installation:

```
shell$ cd /my/path/mysql/bin
```

You can run **mysqladmin** with no arguments to find a complete list of all its features:

```
shell$ ./mysqladmin
```

To find the version:

```
shell$ ./mysqladmin version
./mysqladmin  Ver 7.15 Distrib 3.22.30, for pc-linux-gnu on i686
TCX Datakonsult AB, by Monty


Server version          3.22.30
Protocol version        10
Connection              Localhost via UNIX socket
UNIX socket             /tmp/mysql.sock
Uptime:                 10 min 33 sec


Threads: 1  Questions: 3  Slow queries: 0  Opens: 6  Flush tables: 1  Open
tables: 2
```

To find the status:

```
shell$ ./mysqladmin status
Uptime: 901  Threads: 1  Questions: 4  Slow queries: 0  Opens: 6  Flush
tables: 1  Open tables: 2
```

You can also see all the environment variables with the following:

```
shell$ ./mysqladmin variables
```

To create your first database, use **mysqladmin** to create the database. The **–p** option asks for the password:

```
shell$ ./mysqladmin -p create MYDATABASE
```

Once created, it can be removed, or "dropped" with the following:

```
shell$ ./mysqladmin -p drop MYDATABASE
```

To shutdown the database properly, you would also use **mysqladmin**:

```
shell$ ./mysqladmin -p shutdown
```

You can import and export data easily from MySQL using **mysqldump** and **mysqlimport**. With these tools you can dump the entire database for re-importing into the database later. This is an easy form of backing up all the data in the database.

Other tools that come with the MySQL distribution are:

myisamchk. Checks, optimizes, repairs, and describes the MySQL tables.

make_binary_release. Creates a binary release of MySQL from a compiled version.

msql2mysql. Converts programs written for **msql** to MySQL.

mysqlaccess. Checks access privileges for host, user, and database records from the database.

mysqladmin. Provides general administration for MySQL.

mysqlbug. Files bug reports to MySQL mailing list.

mysqld. The actual MySQL database daemon.

mysqldump. Exports a database to a file.

mysqlimport. Imports a file into the database.

mysqlshow. Shows the information about databases and tables.

mysql_install_db. Script used at the beginning of installation to set up the initial tables.

replace. Script to replace strings; used by **msql2mysql**.

safe_mysqld. Script that keeps the **mysqld** daemon running, and restarts it when it dies.

Troubleshooting

In case of trouble with the MySQL database server, there is a log file in the data directory with a .err extension. This file will most likely contain logging information when errors do occur. If there is no information regarding why it crashed, you might also want to enable the **–log** run time option for **mysqld**. This will also add extra logging information about what the database is doing. There is also a **–debug** option to add more logging information.

A few items to note:

- Make sure you have the latest version in your distribution for the database.

- Make sure you have the latest **glibc** or **libc** (depending on your distribution).

- Check user permissions on all of the files that the database user owns.

- Check the status with **mysqladmin** to make sure the load times do not look abnormal.

- If you have problems connecting make sure that your access control is set up correctly for the user, password, and hostname; and that the server is actually running (can be checked with the **ps** command).

- Make sure no other program took the same port that MySQL runs as.

- If a thread has died, you must kill all other threads before starting the database again.

- Try connecting locally and remotely. If remotely fails, check to make sure the networking options are on. If locally fails, make sure UNIX sockets are turned on.

- Make sure there are enough connections for all of your clients.

- Make sure there is plenty of memory for the database. Very large databases tend to use up resources quickly.

- Make sure the performance settings are set correctly for table sizes. Make sure tables do not grow too large.

- Make sure no significant changes have occurred in the operation of the database since this printing. Refer to the documentation that comes with MySQL for any changes.

Summary

MySQL installation seems pretty daunting at first, but by reviewing the options and taking a course that best suits your needs, you can have the database up and running in no time. MySQL comes in a variety of distributions: binary, RPM, and source. The binary distributions are tailored for specific types of platforms and cannot be used on any other. These are relatively easy to install and may require root access to be installed in the system-level directories. The RPM distributions are the easiest, but only if you have Red Hat Linux. These distributions will even do part of the configuration for you. The last distributions, which we recommend, are the source distributions. These come with a lot of documentation and examples, and can be highly tailored to your liking.

MySQL is constantly in development, as you can see by the number of levels of maturity of the distributions. The stable distributions are recommended for their stability and full range of tested features. The bleeding-edge distributions are for testing out the new features that are being fleshed out in the database. The old deprecated releases are not necessary unless you are a previous user. Keeping up-to-date in the stable distributions, namely 3.22, will provide all the features and stability an application requires.

The actual installation depends on the distribution chosen. The binary and RPM installations require the least amount of work and can be done relatively quickly. The RPM distributions require Red Hat and root privileges. Binary distributions require it only if installed in a system directory. There is no compilation required for these because it is already done for you. The source distribution does not require root access unless placed in a system directory as well. This distribution requires more system tools than the previous distributions, but these should already be installed from your Linux distribution. The only extra step is compilation, which should take more time depending on system resources.

Once installed, you must configure and set up the database for usage. The first stage of setup is to make sure proper security is in place. Nothing can be stressed more strongly than making sure the database is secure and only the users you want access to it can access it, especially if the information being stored is sensitive. Even if it is not, you still do not want users to be able to do harm to the data, such as deleting it.

The first user created when the database is installed is the root user. The password for this user must be set immediately after installation. If not, anyone can connect and have full access to the database. You must also set up a user on the system to run the MySQL daemon. You should not run this daemon as root or you will open yourself up to crackers who try to exploit the daemon to get root privileges. Once this user is created, the files and permissions should be set so only that user has access to the files and can write to them.

With MySQL there are many types of privileges that determine what a user can do with the database. There are more administrative privileges, such as shutting the database down or doing reloads. There are also privileges related to the database and tables such as being able to read the tables and putting new data in them. New users should be created with specific roles in mind. A user can be created that just handles administrative functions. Regular users who manipulate data should only have permissions to do these operations, and leave the more privileged operations. Users also can be restricted from where they originate the connections to the database. You can create users who are allowed to connect locally only, from specific remote hosts or both. There are also special tables that can restrict access to certain tables and from certain hosts that can combine to provide a matrix of privileges that can be very specific to your environment. These privileges are given with the **GRANT** command, and if you know SQL well, you can apply the SQL commands directly to modify these three tables to provide the setup that you need.

Once set up, you need the database to be available as much as possible. The default way to start the MySQL daemon is with **safe_mysqld**. This is actually a script that will monitor the status of the database daemon. If the database were to exit or shutdown, it will automatically restart it. There is also a way to make sure the MySQL daemon is started upon bootup. By creating an **rc** script in the **/etc** directory, you can link it to the different run levels of the machine and make sure that when the machine is rebooted, MySQL is started along with the other programs on the server.

The last few steps of installation require optimizing your distribution. You can compile optimizations in using the compiler, if you have a source distribution. The benefit of having the source is that it allows you to compile with different options to take the best advantage of your platform. There are also hardware methods that can be utilized to speed up the database. Lastly, there are specific runtime flags for the MySQL database daemon that allow you to tweak and modify the variables to further speed up your database. Once you've completed an installation, set up the database users, and even tried working with the performance of the database, you will feel like a database wizard in no time.

FAQs

Q: How do I run more than one MySQL server on my machine?

A: This can be accomplished in two ways:

With the source distribution, you can pass specific flags to configure to allow the database to point to a different location and use a different port:

```
shell$ ./configure  —with-tcp-port=port_number \
—with-unix-socket=file_name \
-prefix=/usr/local/mysql-3.22.9
```

If you do not have the source distribution you may also use runtime flags to **mysqld**:

```
shell$ /my/path/bin/safe_mysqld —socket=file_name —port=port_number
```

You should not have two different daemons modifying the same database path. A different one can be specified with **–datadir**.

Q: How do I replicate my database?

A: For now, MySQL does not have a feature to automatically do this. A simple work-around would be to do a nightly dump of the database and import it to another database. The frequency of this operation depends on how fresh the data needs to be.

Q: How do I backup my database?

A: The **mysqldump** command allows you to save all the tables in the database.

```
shell$ mysqldump —tab=/save/path —opt —full
```

You can also shutdown the server and **tar** up the database directory. To reload the tables back into the database, you can **untar** the files into the database directory or restore the dump.

Q: How do I upgrade to the latest version if I already installed MySQL?

A: You can stop your current database and move the directory to a different name. Then install the distribution like you did before. Afterwards, move your database directory back to the new directory and start up your database.

Q: What happens if I forget my password?

A: You must first shut down the server. Then start up the server with the **–skip-grant-tables** option to *not* use the privileges table. Connect back to the database and either use **GRANT** to reset the password or use SQL commands directly to reset the password on the user table.

Q: How do I enable transactions?

A: Unlike larger-scale databases, MySQL does not have the ability to enable transactions. This will be included in later versions.

Installing and Managing Progress on Linux

Solutions in this chapter:

- **Installing**
- **Configuring**
- **Testing the Database**
- **Database Design**
- **Issues**

Introduction

The Progress database is embedded in literally thousands of the most popular mid-sized packages available today (e.g., qad Inc.'s MFG/Pro, Symix, FiServ's Unifi, and NxTrend's Trend). In fact, Progress is the leading product in the embedded database market space (see http://www.progress.com/services/pressrm/releases/pr_gart-ner_041499.htm for details), and is a major player in the emerging ASP (Association of Shareware Professionals) marketplace. Packages based on the Progress Relational Database Management (RDBM) system are in use by 60 percent of the Fortune 500, and bring in more than $2.5 billion of annual revenue to Progress Partners. Yet Progress Software Corporation (PSC) does not have the instant name recognition that you would expect for a company with $300 million in annual sales and over 80,000 installations in 100 countries to enjoy.

Perhaps this phenomenon is due to PSC's "stealth marketing" strategy of selling primarily through the reseller channel. Progress has always based their sales programs around selling to software developers instead of direct sales to large IT organizations. This has proven extremely successful over their 15-year history since they now have a stable of over 4000 applications developed on top of the database and 4GL. However, since PSC itself must avoid the conflict of selling against their own developers, the names of many Progress partners are more recognizable than Progress itself.

No matter what the marketing strategy, Progress as a platform has a lot to offer. The database has all of the features of a large scale OLTP (Online Transaction Processing) solution, yet does not require a full time database administrator (DBA) to run. Progress gladly scales from a stand-alone PC with 32MB of RAM to the largest IBM, HP, Sun, and Compaq/DEC multiprocessor servers. The 4GL is a complete language that does not require any 3GL code to create a full-scale application. Over 90 percent of all applications contain only 4GL code, and via the runtime application execution environment, are completely transportable across all of the major UNIX platforms, including Linux.

At the time of this writing (first quarter of 2000), PSC has released Progress version 8.3 for Linux. Version 8.3 is the mature deployment platform currently used by most installed Progress packages. The latest Progress version 9 release will be available on Linux when version 9.1 is released in the later part of Q1 2000. Releases prior to v 8.3, while not native, run on Linux through use of the iBCS package and the Progress port for SCO OpenServer. Various parties have successfully run versions 6.2 through 8.2 on Linux in this manner. Those versions are beyond the scope of this book however, and can be investigated through Internet resources as the Progress on Linux FAQ at http://marathon-man.com/pl/Progress-Linux-FAQ.html, and the Progress Email Group

(PEG—www.peg.com). This chapter will focus on the v 8.3 release, its installation, configuration, and management.

Installation

Progress installation is a fairly straightforward three-step process. First, install the executables from media, then change any kernel parameters, and then set up the environment. After installation, you are ready to create your first database.

Install from Media

Installation from media is a simple task of copying the executables from the CD or tape that comes from Progress. Each platform has a slightly different version of how the install scripts work. Linux, like most UNIX platforms, has tape versions available where each section of the tape contains a separate product. The installation script from tape is a straightforward combination of **cpio** to extract files and **dd** to skip over unused products. The CD version is a little different since the files are there without need for extraction. In this case, Progress uses its own file archiving scheme to combine each of the products into a single archive file on the CD. Before we begin the actual install process, we will need to make sure we are ready.

Prerequisites

Installation of the Progress media is a simple process of running the scripts provided on the CD. Before you begin, make sure that you have approximately 100MB of free space for the software. Depending on which products you purchased, less disk may be possible. Also be sure to have the "Progress Software Corporation License Addendum" that came with the products. This is colloquially referred to as the *green sheet*, after the color of the paper on which it is printed.

We will assume that you already have a working computer with Linux already installed and with a properly working CD-ROM drive. If you will be accessing the database in Client/Server mode, then you will need TCP/IP installed. Dumb terminals do not require this. Progress has been officially tested on Red Hat Linux version 6.1, but should run on most distributions with a 2.2.12 or later stable kernel. The specific process described here was tested on the 6.1 Mandrake distribution, which is similar to Red Hat.

Install

Begin the process by placing the CD in the drive and mounting it through Linux. The exact command may vary on custom distributions but is generally of the form:

```
mount /dev/cdrom /mnt/cdrom
```

Be sure to set your current directory to something other than the CD itself. If you forget, the installation script will remind you it cannot be run directly from the CD. Then run the **proinstall** Installation Utility:

```
/mnt/cdrom/proinst
```

You will receive a welcome screen (see Figure 8.1); simply press **Return** to proceed to Product Configuration Data (see Figure 8.2).

Figure 8.1 Installation Welcome screen.

This is the heart of the installation—where you will enter the serial numbers and product keys. Function keys are described on the right-hand side; use the **Tab** key to move between fields. Enter your company name or other unique identifier first. This is not essential—it is not used anywhere other than the installation. Using the green sheet, enter the serial number of the first product. The release number should already be filled in for you so that you can simply tab over this field. You must then enter the three sets of Control numbers for that serial number. Take a moment to verify the codes and then press **Return**. If the Control numbers for the product match the serial number, the screen will confirm your entry as valid. If not, check again for errors.

Figure 8.2 Entering products and control codes.

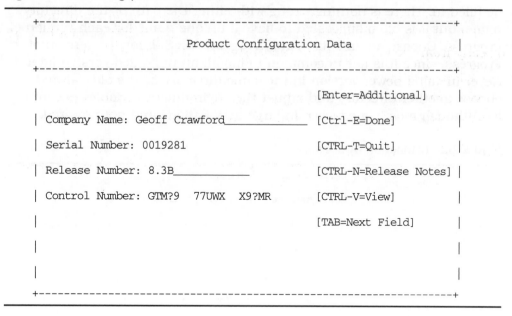

```
+-----------------------------------------------------------------+
|                    Product Configuration Data                   |
+-----------------------------------------------------------------+
|                                       [Enter=Additional]    |
| Company Name: Geoff Crawford_____  [Ctrl-E=Done]         |
| Serial Number: 0019281                [CTRL-T=Quit]         |
| Release Number: 8.3B_____     [CTRL-N=Release Notes] |
| Control Number: GTM?9  77UWX  X9?MR   [CTRL-V=View]         |
|                                       [TAB=Next Field]      |
|                                                            |
|                                                            |
+-----------------------------------------------------------------+
```

Repeat this process of serial numbers for each product found on the green sheet. There is no reason why all products cannot be installed at the same time. After the last product is entered, press **Ctrl-E** to continue with the detailed installation. Some terminal emulators (TinyTERM from Century Software for instance) have mapped **Ctrl-E** to internal functions—you'll have to correct that if you're using such an emulator. Be careful—the **Quit** option (**Ctrl-T**) is meant to cancel the entire installation.

You will be asked to confirm you are done entering all of your products—simply answer **Y**. The next screen will be labeled Type, Device, and Destination, and looks like Figure 8.3. For CD-ROM installations there is no additional Device information needed so we will enter only Type and Destination. Use the arrow key to highlight "Type of Installation" and press **Return**. Use the arrow key again to select **Custom Installation**. The custom installation is not at all difficult, requires only small amounts of additional input, and is always recommended.

Next select **Destination Pathname**. The default value of **/usr/dlc** will be filled in. There is nothing wrong with either the path or the directory name, but it is often suggested to have a unique name for each version of Progress. Choose a name like **/opt/progress/dlc83b** for the version of Progress, since it is not uncommon to install an upgraded version later. Never install a newer version in the same directory as the old—always choose another directory and adjust the environment variables according-ly. Although mostly a concern in large installations and not required,

Figure 8.3 Installation options.

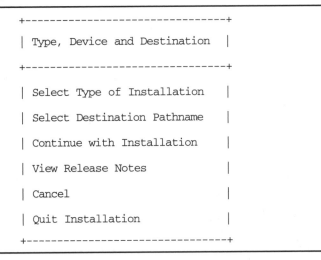

```
               +--------------------------------+
               | Type, Device and Destination   |
               +--------------------------------+

               | Select Type of Installation    |

               | Select Destination Pathname    |

               | Continue with Installation     |

               | View Release Notes             |

               | Cancel                         |

               | Quit Installation              |
               +--------------------------------+
```

there are also performance advantages to having the executables on their own disk drive. In any case, modify the directory name to be in the area set aside during preparation.

You may choose to view the Release Notes at this time, or they can be found in a plain text file on the CD. You are now ready to choose **Continue With Installation**. You are next asked to select the languages seen in Figure 8.4. Use the arrow keys to highlight the primary language you require. Pressing **Return** on the highlighted selection toggles an asterisk to show what has been selected. Then choose the **Make Default** option for this first language. Finish by selecting any other needed lan-guages and then select **Continue With Installation**.

Since this is a Custom install, you will now be given the option to install only parts of each product, or to install a few optional utilities (see Figure 8.5). All of the products entered in the first screen should appear here, with an asterisk by each indicating that they will be installed. You can highlight a product and press **Return** to see a full list of the pack-ages inside each one of the products. In particular, it is recommended to

Figure 8.4 Language selection.

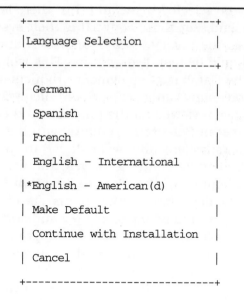

```
               +------------------------------+
               |Language Selection            |
               +------------------------------+

               | German                       |
               | Spanish                      |
               | French                       |
               | English - International      |
               |*English - American(d)        |
               | Make Default                 |
               | Continue with Installation   |
               | Cancel                       |

               +------------------------------+
```

```
     Disk Space Required for Products: 50,394,112 bytes
  Disk Space Required for Installation: 50,785,280 bytes
Disk Space Remaining After Installation: 118,604,800 bytes
```

Figure 8.5 Product option selection.

```
        +------------------------------+-----+
        |   Custom - Select Products   |     |
        +------------------------------+-----+

        |*Enterprise Database (5 USERS)|     |
        |*Client/Networking (5 USERS)  |     |
        |*4GL Development (1 USER)      |     |
        | Install Selected Products    |     |
        | Change Destination Pathname  |     |
        | Cancel                       |     |
        +------------------------------+     |
        | Quit Installation                  |
        +------------------------------------+
```

select all packages unless you are short of disk space. Most packages should already be selected by default, but there is one in particular that may be very useful. For those converting their systems to the native Linux port of Progress, the Legacy v 8.2 Database Utilities is not activated by default, but should be installed anyway. This will be an option underneath any of the Database Deployment products such as *Enterprise Database, WorkGroup Database,* or *Stand Alone Database.*

After you have reviewed all the products and confirmed your selections, choose **Install Selected Products** with the arrow keys and press **Return**. The Installation Utility will ask you to confirm that you are ready to begin installation; just enter **Y** for yes. You will be prompted with one final question about copying scripts to **/usr/bin** (see Figure 8.6). This is a holdover from the days long ago when **/usr/bin** was an appropriate place to put such scripts. It is better to say **No** and add **$DLC/bin** to the PATH of users needing access to these scripts (programmers and DBAs—end users have no need to access the database using these scripts).

After answering this question, Progress will then begin unpacking files from the CD. Depending on the speed of the system and the number of products, this usually takes between 5 and 15 minutes. Afterwards you will receive the final confirmation that the installation from media is complete.

Figure 8.6 Optional shell script copy.

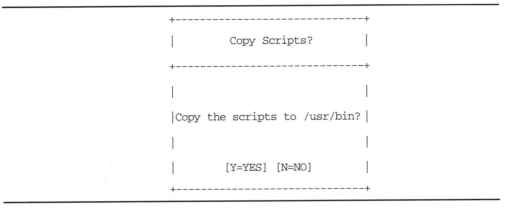

Kernel Parameters

Now that all of the Progress products have been copied from the CD, the Linux kernel may need to be configured. Progress uses two main sets of resources controlled by the Linux kernel: shared memory and semaphores. Before we decide on the exact values of each parameter, it is important to understand a little background on these resources to set them properly.

Shared memory is a facility to set aside RAM for multi-user access. Instead of writing all of the database information directly to disk where each user would perform a slow IO operation, Progress uses faster RAM as a kind of database record depot. Blocks are read from disk into the shared memory area (also known as the *Buffer Pool*) where they are then available to not only the user that requested the data, but to all users of the system. The Progress database engine is multithreaded and takes advantage of SMP if multiple processors are available. Since multiple users simultaneously could attempt to modify shared memory, Progress uses the other resource, semaphores, to lock portions of shared memory as necessary, and to ensure that operations on shared memory are atomic. (Actually, semaphores are only used for "slow" operations; mutex locks, or *latches*, are used for "fast" operations.)

Modified data blocks are eventually written back to disk, and possibly evicted from the buffer pool—but not always immediately. If it sounds like this is dangerous, rest assured the database system has been designed to be rock solid. Although Oracle has a reputation for being crash proof, Progress is actually the highest scorer in that category in user surveys such as VAR Business' Annual Report Cards.

Progress has built in concurrency, crash recovery, and data management schemes to ensure the integrity of the database while keeping frequently used blocks in the pool for possible reuse (and therefore eliminating expensive I/O operations). The details of these schemes are complex and beyond the scope of this book. For more information see the Technical Papers section of the PEG, at http://www.peg.com. The architects of the database engine, commonly referred to as the *Engine Crew*, have written several excellent white papers explaining the various database internals.

Following is a list of each parameter and how to set the value of each one. Most are based on either the number of users in a system, or on the number of databases. The include files **sem.h** and **shm.h** contain descriptions of these parameters in the Linux kernel. Both files generally are found under **/usr/src/linux/include/linux**.

Shared Memory

Shared memory is organized into segments; each individual segment is given a unique identifier. Each Progress database requires at least one segment of shared memory and one identifier to go with it. Take the number of databases you intend to run on the system, and round the number up to the nearest multiple of five for safety—the result is the minimum setting for **SHMMNI**. The default for Red Hat Linux is 10, which should be sufficient for one database.

- **SHMMNI**—Number of shared memory identifiers
- **SHMSEG**—Number of shared memory segments per process
- **SHMMAX**—Maximum size of a shared memory segment

SHMSEG and **SHMMAX** work together as a pair. Since shared memory is organized in segments, the maximum size of shared memory is the number segments times the size of each segment. Progress under v 8.3 will create segments that are the lower of **SHMSEG** or 16,776,214 bytes (16MB). Because Progress currently will never use a segment larger than 16MB, even if **SHMSEG** is set higher, it makes sense to set it to no larger than 16,776,124.

So how much shared memory will be needed? The manuals describe the exact amounts, but invariably the amount of RAM used by the buffer pool dwarfs any other shared memory usage. For performance reasons, try to give each user of a production system an absolute minimum of about 2MB of buffer pool space per user. If at all possible, consider using 4MB and purchasing more memory if needed. Remember, the shared memory must be contained in physical RAM. If you allocate more shared memory than you have physical RAM, Linux will page portions of the buffer pool in and out of swap space to cover the difference. This will have a dramatically negative impact on performance.

Take the number of users of each database and multiply by the amount of RAM you have decided to reserve. Do this for each database, and determine which one will have the maximum amount of shared memory. This is the high-water mark needed to set **SHMSEG**. Divide the maximum RAM by the 16MB we set **SHMMAX** to, and round up. This is the largest number of segments any database will require, and our value for **SHMSEG**.

Semaphores

Semaphores, like shared memory, are organized into a name set with an identifier. Similarly, Progress will require one set of semaphores per database. The calculation for **SEMMNI** is the same as **SHMMNI**—both parameters are usually set to the same value.

- **SEMMNI**—Number of semaphore identifiers
- **SEMMNS**—Number of semaphores system-wide
- **SEMMSL**—Number of semaphores per identifier

Progress uses approximately five semaphores for its own internal use, plus one semaphore for each concurrent user logged into that database. **SEMMSL** needs to be set to the maximum amount of users logged into the database with the most concurrent users. Set it to the maximum number of users in that single database plus the five extra and an additional 10 percent as a safety factor.

SEMMNS in most Linux kernels generally is set to **SEMMNI * SEMMSL**. There is nothing wrong with this, but it does assume that every user will log into every database. If there is only one database there is no real need for any other calculation, but on multiple databases this can be somewhat wasteful. When in doubt, simply let the calculation be. But if you expect to have a very large database and also a very small one, like a development database with only five users compared to the 400 users on the production system, consider modifying **SEMMNS**. A good rule of thumb is to take each database, use **promon** to find out the maximum number of users in each database and add these numbers together. Add an additional five for each database and an additional 10 percent for safety.

Under some UNIX variants there are also Semaphore Undo structures and a Semaphore map (**SEMUME/SEMMAP**), but in Linux these are no longer used.

Other Miscellaneous Parameters

In addition to shared memory and semaphores, there are a couple of other parameters that need to be considered:

- **MAXUMEM**—Maximum memory usage of a process
- **NOFILES**—Maximum number of open files per process
- **NFILES**—Maximum number of open files system-wide
- **NBUFS**—Number of disk buffers

Since each user, and the database process, must connect to the shared memory segment, the amount of memory each Linux process must access can be considerably larger than normal. **MAXUMEM** needs to be set to a level equal to the size of the Progress executable image, plus the largest shared memory area in the system. A good rule is to take **SHMSEG * SHMMAX** (which gives the largest possible amount of shared memory) and add 5MB, or just set it to the amount of physical RAM in the system.

As we will discuss later, some databases will actually be composed of only two or three operating system files. However, larger databases using a multivolume structure are split into many operating system files. When such databases are used, the **NOFILES**, **NFILES**, and **NINODES** parameters may need modification. Under v 8.3 of Progress, the maximum number of files a database can use is 256. (v 9 has the capability of using thousands of files, so be careful to make a better calculation when v 9 becomes available on Linux.) Each user also requires the three standard input/output/error files, plus any temporary and spool files created (as many as 12 file handles, not counting database related files). Therefore, **NOFILES** should never need to be higher than 300.

NFILES is the system-wide number of files, which at its maximum would be the number of users logged in times the number of databases times the number of operating system files in each database. Remember that this is only the amount of Progress usage. Linux itself and other Linux users' open files must be added into this number. The Progress manuals suggest using this maximized number for **NFILES**, but as you can tell from this calculation, that number can become very large very fast. The calculation may be safe, but it assumes each user is logged into each database. In reality, smaller numbers may be more appropriate.

On small sites where there is only one database, this is not generally an issue, but on larger sites this can be quite wasteful. A true value for **NFILES** would calculate the number of concurrent users for each database and multiply by the number of operating system files for that particular database. Each of these values per database would then be added together to create the usage for Progress. Perhaps 10 percent should be added in case of expansion or changes to login patterns. Also add another 10 percent for the operating system file usage.

There is one last Linux parameter to review. Since Progress uses its own buffer pool to manage record access, standard Linux disk buffers are not entirely useful. On systems where RAM is tight, it is often advantageous to reduce the Linux buffers slightly and allocate this towards shared memory. **NBUFS** controls the number of buffers, but caution should be exercised with this parameter. All spool files, program files, and other operating system files must go through the Linux disk buffers. Setting this value lower may allow for better performance of the database, but cause a slowdown in printing and other disk access. If in doubt, reduce this parameter gradually from the original setting. Watch the system carefully for printing slowdowns and pauses while new Progress programs are run. Balance that with the Progress performance tools to see how a larger Buffer Pool affects the database performance. More details on the balance of RAM allocation are in the Configuration section, later.

Environment Setup

Setting up the Linux environment for Progress is a simple matter of establishing a few environment variables and possibly modifying the TCP/IP hosts and services files—tasks that will be familiar to the average Linux system administrator. If a character-based application is going to be used then there also might be modifications to the terminal definition that Progress uses. This terminal setup is in addition to the normal **termcap/terminfo** setup, and on occasion can be more complex than just choosing the right terminal type.

Environment Variables

Progress requires two Linux environment variables—**DLC** and **TERM**. The **DLC** variable should be set to point to the directory where Progress was installed. Typically this would be something like the following (for **bash**):

```
DLC=/opt/progress/dlc83b
TERM=linux
Export DLC TERM
```

This should be done in the system-wide login profile (**/etc/profile**) or alternately in each user's individual **.profile** or **.login** (or whatever is appropriate for the shell in use). Unless there is some compelling reason for a customized setup, all other environment variables Progress requires will take appropriate default values based on **$DLC**. It is advantageous, however, to put the Progress executables in the **PATH**. Add both the **$DLC** directory and **$DLC/bin** to the **PATH** for all database administrators so that the database utilities will be in their path.

Terminal Setup—PROTERMCAP

Progress uses a **curses**-like library called *Vermont Views* (recognized by error messages prefixed with **vv_**) to do screen drawing and painting so the **TERM** value must be set correctly. Progress has its own **termcap**-like configuration file called **PROTERMCAP** that defines the additional terminal attributes that standard **termcap** does not have. Primarily these revolve around the extensive function key and color capabilities that the Progress 4GL supports.

Definitions for many terminals are already provided in the **PROTERM-CAP** file shipped with the product. For Linux, an entry is provided for the Linux console under the **linux** terminal type (ones where control codes reduce the viewable data area). For X Terminal usage, the **xterm** type is assumed. Older space-taking type terminals (Wyse 50, Televideo 925, and so forth) are no longer supported. Watch out for the emulation on some painfully realistic terminal emulators. The original keyboard layout of a real vt100 had only four functions keys, and a real vt220 has predefined hardware uses for the first five function keys. Although some emulators give additional keys, Progress has only the "real" keys in the **PROTERM-CAP** file. You may either need to modify the **PROTERMCAP** or switch to an emulation that has a full set of function keys.

Specific **PROTERMCAP** entries are described in some detail in the Progress technical manuals and are beyond the scope of this book. But in general, here are some tips for working with **PROTERMCAP**. Leave the original configuration file as is. Instead of modifying the original, make a copy of it and then set a Linux environment variable called **PROTERM-CAP** equal to the fully qualified pathname of the new **PROTERMCAP** file (this is a case where there is a reason to customize and override the default settings).

Two other issues that can arise in terminal configuration are the Backspace key and the Linux **interrupt**. Progress expects the backspace character to be **Ctrl-H**, even on DEC terminals where the backspace is really defined as **Ctrl-?** (i.e., the Delete key). Progress also expects to use the Delete key as a **delete character** function, which interferes with some setups where the terminal's Delete key is programmed as the **interrupt**. In either case, use the **stty** command in users' **.profile** to change these values. **Ctrl-C** is the generally accepted alternate for **interrupt** and is compatible with the terminal definitions Progress provides:

```
stty erase ^h intr ^c
```

Client/Server Mode Setup

If your only access is through Telnet terminal emulation, you are what known as a *self-service client*, and there are no additional steps needed. Client/Server mode is not the same as using Telnet to access the Linux machine. If your users are going to access the database in Client/Server mode, an additional file must be edited. Progress requires the TCP/IP address of the machine and a dedicated TCP/IP port for each database accessed over the network. The IP address of the machine should already be set during the TCP/IP setup of the machine. To reserve the TCP/IP port(s), edit **/etc/services**. Each line has the form:

```
name        1000/tcp
```

Create one line for each database, replacing **name** with a unique identifier for each database. You can use the database's actual name for the identifier so it is easy to identify. Choose port numbers above the last one currently in use, and leave at least 500 between each port. This port is not actually the only one used, and through Progress' port assignment scheme, conflicts can sometimes occur if the port numbers for multiple databases are too close. Only a TCP port is needed; the database part of Progress will not use UDP.

Configuration

Configuring a Progress database is not at all difficult. There are several decisions that must be made, and then the actual database is ready to be created. First, we focus on the directory structures Progress uses, and then we discuss the implications of disk space versus disk speed.

Directory Structure

Configuring a directory structure for a Progress database is an important part of preparing to deploy an application. Of course you could just dump everything into a single big ugly directory and not worry about it. This is a solution that is not only ugly, but one that leads to an administrative mess down the road. A well thought-out and organized directory structure is essential to a well-run site. In general, create separate file systems for differently purposed bits of the database and application. That way you can map the file systems onto differently configured disks and tune file system options such as **fs** type, block size, RAID types, and when journaled file systems become available many others to the purpose of the file system. To that end, the following structure in Table 8.1 should be considered:

Table 8.1 Directory Names Table

Directory Name	Purpose
/opt/progress/dlc83b	Establish distinct directories for each release of Progress—this makes updates, testing, and potential rollbacks much easier.
/mnt/db	The **.db**, **.st** and **.d#** extents all go here. This should be a striped and mirrored set of disks with a **fs** block size that works well with the **db** block size and with maximum reliability and recoverability options.
/mnt/bi	
/mnt/ai	The **.bi** and **.ai** file systems should be on mirrored disks, not striped, with maximum reliability and recoverability file system characteristics.
/mnt/logs	You should establish a file system for **lg** files and other monitoring data. Sweep daily logs into this file system nightly. It need not be mirrored or striped; plain old disks are fine. Create an archiving strategy that puts files in directories named by **yyyy.mm.dd** so that you have a searchable history. Archive your **.ai** files in the same manner.
/mnt/source	
/mnt/rcode	
/mnt/tmp	
/mnt/scripts	These file systems should be fast and reliable but need not be highly recoverable—striping and mirroring are appropriate. Full logging (a journaled **fs** option currently unavailable for Linux) is not necessary since you can recover everything from backup, but reliability is important since user sessions may crash if the files stored on these file systems become unavailable.

Continued

Table 8.1 Continued

Directory Name	Purpose
/mnt/recover	You should establish an area to recover a backup to—in most recovery scenarios it is wise to preserve the damaged database in case your backup is damaged or wasn't made properly. This file system should have the same characteristics as the **db** file system.
/mnt/dump	An area for dumping and loading or backup to disk (prior to backing up to tape of course) that is separate from all other areas provides maximum flexibility. Ideally, this area uses disks that are otherwise quiet when a dump and load or backup is in process.

Even if you have a small or lightly used database that doesn't appear to warrant the full treatment of multiple disks and individual tuning of file systems following a file system creation and naming plan like the preceding, this will allow you to change things around and grow more readily in the future. You can always create this layout as a simple directory structure and mount file systems on it as you need them. This design lays the foundation for success moving forward.

Disk Space versus I/O Throughput

Another important consideration when configuring a system to run a database is the physical disk layout and the capabilities of the disk subsystem. If you have a small system that isn't being stressed you can skip this section until you're ready for it. As long as you've followed a design similar to the preceding, you can come back later and apply these techniques as needed.

Capacity of a single disk in gigabytes or sequential throughput in megabytes per second are interesting measurements if you're doing video-on-demand or some other pre-Internet world-domination application. But what you really need to focus on is how many *operations* per second are occurring. Of course the PC media has convinced everyone that the only thing that really matters is the *size* of a disk drive, so if you ever have to explain why you're "wasting" so much space to a bean counter you're going to have to be very patient.

Routine Progress database I/O is going to be in uniform blocks randomly scattered on the disk. The disk holding the database, therefore, needs to concentrate on random I/O. Striped disks are excellent at optimizing random I/O. Mirroring doesn't hurt it any. RAID 5 is a poor choice if there is any noticeable write activity. Thus from a RAID perspective,

RAID 10 (aka RAID 0 + RAID 1) is the ideal choice. JBOD (Just a Bunch Of Disks) is second best, one big enough disk is third best, and RAID 5 should be avoided.

Before Image and After Image file I/O is essentially sequential. Disks perform sequential operations 10 or 20 times faster than random operations. If you mix access types you get random access performance. If the aggregate demand for I/O operations is greater than what the disks can provide then you get disk queuing and bad performance. The first place that this will show up is at long checkpoints (freezes of all users, as in memory copies of data that are periodically synchronized to disk) if you have a *workgroup* license (or if you aren't using the asynchronous page writer features of the *enterprise* license). Dedicating a disk to the **.bi** file allows it to avoid being impacted by other I/O activity and to run at full speed. This is especially important with the workgroup license, and still important with the enterprise license as you start to push the machine's capabilities.

Dedicating a disk to the **.ai** file is important for the same reasons and for an additional reason—after-imaging provides roll forward recovery. If your **.ai** files are on the same media that was damaged in the event from which you're recovering, you have a Catch-22. If at all possible you should spare a disk for after imaging. If you can't then you have only limited protection from serious hardware failures and administrative errors (like accidentally reformatting a disk). You should still use after-imaging—it still protects you from the much more likely user errors (like accidentally deleting all of your customers) through the roll forward to a point-in-time feature. But you aren't getting the full benefit of the feature unless it is on a distinct disk.

Mirroring **.bi** and **.ai** files is a good idea—you don't want to lose either of them for any reason. Mirroring is not a replacement for either. The **.bi** file is essential for successful crash recovery. Mirroring faithfully reproduces human errors such as the previously mentioned "delete all the customers" scenario or something as simple as **rm** * in the wrong directory. Only after-imaging can rescue you from those miscues. Mirroring enhances uptime but it does not protect you from everything.

Striping **.bi** and **.ai** files is not useful—it defeats the sequential nature of the I/O pattern and limits the potential throughput to those files. RAID 5, of course, is completely inappropriate for these files.

Systems with tightly constrained memory or poorly indexed queries might experience heavy I/O rates to the temporary file area defined by the **–T** session startup parameter. This is a file system where Progress creates temp files used for various purposes. These files are normally stored unlinked and are therefore invisible, but they can be made visible by using the **–t** (lowercase) parameter. The major file types found in the **–T** area are:

- **Srta<pid>:** The **sort** file—client-side query resolution and r-code buffering
- **Lbia<pid>:** Local Before Image—subtransaction and variable undo notes
- **DBIa<pid>:** Temporary table buffer overflow

If you cannot use memory to redirect this I/O (the **–mmax** and **–Bt** parameters are the relevant parameters), it is important that the **–T** area have excellent I/O throughput—such as would be found on a striped and mirrored set of disks.

Creating a New Database

Although there are many ways to set up your database, we will concentrate on the best performing methods. Progress provides two different methods of using a database—single-volume and multivolume. Multivolume is an absolute necessity in large-scale environments, but offers many advantages to all users.

Multivolume

Progress has two different types of database layouts available. Single volume databases are the easiest to create but have a maximum size of 2 gigabytes (the limit of an **lseek()** system call). Data extents still have the same 2GB limit in multivolume databases, but they can all be combined for much larger storage capacity. Beginning in version 9 of Progress, all databases will be multivolume. This, combined with the potential performance enhancements due to increased file handles, makes multivolume a recommended choice.

Progress databases are split into four types of files—before-image extents, after-image extents, data extents, and the DB file. Before-imaging is what gives Progress the ability to back out unfinished transactions. The before-simage file are identified by file extensions of **.b1**, **.b2**, etc. or just **.bi** for a single-volume database. After-image extents end in **.a1**, **.a2**, etc., and are the Roll Forward Recovery files. Data extents contain both data and the indexes to the data. Each one of these files is described in a structure file and then pieced together in a collection to form the database. The structure file ends in **.st** and is used to create its binary equivalent, the **.db** file—once the database has been created the **.st** file is not required and can be recreated using the **prostrct** utility—it is, however, handy to keep around for documentation purposes.

The steps to create new databases are defined well in the Progress documentation, but a small example is given here. You first need to create an **.st** file with the list of all extents. Extents are defined by their type (before-image, after-image, data), whether they are fixed length or variable, and if fixed by their size in 1k blocks (or whatever block size database you're creating—1k is the default). There can be only one variable before-image, and one variable data extent. Let's keep the example simple and define a structure file with one fixed and one variable extent for both before-image and data. After-image extents are highly recommended since they give the ability to roll the database forward from the point of last backup to any point in time afterwards. They are not included in this example for the sake of simplicity. Such a structure file would be called something like **mydata.st** and look like this:

```
B    /mnt/bi/mydata.b1    f    10000
B    /mnt/bi/mydata.b2
D    /mnt/db/mydata.d1    f    500000
D    /mnt/db/mydata.d2
```

Note how the first column denotes the extent type, B/D/A, and how the *f* means an extent of fixed size. In this case, if the before-image file grew bigger than 10MB (i.e., 10000 blocks), then the second **.b2** extent would begin to be used. Similarly, the **.d2** extent would be used if the data files grew larger than 500MB. Also, note how the extents are spread across different mount points.

Sizing extents is an exercise in balance. In general, more file handles provide better concurrency, so you would want to choose 10 extents of 200MB instead of 2 extents of 1GB for a 2GB database. You also want to preserve room for growth and keep DBA intervention to add or resize extents to a minimum.

Two steps complete the process. First, the Progress utility **prostrct** is used to translate the structure file into the physical database layout ready to use. Any fixed-length extents will be created in the requested sizes (rounded up to the next 16k). Here is the syntax, using the database structure file created earlier:

```
prostrct create /mnt/db/mydata mydata.st
```

Review the various operating system files created after this step, **.db**, **.b1**, **.b2**, **.d1**, **.d2**, etc. Note that the **.db** file is not described in the structure file, but instead is derived from it. The **.db** will be created in the directory specified by the third parameter passed to the **prostrct** command. These files together create the database, but without the final step there is no internal structure to the database and so is known as a *void* database. To give it structure, copy a blank database into the void by using the **procopy** command:

```
procopy empty /mnt/db/mydata
```

The empty database is a special case of the **procopy** command. It is not necessary to specify the whole path of this structure even though it resides in the DLC directory where the Progress executables were installed. Progress will find the empty database using the **$DLC** environment variable. There are also several alternate versions of the empty database depending on the block size. To create a database using an 8k block size, simply substitute **empty8** for **empty** in the **procopy** command. Remember however, that variable block size is a feature of the Enterprise Database license. All WorkGroup databases are 1k blocks.

The database is now ready for access in single user mode. It is necessary to start a multi-user broker in order to allow more than one user into the database. Simply use the **proserve** command to start this broker. Without any other options, the broker will allow 10 users on the local system to access the database. To allow for more users, use the **–n** option. For network access, use **–H –N –S**. These options and many more performance-related parameters are discussed here later, and are also in the Progress System Administration Reference Manual.

Sizing the Buffer Pool

The largest consumer of RAM in most Progress installations is the **–B** buffer pool. This is a large shared memory area that is used to cache disk blocks in order to improve performance.

Don't tune this per user! Tune it according to how much I/O your disk subsystem can handle. Basically, you're trying to get physical I/O operations down to the point where your disks are between 50 and 25 percent utilized, there are no queues, and the service times are under 20ms. If your disks have an average access time of 10ms, then they can perform 100 random I/O operations per second and can sustain between 25 and 50 I/O operations per second without danger of queuing.

It's true that the number of users is probably related to the number of database access requests. But the relationship between that and the miss ratio is nonlinear. It follows a curve similar to:

$$R = L / \sqrt{C * B}$$

where:

R = Physical I/O operations

L = Logical I/O operations

B = Buffer Pool Size

C = some constant (probably near 1.5)

So there is no X amount of RAM per user rule that you can apply here. Although for getting in the ballpark, 2–4MB per user is usually a good guess. Once you have some data you then can more accurately adjust the value to better meet the target I/O. Figure 8.7 provides an example.

Figure 8.7 Using sample data to meet the Target I/O.

Logical Reads	-B	I/O Ops	Hit Ratio	Miss Ratio
1,000,000	5,000	11,547	98.845%	1.155
1,000,000	10,000	8,165	99.184%	0.816%
1,000,000	15,000	6,667	99.333%	0.667%
1,000,000	20,000	5,774	99.423%	0.577%
1,000,000	25,000	5,164	99.484%	0.516%
1,000,000	30,000	4,714	99.529%	0.471%
1,000,000	35,000	4,364	99.564%	0.436%
1,000,000	40,000	4,082	99.592%	0.408%
1,000,000	45,000	3,849	99.615%	0.385%
1,000,000	50,000	3,651	99.635%	0.365%
1,000,000	55,000	3,482	99.652%	0.348%
1,000,000	65,000	3,203	99.680%	0.320%
1,000,000	70,000	3,086	99.691%	0.309%
1,000,000	75,000	2,981	99.702%	0.298%
1,000,000	80,000	2,887	99.711%	0.289%

Hit Ratio

Running Progress

The typical daily process of running a Progress database generally is not a full-time job. Usually some initial script writing is done for the database startup, backup, and shutdown scripts. Afterwards the most time is spent on gathering data to insure the optimal performance of your system. Many Progress-based systems run for years without any attention from a DBA.

Managing the Database

PSC provides simple scripts for starting, stopping, monitoring, and backing up the database. Although these are generally adequate for an initial development environment, a more sophisticated or customized approach is usually desired for production work.

A helpful first step is to create a small *environment script* that concentrates all of the commonly used Progress and application-related environment variables in a single script that can then be "dotted" or "sourced" in scripts that need it. For instance:

```
# Common Environment Script
#
# To use:
#
# . /mnt/scripts/env

export TMP=/mnt/tmp
export MTH='date '+%m''
export DAY='date +%d'
export LOGS=/mnt/logs/$MTH.$DAY
export SRV='uname'
export SCRIPTS=/mnt/scripts
export DLC=/opt/progress/dlc83b
export DBNAME=/mnt/db/sports

# standard messaging routine

msg()
{
  MSG=$1 ; shift
  echo "$MSG"
  echo 'date' "$MSG" >> $LOGS/start.log

  # If additional arguments were passed then mail the message to
  # those people (the names might be pager addresses)
```

```
[ "$1" != "" ] && {
echo $SRV: 'date' "$MSG" | mailx -s "$MSG" $*
}
}
```

Starting

Smaller sites often use scripts that automatically detect the state of the database and bring it up when the first user attempts to access it. Sometimes they even bring it down automatically when the last user exits. Although convenient, there are several possible pitfalls to this approach. Such a script should *never* delete the **.lk** file. If Progress is telling you that a lock file exists you need to take that message seriously and understand why it is there. It could be that another user has, unbeknownst to you, started a legitimate single-user session (perhaps to perform database maintenance). Deleting that **.lk** file and then accessing the database will result in two sets of processes, potentially updating the database simultaneously without awareness of one another—a situation that would obviously lead to disaster.

Another downside to this approach is that it makes it difficult to gain exclusive access to the database for maintenance or recovery windows. It is good practice to separate database server startup from user session startup and to institute a set of standard controls that are respected by all scripts so that you can safely administer the database when need be. One very helpful technique is to use a *flag* file to gate access to user sessions like so:

```
# Start server
#

. /mnt/scripts/env

# Start something and verify it

strt()
{

  CMD=$1
  USR=$2
  GTX=$3
  WHO=$4

  msg "Starting: $1"
  $CMD >> $LOGS/start.log
  sleep 5
```

```
    ps -fu $USR | grep "$GTX" > /dev/null
    if [ $? = "1" ]; then
      msg "*** $CMD did not start" $WHO
      exit 0
    else
      msg "+++ $CMD started successfully"
    fi

}

# Create logging directory

if [ ! -d $LOGS ]; then
  mkdir $LOGS
  chmod 755 $LOGS
fi

msg "Starting database"
msg "Locking out users"

echo "Starting Database - Please wait" > $TMP/User_Lockout
chmod 644 $TMP/User_Lockout
rm -f $TMP/DB_IS_UP
sleep 5

strt "$DLC/bin/_mprosrv -pf $SCRIPTS/db.pf" \
  progress \
  "[m]prosrv" \
  dba

strt "$DLC/bin/_mprshut $DBNAME -C biw" \
  progress \
  "[b]iw" \
  dba

strt "$DLC/bin/_mprshut $DBNAME -C aiw" \
  progress \
  "[a]iw" \
  dba

strt "$DLC/bin/_mprshut $DBNAME -C apw" \
  progress \
  "[a]pw" \
```

```
   dba

strt "$DLC/bin/_mprshut $DBNAME -C watchdog" \
   progress \
   "[w]atchdog" \
   dba

msg "Creating DB_IS_UP file..."
touch $TMP/DB_IS_UP
chmod 644 $TMP/DB_IS_UP
sleep 5


# Remove user lockout flag file

if [ "$1" != "maintenance" ]; then
   msg "Users allowed into database"
   rm $TMP/User_Lockout
else
   msg "*** Database is up in maintenance mode ***"
   echo "Database is in maintenance mode - Please wait" > $TMP/User_Lockout
fi

sleep 5

msg "Database startup has completed"
```

Starting a Session

Starting a session can be very simple. The technique of placing a message in the lockout file helps users understand the status of the database when it is not available. Sleeping for 30 seconds allows an opportunity to read the message and helps to slow down the rate at which people retry application access. Finally, calling Progress with **exec** helps improve security by preventing users from being able to obtain a shell if this script is run from the login process.

```
# Start session
#

. /mnt/scripts/env        # export TMP=/mnt/tmp

if [ -f $TMP/User_Lockout ]; then
   clear
   cat $TMP/User_Lockout
   sleep 30
```

```
   exit 0
fi


# continue startup...


exec $DLC/bin/_progres -pf $SCRIPTS/standard.pf -T $TMP
```

Using shell **trap** commands is a technique that is sometimes used in an attempt to prevent shell access. This is a bad idea. Progress uses signals for interprocess communication, and interfering with proper signal handling can lead to serious reliability and performance problems.

Shutdown

Shut down a database like so:

```
# Stop server
#


. /mnt/scripts/env        # export TMP=/mnt/tmp


# Create logging directory


if [ ! -d $LOGS ]; then
   mkdir $LOGS
   chmod 755 $LOGS
fi


msg "Stopping database"
msg "Locking out users"


echo "Stopping Database - Please wait" > $TMP/User_Lockout
chmod 644 $TMP/User_Lockout
rm -f $TMP/DB_IS_UP
sleep 5


$DLC/bin/proshut $DBNAME -by >> $LOGS/stop.log 2>&1 &
sleep 60


# Verify that broker has shut down - the -by option
# Does not guarantee shutdown if there are some users
# In the system


ps | grep "[m]prosrv -pf $DBNAME" > /dev/null
```

```
if [ $? = "0" ]; then
        msg "*** DATABASE DID NOT SHUTDOWN WITH JUST -BY" dba
        msg "*** Attempting to force shutdown with -F option..."
        $DLC/bin/proshut $DBNAME -F -by >> $LOGS/stop.log 2>&
fi

ps | grep "[m]prosrv -pf $DBNAME" > /dev/null

if [ $? = "0" ]; then # panic
        msg "*** DATABASE DID NOT SHUTDOWN WITH -F" dba
        cp $DBNAME.lk $LOGS/$DBNAME.xxx
        exit 0
fi

msg "+++ Database is shutdown"

# sweep .lg file into archive

mv $DBNAME.lk $LOGS            # This won't happen unless the
                                      # shutdown is clean...
```

Backup

There are two basic approaches to backing up a Progress database. You can use the Progress-supplied **PROBKUP** program, an external backup routine like **tar** or **cpio**, or a commercial product. *The only way to back up an online database correctly is with* **PROBKUP**. An external backup cannot correctly back up a running Progress database except by shutting it down first.

One excellent method of backing up a Progress database is to combine the two methods by first backing up to disk using **PROBKUP** and then using an external backup command to copy the disk files to tape. Providing that you have enough disk space configured there are several major advantages to this approach:

- Less down time—a backup to disk is much faster than a backup to tape
- Less recovery time—in many recovery scenarios, having the backup files on disk saves time obtaining tapes from offsite locations in addition to the improved speed of restoring from disk rather than tape
- An extra layer of protection—you can never have too many backups

■ The ability to easily combine nondatabase elements of the application onto a single tape

A sample backup script:

```
# Backup
#

. /mnt/scripts/env    # export TMP=/mnt/tmp

if [ -f $TMP/User_Lockout ]; then
  clear
  cat $TMP/User_Lockout
  sleep 30
  msg "*** Backup of active database???" dba
  exit 0
fi

# continue backup...

msg "*** Starting PROBKUP of $DBNAME"

$DLC/probkup $DBNAME /mnt/dump/$DBNAME.bak >> $LOGS/backup.log 2>&1

msg "*** PROBKUP of $DBNAME complete with status $?"

tar cvf /mnt/dump/$DBNAME.bak >> $LOGS/backup.log 2>&1 &

msg "*** Backup of $DBNAME complete with status $?"
```

It is essential that you periodically test your restore procedures to ensure that a valid backup is being created and that your tapes have everything that you need on them. The best way to do this is to restore to a different machine. This verifies the entire process and all of the media. The PEG periodically features sad tales of unfortunate souls who *thought* they were backing up every night who turned out not to have any means of recovery. Don't join them. Verify your backups.

Monitoring

Progress comes with an excellent character-mode database monitor known as **PROMON**. DBAs should become familiar with **PROMON** in its interactive mode and become accustomed to normal ranges of values for their systems. But the true power of monitoring is obtained by consistently collecting a historical view of activity over a long period of time. You can then use that data to validate a hypothesis regarding a problem and act in a much more targeted and reliable manner. The following script can serve as the basis for collecting that data:

```
# Monitor
#

. /mnt/scripts/env     # export TMP=/mnt/tmp

TM='date "%H.%M"'

$DLC/bin/promon $DBNAME > $LOGS/sample.$TM <<- "EOF" 2> /dev/null
    R&D
    5
    3
    300
    1
    9999
    p
    2
    1
    s
    p
    x
EOF
```

This script starts **PROMON**, enters the R&D menu (which is more detailed than the default menu), and adjusts the sampling interval to 300 seconds and the number of lines per page of output to 9999. It then backs up a menu and goes to the Activity → Summary screen, collects the summary since database startup and a sample of activity during a five-minute sample, and exits.

```
01/18/00          Activity: Summary
15:04:35          01/18/00 14:59 to 01/18/00 15:04 (5 min 1 sec)
```

Event	Total	Per Sec		Event	Total	Per Sec
Commits	17951	59.6		DB Reads	26059	86.5
Undos	2	0.0		DB Writes	903	3.0
Record Reads	1219453	4051.3		BI Reads	0	0.0
Record Updates	5144	17.0		BI Writes	554	1.8
Record Creates	9045	30.0		AI Writes	316	1.0
Record Deletes	869	2.8		Checkpoints	0	0.0
Record Locks	77537	257.5		Flushed at chkpt	0	0.0
Record Waits	0	0.0				

```
Rec Lock Waits      0 %    BI Buf Waits       0 %    AI Buf Waits       0 %
Writes by APW     100 %    Writes by BIW     42 %    Writes by AIW     75 %
DB Size:     95384136 K    BI Size:     255984 K    AI Size:     72656 K
Empty blocks:1002347       Free blocks:        0    RM chain:           8
Buffer Hits        99 %    Active trans:      13
```

3 Servers, 679 Clients (679 Local, 0 Remote, 11 Batch), 2 Apws

Running a script like this from **cron** on a regular basis (every half hour is a good start) provides a baseline for monitoring and controlling your database. There is great deal of additional interesting information available from **PROMON**—add as much as you can stand. It is also helpful to gather OS measurements coincident with this data for possible correlation analysis. For instance:

```
cd /mnt/tmp

ls -l DBI* > $LOGS/dbi.$TM
ls -l srt* > $LOGS/srt.$TM
ls -l lbi* > $LOGS/lbi.$TM

cd /mnt

ls -l db bi ai > $LOGS/dblist.$TM

df > $LOGS/df.$TM
who -u > $LOGS/who.$TM
ps aux > $LOGS/ps.$TM
netstat -i > $LOGS/netstat.$TM
vmstat > $LOGS/vmstat.$TM
top -b -n1 > $LOGS/top.$TM
```

The data captured can provide very important clues regarding the state of the system as a whole during the period that a specific sample was gathered.

Monitoring the database and the operating system is only part of the battle—perhaps the most important and most frequently overlooked opportunity for monitoring is the application itself. The user complaint of "it's slow" is surely one of the most frustrating aspects of an administrator's job. "What's slow?" and "How slow is it?" are two key questions that can be very difficult to answer. A simple technique to gain some insight into those questions is to run a background session that measures response time and gathers key application utilization statistics. This requires a small 4GL procedure like this one:

```
/* zippy.p */

define variable l          as character no-undo.
Define variable stime      as integer no-undo.
Define variable endtime    as integer no-undo.
Define variable ttime      as integer no-undo format ">>>>>9".
Define variable utime      as integer no-undo format ">>>>>9".
Define variable rcount     as integer no-undo.
Define variable nxtapp     as integer no-undo initial 100000.
Define variable z          as integer no-undo.
Define variable next_time as integer no-undo initial 21600.  /* 6am */
Define variable curord     as integer no-undo.
Define variable oldord     as integer no-undo format ">>>>>9".
Define variable I          as integer no-undo.
Define variable r          as integer no-undo extent 100.
Define variable w          as integer no-undo extent 5.
Define variable t          as integer no-undo.
Define variable rt         as integer no-undo.
Define variable wt         as integer no-undo.
Define variable mr         as integer no-undo.
Define variable mw         as integer no-undo.
Define variable fname      as character no-undo.

Fname = "/mnt/logs/" +
        String( month( today ), "99" ) + "." +
        string( day( today ), "99" ) + "/zippy.dat".

do while true.

  Pause 30.
  If time < next_time then next.

  Next_time = 300 * integer( time / 300 ).
  Next_time = next_time + 300.    /* increment time by 5 minutes.   */

  /* 100 sort of random record reads of 5 common tables (20 each) */

  r = 0.
  Stime = etime( yes ).
```

```
Do rcount = 1 to 20:

   Stime = etime.

   Find next customer no-lock no-wait no-error.
   Find next order     no-lock no-wait no-error.
   Find next order-line of order no-lock no-wait no-error.
   Find next salesrep no-lock no-wait no-error.
   Find next state no-lock no-wait no-error.

End.

Ttime = etime.
L = " ".
W = 0.
Utime = etime( yes ).

/* 5 writes         */

do I = 1 to 5:
   utime = etime.
   Do for state TRANSACTION:
      find first state exclusive-lock no-wait.
      if available state then
        state.state = state.state.
       else
         l = "x".
   end.
   w[i] = etime - utime.
End.

Utime = etime.
Curord = current-value( next-ord-num ).
Oldord = ( if oldord = 0 then 0 else ( curord - oldord )).
T = 0.
Mw = 0.

Do I = 1 to 5:
   t = t + w[i].
   Mw = max( mw, w[I] ).
End.
Wt = t / 5.
```

```
T = 0.
Mr = 0.

Do I = 1 to 100:
  t = t + r[i].
   Mr = max( mr, r[I] ).
End.
Rt = t / 100.

Output to value( fname ) append.
Put string( time, "HH:MM" ) + " " + l.
Put
   Ttime
   Utime
   Oldord
   " ".
export mr rt mw wt.
Output close.

Oldord = curord.

End.


Return.
```

This program runs in the background connected to the **sports** database. Every five minutes it reads 100 pseudorandom records, writes a record (that shouldn't ever change or be locked), and calculates the number of new orders received in the pervious five-minute interval. Timing statistics and the number of orders are output every five minutes. You can monitor the output using a command such as:

```
$ tail -f /mnt/log/01.12/zippy.dat
```

Spikes in the results indicate interesting events—if the number of orders spikes then the business is busy and it might be reasonable for read and write response times to increase slightly. Big jumps in response times with or without corresponding jumps in business activity tend to indicate that there is a problem in the environment that needs to be addressed—it might mean, for instance, that another application which is sharing the disks is stressing them to the point that your Progress application is being affected. Or it might mean that you are running near the capacity of the current configuration and that tuning or upgrades are in order.

Gathering performance data that includes business-relevant metrics (such as the number of orders) and being able to cross-reference that data helps greatly when you need to make the case for an upgrade. Or it can help you look for other solutions—if there is no increase in business activity why should performance problems be popping up? Maybe there is something misconfigured or badly designed somewhere.

Troubleshooting

Very little goes wrong with a Progress database. Most issues have to do with managing those crazy users. The following topics are some of the more likely scenarios.

Hung Users, Runaways, and Other Psychos

The simplest (and safest) way to handle **_progress** processes (self-service user sessions) needing some sort of external attention is to wait for them to finish.

If that isn't an option, then in all cases your next step should be to have the user slowly back away from the keyboard keeping their hands in sight at all times. This (hopefully) prevents any problems arising from simultaneous conflicting attempts to remedy the situation. Then your best bet is **kill -2 (SIGINT)**. **Kill -2** simply raises the **STOP** condition in the target 4GL procedure and causes the **-p** startup procedure to be rerun. The process won't die but it won't be doing anything bad either. And if the problem is something along the lines of "I'm hung" the user will probably get their session back without having to go through a UNIX login again (if it's a network or hung PC problem you're out of luck).

If **kill -2** isn't what you need—perhaps because you limit users to one login each and there is a network problem so the idle session is blocking access—then you should still use **kill -2** to get the process to a stable state. Once it is stabilized (the **.lg** file says that any transaction backout is complete and it is no longer accumulating CPU time and performing I/O operations) then **kill -1 (SIGHUP)** should very safely terminate it just as if the user had shut off their terminal. **Kill -15 (SIGTERM)** has much the same effect.

Using a series of **kill** commands isn't a good idea unless you put plenty of time between them and monitor both the **.lg** file and the process status. If you interrupt Progress' cleanup routines and the interruption to an interrupt isn't handled correctly you could easily crash the database.

Trapping signals with the shell **trap** command is a bad idea. It will defeat the proper operation of these signals and lead to a very unstable system. If you shell out of a **_progres** session, type **trap**, and get any output back, then your system is at risk. The most common problem in this scenario is a *runaway* process—a process that attempts to consume all available CPU. If you have traps get rid of them.

Kill -8 (SIGFPE) varies in behavior depending on the release of Progress. In some releases it just acts like an unhandled signal—that is, it dumps core and the process dies without any serious attempt to cleanup, which is essentially the same as **kill -9**. This is bad because you could be holding a latch, thereby bringing down the database. In more recent releases (including the Linux 8.3b release) it cleans up as if **SIGHUP** were sent, but also creates a **procore** file.

Kill -10 (SIGUSR1) in recent releases causes the process to create a **procore** file and a **protrace** file without otherwise impacting the process (the process keeps on running). This is a very neat feature although it's not well supported (it isn't documented anywhere and Tech Support is often ignorant of its existence). The protrace file is very handy—it contains a 4GL stack trace including line numbers showing where the process was at the time that it was signaled. This is very handy for tracking down what a user was (really) doing when they became "hung."

Kill -9 (SIGKILL) is never a good idea. It also isn't ever necessary. There is a myth that **kill -9** is "good" because it "always works." This isn't true—a process blocked in certain states (such as **D** or disk-wait) will not respond to anything—including **kill -9**.

When you use **kill –9**, the killed process cannot clean up (this is a UNIX feature—**kill -9** is defined as being *uncatchable*). Watchdog notices that the client is gone and then attempts to shut down the session and clean up on behalf of the client. Watchdog succeeds at cleaning up almost all the time. Sometimes a critical resource is being held (protected by a latch) and there is no way to clean up because the necessary data was in the vanished memory space of the client. In that event watchdog brings down the database (if you aren't running a watchdog process the broker will perform this function). That isn't as big an issue as it sounds—if a latch was being held (and they always are when watchdog crashes the database) then nobody was doing anything except spinning on it anyway so your users are effectively frozen—they just haven't noticed yet.

The corruption that some people think that they see after using **kill -9** comes from some of the other excitement that often happens along with it. In no event does "bad data" get written to disk either in the **.bi** file or the **.db** file as a direct result of any sort of a **kill** command. Rash actions such as deleting live **.lk** files, misconfiguring the location of the **.bi** file, unwisely using **dbrpr**, or using the **-F** option *can* lead to data corruption (you have to ignore a lot of warning messages to succeed). Environments where **kill -9** is used are usually very uncontrolled and chaotic. Lots of stuff happens that isn't reported or well thought out and it's difficult to get to the bottom of things. So **kill -9** gets blamed.

So in summary, **kill -9** will certainly crash your database sooner or later—it's like playing Russian Roulette. It will not, by itself, corrupt your database. It does, however, lay the groundwork for other activities to be executed, which may damage your data. If you feel that you must kill a process first, use **kill -2**, then, if necessary, **kill -1**. If you need more than that then something is very seriously wrong and you should get help.

Strengths and Weaknesses

Like all products, Progress is not perfect. Although it offers a large set of features that only the enterprise class databases have, it does lack some of the most expensive options available on the "Big Four." Here is a discussion of where Progress shines, and where it is lacking.

The 4GL

In many ways the Progress 4GL (fourth generation language) is both its greatest strength and a weakness combined. The 4GL is a procedural language designed to write an entire application. From the very start PSC has made good on that promise as witnessed by the number of applications available from their partners, each without any significant usage of 3GL (third generation language). These are not just small products either, but industry-leading products from software houses like FiServ; qad, inc.; Symix; and NxTrend.

On the other hand, 4GLs are seen as proprietary and closed. Progress's product is no exception, and in fact, the lack of reasonable ODBC drivers has until recently added to the closed nature of the product. To some extent this is a red herring since in fact all databases have their own proprietary SQL extensions, and code transportability is limited to only a small subset of the application.

OLTP Oriented

From the start, the database engine was built to be a transaction engine. In fact, unlike other databases, it is impossible to modify data and not use a transaction—very high data integrity results. The 4GL also has features that make sense in an OLTP world. SQL traditionally is set related, meaning records are gathered together a set at a time and then processed. For online applications, this is not as efficient or natural as the 4GL that focuses on accessing a single record and making it available to the application immediately.

There is a down side to the pure OLTP model however, and that is Decision Support. Set-oriented access by far outperforms individual record retrieval when large report and forecasting is the goal. ODBC report writers almost always expect such features as well as fast SQL execution. Progress does support the older SQL 88 specification, but it is not optimized for this type of access. Reports still run workable, but in many cases inefficient and poorly written SQL, and computer-generated SQL in particular, does not run nearly as fast as native 4GL for the same reports.

This is in a state of change, though. Version 9 has been slowly introducing the newly written SQL-92 engine. PSC has written an entirely new product that sits on top of the same storage manager as the current 4GL product. The new product not only follows the newer language standard, it is optimized for SQL execution. This new product will become commercial with version 9.1 of Progress.

Bullet-Proof Crash Recovery

In the Progress sales force, there is an old story of how representatives were trained to prove the reliability of the database. Demonstrations were done on portable computers running DOS. There has always been concern on that platform about the operating system clobbering open files. While in the middle of the demonstration, sales reps would purposefully pull the power cord from the wall, without battery power, and crash the machine. Without exception, the database would be undamaged and crash recovery successful. The technology that goes into Progress' transaction processing is the same one that keeps the database going without fear of power failure corrupting the database. This should not be seen as a panacea for hardware failure. All databases will lose data if the physical media is unrecoverable by the hardware.

Cost of Ownership

Progress is priced in the range that ordinary companies can afford—not only in terms of the initial purchase, but also in terms of what it takes to keep a system running. Most Progress installations today do not have a full time database administrator. The database does not need to be reconfigured in many cases unless a significant increase in the number of users occurs. Most Progress administrators share their time between an hour or two monitoring their database and other mundane system administration related tasks. A system that can scale to several thousand users and be operational with minimal database administration is a remarkable achievement.

PSC authorized the Aberdeen Group to evaluate both initial and long-term costs to run the Progress database compared to databases aimed at both large and small environments. The results can be viewed at the Progress web site, http://www.peg.com.

Word Indexes

One of the forgotten gems in the Progress database is a feature known as the *Word Index*. Character data can be used to create a presorted index identifying all of the words contained inside the data. This is not a particularly sophisticated text retrieval feature, but a low-cost way to provide advanced searches on databases of newsgroup posts, legal briefs, and knowledge-base entries. Access to the index is provided by the single 4GL function **CONTAINS**.

Internationalization

Internationalization covers a wide variety of topics from Double Byte enabled versions of Progress for the Asian character sets, to language translations of the Progress error messages, to regionalized date and numeric formats, and collation tables providing sort capabilities based on national character sets. Progress has all of these features through a rich set of character handling features.

In addition, Progress makes an additional cost optional product called Translation Manager. Its primary function is to scan Progress 4GL source code and determine the strings used in the application for various messages and screen labels. This list can then be given to a professional translator without ever having to know anything about computers. Multiple copies of the translated strings can then be kept, and swapped in and out through the Translation Manager product.

24 by 7 Operation

Progress added an online backup feature in several releases prior to the current one. However, there are still several features missing in the product currently available for Linux. The Linux 8.3 version does not allow you to keep the database online during index reorganization. Activation and deactivation of indexes and most other database schema changes currently may not be conducted online.

Progress slowly has been adding features to mitigate some of these issues. For example, new fields can now be added without reorganizing the entire table. In addition, version 9 now offers an online table move and an online index build. The Linux platform is scheduled to be ported during the introduction of Progress 9.1.

No BLOBs

Binary Large Objects (BLOBs) are pieces of data like movie and audio clips, or geospatial data. Progress currently does not support these and has plans for only minimal support in the future. Support for smaller objects, up to 32k bytes, is available and so is using the database as an index of the BLOBs stored as file pointers. However, if you have requirements for heavy multimedia storage, then Progress is not a likely candidate.

No Parallel Queries

A handful of the highest end database systems have incorporated the ability to process a single database query across multiple CPUs. The technology behind this has proven to be extremely costly and time-consuming to debug. Today's massively parallel CPU architectures can certainly produce huge amounts of CPU resources. However, the cost of such machines and the cost of creating the technology puts it out of the reach of the average medium-sized computer department. Costs aside, there is also no guarantee that the individual queries you may have will benefit from processing on more than one CPU. Many cases show that the I/O operations become the bottle-neck instead of the CPU. In those cases, all the money spent on a Parallel Query system would be wasted.

No Distributed Lock Manager

To provide full transactional roll back between multiple databases, a feature called 2-Phase Commit is needed. This was introduced shortly after introducing the capability of one Progress session to be connected to multiple databases at the same time. There is no issue if those databases are located on one single system, since the 2-Phase Commit scheme involves shared data in main memory. But if those databases are located on different machines, the method no longer works. For such a feature to exist, a Distributed Lock Manager is needed. The theory and practice of this type of software is complex and expensive to build. It is even more expensive to continue to manage and run. PSC has taken the stance that the expense of such a Lock Manager would be too much for a client base accustimed to a high ROI database. Consequently, systems needing products like Tuxedo and TopEnd are not candidates for Progress.

For IT Professionals

A Simple CGI Interface to Progress

The standard http server to CGI process simply provides **stdin** and **stdout** to a program, and that program can be anything at all. The following shell script simply passes **stdin** down a well-known FIFO that, as it happens, has a Progress 4GL procedure running in the background reading it (that's why it's well-known... the procedures have agreed in advance to use it). It then reads a response from a

Continued

FIFO that it created and told the Progress server program to use. The point of that is to make sure that the response goes back to the correct user—see Chapter 3 of the Progress External Interfaces Guide for some of the considerations. The Progress program accepts requests and responds to them—the sample form and response are, obviously, silly but are easily modified to do something more interesting:

```sh
#!/bin/sh
#
# cgi-bin/xxx


PIPE=/tmp/cgi$$          # where to send the response
rm -f $PIPE              # make sure that no old one
                        #is hanging around
/bin/mknod $PIPE p      # create the named pipe
chmod 666 $PIPE         # make it writable
read INPUT              # read the form


# add the name of the named pipe to send the response
# down to the front of the form data and write the
# whole mess to the "well known" pipe /tmp/cgi-pipe


echo "${PIPE}&${INPUT}" > /tmp/cgi-pipe


cat < $PIPE             # read the response and echo
                        # it to the server
rm -f $PIPE             # clean up
```

The Progress 4GL part looks like this:

```
/* websrvr.p */


define variable I as integer no-undo.
define variable req as character no-undo.
define variable outpipe as character no-undo.


/* uncomment this if you want the progress daemon to
create the pipe...
```

Continued

```
unix silent value( "rm -f /tmp/cgi-pipe" ).
unix silent value( "/bin/mknod /tmp/cgi-pipe p" ).
*/

do while true:

  input from value( "/tmp/cgi-pipe" ) no-echo.
  import unformatted req.
  outpipe = substring( req, 1, index( req, "&" ) - 1 ).
  output to value( outpipe ) unbuffered.
  put unformatted "Content-type: text/html" skip(1).
  put unformatted skip(1).

  /* do something useful like parse the form, query
     the db and
   * provide a response...
   */

  I = I + 1.

  put unformatted
    "<html><head><title>Bogus
         Response</title></head></html>" +
    "<body><p>" +
    "Sample Bogus Response #" + string( I, ">>>>9" ) +
    "</p></body></html>".
  output close.
  input close.

  end.

return.
```

The relevant HTML looks like this:

```
<form action="cgi-bin/xxx" method="post">
    What? <input name="something" size="30"
    maxlength="30">
```

Continued

```
      <input type="submit" value="submit">
</form>
```

A not-very-sophisticated script to launch the daemon:

```
# Start daemon
#


. /mnt/scripts/env    # export TMP=/mnt/tmp


if [ -f $TMP/User_Lockout ]; then
  clear
  cat $TMP/User_Lockout
  sleep 30
  exit 0
fi


# startup


sh -c "eval nohup $DLC/bin/_progres -b  p websrvr.p
    >> $LOG 2>&1 &"
```

Together these demonstrate a simple and straightforward method of accessing Progress via a web-based interface. Obviously there are security and scalability issues with this approach, but for quick and dirty internal use this approach is very powerful.

Here is an example of a simple HTML table being built out of data in the **sports** database shipped with the product. This creates a list of Customer Information:

```
/* sportssrvr.p */


define variable I as integer no-undo.
define variable req as character no-undo.
define variable outpipe as character no-undo.


/* uncomment this if you want the progress daemon to
    create the pipe...
unix silent value( "rm -f /tmp/cgi-pipe" ).
unix silent value( "/bin/mknod /tmp/cgi-pipe p" ).
*/
```

Continued

```
do while true:

  input from value( "/tmp/cgi-pipe" ) no-echo.
  import unformatted req.
  outpipe = substring( req, 1, index( req, "&" ) - 1 ).
  output to value( outpipe ) unbuffered.
  put unformatted "Content-type: text/html" skip(1).
  put unformatted skip(1).

  /* do something useful like parse the form, query
   * the db and       provide a response...
   */

  I = I + 1.

  put unformatted
    "<html><head><title>Customer
        List</title></head></html>" +
    "<body><br><br><B><I>Customers:</B></I><br>"

"<table><th>Number</th><th>Name</th><th>Address</th>"

"<th>City</th><th>State</th><th>Zip</th><th>Country>
 </th>".
  for each customer no-lock:
    put unformatted "<tr>"
                    "<td>" customer.cust-num "</td>"
                    "<td>" customer.name "</td>"
                    "<td>" customer.address "</td>"
                    "<td>" customer.city "</td>"
                    "<td>" customer.state "</td>"
                    "<td>" customer.postal-code "</td>"
                    "<td>" customer.country "</td>"
                    "</tr>".
  end.
```

Continued

```
    put unformatted "</table></body></html>".
       output close.
       input close.


    end.


    return.
```

Summary

The Progress database has proven itself over the years to be an extremely reliable product, while easy to use and administer. The installation is little more than a copy from media and the setup of a few variables. Although there are many advanced features such as Roll Forward Recovery, and 2-Phase commit, these are not mandatory and administration is simple. The many startup options allow for customizing Progress operations, increasing performance, and balancing resource utilization. Although Progress is an excellent choice for cost-sensitive small and medium companies, some large companies may require additional 24x7 operation features not provided in the v 8.3 release provided on Linux. Other than these highest end features, Progress provides all of the really important features that the big-name databases do at a much smaller cost.

FAQs

Q: How old is Progress Software Corporation?

A: PSC started out as a company called Data Language Corp. in 1981. This is the origin of the DLC variable used during installation. The product has always been called Progress since its commercial introduction in 1983. In keeping with that name recognition, the name of the company was changed in 1987. PSC went public in 1991 and is traded on Nasdaq as PRGS.

Q: What is the difference between the WorkGroup and Enterprise versions of the database?

A: WorkGroup was designed to be used by a maximum of 35 users, and is available only up to the 50-user count level. Almost all of the high-end performance features like variable database blocks, background page writers, and **–spin** parameter are not available. All of the basic features of Roll Forward Recovery, Crash Proof, Networkable, multiple database connections in a single connection, and 2-Phase Commit are common to both databases. But users of any kind will be looking to buy Enterprise if performance is of any concern.

Q: Is Progress available internationally?

A: Yes; in fact, Progress has offices throughout the world. In some cases where Progress does not have its own presence, national distribution networks have been set up. Each office has different policies and price schedules so be sure to speak with your local office. A list is available on the Progress web site.

Q: Is there a recommended RAID level for use with Progress?

A: There is no recommended parity-based RAID (2,3,4,5,7, ...). Parity-based RAID results in a parody of performance. It exists to make you a repeat customer of the RAID vendor, because you will continually need upgrades and enhancements to eke out reasonable performance from such a system. RAID 0 (striping) and RAID 1 (mirroring) are not parity-based and are, therefore, good choices (especially when combined). You have to add RAM and lie about the completion of I/O requests ("write back" cache vs "write through" cache) to improve parity-based RAID performance, whereas you can improve the performance of striped and mirrored systems by adding disks. Disk is cheaper than RAM (especially the RAM required for RAID arrays and big time servers) and you can add lots more of them (there are always severe limits on how much RAM you can add even if you have a bottomless budget...). And then there is the question of what happens to the data in that RAM when the power fails. If a write back cache is enabled (and it has to be to get decent performance out of parody based RAID), one little slip and your database is in jeopardy (battery backups have been known to fail) because the array lied to Progress about what is really on disk, which makes crash recovery very questionable.

Just say **No** to RAID 5 (and its cousins).

Q: Why doesn't Progress work with RAID 5?

A: Progress does work with RAID 5. But like every other database, it works much, much faster with other disk technologies. Progress has no awareness of the sort of RAID system that you use. Only your users will be able to tell.

Q: I'm currently using Progress by installing the SCO binaries and iBCS. What do I need to do to switch to the native Linux port?

A: First, call your PSC Sales Representative and get the license switched to the Linux platform, and install the native binaries as described in this chapter. Make sure you choose a separate directory for this version of Progress. Modify your environment variables, particularly the **$DLC** variable, and the rest of your existing start up/shutdown/backup/etc. scripts should be ready to go. If you are already using the v 8.3 format for SCO, there should be no database conversion necessary. If you are using version 8.2, it should only be a matter of truncating the **.bi** file **proutil dbname –C truncate bi**. Both of these methods are not guaranteed by Progress, however. For versions of Progress older than v 8.2, or for safety, create a new v 8.3 database with the Linux binaries and dump and load between the two databases.

Q: I know Progress 4GL supports graphical programming under MS Windows, and I know Progress supports Linux as a host-based character client. But can I program under X Windows as well?

A: Yes, but only with the older version 7 of Progress that is not a native port to Linux (in other words, the SCO binaries using the iBCS emulation). At the time version 8 was under construction, the marketing team reviewed the number of licenses sold to UNIX GUI environments and found the numbers to be small. A marketing decision was made to freeze the X Windows support at the Progress V7 level. This was also at a time when X Windows meant special X-Terminal hardware, or expensive third-party PC emulation of X Windows. Linux popularity was not what it is today, and the number of X Windows capable computers has grown accordingly since then. By all means call your Progress Sales Representative and express interest in reviving support for X Windows.

Q: I heard that after-imaging is a performance drain. Do I really need it? After all, I back up the database anyway.

A: After-imaging will save you. Running after-imaging allows you to restore a database right up to the minute before the crash. Even if you back up your entire system on a nightly basis, you run the risk of crashing at the end of the day. Your entire day's worth of work is gone if you are not running after-imaging. Always ask the question, "Can I afford to lose data from the time the last backup was done?" Few 24x7 and other mission-critical systems will say the data loss is acceptable.

Q: The Progress documentation says I can administer the database through the Dictionary even though I have only run-time clients. How can I get to the Dictionary?

A: The Dictionary code is supplied as encrypted source. Simply start your Progress session with the **–rx** parameter for encrypted source mode.

Q: When I start my Progress session it says "This Version Of Progress Requires A Startup Procedure." What's wrong?

A: There are several possibilities. This occurs when you have started a Progress session and attempted to get to the Procedure Editor. The Client/Networking product is meant to run only compiled code or encrypted source. You will not be able to compile new programs with this Progress client; you need Query/Runtime or the 4GL client. If you purchased one of those products and the message still appears, check the **$DLC** and **$PROCFG** variables for errors. Progress looks at the **progress.cfg** file to determine which products are installed, and if it cannot find this file it assumes you do not have the proper licenses. A corrupted **progress.cfg** file will also cause this, and so will the session startup parameter **–rr**

## Chapter 9

PostgreSQL on Linux

Solutions in this chapter:

- Installation
- Configuration
- Issues
- Troubleshooting

Introduction

Every computer system in the world needs a database to store and retrieve information. The primary reason you use the computer is to store, retrieve, and process information, and to do all these very quickly, thereby saving you time. At the same time, the system must be simple, robust, fast, reliable, economical, and very easy to use. A database is the most vital system, because it stores mission-critical information of every company in the world. Industries like telecom, automobile, banks, airlines, etc. will not function efficiently without a database system. The most popular database systems are based on the International Standard Organization (ISO) SQL specifications and ANSI SQL (American) standards. The current specifications widely used in the industry are ISO/ANSI SQL 1992/98. Without a standard like ANSI/ISO SQL, it would be very difficult for the customer to develop an application once, and run it on all the database systems. An end user wants to develop an application only once, using ISO SQL, ODBC, JDBC, and then be able to deploy it on all variety of database systems.

PostgreSQL is the most advanced *open source code* object relational database in the world. Postgres, developed originally in the UC Berkeley Computer Science Department, pioneered many of the object-relational concepts. It provides SQL92/SQL3 language support, transaction integrity, user-defined functions, stored procedures, triggers, and type extensibility. PostgreSQL is a free and open-source descendant of this original Berkeley code. Millions of PostgreSQL databases are installed as database servers, Web database servers, and application database servers. It is a very sophisticated object relational database system (ORDBMS).

PostgreSQL runs on Solaris, SunOS, HPUX, AIX, Linux, Irix, Digital Unix, BSDi, NetBSD, FreeBSD, SCO UNIX, NEXTSTEP, Unixware, and almost all flavors of UNIX. A port to Microsoft Windows NT has been done using the Cygnus cygwin32 package.

- Title: PostgreSQL SQL RDBMS Database (Object Relational Database Management System)
- Current Version: 7.0
- Age: In development since 1985, PostgreSQL is now 15 years old.
- Authors: PostgreSQL was developed by millions of people in universities and companies on the Internet for the past 15 years.

MySQL is another open-source, quasi-commercial database system, but it supports important features like transactions.

Internet Power Drives PostgreSQL

The Internet, which started as a defense project, became so widespread that it connected people living on all continents of the globe. That promoted a rapid exchange of information, intelligent ideas, and research topics across continents around the globe. The result was that the Internet became the world's largest "generator" of software. The software development methodology changed from closed-source to open-source code, and the Internet facilitated such a system.

The Internet was used to help create the operating system *Linux*, which became immensely popular. With the success of Linux, many people decided to carry forward the idea on computer applications such as database systems, spreadsheets, and so on. Instead of starting a system from scratch, developers on the Internet took the University of California's public-domain Postgres code and started making changes and enhancements to it, resulting in PostgreSQL.

The Internet is the real engine that drives PostgreSQL. The laws of physics and statistics are also partly responsible for the success of PostgreSQL—they favor open source code systems like PostgreSQL and Linux. As Internet speed is increasing every day, and the Internet is becoming more and more reliable, the open source code system will gain very rapid momentum. By applying the principles of statistics, mathematics, and science to software quality, you get the best quality of software only in an open source code system like PostgreSQL, whose source code is open to the Internet, the "information superhighway." The more people working on the code, the better will be the quality of software. The open source code model greatly reduces duplication of work, reduces the cost of development, saves time in distribution, and follows the modern economic laws of optimizing the national and global resources. Once others have produced a software package, you do not need to waste your valuable time redoing something already well done.

You get many features with PostgreSQL since it follows the open source code development model. The pace of software development on the Internet is very rapid because an extremely vast network of computers and people are involved in the process. Future trends indicate that most of the software development will take place on the so-called information superhighway, which spans the whole globe. In the coming years, Internet growth will be explosive, which will further fuel rapid adoption of PostgreSQL by the industry.

Since a lot of work had been done on PostgreSQL during the past 15 years, it does not make sense to recreate from scratch another database system that satisfies ANSI/ISO SQL. It will be a great advantage to take the existing code and add missing features or enhancements to PostgreSQL, and start using it immediately.

Demand for Internet products like PostgreSQL is predicted to grow exponentially, since it is capable of maintaining a high quality, low cost, extremely large user and developer base. Those nations not using Internet products will be seriously missing the worldwide Internet revolution, and will be left far behind other countries, because the Internet itself is the world's largest "software company."

Getting PostgreSQL

If you plan to use PostgreSQL on Linux operating systems, you can buy either the Red Hat Linux CD-ROM, Debian Linux CD-ROM, or Slackware Linux CD-ROM, which already contain the PostgreSQL in package form (both source code and binaries), or you can purchase them online from one of these Web sites:

- Linux System Labs: http://www.lsl.com/
- Red Hat: http://www.redhat.com/
- Cheap Bytes Inc.: http://www.cheapbytes.com/
- Debian: http://www.debian.org/vendors.html

The PostgreSQL organization is also selling the PostgreSQL CD-ROM, which contains the complete source code and binaries for many UNIX operating systems as well as full online documentation:

- PostgreSQL CD-ROM from the main Web site:
  http://www.postgresql.org

If you want to download from the Internet, visit the following sites:

- PostgreSQL source RPM and binaries RPM:
  http://www.ramifordistat.net/postgres
- The maintainer of PostgreSQL RPMs is Lamar Owen:
  lamar.owen@wgcr.org
- PostgreSQL source RPM and binaries RPM:
  http://www.postgresql.org
  Click Latest News and click Red Hat RPMs.
- PostgreSQL source RPM and binaries RPM:
  http://www.redhat.com/pub/contrib/i386/
  Ftp site: ftp://ftp.redhat.com/pub/contrib/i386/
- Binaries site for Solaris, HPUX, AIX, IRIX, and Linux:
  ftp://ftp.postgresql.org/pub/bindist

PostgreSQL Quick-Install Instructions

Even though PostgreSQL is the most advanced and most sophisticated database system in the world, installing PostgreSQL is not at all complex, and in fact, installation takes less than five minutes with binary RPMs. PostgreSQL needs a bare minimum of 40MB disk space and 8MB of RAM. But nowadays, even low-cost PC systems are shipping with 10GB hard-disks and 64MB RAM. This section gives you a bird's-eye view of the installation process. If you have had some experience with Linux and Red Hat RPM packages, you can complete PostgreSQL installation in just five minutes by simply following the next steps. If you are a novice to Linux/UNIX, then cross-reference this section with the next section, "Detailed Instructions," which explains in detail each one of the steps.

On Red Hat Linux systems, use the following steps. On Debian Linux, the steps will be similar, but replace **.rpm** with **.deb**. On Debian Linux, if you do not have PostgreSQL packages then you can convert Red Hat PostgreSQL RPM packages to Debian packages using the rpm2deb program.

Login as root and give the following commands at the **bash** prompt:

```
# cd /mnt/cdrom/Red Hat/RPMS

# man rpm

# ls postgre*.rpm (to see list of packages)

# rpm -qpi postgre*.rpm | less (to see info of package)

# rpm -qpl postgre*.rpm | less (to see list of files inside each package)

# ps -auxw | grep postmaster
```

If the postmaster is running then exit all the PostgreSQL applications and stop the postmaster process.

```
# cat /etc/passwd | grep postgres
```

> **NOTE**
>
> If you see a postgres user, you may need to back up and clean up the **postgres** home directory ~**postgres** and delete the UNIX user postgres, or rename the UNIX user postgres to something like postgres2. It must be a clean-slate install.

Install the required **postgresql** packages—you must install all packages of clients, data, and server for **pgaccess** to work.

To start PostgreSQL during booting:

```
# man chkconfig
```

```
# chkconfig --add postgresql
```

To start up postgres server right now:

```
# /etc/rc.d/init.d/postgresql start
```

To give display access for pgaccess do the following:

```
# man xhost
# xhost +
# su - postgres
bash$ man createdb
bash$ createdb mydatabase
bash$ man psql
bash$ psql mydatabase
..... in psql press up/down arrow keys for history line editing or give \s

bash$ export DISPLAY=<hostname>:0.0
bash$ man pgaccess
bash$ pgaccess mydatabase
```

Now you can start banging away SQL commands at **psql** or **pgaccess**! To read all the FAQs, User, Programmer, Admin guides, and tutorials, use:

```
bash$ cd /usr/doc/postgresql*
```

Here you will see all the documents for PostgreSQL. You can read the compressed postscript file using the following command:

```
bash$ man gv
```

```
bash$ gv admin.ps.gz
```

If the preceding steps do not work for you, you can get additional information from *Installation Steps* at http://www.ramifordistat.net/ postgres. Lamar Owen is the maintainer of PostgreSQL RPMs; his e-mail address is lamar.owen@wgcr.org. Also familiarize yourself with the RPM Package Manager in order to manage the PostgreSQL installations. Download the *Maximum RPM* textbook from http://www.rpm.org, and look for the filename **maximum-rpm.ps.gz**. Read it on Linux using the **gv** command:

```
bash$ gv maximum-rpm.ps.gz
```

Detailed Installation

This section is the detailed explanation of each one of the steps in the section "PostgreSQL Quick-Install Instructions."

Insert the latest Red Hat Linux CD-ROM into the caddy and log in as root. Give the following commands at the **bash** prompt:

```
# mount /mnt/cdrom
```

This will mount the CD-ROM on the directory **/mnt/cdrom**. Now change to the directory where all the RPMs are located:

```
# cd /mnt/cdrom/Red Hat/RPMS
```

You need to know some basics about the RPM packages and the Linux command **rpm**. To see online documentation that explains the options and usage of **rpm**, issue the following command:

```
# man rpm
```

PostgreSQL RPMs are generally named as **postgresql-aaa-x.x.x-r.rpm**, where **aaa** is the package, like **jdbc** or **server**; **x.x.x** is the version number, like 7.0.0; and **r** is the package release, like **1**, **2**, **3**, and so on. To see the list of PostgreSQL RPMs:

```
# ls postgre*.rpm
postgresql-6.5.2-1.i386.rpm
postgresql-devel-6.5.2-1.i386.rpm
postgresql-jdbc-6.5.2-1.i386.rpm
postgresql-odbc-6.5.2-1.i386.rpm
postgresql-perl-6.5.2-1.i386.rpm
postgresql-python-6.5.2-1.i386.rpm
postgresql-server-6.5.2-1.i386.rpm
postgresql-tcl-6.5.2-1.i386.rpm
postgresql-test-6.5.2-1.i386.rpm
```

To read the information about the PostgreSQL RPM use the **-i rpm** option and **pipe it to less** command so that you scroll page by page. See the online manual page by typing **man less**.

```
# rpm -qpi postgre*.rpm | less
Name        : postgresql            Relocations: /usr
Version     : 6.5.2                      Vendor: Red Hat Software
Release     : 1                      Build Date: Sun 26 Sep 1999
                                                 03:41:44 PM CDT
Install date: (not installed)        Build Host: porky.devel.redhat.com
Group       : Applications/Databases Source RPM: postgresql-6.5.2-1.src.rpm
Size        : 7354692                   License: BSD
```

```
Packager      : Red Hat Software <http://developer.redhat.com/bugzilla>
URL           : http://www.ramifordistat.net/
Summary       : The PostgreSQL server programs.
Description : Postgresql includes the programs needed to create and run
a PostgreSQL server, which will in turn allow you to create and maintain
PostgreSQL databases.  PostgreSQL is an advanced Object-Relational database
management system (DBMS) that supports almost all SQL constructs.
```

Sometimes it is a good idea to check the list of files inside the RPM package. To see the list of files in the PostgreSQL RPMs:

```
# rpm -qpl postgre*.rpm | less
```

The RPM option **-q** is query mode, **-p** is package, and **-l** is list files.

If PostgreSQL already exists on your system and if the database is running on the default port, then you *must* first stop the postmaster process. To see if any PostgreSQL process is running type:

```
# ps -auxw | grep postmaster
```

If the postmaster is running, exit all the PostgreSQL applications and stop the postmaster process. You can stop the postmaster by giving the following command:

```
# /etc/rc.d/init.d/postgresql stop
```

The PostgreSQL installation must always be a "clean slate" installation in that your system can not have prior installations of PostgreSQL. If you do have an installation of PostgreSQL, you may need to move or rename it so that there is no "name collision." PostgreSQL is usually installed under the Postgres UNIX user ID. Now check to see if there is already a UNIX user by the name of postgres on your Linux system. Type:

```
# cat /etc/passwd | grep postgres
postgres:x:40:233:PostgreSQL Server:/var/lib/pgsql:/bin/bash
```

If you see a postgres user then you may need to back up and clean up the Postgres home directory **~postgres** and delete the UNIX user postgres, or rename the UNIX user postgres to something like postgres2.

Install the required **postgresql** packages, but if you have enough hard disk space, install all PostgreSQL RPMs.

```
# rpm -i postgre*.rpm
```

If you want the Linux system to start up the PostgreSQL database automatically during the system booting, add PostgreSQL to system init startup scripts using the Linux command **chkconfig**. To read the online manual type:

```
# man chkconfig
```

```
# chkconfig --add postgresql
```

This will add the following soft links in /etc/rc?.d directory to the file /etc/rc.d/init.d/postgresql:

```
init.d/postgresql
rc0.d/K15postgresql
rc1.d/K15postgresql
rc2.d/K15postgresql
rc3.d/S85postgresql
rc4.d/S85postgresql
rc5.d/S85postgresql
rc6.d/K15postgresql
```

Now that all the PostgreSQL system files are in place, start the Postgres server right now by typing the command:

```
# /etc/rc.d/init.d/postgresql start
```

This will start the Linux process **postmaster**, which will be listening for the requests on the TCP port **5432**. To see the running process, type:

```
# ps -auxw | grep postmaster
```

Now you are ready to use the PostgreSQL interface applications. The two most widely used PostgreSQL user interfaces are **pgaccess** and **psql**. **psql** is a command-line, terminal-based interactive program and the **pgaccess** is an X Windows GUI-based application written in Tcl/Tk program. It is extremely user friendly and you can use mouse buttons to click on various functions to create tables and databases, run queries and reports, and so on. Since **pgaccess** is an X Windows application, you must give permission to other UNIX users to use the X Windows server display. To give X Windows display access for **pgaccess** to other UNIX users, type:

```
# xhost +
```

The + after **xhost** means give display access to all the UNIX users on your system. Refer to a standard X Windows textbook for more help, and see also the online manual page:

```
# man xhost
```

Login as postgres by typing:

```
# su - postgres
```

See **man su** for details on the **su** (Switch User) command.

Now you are logged in as the postgres user. The prompt sign changes from **#** to **bash$**. Now type:

```
bash$ id
postgres(uid=10 gid=4)
```

You are ready to create your first database! You do so by using the command **createdb**. See the online manual page on **createdb**:

```
bash$ man createdb

bash$ createdb mydatabase
```

This will create a database named **mydatabase**. After creating the database, you can access the database through the **psql** interface. See the online document by typing:

```
bash$ man psql
```

and access **mydatabase** by typing:

```
bash$ psql mydatabase
```

This will put you inside the **psql** program at the **psql** prompt. Inside **psql** you press up and down arrow keys for history line editing, or alternatively, use the **\s** command. Now you can enter all the standard SQL commands at the **psql** prompt. Refer to a SQL tutorial or SQL textbook for more help.

Exit the **psql** program by typing the **\q** command. This will put you back at the **bash$** prompt.

Now, to use the **pgaccess** interface to PostgreSQL you should export a Linux environment variable called **DISPLAY**:

```
bash$ export DISPLAY=<hostname>:0.0
```

where **hostname** is the name of the Linux host as given in the file **/etc/hosts**, or the IP address of the host. For example, on my machine I type:

```
bash$ export DISPLAY=elmo:0.0
```

or alternatively, I type:

```
bash$ export DISPLAY=198.210.32.110:0.0
```

where **198.210.32.110** is the IP address of the host named **elmo**. See the manual page on **pgaccess** by typing:

```
bash$ man pgaccess
```

and access your **mydatabase** database by typing:

```
bash$ pgaccess mydatabase
```

This will pop up a convenient GUI application on your X Windows system (KDE or GNOME). There is also a help button, which gives more details about **pgaccess**.

Now you can start banging away SQL commands at **psql** or **pgaccess**!

All the documentation is installed in the **/usr/doc** directory on a Red Hat Linux system. To read all the FAQs, User, Programmer, and Admin Guides and Tutorials, type:

```
bash$ cd /usr/doc/postgresql-6.5.2
```

You can read the compressed postscript file using the following command:

```
bash$ gv admin.ps.gz
```

See also the online document on the **gv** command:

```
bash$ man gv
```

If the preceding steps do not work for you, then you can get additional information from *Installation Steps*, at http://www.ramifordistat.net/postgres. Lamar Owen is the maintainer of PostgreSQL RPMs, and his e-mail address is lamar.owen@wgcr.org. Also familiarize yourself with the Red Hat RPM package manager in order to manage the PostgreSQL installations. Download the *Maximum RPM* textbook from http://www.rpm.org and look for the filename **maximum-rpm.ps.gz**. Read it on Linux using the **gv** command:

```
bash$ gv maximum-rpm.ps.gz
```

Installation of the Source Distribution

In addition to these tools, you will also need the GNU tools **gcc** and **make**. You can determine if you have these tools with the following commands:

```
shell$ which gcc
/usr/bin/gcc
shell$ which make
/usr/bin/make
```

The **gcc** that is installed must be version 2.81 or later. You can determine your version with the following:

```
shell$ gcc -v
Reading specs from /usr/lib/gcc-lib/i386-redhat-linux/egcs-2.91.66/specs
gcc version egcs-2.91.66 19990314/Linux (egcs-1.1.2 release)
```

If this is not the correct version, refer to your Linux distribution documentation to find out how to upgrade. Also, visit the GNU Web site listed earlier for help in the installation of these tools. Commands were tested on Red Hat Linux version 5.2 using the **bash** shell. Except where noted, they will probably work on most systems. Commands like **ps** and **tar** may vary wildly between platforms on what options you should use. Use common sense before entering these commands.

If you haven't gotten the PostgreSQL distribution, get it from ftp.postgresql.org and unpack it:

```
$ cd /usr/src
$ gzip -cd /tmp/postgresql/-7.0.tar.g2 |tar xvf -
```

Before You Start

Building PostgreSQL requires the GNU **make** command. It will not work with other **make** programs. On GNU/Linux systems, GNU **make** is the default tool; on other systems you may find that GNU **make** is installed under the name **gmake**. We will use that name from now on to indicate GNU **make**, no matter what name it has on your system. To test for GNU **make**, enter:

```
$ gmake -version
```

If you need to get GNU **make**, you can find it at ftp://ftp.gnu.org. Up to date information on supported platforms is at http://www.postgresql. org/docs/admin/ports.htm. In general, most UNIX-compatible platforms with modern libraries should be able to run PostgreSQL. In the **doc** subdirectory of the distribution are several platform-specific FAQ and README documents you might wish to consult if you are having trouble.

Although the minimum required memory for running PostgreSQL can be as little as 8MB, there are noticeable speed improvements when expanding memory up to 96MB or beyond. The rule is you can never have too much memory.

Check that you have sufficient disk space. You will need about 30MB for the source tree during compilation and about 5MB for the installation directory. An empty database takes about 1MB; otherwise, they take about five times the amount of space that a flat text file with the same data would take. If you run the regression tests you will temporarily need an extra 20MB.

To check for disk space, use

```
$ df -k
```

Considering today's prices for hard disks, getting a large and fast hard disk should probably be in your plans before putting a database into production use.

Step-by-Step Procedure

For a fresh install, or when upgrading from previous releases of PostgreSQL:

1. Create the PostgreSQL superuser account—the server will run as this user. For production use you should create a separate, unprivileged account (postgres is commonly used). If you do not have root access or just want to play around, your own user account is enough.

   Running PostgreSQL as root, bin, or any other account with special access rights is a security risk and therefore won't be allowed. You do not need to do the building and installation itself under this account (although you can). You will be told when you need to log in as the database superuser.

2. If you are not upgrading an existing system, skip ahead to step 4.

   You now need to back up your existing database. To dump your fairly recent post-6.0 database installation, type:

   ```
   $ pg_dumpall > db.out
   ```

   If you wish to preserve object ids (OIDs), use the **-o** option when running **pg_dumpall**. However, unless you have a special reason for doing this (such as using OIDs as keys in tables), don't do it.

   Make sure to use the **pg_dumpall** command from the version you are currently running. However, do not use the **pg_dumpall** script from 6.0 or everything will be owned by the PostgreSQL superuser. In that case you should grab **pg_dumpall** from a later 6.x.x release. Version 7.0's **pg_dumpall** will not work on older databases. If you are upgrading from a version prior to Postgres95 v1.09, you must back up your database, install Postgres95 v1.09, restore your database, and then back it up again.

WARNING

You must make sure that your database is not updated in the middle of your backup. If necessary, bring down postmaster, edit the permissions in file **/usr/local/pgsql/data/pg_hba.conf** to allow only you on, then bring postmaster back up.

3. If you are upgrading an existing system, kill the database server now. Type:

```
$ ps ax|grep postmaster
```

This should list the process numbers for a number of processes, similar to this:

```
1032   ?    S    0:00 /usr/bin/postmaster -i -S -D/var/lib/pgsql
1089   pts/3 S    0:00 grep postmaster
```

Type the following line, with **pid** replaced by the process ID for process postmaster (**263** in this case). (Do not use the ID for the process **grep postmaster**.)

```
$ kill pid
```

TIP

On systems that have PostgreSQL started at boot time, there is probably a startup file that will accomplish the same thing. For example, on a Red Hat Linux system, you might find that:

```
$ /etc/rc.d/init.d/postgres.init stop
```

works. Also move the old directories out of the way. Type the following:

```
$ mv /usr/local/pgsql /usr/local/pgsql.old
```

or replace your particular paths.

4. Configure the source code for your system. It is at this step that you can specify your actual installation path for the build process and make choices about what gets installed. Change into the **src** subdirectory and type:

```
$ ./configure
```

followed by any options you might want to give it. For a first installation, you should be able to do fine without any. For a complete list of options, type:

```
/configure --help
```

Some of the more commonly used options are:

- **prefix=BASEDIR** Selects a different base directory for the installation of PostgreSQL. The default is **/usr/local/pgsql**.
- **enable-locale** Lets you use locales.
- **enable-multibyte** Allows the use of multibyte character encodings. This is primarily for languages like Japanese, Korean, or Chinese.
- **with-perl** Builds the Perl interface. Please note that the Perl interface will be installed into the usual place for Perl modules (typically under **/usr/lib/perl**), so you must have root access to use this option successfully.
- **with-odbc** Builds the ODBC driver package.
- **with-tcl** Builds interface libraries and programs requiring Tcl/Tk, including libpgtcl, pgtclsh, and pgtksh.

5. Compile the program. Type:

```
$ gmake
```

The compilation process can take anywhere from 10 minutes to an hour. Your mileage will most certainly vary. The last line displayed hopefully will be as follows:

```
All of PostgreSQL is successfully made. Ready to install.
```

Remember, **gmake** may be called **make** on your system.

6. Install the program. Type:

```
$ gmake install
```

7. Tell your system how to find the new shared libraries—this method varies between platforms. What tends to work everywhere is to set the environment variable **LD_LIBRARY_PATH**:

```
$ LD_LIBRARY_PATH=/usr/local/pgsql/lib
```

```
$ export LD_LIBRARY_PATH
```

You might want to put this into a shell startup file such as **~/.bash_profile**.

On some systems the following is the preferred method, but you must have root access. Edit file **/etc/ld.so.conf** to add a line:

```
/usr/local/pgsql/lib
```

Then run the command **/sbin/ldconfig**.

When in doubt, refer to the manual pages of your system. If you get a message like the following:

```
./psql: error in loading shared libraries
```

```
libpq.so.2.1: cannot open shared object file: No such file or
directory
```

then the preceding step was necessary—simply do this step now.

8. Create the database installation. To do this you must log in to your PostgreSQL superuser account. It will not work as root.

```
$ mkdir /usr/local/pgsql/data
$ chown postgres /usr/local/pgsql/data
$ su - postgres
$ /usr/local/pgsql/initdb -D /usr/local/pgsql/data
```

The **-D** option specifies the location where the data will be stored. You can use any path you want—it does not have to be under the installation directory. Just make sure that the superuser account can write to the directory (or create it) before starting **initdb**. (If you have already been doing the installation up to now as the PostgreSQL superuser, you may have to log in as root temporarily to create the data directory.)

9. The preceding step tells you how to start up the database server—do so now.

```
$ /usr/local/pgsql/bin/postmaster -D /usr/local/pgsql/data
```

This will start the server in the foreground. To make it detach to the background, use the **–S** option.

10. If you are upgrading from an existing installation, dump your data back in:

```
$ /usr/local/pgsql/bin/psql < db.out
```

You also might want to copy over the old pg_hba.conf file and any other files you might have had set up for authentication, such as password files.

This concludes the installation proper. To make your life more productive and enjoyable, look at the following optional steps and suggestions.

■ Life will be more convenient if you set up some environment variables. First, you probably want to include **/usr/local/pgsql/bin** (or equivalent) into your PATH. To do this, add the following to your shell startup file, such as **~/.bash_profile** (or **/etc/profile**, if you want it to affect every user):

```
PATH=$PATH:/usr/local/pgsql/bin
```

- Furthermore, if you set PGDATA in the environment of the PostgreSQL superuser, you can omit the **-D** option for **postmaster** and **initdb**.

- You probably want to install the **man** and HTML documentation. Type:

  ```
  $ cd /usr/src/pgsql/postgresql-7.0/doc
  $ gmake install
  ```

- This will install files under **/usr/local/pgsql/doc** and **/usr/local/pgsql/man**. To enable your system to find the man documentation, you need to add a line like the following to a shell startup file:

  ```
  MANPATH=$MANPATH:/usr/local/pgsql/man
  ```

- The documentation is also available in Postscript format. If you have a Postscript printer or if your machine is already set up to accept Postscript files using a print filter, to print the User's Guide type the following:

  ```
  $ cd /usr/local/pgsql/doc
  $ gunzip -c user.ps.tz | lpr
  ```

- Here is how you might do it if you have **Ghostscript** on your system and are writing to a laserjet printer:

```
$ alias gshp='gs -sDEVICE=laserjet -r300 -dNOPAUSE'
$ export GS_LIB=/usr/share/ghostscript:/usr/share/ghostscript/fonts
$ gunzip user.ps.gz
$ gshp -sOUTPUTFILE=user.hp user.ps
$ gzip user.ps
$ lpr -l -s -r manpage.hp
```

- If in doubt, confer with your manuals or your local expert. The Administrator's Guide probably should be your first reading if you are completely new to PostgreSQL, since it contains information about how to set up database users and authentication.

- Usually, you will want to modify your computer so that it will start the database server automatically, whenever it boots. This is not required; the PostgreSQL server can be run successfully from nonprivileged accounts without root intervention.

- Different systems have different conventions for starting up daemons at boot time, so you are advised to familiarize yourself with them. Most systems have a file called **/etc/rc.local** or **/etc/rc.d/rc.local**, which is almost certainly not a bad place to put such a command. Whatever you do, **postmaster** must be run by the PostgreSQL superuser (postgres) and not by root or any other user. Therefore you probably always want to form your command lines along the lines of **su -c '...' postgres**.

- It is advisable to keep a log of the server output. To start the server that way, try:

```
nohup su -c 'postmaster -D /usr/local/pgsql/data > server.log 2>&1' postgres &
```

Here are a few more operating system-specific suggestions.

- Edit file **rc.local** on NetBSD or file **rc2.d** on SPARC Solaris 2.5.1 to contain the following single line:

```
su postgres -c "/usr/local/pgsql/bin/postmaster -S -D
    /usr/local/pgsql/data"
```

- In the FreeBSD 2.2-RELEASE, edit **/usr/local/etc/rc.d/pgsql.sh** to contain the following lines and make it **chmod 755** and **chown root:bin**:

```
#!/bin/sh
[ -x /usr/local/pgsql/bin/postmaster ] && {
    su -l pgsql -c 'exec /usr/local/pgsql/bin/postmaster
        -D/usr/local/pgsql/data
        -S -o -F > /usr/local/pgsql/errlog' &
    echo -n ' pgsql'

}
```

- You may put the line breaks as shown here. The shell is smart enough to keep parsing beyond end-of-line if there is an expression unfinished. The exec saves one layer of shell under the postmaster process so the parent is **init**.

- In Red Hat Linux, add a file **/etc/rc.d/init.d/postgres.init**, which is based on the example in **contrib/linux/**. Then make a softlink to this file from **/etc/rc.d/rc5.d/S98postgres.init**.

- Run the regression tests to verify that PostgreSQL runs on your machine in the way the developers expected it to. You definitely should do this before putting a server into production use. The file **/usr/src/pgsql/postgresql-7.0/src/test/regress/README** has detailed instructions for running and interpreting the regression tests.

PostgreSQL Examples RPM

Examples RPM contains various programs to validate the installation of PostgreSQL at your site. They are also needed to do testing of various interfaces to PostgreSQL. Install the **postgresql** examples directory from one of the following sources:

- Linux CD-ROM: postgresql-*examples.rpm
- Get postgresql-*examples.rpm from http://www.aldev.8m.com or http://www.aldev.webjump.com
- PostgreSQL source code tree postgresql*.src.rpm: look for examples, testing, or tutorial directories

Testing Tcl/Tk Interface

An example of the Tcl/Tk interface is the **pgaccess** program. It requires X Windows to be running. You can use KDE, GNOME, or Motif window. Read the file **/usr/bin/pgaccess** using a text editor like **vi**, **gvim**, or **view**:

```
# man xhost
# xhost +
# su - postgres
bash$ view /usr/bin/pgaccess
bash$ export DISPLAY=<hostname of your machine>:0.0
bash$ createdb mydb
bash$ pgaccess mydb
```

This will bring up a beautiful GUI showing various buttons for creating forms, tables, queries, reports, etc. For more information on **pgaccess**, visit http://www.flex.ro/pgaccess. If you have any comments or suggestions for improvements, send e-mail to teo@flex.ro.

Testing Python Interface—PyGreSQL

After installing PostgreSQL Examples RPM, do the following:

```
bash$ cd /usr/lib/pgsql/python
bash$ createdb thilo
bash$ psql thilo
thilo=> create table test (aa char(30), bb char(30) );
bash$ /usr/bin/python
>>> import _pg
>>> db = _pg.connect('thilo', 'localhost')
```

```
>>> db.query("INSERT INTO test VALUES ('ping', 'pong')")
>>> db.query("SELECT * FROM test")
eins|zwei
----+----
ping|pong
(1 row)
>>>CTRL+D
bash$
..... Seems to work - now install it properly
bash$ su - root
# cp /usr/lib/pgsql/python/_pg.so /usr/lib/python1.5/lib-dynload
```

Testing the Perl Interface

After installing PostgreSQL Examples RPM, do the following.

```
bash$ cd /usr/doc/postgresql-7.0.0/examples/perl5
```

```
bash$ perl ./example.pl
```

> ## NOTE
>
> If this command does not work, try the following. Global var @INC should include the Pg.pm module in directory **site_perl**, so use the **-I** option:
>
> ```
> bash$ perl -I/usr/lib/perl5/site_perl/5.005/i386-linux-thread ./example.pl
> ```
>
> You ran the Perl, which is accessing PostgreSQL database! Read the **example.pl** file for information on using the Perl interface.

Testing the libpq and libpq++ Interfaces

After installing PostgreSQL Examples RPM, do the following:

```
bash$ cd /usr/doc/postgresql-7.0.0/examples/libpq++
bash$ su root    -> to change ownership of examples
# chown -R postgres /usr/doc/postgresql-7.0.0/examples
# exit
bash$ g++ testlibpq0.cc -I/usr/include/pgsql -I/usr/include/pgsql/libpq++
-lpq++ -lpq -lcrypt
bash$ ./a.out
```

Ignore error messages if you get any—as below:

```
> create table foo (aa int, bb char(60));
No tuples returned...
status = 1
Error returned: fe_setauthsvc: invalid name: , ignoring...
> insert into foo values ('4535', 'vasu');
No tuples returned...
status = 1
Error returned: fe_setauthsvc: invalid name: , ignoring...
> select * from foo;
aa    |bb    |
-----|-----|
4535 |vasu |
Query returned 1 row.
>
>CTRL+D
bash$
```

You ran direct C/C++ interfaces to the PostgreSQL database!

Testing Java Interfaces

After installing PostgreSQL Examples RPM, install the following:

- Get JDK jdk-*glibc*.rpm from
  ftp://ftp.redhat.com/pub/contrib/i386 or from
  http://www.blackdown.org

- Get postgresql-jdbc-*.rpm
  ftp://ftp.redhat.com/pub/contrib/i386

```
bash$ cd /usr/doc/postgresql-7.0.0/examples/jdbc
bash$ echo $CLASSPATH
 --> Should show  CLASSPATH=/usr/lib/jdk-x.x.x/lib/classes.zip
```

where x.x.x is proper version numbers:

```
bash$ export CLASSPATH=$CLASSPATH:.:/usr/lib/pgsql/jdbc7.0-1.2.jar
```

Edit all psql.java files and comment out the package line.

```
bash$ javac psql.java
bash$ java psql jdbc:postgresql:template1 postgres < password>[1]
 select * from pg_tables;
tablename        tableowner      hasindexes       hasrules
pg_type postgres            true      false      false
pg_attribute     postgres            true      false      false
```

```
[2]
CTRL+C
bash$
```

You ran direct Java interfaces to the PostgreSQL database!

Testing the ecpg Interface

After installing PostgreSQL Examples RPM, do the following:

```
bash$ cd /usr/doc/postgresql-7.0.0/examples/ecpg
bash$ ecpg test1.pgc -I/usr/include/pgsql
bash$ cc test1.c -I/usr/include/pgsql -lecpg -lpq -lcrypt
bash$ createdb mm
bash$ ./a.out
```

You ran Embedded C-SQL to the PostgreSQL database!

Testing the ODBC Interface

Get the **win32 pgsql odbc** driver from http://www.insightdist.com/ psqlodbc/. Also see **/usr/lib/libpsqlodbc.a**.

Test the driver by running a Windows program accessing the PostgreSQL database.

Testing MPSQL Motif-Worksheet Interface

Get the RPMs from http://www.mutinybaysoftware.com and follow the instructions for testing the interface.

Testing SQL Examples—User-Defined Types and Functions

After installing PostgreSQL Examples RPM, do the following:

```
bash$ cd /usr/doc/postgresql-7.0.0/examples/sql
bash$  make
bash$  sql_exe
```

Verification of PostgreSQL Install

To verify the top quality of PostgreSQL, run the Regression test package. Login as root:

```
#  su - root
# rpm -i postgresql*test.rpm
```

Also, see the README file or install the source code tree which has the regress directory:

```
# rpm -i postgresql*.src.rpm
# cd /usr/src/redhat/SPECS
# more postgresql*.spec
```

to see what system RPM packages you need to install. Run the following to prepare the package:

```
# rpm -bp postgresql*.spec
```

The regression test needs the makefiles and some header files like ***fmgr*.h** which can be built by typing:

```
# rpm —short-circuit -bc postgresql*.spec
```

Abort the build by pressing **Ctrl+C**, when you see **make -C common SUBSYS.o**. At this time, the configuration is successful, and all makefiles and headers are created. You do not need to proceed any further:

```
# cd /usr/src/redhat/BUILD
# chown -R postgres postgresql*
# su - postgres
bash$ cd /usr/src/redhat/BUILD/postgresql-7.0.0/src/test/regress
bash$ more README
bash$ make clean; make all runtest
bash$ more regress.out
```

Emergency Bug Fixes

Sometimes emergency bug fix patches are released after the GA release of PostgreSQL. You can apply these optional patches depending upon the needs of your application. Follow these steps to apply the patches. First, change the directory to the **postgresql** source directory.

```
# su - root
# rpm -i postgresql*.src.rpm
# cd /usr/src/postgresql7.0.0
# man patch
# patch -p0 < patchfile
# make clean
# make
```

The patch files are located in PostgreSQL patches: ftp://ftp.postgresql.org/pub/patches.

How Can I Trust PostgreSQL?

There is a scientific way to validate the reliability of the PostgreSQL system. To validate PostgreSQL, a regression test package (**src/test/regress**) is included in the distribution. The regression test package will verify the standard SQL operations as well as the extensibility capabilities of PostgreSQL. The test package already contains hundreds of SQL test programs.

You should use the computer's high-speed power to validate the PostgreSQL, instead of using human brain power. Computers can carry out software regression tests millions or even billions of times faster than humans can. Modern computers can run billions of SQL tests in a very short time. In the near future the speed of computers will be several zillion times faster than the human brain! Hence, it makes sense to use the power of computers to validate the software.

You can add more tests just in case you need to, and can upload to the primary PostgreSQL Web site if you feel that it will be useful to others on the Internet. The regression test package helps build customer confidence and trust in PostgreSQL, and facilitates rapid deployment of PostgreSQL on production systems.

The regression test package can be taken as a very solid technical document, mutually agreed upon between the developers and end users. PostgreSQL developers extensively use the regression test package during the development period and also before releasing the software to the public to ensure good quality.

Capabilities of PostgreSQL are directly reflected by the regression test package. If a functionality, syntax, or feature exists in the regression test package, then it is supported; all others not listed in the package may not be supported by PostgreSQL! You may need to verify those and add them to the regression test package.

System Layout

If you installed the PostgreSQL RPM, then the **pgsql** directory will be in **/var/lib/pgsql**, and the **doc** directory will be in **/usr/doc/postgresql-x-x-x**, where **x-x-x** is the version number of PostgreSQL. Therefore, you should add this directory to your shell command path. If you use a variant of the Berkeley C shell, such as **csh** or **tcsh**, you would add:

```
set path = ( /usr/local/pgsql/bin path )
```

in the .login file in your home directory. If you use a variant of the Bourne shell, such as **sh**, **ksh**, or **bash**, then you would add:

```
PATH=/usr/local/pgsql/bin:$PATH
export PATH
```

to the **.profile** file in your home directory. From now on, we will assume that you have added the Postgres bin directory to your path. In addition, we will make frequent reference to "setting a shell variable" or "setting an environment variable" throughout this document. If you did not fully understand the last paragraph on modifying your search path, you should consult the UNIX manual pages that describe your shell before going any further.

If you have not set things up in the default way, you may have some more work to do. For example, if the database server machine is a remote machine, you will need to set the **PGHOST** environment variable to the name of the database server machine. The environment variable **PGPORT** also may have to be set. The bottom line is this: If you try to start an application program and it complains that it cannot connect to the post-master, you must go back and make sure that your environment is set up properly.

Kerberos Authentication

Kerberos is an industry-standard secure authentication system suitable for distributed computing over a public network.

Availability

The Kerberos authentication system is not distributed with Postgres. Versions of Kerberos typically are available as optional software from operating system vendors. In addition, a source code distribution may be obtained through MIT Project Athena.

NOTE

You may wish to obtain the MIT version even if your vendor provides a version, since some vendor ports have been deliberately crippled or rendered noninteroperable with the MIT version.

Users located outside the U.S. and Canada are warned that distribution of the actual encryption code in Kerberos is restricted by U.S. Government export regulations.

Inquiries regarding your Kerberos should be directed to your vendor or to MIT Project Athena. Note that FAQLs (Frequently-Asked Questions Lists) periodically are posted to the Kerberos mailing list (send mail to subscribe), and to the USENET news group.

Installation

Installation of Kerberos itself is covered in detail in the Kerberos installation notes. Make sure that the server key file (the **srvtab** or **keytab**) is somehow readable by the Postgres account.

Postgres and its clients can be compiled to use either Version 4 or Version 5 of the MIT Kerberos protocols by setting the KRBVERS variable in the file **src/Makefile.global** to the appropriate value. You can also change the location where Postgres expects to find the associated libraries, header files, and its own server key file.

After compilation is complete, Postgres must be registered as a Kerberos service. See the Kerberos operations notes and related manual pages for more details on registering services.

Operation

After initial installation, Postgres should operate in all ways as a normal Kerberos service. For details on the use of authentication, see the *PostgreSQL User's Guide* reference sections for **postmaster** and **psql**.

In the Kerberos Version 5 books, the following assumptions are made about user and service naming (also, see Table 9.1):

- User principal names (anames) are assumed to contain the actual UNIX/Postgres username in the first component.
- The Postgres service is assumed to have two components, the service name and a hostname, canonicalized as in Version 4 (i.e., with all domain suffixes removed).

Table 9.1 Kerberos Examples

Parameter	Example
user	frew@S2K.ORG
user	aoki/HOST=miyu.S2K.Berkeley.EDU@S2K.ORG
host	postgres_dbms/ucbvax@S2K.ORG

Support for Version 4 will disappear sometime after the production release of Version 5 by MIT.

Runtime Environment—Using Postgres from UNIX/Linux

All Postgres commands that are executed directly from a UNIX shell are found in the directory **.../bin**. Including this directory in your search path will make executing the commands easier.

A collection of system catalogs exists at each site. These include a class (**pg_user**) that contains an instance for each valid Postgres user. The instance specifies a set of Postgres privileges, such as the ability to act as Postgres superuser, the ability to create and destroy databases, and the ability to update the system catalogs. A UNIX user cannot do anything with Postgres until an appropriate instance is installed in this class. Further information on the system catalogs is available by running queries on the appropriate classes.

Starting Postmaster

Nothing can happen to a database unless the postmaster process is running. As the site administrator, there are a number of things you should remember before starting the postmaster. These are discussed in the installation and configuration sections of this manual. However, if Postgres has been installed by following the installation instructions exactly as written, the following simple command is all you should need to start the postmaster:

```
% postmaster
```

The postmaster occasionally prints out messages that are often helpful during troubleshooting. If you wish to view debugging messages from the postmaster, you can start it with the **-d** option and redirect the output to the log file:

```
$ postmaster -d >pm.log 2>&1 &
```

If you do not wish to see these messages, you can type:

```
% postmaster -S
```

and the postmaster will be "S"ilent. Notice that there is no ampersand (&) at the end of the last example, so postmaster will be running in the foreground.

Using pg_options

The optional file **data/pg_options** contains runtime options used by the back-end to control trace messages and other back-end tunable parameters. The file is reread by a back-end when it receives a SIGHUP signal, making it possible to change runtime options on the fly without needing to restart Postgres. The options specified in this file might be debugging flags used by the trace package (**backend/utils/misc/trace.c**), or numeric parameters that can be used by the back-end to control its behavior.

All **pg_options** are initialized to zero at back-end startup. New or modified options will be read by all new back-ends when they are started. To make effective any changes for all running back-ends, we need to send a SIGHUP to the postmaster. The signal will be sent automatically to all the back-ends. We can also activate the changes for a specific back-end by sending the SIGHUP directly to it.

pg_options can also be specified with the **-T** switch of Postgres:

```
postgres options -T "verbose=2,query,hostlookup-"
```

The functions used for printing errors and debug messages can now make use of the syslog(2) facility. Messages printed to **stdout** or **stderr** are prefixed by a timestamp also containing the back-end **pid**:

```
#timestamp            #pid      #message
980127.17:52:14.173 [29271] StartTransactionCommand
980127.17:52:14.174 [29271] ProcessUtility: drop table t;
980127.17:52:14.186 [29271] SIIncNumEntries: table is 70% full
980127.17:52:14.186 [29286] Async_NotifyHandler
980127.17:52:14.186 [29286] Waking up sleeping backend process
980127.19:52:14.292 [29286] Async_NotifyFrontEnd
980127.19:52:14.413 [29286] Async_NotifyFrontEnd done
980127.19:52:14.466 [29286] Async_NotifyHandler done
```

This format improves readability of the logs and allows people to understand exactly which back-end is doing what and at which time. It also makes it easier to write simple **awk** or **perl** scripts, which monitor the log to detect database errors or problems, or to compute transaction time statistics.

Messages printed to **syslog** use the log facility **LOG_LOCAL0**. The use of **syslog** can be controlled with the **syslog pg_option**. Unfortunately many functions directly call **printf()** to print their messages to **stdout** or **stderr**, and this output can't be redirected to **syslog** or have timestamps in it. It is advisable that all calls to **printf** be replaced with the **PRINTF** macro and output to **stderr** be changed to use **EPRINTF** instead so that we can control all output in a uniform way.

The format of the **pg_options** file is as follows:

```
# comment
option=integer_value  # set value for option
option                # set option = 1
```

```
option+                 # set option = 1
option-                 # set option = 0
```

Note that **keyword** can also be an abbreviation of the option name defined in **backend/utils/misc/trace.c**.

For example, my **pg_options** file contains the following values:

```
verbose=2
query
hostlookup
showportnumber
```

Recognized Options

The options currently defined are as follows:

all Global trace flag. Allowed values are:

0 Trace messages enabled individually.

1 Enable all trace messages.

-1 Disable all trace messages.

verbose Verbosity flag. Allowed values are:

0 No messages. This is the default.

1 Print information messages.

2 Print more information messages.

query Query trace flag. Allowed values are:

0 Don't print query.

1 Print a condensed query in one line.

4 Print the full query.

plan Print query plan.

parse Print parser output.

rewritten Print rewritten query.

parserstats Print parser statistics.

plannerstats Print planner statistics.

executorstats Print executor statistics.

shortlocks Currently unused, but needed to enable features in the future.

locks Trace locks.

userlocks Trace user locks.

spinlocks Trace spin locks.

notify Trace notify functions.

malloc Currently unused.

palloc Currently unused.

lock_debug_oidmin Minimum relation OID traced by locks.

lock_debug_relid OID, if not zero, of relation traced by locks.

lock_read_priority Currently unused.

deadlock_timeout Deadlock check timer.

syslog **syslog** flag. Allowed values are:
>**0** Messages to **stdout/stderr**.
>**1** Messages to **stdout/stderr** and **syslog**.
>**2** Messages only to **syslog**.

hostlookup Enable hostname lookup in **ps_status**.

showportnumber Show port number in **ps_status**.

notifyunlock Unlock of **pg_listener** after notify.

notifyhack Remove duplicate tuples from **pg_listener**.

Security

Database security is addressed at several levels:

- Database file protection. All files stored within the database are protected from reading by any account other than the Postgres superuser account.
- Connections from a client to the database server are, by default, allowed only via a local UNIX socket, not via TCP/IP sockets. The back-end must be started with the **-i** option to allow nonlocal clients to connect.
- Client connections can be restricted by IP address and/or username via the **pg_hba.conf** file in **PG_DATA**.
- Client connections may be authenticated via other external packages.

- Each user in Postgres is assigned a username and (optionally) a password. By default, users do not have write access to databases they did not create.
- Users may be assigned to groups, and table access may be restricted based on group privileges.

User Authentication

Authentication is the process by which the back-end server and postmaster ensure that the user requesting access to data is in fact who he or she claims to be. All users who invoke Postgres are checked against the contents of the **pg_user** class to ensure that they are authorized to do so. However, verification of the user's actual identity is performed in a variety of ways:

- **From the user shell:** A back-end server started from a user shell notes the user's (effective) user id before performing a **setuid** to the user id of user **postgres**. The effective user id is used as the basis for access control checks. No other authentication is conducted.
- **From the network:** If the Postgres system is built as distributed, access to the Internet TCP port of the postmaster process is available to anyone. The DBA configures the **pg_hba.conf** file in the **PGDATA** directory to specify what authentication system is to be used according to the host making the connection, and to which database it is connecting. See **pg_hba.conf(5)** for a description of the authentication systems available. Of course, host-based authentication is not foolproof in UNIX, either. It is possible for determined intruders to masquerade as the origination host. Those security issues are beyond the scope of Postgres.

Host-Based Access Control

Host-based access control is the name for the basic controls PostgreSQL exercises on clients that are allowed to access a database, and on how the users on those clients must authenticate themselves.

Each database system contains a file named **pg_hba.conf**, in its **PGDATA** directory, which controls who can connect to each database.

Every client accessing a database must be covered by one of the entries in **pg_hba.conf**. Otherwise, all attempted connections from that client will be rejected with a **User authentication failed** error message.

The general format of the **pg_hba.conf** file is a set of records, one per line. Blank lines and lines beginning with a hash character (#) are ignored. A record is made up of a number of fields, separated by spaces and/or tabs.

Connections from clients can be made using UNIX domain sockets or Internet domain sockets (i.e., TCP/IP). Connections made using UNIX domain sockets are controlled using records of the following format:

```
local database authentication method
```

where:

> **database** specifies the database to which this record applies. The value **all** specifies that it applies to all databases.
>
> **authentication method** specifies the method a user must use to authenticate themselves when connecting to that database using UNIX domain sockets. The different methods are described next.

Connections made using Internet domain sockets are controlled using records of the following format:

```
host database TCP/IP address TCP/IP mask authentication method
```

The **TCP/IP address** is logically and'ed to both the specified TCP/IP mask and the TCP/IP address of the connecting client. If the two resulting values are equal, the record is used for this connection. If a connection matches more than one record, the earliest one in the file is used. Both the TCP/IP address and the TCP/IP mask are specified in dotted decimal notation.

If a connection fails to match any record then the reject authentication method is applied (see next).

Authentication Methods

The following authentication methods are supported for both UNIX and TCP/IP domain sockets:

> **trust** The connection is allowed unconditionally.
>
> **reject** The connection is rejected unconditionally.
>
> **crypt** The client is asked for a password for the user. This is sent encrypted (using **crypt(3)**) and compared against the password held in the **pg_shadow** table. If the passwords match, the connection is allowed.
>
> **password** The client is asked for a password for the user. This is sent in clear and compared against the password held in the **pg_shadow** table. If the passwords match, the connection is allowed. An optional password file may be specified after the password keyword, which is used to match the supplied password rather than the **pg_shadow** table. See **pg_passwd**.

The following authentication methods are supported for TCP/IP domain sockets only:

krb4 Kerberos V4 is used to authenticate the user.

krb5 Kerberos V5 is used to authenticate the user.

ident The ident server on the client is used to authenticate the user (RFC 1413). An optional map name may be specified after the **ident** keyword, which allows ident usernames to be mapped onto Postgres usernames. Maps are held in the file **$PGDATA/pg_ident.conf**.

Here are some examples:

```
# Trust any connection via Unix domain sockets.
local     trust
# Trust any connection via TCP/IP from this machine.
host    all    127.0.0.1    255.255.255.255         trust
# We don't like this machine.
host    all    192.168.0.10    255.255.255.0         reject
# This machine can't encrypt so we ask for passwords in clear.
host    all    192.168.0.3    255.255.255.0         password
# The rest of this group of machines should provide encrypted passwords.
host    all    192.168.0.0    255.255.255.0         crypt
```

Creating Users

To define a new user, run the **createuser** utility program.

To assign a user or set of users to a new group, you must define the group itself, and assign users to that group. In Postgres, these steps are not currently supported with a **create group** command. Instead, the groups are defined by inserting appropriate values into the **pg_group** system table, and then using the **grant** command to assign privileges to the group.

Creating Groups

Currently, there is no easy interface to set up user groups. You have to explicitly insert/update the **pg_group** table. For example:

```
jolly=> insert into pg_group (groname, grosysid, grolist)
jolly=>       values ('posthackers', '1234', '{5443, 8261}');
INSERT 548224
jolly=> grant insert on foo to group posthackers;
CHANGE
jolly=>
```

The fields in **pg_group** are:

groname The group name. This name should be purely alphanumeric; do not include underscores or other punctuation.

grosysid The group id. This is an int4, and should be unique for each group.

grolist The list of **pg_user** IDs that belong in the group. This is an int4[].

Access Control

Postgres provides mechanisms to allow users to limit the access to their data that is provided to other users.

Database superusers Database superusers (that is, users who have **pg_user.usesuper** set) silently bypass all of the access controls described next with two exceptions: manual system catalog updates are not permitted if the user does not have **pg_user.usecatupd** set, and destruction of system catalogs (or modification of their schemas) is never allowed.

Access privilege The use of access privilege to limit reading, writing, and setting of rules on classes is covered in **grant/revoke(l)**.

Class removal and schema modification Commands that destroy or modify the structure of an existing class, such as alter, drop table, and drop index, only operate for the owner of the class. As mentioned earlier, these operations are never permitted on system catalogs.

Functions and Rules

Functions and rules allow users to insert code into the back-end server that other users may execute without knowing it. Hence, both mechanisms permit users to Trojan-horse others with relative impunity. The only real protection is tight control over who can define functions (for example, write to relations with SQL fields) and rules. Audit trails and alerters on **pg_class**, **pg_user**, and **pg_group** are also recommended.

Functions

Functions written in any language except SQL run inside the back-end server process with the permissions of the user postgres (the back-end server runs with its real and effective user id set to postgres). It is possible for users to change the server's internal data structures from inside of trusted functions. Hence, among many other things, such functions can circumvent any system access controls. This is an inherent problem with user-defined C functions.

Rules

Like SQL functions, rules always run with the identity and permissions of the user who invoked the back-end server.

Caveats

There are no plans to explicitly support encrypted data inside of Postgres (though there is nothing to prevent users from encrypting data within user-defined functions). There are no plans to explicitly support encrypted network connections either, pending a total rewrite of the front-end/back-end protocol.

Usernames, group names, and associated system identifiers (e.g., the contents of **pg_user.usesysid**) are assumed to be unique throughout a database. Unpredictable results may occur if they are not.

Secure TCP/IP Connection

You can use **ssh** to encrypt the network connection between clients and a Postgres server. Done properly, this should lead to an adequately secure network connection.

The documentation for **ssh** provides most of the information to get started. Please refer to http://www.heimhardt.de/htdocs/ssh.html for better insight.

Running a Secure Tunnel via ssh

A step-by-step explanation can be done in just two steps.

- Establish a tunnel to the back-end machine, like this:

    ```
    ssh -L 3333:wit.mcs.anl.gov:5432 postgres@wit.mcs.anl.gov
    ```

- The first number in the **-L** argument, **3333**, is the port number of your end of the tunnel. The second number, **5432**, is the remote end of the tunnel—the port number your back-end is using. The name or the address in between the port numbers belongs to the server machine, as does the last argument to **ssh** that also includes the optional username. Without the username, **ssh** will try the name you are currently logged on as on the client machine. You can use any username the server machine will accept, not necessarily those related to postgres.

■ Now that you have a running **ssh** session, you can connect a postgres client to your local host at the port number you specified in the previous step. If it's **psql**, you will need another shell because the shell session you used in Step 1 is now occupied with **ssh**.

```
psql -h localhost -p 3333 -d mpw
```

■ Note that you have to specify the **-h** argument to cause your client to use the TCP socket instead of the UNIX socket. You can omit the port argument if you chose **5432** as your end of the tunnel.

Adding and Deleting Users

The **createuser** command enables specific users to access Postgres. **destroyuser** removes users and prevents them from accessing Postgres.

These commands only affect users with respect to Postgres; they have no effect on a user's other privileges or status with regards to the underlying operating system.

```
bash# su - postgres
bash$ man createuser
bash$ createuser
```

Disk Management—Supporting Large Databases

PostgreSQL can support extremely large databases with sizes greater than 200GB. Performance of 32-bit CPU machines will decline rapidly when the database size exceeds 5GB. You can run a 30GB database on a 32-bit CPU, but the performance will be degraded. Machines with 32-bit CPUs impose a limitation of 2GB on RAM (though newer versions of Linux can extend this a little bit farther), 2GB on file system sizes, and other limitations on the operating system. Use the special file systems for Linux made by SGI, IBM, HP, or ext3-fs to support file sizes greater than 2GB on 32-bit Linux machines.

For extremely large databases, it is strongly advised to use 64-bit machines like Digital Alpha CPU, Sun Ultra-SPARC 64-bit CPU, Silicon graphics 64-bit CPU, Intel Itanium IA-64 CPU, HPUX 64bit machines, or IBM 64-bit machines. Compile PostgreSQL under a 64-bit CPU and it can support huge databases and large queries. Performance of PostgreSQL for queries on large tables and databases will be several times faster than PostgreSQL on 32-bit CPU machines. Advantages of 64-bit machines are that you get very large memory addressing space; and the operating system can support very large file systems, provide better performance with large databases, and can efficiently utilize much larger amounts of physical memory.

Alternate Locations

It is possible to create a database in a location other than the default location for the installation. Remember that all database access actually occurs through the database back-end, so that any location specified must be accessible by the back-end.

Alternate database locations are created and referenced by an environment variable, which gives the absolute path to the intended storage location. This environment variable must have been defined before the back-end was started, and must be writeable by the postgres administrator account. Any valid environment variable name may be used to reference an alternate location, although using a variable name with a prefix of PGDATA is recommended to avoid confusion and conflict with other variables.

NOTE

In previous versions of Postgres, it was also permissible to use an absolute pathname to specify an alternate storage location. The environment variable style of specification is preferred since it allows the site administrator more flexibility in managing disk storage. If you prefer using absolute paths, you may do so by defining ALLOW_ABSOLUTE_DBPATHS and recompiling Postgres. To do this, either add the line:

```
#define ALLOW_ABSOLUTE_DBPATHS 1
```

to the file **src/include/config.h,** or by specifying:

```
CFLAGS+= -DALLOW_ABSOLUTE_DBPATHS
```

in your **Makefile.custom.**

Remember that database creation actually is performed by the database back-end. Therefore, any environment variable specifying an alternate location must have been defined before the back-end was started. To define an alternate location, **PGDATA2**, pointing to **/home/postgres/data**, first type:

```
% setenv PGDATA2 /home/postgres/data
```

to define the environment variable to be used with subsequent commands. Usually, you will want to define this variable in the Postgres superuser's **.profile** or **.cshrc** initialization file to ensure that it is defined upon system startup. Any environment variable can be used to reference an alternate location, although it is preferred that the variables be prefixed with **PGDATA** to eliminate confusion and the possibility of conflicting with, or overwriting, other variables.

To create a data storage area in **PGDATA2**, ensure that **/home/postgres** already exists and is writeable by the postgres administrator. Then from the command line, type:

```
% setenv PGDATA2 /home/postgres/data
% initlocation $PGDATA2
Creating Postgres database system directory /home/postgres/data

Creating Postgres database system directory /home/postgres/data/base
```

To test the new location, create a database test by typing:

```
% createdb -D PGDATA2 test
% dropdb test
```

Managing a Database

If the Postgres postmaster is up and running, we can create some databases to experiment with. Here, we describe the basic commands for managing a database.

Creating a Database

Let's say you want to create a database named **mydb**. You can do this with the following command:

```
% createdb dbname
```

Postgres allows you to create any number of databases at a given site, and you automatically become the database administrator of the database you just created. Database names must have an alphabetic first character and are limited to 31 characters in length. Not every user has authorization to become a database administrator. If Postgres refuses to create databases for you, then the site administrator needs to grant you permission to create databases. Consult your site administrator if this occurs.

Accessing a Database

Once you have constructed a database, you can access it by:

- Running the Postgres terminal monitor program (psql), which allows you to interactively enter, edit, and execute SQL commands.
- Writing a C program using the **libpq** subroutine library. This allows you to submit SQL commands from C and get answers and status messages back to your program. This interface is discussed further in the PostgreSQL Programmer's Guide.

You might want to start up **psql**, to try out the examples in this manual. It can be activated for the **dbname** database by typing the command:

```
% psql dbname
```

You will be greeted with the following message:

```
Welcome to the Postgres interactive sql monitor:

  type \? for help on slash commands
  type \q to quit
  type \g or terminate with semicolon to execute query
You are currently connected to the database: dbname


dbname=>
```

This prompt indicates that the terminal monitor is listening to you and that you can type SQL queries into a workspace maintained by the terminal monitor. The **psql** program responds to escape codes that begin with the backslash character (\). For example, you can get help on the syntax of various Postgres SQL commands by typing:

```
dbname=> \h
```

Once you have finished entering your queries into the workspace, you can pass the contents of the workspace to the Postgres server by typing:

```
dbname=> \g
```

This tells the server to process the query. If you terminate your query with a semicolon, the **\-g** is not necessary. **psql** will process semicolon terminated queries automatically. To read queries from a file instead of entering them interactively, type:

```
dbname=> \i filename
```

To get out of **psql** and return to UNIX, type:

```
dbname=> \q
```

and **psql** will quit and return you to your command shell. (For more escape codes, type **\-h** at the monitor prompt.) White space (that is, spaces, tabs, and newlines) may be used freely in SQL queries. Single-line comments are denoted by two dashes (—). Everything after the dashes up to the end of the line is ignored. Multiple-line comments, and comments within a line, are denoted by /* ... */, a convention borrowed from Ingres.

Destroying a Database

If you are the database administrator for the database **mydb**, you can destroy it using the following UNIX command:

```
% dropdb dbname
```

This action physically removes all of the UNIX files associated with the database and cannot be undone, so this should be done with a great deal of forethought.

It is also possible to destroy a database from within an SQL session by using:

```
> drop database dbname
```

Backup and Restore

Postgres provides two utilities to back up your system: **pg_dump** to back-up individual databases, and **pg_dumpall** to back up your installation in one step.

An individual database can be backed up using the following command:

```
% pg_dump dbname > dbname.pgdump
```

and can be restored using:

```
cat dbname.pgdump | psql dbname
```

This technique can be used to move databases to new locations, and to rename existing databases.

WARNING

Every database should be backed up on a regular basis. Since Postgres manages its own files in the file system, it is not advisable to rely on system backups of your file system for your database backups; there is no guarantee that the files will be in a usable, consistent state after restoration.

Large Databases

Since Postgres allows tables larger than the maximum file size on your system, it can be problematic to dump the table to a file, because the resulting file likely will be larger than the maximum size allowed by your system.

As **pg_dump** writes to **stdout**, you can just use standard *nix tools to work around this possible problem:

- Use compressed dumps:

```
% pg_dump dbname | gzip > filename.dump.gz
```

  reload with:

```
% createdb dbname
```

```
% gunzip -c filename.dump.gz | psql dbname
```

  or

```
% cat filename.dump.gz | gunzip | psql dbname
```

- Use split:

```
% pg_dump dbname | split -b 1m - filename.dump.
```

  reload with:

```
% createdb dbname
```

```
% cat filename.dump.* | pgsql dbname
```

Of course, the name of the file (**filename**) and the content of the **pg_dump** output need not match the name of the database. Also, the restored database can have an arbitrary new name, so this mechanism is also suitable for renaming databases.

Using the KVM Switch with PostgreSQL

You can stack up multiple CPU boxes and connect to just one monitor and use the KVM (Keyboard, Video, Monitor) switch box to select the host. This saves space, avoids a lot of clutter, and also eliminates monitor, keyboard, and the mouse (saving anywhere from $100 to $500 US per set).

Using this switch box, you can stack up many PostgreSQL servers (development, test, production), Web servers, ftp servers, intranet servers, mail servers, and news servers in a tower shelf. The switch box can be used for controlling Windows 95/NT or OS/2 boxes as well.

Please check out these sites:

- DataComm Warehouse Inc. at 1–800–328–2261 (http://www.warehouse.com). They supply all varieties of computer hardware: a 4-port Manual KVM switch (PS/2) is about $89.99 (Part No. DDS1354).
- Network Technologies Inc. (http://www.networktechinc.com/servswt.html). They list server switchers and video-only switches ($120/PC 8 ports).
- Scene Double Inc., England (http://www.scene.demon.co.uk/qswitch.htm).
- Cybex Corporation (http://www.cybex.com).
- Raritan Inc. (http://www.raritan.com).
- RealStar Solutions Inc. (http://www.real-star.com/kvm.htm).
- Belkin Inc. (http://www.belkin.com).
- Better Box Communications Ltd. (http://www.betterbox.com/info.html).
- The nearest hardware store. Ask for a server switch, also known as a KVM auto switch.

Use the Yahoo! search engine to find more companies with server switches or KVM switches.

It is strongly recommended to have a dedicated UNIX box for each PostgreSQL database server, for better performance. No other application program/processes should run on this box. You do not need a color monitor for the database server, as you can do remote administration from a color PC workstation. Using a KVM switch, you can control many CPU boxes by just one monitor and one keyboard!

Troubleshooting—Postmaster Startup Failures

There are several common reasons for the postmaster to fail to start up. Check the postmaster's log file, or start it by hand (without redirecting standard output or standard error) to see what complaint messages appear. Some of the possible error messages are reasonably self-explanatory, but here are some that are not:

```
FATAL: StreamServerPort: bind() failed: Address already in use

        Is another postmaster already running on that port?
```

This usually means just what it suggests: you accidentally started a second postmaster on the same port where one is already running. However, if the kernel error message is not "Address already in use" or some variant of that wording, there may be a different problem. For example, trying to start a postmaster on a reserved port number may draw something like:

```
$ postmaster -i -p 666
FATAL: StreamServerPort: bind() failed: Permission denied
        Is another postmaster already running on that port?


IpcMemoryCreate: shmget failed (Invalid argument) key=5440001,
size=83918612, permission=600
FATAL 1:  ShmemCreate: cannot create region
```

A message like this probably means that your kernel's limit on the size of shared memory areas is smaller than the buffer area that Postgres is trying to create. (Or it could mean that you don't have SysV-style shared memory support configured into your kernel at all.) As a temporary workaround, you can try starting the postmaster with a smaller-than-normal number of buffers (**-B** switch). You eventually will want to reconfigure your kernel to increase the allowed shared memory size, however. You may see this message when trying to start multiple postmasters on the same machine, if their total space requests exceed the kernel limit.

```
IpcSemaphoreCreate: semget failed (No space left on device) key=5440026,

num=16, permission=600
```

A message like this does not mean that you've run out of disk space; it means that your kernel's limit on the number of SysV semaphores is smaller than the number Postgres wants to create. As before, you may be able to work around the problem by starting the postmaster with a reduced number of back-end processes (**-N** switch), but eventually you'll want to increase the kernel limit.

Client Connection Problems

Once you have a running postmaster, trying to connect to it with client applications can fail for a variety of reasons. The sample error messages shown here are for clients based on recent versions of **libpq**; clients based on other interface libraries may produce other messages with more or less information.

```
connectDB() — connect() failed: Connection refused
Is the postmaster running (with -i) at 'server.joe.com' and accepting
connections on TCP/IP port '5432'?
```

This is the generic "I couldn't find a postmaster to talk to" failure. It looks like the earlier example, when TCP/IP communication is attempted, or like the following, when attempting UNIX-socket communication to a local postmaster:

```
connectDB() — connect() failed: No such file or directory
Is the postmaster running at 'localhost' and accepting connections
on Unix socket '5432'?
```

The last line is useful in verifying that the client is trying to connect to where it is intended. If there is, in fact, no postmaster running there, the kernel error message typically will be either "Connection refused" or "No such file or directory," as illustrated. (It is particularly important to realize that "Connection refused" in this context does not mean that the postmaster got your connection request and rejected it—that case will produce a different message, as shown next.) Other error messages such as "Connection timed out" may indicate more fundamental problems, like lack of network connectivity.

```
No pg_hba.conf entry for host 123.123.123.123, user joeblow, database testdb
```

This is what you are most likely to get if you succeed in contacting a postmaster, but it doesn't want to talk to you. As the message suggests, the postmaster refused the connection request because it found no authorizing entry in its **pg_hba.conf** configuration file.

```
Password authentication failed for user 'joeblow'
```

Messages like this indicate that you contacted the postmaster, and it's willing to talk to you, but not until you pass the authorization method specified in **the pg_hba.conf** file. Check the password you're providing, or check your Kerberos or IDENT software if the complaint mentions one of those authentication types.

```
FATAL 1:  SetUserId: user 'joeblow' is not in 'pg_shadow'
```

This is another variant of authentication failure: no Postgres **create_user** command has been executed for the given username.

```
FATAL 1:  Database testdb does not exist in pg_database
```

There's no database by that name under the control of this postmaster. Note that if you don't specify a database name, it defaults to your Postgres username, which may or may not be the right thing.

Debugging Messages

The postmaster occasionally prints out messages that are often helpful during troubleshooting. If you wish to view debugging messages from the postmaster, you can start it with the **-d** option and redirect the output to the log file:

```
% postmaster -d > pm.log 2>&1 &
```

If you do not wish to see these messages, you can type:

```
% postmaster -S
```

and the postmaster will be "S"ilent. Notice that there is no ampersand (&) at the end of the last example so postmaster will be running in the foreground.

pg_options

The optional file **data/pg_options** contains runtime options used by the back-end to control trace messages and other back-end tunable parameters. What makes this file interesting is the fact that it is reread by a back-end when it receives a SIGHUP signal, making it possible to change runtime options on the fly without needing to restart Postgres. The options specified in this file might be debugging flags used by the trace package (**backend/utils/misc/trace.c**) or numeric parameters that can be used by the back-end to control its behavior. New options and parameters must be defined in **backend/utils/misc/trace.c** and **backend/include/utils/trace.h**.

pg_options can also be specified with the **-T** switch of Postgres:

```
postgres options -T "verbose=2,query,hostlookup-"
```

The functions used for printing errors and debug messages can now make use of the **syslog(2)** facility. Messages printed to **stdout** or **stderr** are prefixed by a timestamp containing the back-end pid:

```
#timestamp          #pid     #message
980127.17:52:14.173 [29271]  StartTransactionCommand
980127.17:52:14.174 [29271]  ProcessUtility: drop table t;
980127.17:52:14.186 [29271]  SIIncNumEntries: table is 70% full
980127.17:52:14.186 [29286]  Async_NotifyHandler
980127.17:52:14.186 [29286]  Waking up sleeping backend process
980127.19:52:14.292 [29286]  Async_NotifyFrontEnd
980127.19:52:14.413 [29286]  Async_NotifyFrontEnd done
980127.19:52:14.466 [29286]  Async_NotifyHandler done
```

This format improves readability of the logs and allows people to understand exactly which back-end is doing what, and at which time. It also makes it easier to write simple **awk** or **perl** scripts that monitor the log to detect database errors or problems, or to compute transaction time statistics.

Messages printed to **syslog** use the log facility **LOG_LOCAL0**. The use of **syslog** can be controlled with the **syslog pg_**option. Unfortunately many functions directly call **printf()** to print their messages to **stdout** or **stderr**, and this output can't be redirected to **syslog** or have timestamps in it. It would be advisable that all calls to **printf** be replaced with the **PRINTF** macro, and output to **stderr** be changed to use **EPRINTF** instead so that we can control all output in a uniform way.

The format of the **pg_options** file is as follows:

```
# comment
option=integer_value   # set value for option
option                 # set option = 1
option+                # set option = 1
option-                # set option = 0
```

Note that **keyword** can also be an abbreviation of the option name defined in **backend/utils/misc/trace.c**.

Refer to the section "Using pg_options" for a complete list of option keywords and possible values.

Technical Support

The PostgreSQL organization is selling technical support to companies, and the revenue generated is being used for maintaining primary Web sites and several mirror sites (Web and ftp) around the world. The revenue is also being used for R&D and to produce printed documentation, guides, and textbooks, which will help customers.

You can also get help from professional consulting firms such as Red Hat, Anderson, and WGS (Work Group Solutions). Contact them for help, because they have very good expertise in C and C++ (PostgreSQL is written in C):

- Red Hat Corp; database consulting division, at http://www.redhat.com
- Work Group Solutions, at http://www.wgs.com
- Anderson Consulting, at http://www.ac.com

You can also use mailing lists and Usenet newsgroups. If you have any technical question or encounter any problem you can e-mail to:

- pgsql-questions@postgresql.org
- Newsgroup comp.databases.postgresql.general
- Newsgroup comp.databases.postgresql.hackers
- Newsgroup comp.databases.postgresql.doc
- Newsgroup comp.databases.postgresql.bugs
- Newsgroup linux.postgres
- Other Mailing lists at http://www.postgresql.org

and expect an e-mail answer in less than a day. As the user-base of the Internet product is very vast, and users support other users, the Internet will be capable of giving technical support to billions of users easily. E-mail support is much more convenient than telephone support, because you can cut and paste error messages, program output, etc., and easily transmit to mailing lists and newsgroups.

Mailing Lists

To follow are a series of PostgreSQL mailing lists which you can sign on to, to keep abreast of PostgreSQL news, information, and answers to questions.

E-mail Account for PostgreSQL

Get free e-mail accounts from the following sources:

- In Yahoo!, http://www.yahoo.com, click on e-mail
- In Lycos, http://www.lycos.com, click on new e-mail accounts
- In hotmail, http://www.hotmail.com, click on new e-mail accounts

Subscribe to the PostgreSQL mailing list. Yahoo! has the additional feature of creating a separate folder for PostgreSQL e-mails, so that your regular e-mail is not cluttered. Select menu Email | Options | Filters and pick a separate folder for e-mail. With this e-mail account you can access mail from anywhere in the world as long as you have access to a Web page.

If you have any other e-mail, you can use "Mail Filters" to receive the PostgreSQL mail into a separate folder automatically. This will avoid mail cluttering.

English Mailing List

See the Mailing Lists Item on the main Web page at:

- http://www.postgresql.org/
- pgsql-questions@postgresql.org for e-mail questions
- pgsql-hackers@postgresql.org for developers
- pgsql-ports@postgresql.org for port-specific questions
- pgsql-docs@postgresql.org for documentation questions

You will get a reply by e-mail in less than a day.

You can also subscribe to mailing lists. To subscribe or unsubscribe from the list, send mail to:

- pgsql-questions-request@postgresql.org
- pgsql-hackers-request@postgresql.org
- pgsql-ports-request@postgresql.org
- pgsql-docs-request@postgresql.org

The body of the message should contain the single line **subscribe** or **unsubscribe**.

Archive of Mailing List

Mailing lists are also archived in HTML format at the following location:

- Datewise listing available via Mhonarc, via the WWW at http://www.postgresql.org/mhonarc/pgsql-questions
- ftp://ftp.postgresql.org directory is **/pub/majordomo**

There is also a search engine available on the main PostgreSQL Web site, specifically for **pgsql** questions.

Spanish Mailing List

Now there is an unofficial list of postgreSQL in Spanish. To subscribe, the user has to send a message to:

majordomo@tlali.iztacala.unam.mx

The body of the message should contain the single line:

inscripcion pgsql-ayuda

GUI Front-End Tool for PostgreSQL

After installing PostgreSQL, you may want to install other packages and tools such as GUI front-ends to start using the database system. The Web browser will be the most popular GUI front-end in the future. A major portion of code should be written in Web server scripting (and compiling) language PHP+Zend compiler, HTML, DHTML, and with a little bit of JavaScript and Java-Applets on the Web-client side. It is recommended that you migrate your legacy Windows 95/NT applications to a PHP+Zend compiler.

The best tools, in order of preference, are:

- PHP script and Zend compiler at PHP+Zend compiler
- X-Designer supports C++, Java and MFC at http://www.ist.co.uk/xd

- Qt for Windows95 and UNIX at http://www.troll.no and ftp://ftp.troll.no
- Code Crusader is on the Linux CD-ROM, freeware-based on MetroWorks Code Warrior at http://www.kaze.stetson.edu/cdevel/code_crusader/about.html
- Code Warrior from MetroWorks at http://www.metrowerks.com
- GNU Prof C++ IDE from (Red Hat) Cygnus at http://www.cygnus.com
- Borland C++ Builder for Linux at http://www.inprise.com
- Borland Java JBuilder for Linux at http://www.inprise.com

Language choices, in order of preference, are:

- PHP Web server scripting, HTML, DHTML with Javascript client scripting and Java Applets
- Perl scripting language using Perl-Qt or Perl-Tk Perl Database Interface

In the popular C++ (GNU g++) programming language:

- Fast CGI (written in GNU C++) with Javascript/Java Applets as Web-GUI front-end
- GNU C++ and QtEZ or QT
- GNU C++ with Lesstiff or Motif
- Java language, but its programs run very slow (20 times slower than C++) and it has license fees.

Other tools are available: PostgreSQL has a Tcl/Tk interface library in the distribution called pgTcl. See also:

- Lesstiff Motif tool: ftp://ftp.redhat.com/pub/contrib/i386/lesstiff*.rpm
- Tcl/Tk: http://www.scriptics.com
- Object-oriented extension of Tcl called INCR: http://www.tcltk.com
- Java FreeBuilder: ftp://ftp.redhat.com/pub/contrib/i386/free*.rpm
- SpecTCL: ftp://ftp.redhat.com/pub/contrib/i386/spec*.rpm
- Java RAD Tool for PostgreSQL Kanchenjunga: http://www.man.ac.uk/~whaley/kj/kanch.html

ODBC, JDBC, and UDBC Drivers

PostgreSQL users may ask the DBA to install the database access drivers such as ODBC, UDBC, and so on. ODBC (Open DataBase Connectivity), established by Microsoft, is a popular standard for accessing information from various databases from different vendors. Applications written using the ODBC drivers are guaranteed to work with various databases like PostgreSQL, Oracle, Sybase, and Informix.

- PostODBC is already included in the distribution, on the PostgreSQL CD-ROM. See the main Web site, http://www.postgresql.org.
- Open Link Software Corporation (http://www.openlinksw.com) is selling ODBC for PostgreSQL and other databases. Open Link also is giving away free ODBC (limited seats)—check them out.
- Insight ODBC for PostgreSQL (http://www.insightdist.com/psqlodbc). This is the official PostODBC site.
- FreeODBC package (http://www.ids.net/~bjepson/freeODBC/). This is a free version of ODBC.

UDBC is a static version of ODBC, independent of driver managers and DLL support, used to embed database connectivity support directly into applications.

- Open Link Software Corporation (http://www.openlinksw.com) is selling UDBC for PostgreSQL and other databases. Open Link also is giving away free UDBC (limited seats)—check them out.

Java is a platform-independent programming language developed by Sun Microsystems. Java programmers are encouraged to write database applications using JDBC (Java DataBase Connectivity) to facilitate portability across databases like PostgreSQL, Oracle, and Informix. If you write Java applications you can get JDBC drivers for PostgreSQL from the following sites:

- JDBC driver is already included in the PostgreSQL distribution in **postgresql-jdbc*.rpm**.
- http://www.demon.co.uk/finder/postgres/index.html is Sun's Java connectivity to PostgreSQL.
- ftp://ftp.ai.mit.edu/people/rst/rst-jdbc.tar.gz.
- http://www.openlinksw.com Open Link Software Corporation is selling JDBC for PostgreSQL and other databases. Open Link also is giving away free JDBC (limited seats)—check them out.
- JDBC UK site, at http://www.retep.org.uk/postgres.
- JDBC FAQ site, at http://eagle.eku.edu/tools/jdbc/faq.html.

The JDBC home, guide, and FAQ are located at:

- JDBC home: http://splash.javasoft.com/jdbc
- JDBC guide:
  http://www.javasoft.com/products/jdk/1.1/docs/guide/jdbc
- JDBC FAQ: http://javanese.yoyoweb.com/JDBC/FAQ.txt

See the section, *Testing Java PostgreSQL Interface*, later in this chapter. Java programmers can find these for PostgreSQL very useful.

- ftp://ftp.redhat.com/pub/contrib/i386 and see postgresql-jdbc-*.rpm
- http://www.blackdown.org

Perl and DBI Interfaces

Perl (Practical Extraction and Report Language) is available on each and every operating system and hardware platform in the world. You can use Perl on Windows95/NT, Apple Macintosh iMac, all flavors of UNIX (Solaris, HPUX, AIX, Linux, Irix, SCO, etc.), mainframe MVS, desktop OS/2, OS/400, Amdahl UTS, and many others.

Perl 5 Interface for PostgreSQL

Perl interface for PostgreSQL is included in the distribution of PostgreSQL. Check in the **src/pgsql_perl5** directory.

- Pgsql_perl5, contact by e-mail: E.Mergl@bawue.de
- Another source from ftp://ftp.kciLink.com/pub/PostgresPerl-1.3.tar.gz
- Perl home page: http://www.perl.com/perl/index.html
- Perl tutorial; look for Tutorial title at: http://reference.perl.com/
- Perl FAQ is at:
  http://www.yahoo.com/Computers_and_Internet/Programming_Languages/Perl/
- Perl GUI User Interfaces Perl-Qt RPM:
  ftp://ftp.redhat.com/pub/contrib/i386 and look for PerlQt-1.06-1.i386.rpm
- Perl GUI User Interfaces Perl-Qt:
  http://www.accessone.com/~jql/perlqt.html
- Perl GUI User Interfaces Perl-XForms:
  ftp://ftp.redhat.com/pub/contrib/i386 and look for Xforms4Perl-0.8.4-1.i386.rpm

- Perl GUI User Interfaces Perl-Tk:
  ftp://ftp.redhat.com/pub/contrib/i386
- Perl GUI kits: http://reference.perl.com/query.cgi?ui
- Perl Database Interfaces:
  http://reference.perl.com/query.cgi?database
- Perl to C translator: http://www.perl.com/CPAN-
  local/modules/by-module/B/ and look for Compiler-a3.tar.gz
- Bourne shell to Perl translator:
  http://www.perl.com/CPAN/authors/id/MERLYN/sh2perl-
  0.02.tar.gz
- awk to Perl a2p and sed to Perl s2p is included with the Perl
  distribution.
- See also the newsgroups for PERL at comp.lang.perl.*

What Is Perl DBI?

The Perl Database Interface (DBI) is a database access Application
Programming Interface (API) for the Perl Language. The Perl DBI API specification defines a set of functions, variables, and conventions that provide a consistent database interface independent of the actual database
being used.

- DBI FAQ author Descartes Hermetica is at
  descarte@hermetica.com.

DBI Driver for PostgreSQL DBD-Pg-0.89

Get DBD-Pg-0.89.tar.gz from the following sites:

- DBD-Pg-0.89: http://www.perl.com/CPAN/modules/by-
  module/DBD/
- Comprehensive Perl Archive Network CPAN:
  http://www.perl.com/CPAN
- DBI drivers list and DBI module pages:
  http://www.hermetica.com/technologia/perl/DBI
- DBI information is at http://www.fugue.com/dbi/
- Primary ftp site: ftp://ftp.demon.co.uk/pub/perl/db
- Miscellaneous DBI link: http://www-ccs.cs.umass.edu/db.html
- Miscellaneous DBI link:
  http://www.odmg.org/odmg93/updates_dbarry.html
- Miscellaneous DBI link: http://www.jcc.com/sql_stnd.html
- PostgreSQL database: http://www.postgresql.org

Technical Support for DBI

Send comments and bug reports to E.Mergl@bawue.de. Include the output of **perl -v** and **perl -V**, the version of PostgreSQL, the version of DBD-Pg, and the version of DBI in your bug report.

What Is DBI, DBperl and Perl?

To quote Tim Bunce, the architect and author of DBI:

"DBI is a database access Application Programming Interface (API) for the Perl Language. The DBI API Specification defines a set of functions, variables and conventions that provide a consistent database interface independent of the actual database being used."

In simple language, the DBI interface allows users to access multiple database types transparently. So, if you are connecting to an Oracle, Informix, mSQL, Sybase, or whatever database, you don't need to know the underlying mechanics of the 3GL layer. The API defined by DBI will work on all these database types.

A similar benefit is gained by the ability to connect to two different databases of different vendors within the one Perl script; that is, I want to read data from an Oracle database and insert it back into an Informix database, all within one program. The DBI layer allows you to do this simply and powerfully.

DBI Specifications

There are a few information sources on DBI:

- DBI Specification:
  http://www.hermetica.com/technologia/perl/DBI/doc/dbispec
- Information from DBI mailing lists:
  http://www.hermetica.com/technologia/perl/DBI/tidbits
- DBI Perl Journal Web site: http://www.tpj.com
- *The Perl5 Database Interface*, a book to be written by Alligator Descartes and published by O'Reilly and Associates.

The mailing lists that users may participate in are:

- Mailing lists: http://www.fugue.com/dbi
- dbi-announce e-mail: dbi-announce-request@fugue.com with a message body of **subscribe**
- dbi-users general discussion e-mail: dbi-users-request@fugue.com with a message body of **subscribe**
- US Mailing List Archives: http://outside.organic.com/mail-archives/dbi-users/
- European Mailing List Archives: http://www.rosat.mpe-garching.mpg.de/mailing-lists/PerlDB-Interest

For commercial support and training, see:

- http://www.perl.co.uk/tpc

Tutorial for PostgreSQL

A PostgreSQL DBA should have a solid understanding of the SQL commands. The DBA uses SQL to directly manipulate the PostgreSQL system tables. An SQL tutorial is also distributed with PostgreSQL. The SQL tutorial scripts are in the directory **src/tutorial**.

Internet URL Pointers

The SQL tutorial can be found at http://w3.one.net/~jhoffman/sqltut.htm. Mail comments or suggestions to Jim Hoffman at jhoffman@one.net. He suggests the following sites:

- SQL Reference:
  http://www.contrib.andrew.cmu.edu/~shadow/sql.html
- Ask the SQL Pro: http://www.inquiry.com/techtips/thesqlpro/
- SQL Pro's Relational DB Useful Sites:
  http://www.inquiry.com/techtips/thesqlpro/usefulsites.html
- Programmer's Source:
  http://infoweb.magi.com/~steve/develop.html
- DBMS Sites: http://info.itu.ch/special/wwwfiles. Go here and see file comp_db.html
- DB Ingredients:
  http://www.compapp.dcu.ie/databases/f017.html
- Web Authoring: http://www.stars.com/Tutorial/CGI/
- Computing Dictionary: http://wfn-shop.princeton.edu/cgi-bin/foldoc
- DBMS Lab/Links: http://www-ccs.cs.umass.edu/db.html
- SQL FAQ:
  http://epoch.CS.Berkeley.EDU:8000/sequoia/dba/montage/FAQ. Go here and see file SQL_TOC.html
- SQL Databases:
  http://chaos.mur.csu.edu.au/itc125/cgi/sqldb.html
- RIT Database Design Page:
  http://www.it.rit.edu/~wjs/IT/199602/icsa720/icsa720postings.html
- Database Jump Site: http://www.pcslink.com/~ej/dbweb.html
- Programming Tutorials on the Web:
  http://www.eng.uc.edu/~jtilley/tutorial.html

- Development Resources:
  http://www.ndev.com/ndc2/support/resources.htp
- Query List: http://ashok.pair.com/sql.htm
- MAGE SQL Miscellaneous:
  http://jazz.external.hp.com/training/sqltables/main.html
- Internet Resource List http://www.eit.com/web/netservices.html

PostgreSQL URL References

The main site is at http://www.postgreSQL.org. The PostgreSQL
Database HOWTO is at http://www.metalab.unc.edu/LDP/HOWTO/
PostgreSQL-HOWTO.html.

To read why Linux is better as a database server as compared with
Windows 95/NT, see http://www.aldev.8m.com or
http://www.aldev.webjump.com.

Summary

After researching all the available databases that are free, with available
source code, it was found that only PostgreSQL is the most mature, most
widely used and robust RDBMS SQL free database (object relational) in
the world.

PostgreSQL is very appealing because a lot of work has already been
done. It has ODBC and JDBC drivers; using these makes it possible to
write applications independent of the databases. The applications written
in PostgreSQL using ODBC and JDBC drivers are easily portable to other
databases like Oracle, Sybase, and Informix, and vice versa.

You may ask, why PostgreSQL? The answer is, since it takes a lot
more time to develop a database system from scratch, it makes sense to
pick up a database system that satisfies the following conditions:

- Source code is available (must be an Open Source Code system)
- Has no license strings, no ownership strings attached to it
- Can be distributed on the Internet
- Has been in development for several years
- Satisfies standards like ISO/ANSI SQL 92 (and SQL 89)
- Can satisfy future needs like SQL 3 (SQL 98)
- Has advanced capabilities

And it just so happens that PostgreSQL satisfies all these conditions
and is the appropriate software for this situation.

FAQs

Q: Why does **initdb** fail?

A: Check that you don't have any of the previous version's binaries in your path. (If you see the message **WARN:heap_modifytuple: repl is \ 9**, this is the problem.) Check to see that you have the proper paths set, and that the postgres user owns the proper files.

Q: How do I install PostgreSQL somewhere other than **/usr/local/pgsql**?

A: The simplest way is to specify the **—prefix** option when running configure. If you forgot to do that, you can edit **Makefile.global** and change **POSTGRESDIR** accordingly, or create a **Makefile.custom** and define **POSTGRESDIR** there.

Q: When I start the postmaster, I get a *Bad System Call* or core dumped message. Why?

A: It could be a variety of problems, but first check to see that you have System V extensions installed on your kernel. PostgreSQL requires kernel support for shared memory and semaphores.

Q: When I try to start the postmaster, I get *IpcMemoryCreate* errors. Why?

A: You either do not have shared memory configured properly in the kernel or you need to enlarge the shared memory available in the kernel. The exact amount you need depends on your architecture and how many buffers and back-end processes you configure postmaster to run with. For most systems, with default numbers of buffers and processes, you need a minimum of ~1MB.

Q: When I try to start the postmaster, I get *IpcSemaphoreCreate* errors. Why?

A: If the error message is *IpcSemaphoreCreate: semget failed (No space left on device)* then your kernel is not configured with enough semaphores. Postgres needs one semaphore per potential back-end process. A temporary solution is to start the postmaster with a smaller limit on the number of back-end processes. Use **-N** with a parameter less than the default of 32. A more permanent solution is to increase your kernel's **SEMMNS** and **SEMMNI** parameters.

If the error message is something else, you might not have semaphore support configured in your kernel at all.

Q: How do I prevent other hosts from accessing my PostgreSQL database?

A: By default, PostgreSQL only allows connections from the local machine using UNIX domain sockets. Other machines will not be able to connect unless you add the **-i** flag to the postmaster, and enable host-based authentication by modifying the file **$PGDATA/pg_hba.conf** accordingly. This will allow TCP/IP connections.

Q: Why can't I connect to my database from another machine?

A: The default configuration allows only UNIX domain socket connections from the local machine. To enable TCP/IP connections, make sure the postmaster has been started with the **-i** option, and add an appropriate host entry to the file **pgsql/data/pg_hba.conf**. See the **pg_hba.conf** manual page.

Q: Why can't I access the database as the root user?

A: You should not create database users with user id 0 (root). They will be unable to access the database. This is a security precaution because of the ability of any user to dynamically link object modules into the database engine.

Q: All my servers crash under concurrent table access. Why?

A: This problem can be caused by a kernel that is not configured to support semaphores.

Q: How do I tune the database engine for better performance?

A: Certainly, indices can speed up queries. The **explain** command allows you to see how PostgreSQL is interpreting your query, and which indices are being used.

If you are doing a lot of inserts, consider doing them in a large batch using the **copy** command. This is much faster than individual inserts. Second, statements not in a **begin work/commit** transaction block are considered to be in their own transaction. Consider performing several statements in a single transaction block. This reduces the transaction overhead. Also consider dropping and recreating indices when making large data changes.

There are several tuning things that can be done. You can disable **fsync()** by starting the postmaster with a **-o -F** option. This will prevent **fsync()**s from flushing to disk after every transaction.

You can also use the postmaster **-B** option to increase the number of shared memory buffers used by the back-end processes. If you make this parameter too high, the postmaster may not start up because you've exceeded your kernel's limit on shared memory space. Each buffer is 8K and the default is 64 buffers.

You can also use the back-end **-S** option to increase the maximum amount of memory used by each backend process for temporary sorts. The **-S** value is measured in kilobytes, and the default is 512 (i.e., 512K). It is unwise to make this value too large, or you may run out of memory when a query invokes several concurrent sorts.

You can also use the **cluster** command to group data in base tables to match an index. See the **cluster(l)** manual page for more details.

Q: What debugging features are available in PostgreSQL?

A: PostgreSQL has several features that report status information that can be valuable for debugging purposes.

First, by running configure with the **—enable-cassert** option, many **assert()**s monitor the progress of the back-end and halt the program when something unexpected occurs.

Both postmaster and postgres have several debug options available. First, whenever you start the postmaster, make sure you send the standard output and error to a log file, like:

```
cd /usr/local/pgsql

./bin/postmaster >server.log 2>&1 &
```

This will put a **server.log** file in the top-level PostgreSQL directory. This file contains useful information about problems or errors encountered by the server. Postmaster has a **-d** option that allows even more detailed information to be reported. The **-d** option takes a number that specifies the debug level. Be warned that high debug level values generate large log files.

You can actually run the postgres back-end from the command line, and type your SQL statement directly. This is recommended *only* for debugging purposes. Note that a newline terminates the query, not a semicolon. If you have compiled with debugging symbols, you can use a debugger to see what is happening. Because the back-end was not started from the postmaster, it is not running in an identical environment and locking/back-end interaction problems may not be duplicated. Some operating systems can attach to a running back-end directly to diagnose problems.

The postgres program has **-s**, **-A**, and **-t** options that can be very useful for debugging and performance measurements.

You can also compile with profiling to see what functions are taking execution time. The back-end profile files will be deposited in the **pgsql/data/base/dbname** directory. The client profile file will be put in the current directory.

Q: I get *Sorry, too many clients* when trying to connect. Why?

A: You need to increase the postmaster's limit on how many concurrent back-end processes it can start.

In Postgres 6.5.*, the default limit is 32 processes. You can increase it by restarting the postmaster with a suitable **-N** value. With the default configuration, you can set **-N** as large as 1024; if you need more, increase **MAXBACKENDS** in **include/config.h** and rebuild. You can set the default value of **-N** at configuration time, if you like, using configure's **—with-maxbackends** switch.

Note that if you make **-N** larger than 32, you should consider increasing **-B** beyond its default of 64. For large numbers of back-end processes, you are also likely to find that you need to increase various UNIX kernel configuration parameters. Things to check include the maximum size of shared memory blocks, **SHMMAX**; the maximum number of semaphores, **SEMMNS** and **SEMMNI**; the maximum number of processes, **NPROC**; the maximum number of processes per user, **MAXUPRC**; and the maximum number of open files, **NFILE** and **NINODE**. The reason that Postgres has a limit on the number of allowed back-end processes is so that you can ensure that your system won't run out of resources.

In Postgres versions prior to 6.5, the maximum number of back-ends was 64, and changing it required a rebuild after altering the **MaxBackendId** constant in **include/storage/sinvaladt.h**.

Q: What are the **pg_tempNNN.NN** files in my database directory?

A: They are temporary files generated by the query executor. For example, if a sort needs to be done to satisfy an ORDER BY, and the sort requires more space than the back-end's **-S** parameter allows, then temp files are created to hold the extra data.

The temp files should go away automatically, but might not if a back-end crashes during a sort. If you have no transactions running at the time, it is safe to delete the **pg_tempNNN.NN** files.

Q: How do I set up a **pg_group**?

A: Currently, there is no easy interface to set up user groups. You have to explicitly insert/update the **pg_group** table. For example:

```
jolly=> insert into pg_group (groname, grosysid, grolist)
jolly=>     values ('posthackers', '1234', '{5443, 8261}');
INSERT 548224
jolly=> grant insert on foo to group posthackers;
CHANGE
jolly=>
```

The fields in **pg_group** are:

groname: The group name. This should be purely alphanumeric—do not include underscores or other punctuation.

grosysid: The group id. This is an int4, and should be unique for each group.

grolist: The list of **pg_user** ids that belong on the group. This is an int4[].

## Chapter 10

Developing a Web-Based Application

Solutions in this chapter:

- **Web Application Platforms**
- **Getting Started**
- **Design Goals**
- **Designing a Schema**
- **Data Flow**
- **PHP Database Connectivity**

Introduction

In this chapter, we discuss a complete build-up of a Web-based application from start to finish—that of the popular "shopping-cart" storefront application (see Figure 10.1). Due to space considerations, this application will not include a full treatment of security issues, but we will discuss the issues inherent in an application such as this. (Future revisions will be security hardened.) The complete application—with source code, the database dump, and installation instructions—is available under the GNU Public License version 2 (GPLv2) at http://www.syngress.com or http://www.sourceforge.net.

Figure 10.1 A shopping-cart storefront application.

Web Application Platforms

The Web application platforms available today include JSP, PHP, Cold Fusion, Zope, ASP, and many others. We'll discuss how they relate to each other, and how they each relate to Linux.

Active Server Pages

Microsoft's Active Server Pages (ASP) are designed for Windows NT/2000 but can run also (better, in fact) on many UNIX/Linux platforms, including Red Hat Linux, via Chili!Soft's excellent emulator. ASP has the ability to use any Component Object Model (COM) object, but COM objects are a Microsoft technology. Microsoft's own Internet Information Services (IIS) and Visual Studio presents an excellent development environment, but is plagued with reliability and security issues and typically is not compatible with Web servers other than IIS unless Chili!ASP is used. You can find more information at Chili!Soft's Web site at http://www.chilisoft.com.

Cold Fusion

Allaire's Cold Fusion is another proprietary product that is easy to learn and use; although it traditionally has been available for Windows NT only, Allaire has recently begun converting it to various UNIX flavors, including HP-UX, Solaris, and Linux. Cold Fusion uses custom HTML-like embedded tags mixed with standard HTML to build a customized, database-driven page. You can find more information at http://www.allaire.com.

Java Server Pages

Sun's Java Server Pages is a relative newcomer to the Web application platform arena, but offers the vast power of Sun's Java language. Although replete with complexity as well as features, it is an excellent choice if your organization is standardizing on Java and CORBA. JSP is available for any platform that a Java interpreter is available, which includes Linux, UNIX, and Windows NT. Go to http://www.sun.com for more information.

Zope

Zope is an excellent Open Source Web application platform that incorporates a hierarchical, object-oriented database with built-in permissions and a Web-based development environment. It also has modules that connect to major database engines, and offers all the advantages of traditional relational databases as well as object-oriented databases, as well as many of the advantages of PHP. It also offers a flow-down inheritance scheme and a built-in permission strategy. Development on Zope, like most Open Source projects, proceeds very rapidly, and it's definitely worth checking out. As a complex and full-featured product with an integrated security model, it's not quite as fast as PHP. You can find more information at http://www.zope.org.

Scripting Languages

There are many Open Source scripting languages, such as Perl, Python, and TCL, that offer scripting capabilities. Many of them can be integrated into Apache and other Web servers, avoiding the security and performance issues that occur with CGI. These languages are an excellent choice for Web development, especially if you are already proficient in them. You can visit any of the following sites for more information: http://www.perl.com, http://www.python.org, and http://www.tcl.com.

PHP

PHP is an extremely popular Open Source application language that is designed to compete directly with ASP and JSP. It offers modules for IMAP, POP3, LDAP, XML, PDF, PostScript, FTP, WebDAV, Oracle, MySQL, mSQL, Informix, PostgreSQL, Sybase, and too many other database engines to mention here. It runs on Linux, UNIX, and Windows NT. Because PHP is freely available, with source code, and included with Red Hat Linux, we will develop the application build-up in PHP against the excellent MySQL database engine. According to Netcraft, PHP is powering over one million Web servers and growing very fast. Go to http://www.php.net for more information.

Apache

By far the most popular Web server platform is Apache (http://www.apache.org), with approximately 60 percent of the market share according to NetCraft. Microsoft's IIS comes in a distant second with 22 percent of the market share. Apache offers great performance, although performance is not its only advantage. There is a wealth of add-ons and modules available; it's extremely stable and offers good security; it runs on all popular operating systems; it's very scalable; and it's free and Open Source.

Apache is based on the NCSA Web server. The developers of Apache were unsatisfied with the rate of development on the NCSA Web server, and so released their own patched-up version, a Patchy Web Server. In the years since, Apache has developed into a robust and well-supported platform. Security bugs are fixed in a matter of hours, as everyone has the source code and can contribute a fix back to the development team.

PHP and Perl, as well as most other Open Source languages and platforms, are available as plug-in modules to Apache. Although PHP can run with other Web servers, we will discuss PHP running as an Apache module, because there are other security constraints involved with running it via CGI.

Getting Started

Consult your Red Hat manual for instructions on installing PHP, MySQL, and Apache RPM packages. For most recent versions of Red Hat, these RPMs are included on the CDs, and will not need to be downloaded.

We recommend downloading and installing phpMyAdmin (see Figure 10.2) to ease the development of the new database system. phpMyAdmin is a Web-based database manager for MySQL databases and offers the distinct advantage of complete source code, which you can use when developing your own PHP-based applications.

Also, you may download and install the actual application, available for free at http://www.syngress.com or http://www.sourceforge.net.

Figure 10.2 Utilizing phpMyAdmin to develop a new database system.

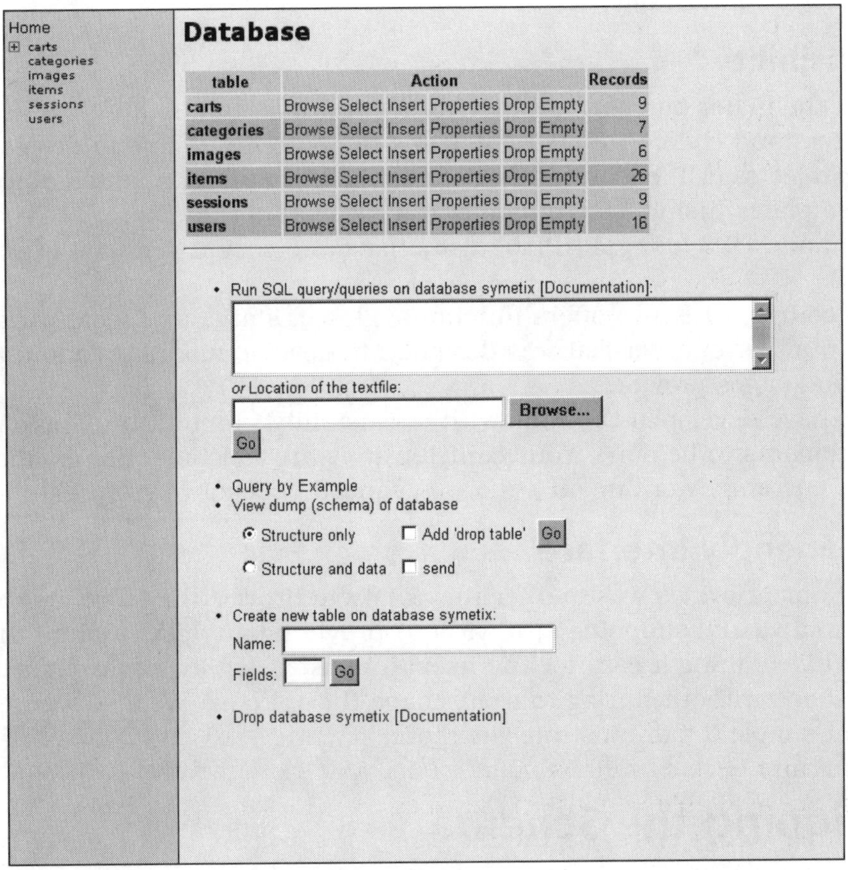

Design Goals

We had certain goals in mind when designing our shopping cart application, including easy maintenance and extensibility, clarity of code, and a user-friendly interface.

Clarity

Because clarity is a focal point, we have decided not to include any sophisticated session identifier generation systems. We have also developed the entire application in a single PHP script. Everything is available through this one script, so the browser's base URL never changes as he or she proceeds through the site. To tell one user from another, we set a single cookie on each user's computer, which contains a unique session identifier. This session identifier increments with each new computer as it connects (i.e., 1,2,3...), so there is never a conflict. There is a security flaw with this scheme, though, which we will discuss in the security section later in this chapter.

Extensibility

One of the major barriers to extensibility and maintainability is difficult-to-understand code. PHP offers features to make it possible to develop large projects. PHP has a number of advanced features, such as objects and templates (using FastTemplate) that we will not use here. PHP4 (Zend) and PHP3 (using PHPLib) also offer more secure versions of session control.

Of course, PHP also offers functions; global, static, and local variables; and a number of other features designed to develop modular code that most languages provide.

We have developed the code with extensibility in mind, but some more work remains to be done. Your contributions are welcome. For example, we are currently working on a more advanced checkout system.

User-Friendly Interface

One of our priorities was to offer the ability to browse the store and add items to a virtual shopping cart without providing any personal information, while making it easy for the user to register, log-in, or purchase those items without having to repurchase those items. We also wanted to make it simple to administrate the store.

Designing the Schema

Currently in open-source development is a full, free, secure version of this database. Details are available at www.syngress.com or www.source-forge.net. This code is not designed to be secure and we strongly recommend you do not implement it in a production environment. As we will discuss in the security section, we know of some security flaws that must be patched before production usage.

Out of our design goals for our application, we developed a database structure (see Figure 10.3). This database structure, encompassing six tables, is designed to offer a clear, lucid definition of the data that will be used by the database. Please refer to it in the discussion that follows.

Figure 10.3 The database structure.

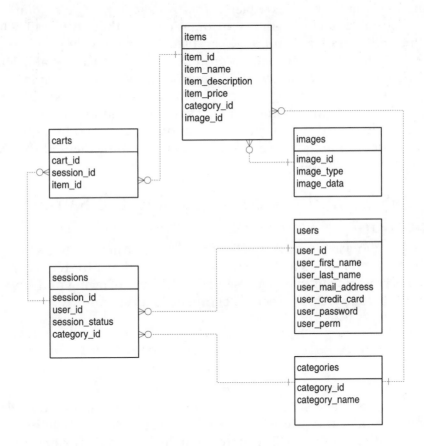

Data Flow

When the user first connects to the Web site, a session is created for him and he is provided with a cookie that contains a single value, **session_id**. This **session_id** contains a unique number that is keyed to the primary key of the session's database. (In this case, we are simply allowing MySQL to auto-increment the primary key; we do not recommend that this practice be followed for reasons explained in the security section.)

After the session is created, the user has a **session_status** of 0. This **session_status** means that the user is just browsing and has not authenticated. Since the user must authenticate before purchasing any items, he or she doesn't have a checkout button. The user is allowed to browse and add items to the shopping cart (the carts database) without authenticating. Upon authentication (or registration), the **session_status** is increased to 1, which means that the user now has a checkout button. Also, the **user_id** is placed in the session database.

When the user clicks checkout, the **session_status** is increased to 2, meaning that the user has completed the transaction. At this point, it would be possible to send e-mails automatically to the buyer and seller indicating that a transaction has taken place. (For security purposes, an unencrypted credit card number should *never* be sent via e-mail.) The best thing to send via e-mail would be a unique URL (for example, http://www.shoppingcart.org/view_session_id=323), which would send the viewer to a page that wouldn't allow someone who intercepted this e-mail to get any sensitive information, or to one that would be protected behind a login. For simplicity's sake, we have not implemented this code in this sample application.

PHP, MySQL, and Apache: Installing the Sample Application

This application will work with PHP compiled as either a module for Apache (**mod_php**) or as a CGI module. To verify that PHP has been installed correctly with your Web server, enter the following and save it as **test.php3** in your Web browser's DocumentRoot directory:

```
<?php

phpinfo();

?>
```

When you browse to http://webserver/test.php3, you should see a large information page stating all kinds of information about your PHP installation. Under the extensions section, verify that a MySQL extension is loaded. If it is not, you will need to compile the MySQL extension.

To create the database schema, a database needs to be created and the database dump needs to be loaded. All the tables for the application fit into one database. If your database is not already created, select a database name and enter the following command:

```
servername:~$ mysql -u username -p
Enter password:
Welcome to the MySQL monitor.  Commands end with ; or \g.
Your MySQL connection id is 106270 to server version: 3.22.27
```

```
Type 'help' for help.mysql> CREATE DATABASE shopcart
```

Please alter the code within Appendix A and Appendix B according to the instructions in the paragraphs that follow.

Import the dump file into MySQL using the following command:

```
servername:~$ mysql -u username -p shopcart <shopcart.sql
```

Finally, edit the **init_db_variables()** function in the **index.php3** file (found in Appendix A) to match your database server name, username, password, and database name.

Browse to http://webserver/ and ensure that the shopping cart screen displays without errors. If you get a directory listing or "Permission Denied," you may need to add **index.php3** to your DirectoryIndex listing in Apache's httpd.conf. Alternatively, you could create an HTTP refresh page named **index.html** and have it immediately transfer the browser to **index.php3**.

PHP Database Connectivity: Making the Connection

In the function **connect_db()**, we connect to the database server and select the database we plan to use. To make it easy to port this application to another database server, we have separated the variables into **init_db_variables()**.

```
MYSQL_CONNECT($db_server,$db_username,$db_password) OR DIE("Unable to
connect to database");
```

```
@MYSQL_SELECT_DB("symetix") or die("Unable to select database");
```

Reading Data from the Database

In **browse_column()**, there is a simple example of reading data from the database:

```
$result=mysql_query("SELECT * FROM items WHERE category_id=$category_id");

$num_results=mysql_num_rows($result);
```

In the first statement, we run a simple SQL SELECT statement against the **items** table. The results are stored in the **$result** variable. In the second statement, we are taking a count of the number of results we received.

```
$row=mysql_fetch_array($result))
```

In this statement, we are extracting the first record that was in our result set. We can then extract each field from that record using the following command:

```
$item_id=$row["item_id"];
```

In this case, we are merely setting the variable **$item_id** equal to the information that is contained in the current row of **$results**, in the field named **item_id**. There are many more ways to extract data from a result string as well. PHP is loosely typed, which means that there is little distinction between variables that hold various types of information, such as number versus text; PHP makes the determination from the context of the variable. This makes it very easy to code for. Of course, if you wish, you can always force a variable to be a particular type by using the **settype()** function.

Security

It would be easy for a cracker simply to note that he was session #444 and simply change his personal cookie so that his session would become session #443, effectively hijacking another user's session. The way most shopping cart and other secure Web applications combat this is by generating a unique and difficult-to-guess session id using a combination of the date, time, a random number, the user's IP address or host name, and so on. A complicated and sophisticated scheme would be virtually unbreakable.

For IT Professionals

Does Linux Really Offer Advantages Over NT/2000 for Web Serving?

Linux offers all the traditional advantages of UNIX such as stability, scalability, and reliability, but it also offers ease-of-use, a large number of powerful and full-featured utilities, a large amount of free software that's useful, and a design paradigm that sets it apart from NT/2000. In Linux, as in UNIX, the emphasis is placed on building small, modular programs that can be quickly linked together from the command line. Although Microsoft has been trying to move in that direction for many years (i.e., COM/DCOM/DNA), most of their applications and tools are still large, monolithic applications that generally try to do everything all by themselves. In contrast, Linux tools are designed to work together. Metaphorically speaking, this

Continued

means that if a particular brick that you're using to build your tower isn't the right color, you can pull out that brick and replace it with another without having the entire structure collapse on your head.

One of the only advantages that Microsoft has over Linux is in the ease-of-use of their development tools. However, even this advantage is subject to debate. Because the Microsoft tools make it so easy to rapidly develop an application, design tends to suffer or be discarded altogether as a continuous running prototype is developed. As any DBA will attest, proper database design is absolutely crucial before actually beginning any coding. Microsoft tools attempt to shield the user from the actual complexity of the task at hand. Generally speaking, though, this is a direction that Linux is moving in; for example, KDE, one of the most popular Linux desktops (windows managers), is widely known as being easier to use than even Windows 98.

Finally, Linux and UNIX enjoy a huge lead over NT, both in terms of actual large-site installations, and in terms of developer support. While there are thousands and thousands of Visual Basic programmers who have made the transition to Web-based development, Visual Basic itself was never designed to handle the demands that Web development places on it. Also, because the Visual Basic tools and Visual Studio relieve the programmer of many design constraints, many VB programmers never learn proper coding procedures or database interfaces. While this may not be a problem for small applications, limitations and design flaws become readily apparent as an application grows.

Aside from Microsoft, very few IT professionals contest that Linux is a much more stable and full-featured platform than NT/2000. There is also an upgrade path to other, non-Intel platforms that NT doesn't offer. For example, Linux is available on every major platform available, including Sun's Sparc, Compaq's Alpha, Apple's PowerPC, HP's PA-RISC, and Intel's upcoming IA-64 processors. If those machines aren't large enough for you, IBM is porting Linux to their largest mainframes. In addition to very large machine-support, Linux has been ported all the way down to 3Com's Palm Pilot and Linus Torvalds is developing a special version of Linux for the upcoming Transmeta Crusoe processor that promises to revolutionize portable computing with extraordinary battery life and self-optimizing processor architecture.

The reality is that by choosing Linux, you've made the right move. Open Source is here to stay and the entire industry has recognized and is committing to that fact.

Summary

In this chapter, a shopping cart application was built using PHP and MySQL. We look forward to hearing of any implementations of this code. The complete application—with source code, the database dump, and installation instructions—is available for free under the GNU Public License version 2 (GPLv2) at www.syngress.com or www.sourceforge.net. If you are not familiar with the GPL, a description, as well as the text of the license, is available at http://www.gnu.org/copyleft/gpl.html.

FAQ

Q: We don't have any PHP expertise in our organization, but we do have some Perl experts. Are there other open source shopping cart applications available?

A: Yes. One of the most complete shopping cart applications is Minivend, written in Perl (http://www.minivend.com). Another excellent Perl-based shopping cart application is OpenCart, developed and used by Walnut Creek CDROM (http://www.cdrom.com, http://www.opencart.com/). For many more examples, including others in both PHP as well as other languages, check out Freshmeat.Net (http://www.freshmeat.net).

Q: Which Web server is the fastest?

A: That depends on what you're serving and, of course, who you ask. In general, for serving static, traditional Web pages (such as the traditional HTML page) and not those generated by PHP, ASP, or other languages, the simplest Web server will be the fastest. More sophisticated servers include caching and other performance features to enhance the speed of the more processing-intensive functions (such as dynamic page generation), but these features themselves incur a certain amount of overhead if they are not needed. Generally speaking, security functions slow down a server greatly as well. So, if speed is the main objective, you would need to weigh the various options carefully, and balance them against your needs. In general, Apache is the best solution for most uses as it offers an excellent balance of features and performance.

Q: Do I need any particular permissions to use the shopping cart application provided in this chapter?

A: The shopping cart application was designed on a server that was hosted by Hurricane Electric at http://www.he.net. No root access or otherwise unusual access was required.

Q: Where would I find PHP professionals?

A: If you're having difficulty finding qualified PHP professionals, it's best to seek them out where they lurk. The recommended ways are to post a message on the jobs boards at http://phpbuilder.com or http://www.schaffner.net/emp/. Alternatively, you could send a message to one of the PHP mailing lists.

PHP Script for Shopping Cart Application

```php
<?PHP

// Shopping Cart Application
// By Jamie Becker
// Copyright (c) 2000, Jamie Becker, jamiebecker@ring0.com

// This program is free software; you can redistribute it and/or
// modify it under the terms of the GNU General Public License
// as published by the Free Software Foundation; either version 2
// of the License, or (at your option) any later version.

// This program is distributed in the hope that it will be useful,
// but WITHOUT ANY WARRANTY; without even the implied warranty of
// MERCHANTABILITY or FITNESS FOR A PARTICULAR PURPOSE.  See the
// GNU General Public License for more details.

// You should have received a copy of the GNU General Public License
// along with this program; if not, write to the Free Software
// Foundation, Inc., 59 Temple Place - Suite 330, Boston, MA  02111-1307,
// USA.

// Please see www.gnu.org or www.fsf.org for the full text of the license.

// Source Code modified <80 cols. (JamieBecker,2/16/99)

// strongly recommend this function be separated into a separate, non-public
// file and included here.

function init_db_variables()
{
global $db_server;
global $db_username;
global $db_password;
$db_server='localhost';
$db_username='username';
$db_password='password';
$db_name='shopcart';
}

function set_color_theme()
{
// Set color scheme
global $body_background_color;
```

```
global $body_font_color;
global $top_header_color;
global $top_header_font_color;
global $top_header_company_font_color;
global $main_index_tab_color;
global $main_index_tab_font_color;
global $index_tab_color;
global $index_tab_font_color;
global $dividing_hline_color;
global $dividing_vline_color;
global $shopping_cart_color;
global $shopping_cart_font_color;
global $browse_color;
global $browse_font_color;
global $shopping_cart_width; // minimum width
global $shopping_cart_height; // minimum height
global $company_name;
global $search_categories; // if $search_categories=='current', only the
// current category will be searched.
global $table_row_rows;
global $table_row_cols;
$table_row_rows=5;
$table_row_cols=30;
$body_background_color='336699';
$body_font_color='000000';
$top_header_color='336699';
$top_header_font_color='EEEEEE';
$top_header_company_font_color='EEEEEE';
$main_index_tab_color='990000';
$main_index_tab_font_color='EEEEEE';
$index_tab_color='003366';
$index_tab_font_color='EEEEEE';
$dividing_hline_color='990000';
$dividing_vline_color='990000';
$shopping_cart_color='336699';
$shopping_cart_font_color='FFFFFF';
$browse_color='FFFFFF';
$browse_font_color='336699';
$shopping_cart_width='100'; // minimum width
$shopping_cart_height='0'; // minimum height
$company_name='phpshopcart.sourceforge.net';
// if $search_categories=='current', only the current category will be
// searched.
```

```php
// $search_categories=='current';
}


// Initiate connection to database
// userid and password should be stored in a separate, non-public file and be
// include()'d here.
function connect_db()
{
global $db_server;
global $db_username;
global $db_password;
MYSQL_CONNECT($db_server,$db_username,$db_password) OR DIE("Unable to
connect to database");
@MYSQL_SELECT_DB($db_name) or die("Unable to select database");
}


// If an image is requested, display the image and exit. Exit is critical!
function display_image()
{
    global $image_id;
    $result=mysql_query("SELECT * FROM images WHERE image_id=$image_id");
    WHILE ($row=mysql_fetch_array($result))
    {
    $image_type=$row["image_type"];
    $image_data=$row["image_data"];
    }
    header("Content-type: $image_type");
    print $image_data;
    exit();
}


// Set up cookies
function init_cookies()
{
global $session_id;
if (!isset($session_id)):
    // session_status values:
    // 0 - not logged in, just browsing...
    // 1 - logged in
    // 2 - purchase completed.
    $query = "INSERT INTO sessions (session_status) VALUES(0')";
    $result = MYSQL_QUERY($query);
    $session_id=mysql_insert_id();
```

```
        setcookie("session_id",$session_id);
        // Warning - note that this is inherently insecure. For example, it would
        // be easy to simply increment your cookie ID on your browser and hijack
        // someone's session. It would be better to generate a pseudorandom
        // number or a unique ID that couldn't be easily guessed. DO NOT
        // implement this on a production machine.
endif;
}


// Register User in Database
function register_user()
{
global $register_form;
global $user_id;
global $user_first_name;
global $user_last_name;
global $user_mail_address;
global $user_credit_card;
global $user_password;
global $session_id;
If ($register_form!=""):
        // Verify that information is accurate and acceptable for input
        // into the database.
        // (Insert your info checking routines here)
        // Insert the information into database.
        $fields="user_first_name, user_last_name, user_mail_address, ";
        $fields=$fields."user_credit_card, user_password";
        $values="'$user_first_name', $user_last_name', '$user_mail_address', ";
        $values=$values."'$user_credit_card', '$user_password'";
        $query = "INSERT INTO users ($fields) VALUES($values)";
        $result = MYSQL_QUERY($query);
        $user_id=mysql_insert_id();
        $query="UPDATE sessions SET user_id = '$user_id' WHERE session_id = ";
        $query=$query."'$session_id'";
        $result=MYSQL_QUERY($query);
Endif;
}


// Log out user
function logout_user()
{
global $session_id;
global $session_status;
```

```
global $login_success;
global $logout;
If ($logout):
    $query="UPDATE sessions SET user_id = '' WHERE session_id = '$session_id'";
    $result=MYSQL_QUERY($query);
    $query="UPDATE sessions SET session_status = '0' WHERE session_id = ";
    $query=$query."'$session_id'";
    $result=MYSQL_QUERY($query);
    $session_status=0;
    $login_success=0;
Endif;
}


// Log in user
function login_user()
{
global $login;
If ($login):
    global $user_id;
    global $user_password;
    global $session_id;
    global $session_status;
    global $login_success;
    $query="SELECT user_password from users WHERE user_id='$user_id'";
    $result=mysql_query($query);
    $num_results=mysql_num_rows($result);
    If ($num_results!=0):
        $row=mysql_fetch_array($result);
        $test_password=$row["user_password"];
        If ($test_password == $user_password):
            $query = "UPDATE sessions SET user_id = '$user_id' WHERE session_id =";
            $query = $query." '$session_id'";
            $result = MYSQL_QUERY($query);
            $query = "UPDATE sessions SET session_status = '1' WHERE session_id =";
            $query = $query." '$session_id'";
            $result = MYSQL_QUERY($query);
            $session_status=1;
            $login_success=1;
        Else:
            $login_success=0;
        Endif;
    Else:
        $login_success=0;
```

```
    Endif;
Endif;
}


// See if User has logged in yet and read info if so.
function read_user_info()
{
global $user_id;
global $user_first_name;
global $user_last_name;
global $user_mail_address;
global $user_credit_card;
global $user_password;
global $user_perm;
global $session_status;
global $session_id;
global $uc_user_first_name;
$query="SELECT user_id from sessions WHERE session_id=$session_id";
$result=mysql_query($query);
$num_results=mysql_num_rows($result);
If ($num_results==1):
    $row=mysql_fetch_array($result);
    $user_id=$row["user_id"];
    $result=mysql_query("SELECT * from users WHERE user_id=$user_id");
    $num_results=mysql_num_rows($result);
    If ($num_results==1):
        $row=mysql_fetch_array($result);
        $user_id=$row["user_id"];
        $user_first_name=$row["user_first_name"];
        $uc_user_first_name=ucwords($user_first_name);
        $user_last_name=$row["user_last_name"];
        $user_mail_address=$row["user_mail_address"];
        $user_credit_card=$row["user_credit_cart"];
        $user_password=$row["user_password"];
        $user_perm=$row["user_perm"];
        $session_status=1;
        $query = "UPDATE sessions SET session_status = '1' WHERE session_id =";
        $query = " '$session_id'";
        $result = MYSQL_QUERY($query);
    Endif;
Endif;
}
```

```
// Layout Page
function layout_page()
{
global $company_name;
global $body_background_color;
global $body_font_color;
Print "<HTML>\n";
Print "<HEAD>\n";
Print "<TITLE>\n$company_name</TITLE>\n";
Print "</HEAD>\n";
Print "<BODY MARGINWIDTH=0 MARGINHEIGHT=0 LEFTMARGIN=0 TOPMARGIN=0 ";
Print "TEXT='$body_font_color' VLINK='$body_font_color' ";
Print "BGCOLOR='#$body_background_color' ";
Print "ALINK='$body_font_color' LINK='$body_font_color'>\n";
}


// Select initial category
function init_category()
{
global $category_id;
global $session_id;
// get category id from current session, if it exists.
If ($category_id=="" || $category_id=="0"):
    $query="SELECT category_id from sessions WHERE session_id=$session_id";
    $result=mysql_query($query);
    $row=mysql_fetch_array($result);
    $category_id=$row["category_id"];
Else:
    // this would get executed if category id was set on the URL, for example
    // when changing categories.
    $query = "UPDATE sessions SET category_id = '$category_id' WHERE ";
    $query = $query."session_id = '$session_id'";
    $result = MYSQL_QUERY($query);
Endif;
// If $category_id is still 0 or "", then go ahead and set it to 1.
If ($category_id=="" || $category_id=="0"):
    $category_id='1';
    $query = "UPDATE sessions SET category_id = '$category_id' WHERE ";
    $query = $query."session_id = '$session_id'";
    $result = MYSQL_QUERY($query);
Endif;
}
```

```
// Draw Header Table
function header_table()
{
global $top_header_color;
global $top_header_font_color;
global $top_header_company_font_color;
global $company_name;
global $search;
global $category_id;
global $session_status;
global $uc_user_first_name;
global $PHP_SELF;
Print "<TABLE BORDER=0 WIDTH='100%' CELLSPACING='0' CELLPADDING='0' ";
Print "BGCOLOR='#$top_header_color'>\n";
// Print "<TR><TD>\n<IMG SRC='img/clear.gif'>\n</TD>\n</TR>\n";
Print "<TR><TD ALIGN='LEFT'>";
Print "<FONT FACE='Helvetica, Verdana, Arial' SIZE=+4 COLOR=";
Print "'$top_header_company_font_color'><EM>$company_name</EM></FONT></TD>\n";
If ($session_status == 1):
    Print "<TD COLSPAN=2 ALIGN='CENTER'><FONT FACE=";
    Print "'Helvetica, Verdana, Arial' COLOR='$top_header_font_color'>";
    Print "Welcome, $uc_user_first_name!</FONT></TD>\n";
Endif;
Print "<TD ALIGN='RIGHT'><FONT FACE='Helvetica, Verdana, Arial'";
Print "COLOR='$top_header_font_color' SIZE=-2><FORM ACTION='$PHP_SELF'";
Print " METHOD=POST>\n";
Print "<INPUT TYPE=text NAME='search' VALUE='$search'>";
Print "<INPUT TYPE=hidden NAME='current_category_id' VALUE='$category_id'>";
Print "<INPUT TYPE=SUBMIT VALUE='Search'></FORM></FONT></TD></TR>\n";
Print "</TABLE>\n";
}


// Draw dividing line
function divide_lineh()
{
global $dividing_hline_color;
Print "<TABLE WIDTH=100% BORDER=0 CELLSPACING='0' CELLPADDING='0'>\n";
Print "<TR>\n<TD HEIGHT=1 WIDTH='100%' BGCOLOR='#$dividing_hline_color'>\n";
Print "<IMG SRC='img/clear.gif' HEIGHT=1 WIDTH=1></TD>\n</TR>\n";
Print "</TABLE>\n";
}


// Draw dividing line
```

```php
function divide_colv()
{
global $dividing_vline_color;
Print "<TD HEIGHT='100%' ROWSPAN=1 WIDTH='1' ";
Print "BGCOLOR='#$dividing_vline_color'>";
Print "<IMG SRC='img/clear.gif' HEIGHT=1 WIDTH=1></TD>\n";
}


// Checkout!!! Another successful sale!
function checkout()
{
global $session_status;
global $session_id;
$session_status=2;
$query = "UPDATE sessions SET session_status = '2' WHERE session_id = ";
$query = $query."'$session_id'";
$result = MYSQL_QUERY($query);
If ($result):
    Print "<H3>Checkout Successful! Thank you!</H3><HR><BR>";
Else:
    Print "<H3>Checkout Failed! Thank you!</H3><HR><BR>";
Endif;
}


// Start table for shopping cart and browse columns
function start_shop_browse_table()
{
global $browse_color;
Print "<TABLE BORDER=0 WIDTH='100%' CELLSPACING='0' CELLPADDING='0'";
Print " BGCOLOR='#$browse_color'>\n<TR>\n";
}


// Start Shopping Cart Column
function start_shop_column()
{
global $shopping_cart_color;
global $shopping_cart_height;
global $shopping_cart_width;
Print "<TD BGCOLOR='#$shopping_cart_color' HEIGHT='$shopping_cart_height'";
Print " WIDTH='$shopping_cart_width' VALIGN=TOP>";
}


// Delete an item from the cart before display.
```

```php
function delete_item()
{
global $delete_cart_id;
If ($delete_cart_id!=""):
    // Delete item from the carts database
    $query = "DELETE FROM carts WHERE cart_id='$delete_cart_id'";
    $result = MYSQL_QUERY($query);
Endif;
}


// Buy (Add) an item to the cart before display.
function buy_item()
{
global $buy_item_id;
global $session_id;
If ($buy_item_id!=""):
    // Insert this buy item into the carts database
    $query = "INSERT INTO carts (session_id,item_id) VALUES('$session_id',";
    $query = $query."'$buy_item_id')";
    $result = MYSQL_QUERY($query);
Endif;
}


// Print Shopping Cart contents
function print_shopping_cart()
{
    global $session_id;
    global $shopping_cart_font_color;
    global $shopping_cart_width;
    global $PHP_SELF;
    global $session_status;
    global $uc_user_first_name;
    global $user_perm;
    global $total;
    global $items_in_cart;
    $query="SELECT items.item_id, items.item_name, items.item_price, ";
    $query=$query."carts.cart_id FROM items, carts WHERE carts.session_id ";
    $query=$query."='$session_id' AND carts.item_id=items.item_id ORDER BY ";
    $query=$query." items.item_name";
    $result=mysql_query($query);
    If (mysql_num_rows($result)>0):
        If ($session_status>0):
                Print "<FONT FACE='Helvetica, Verdana, Arial' COLOR=";
```

```
                    Print "'$shopping_cart_font_color'>$uc_user_first_name's ";
            Print "Selections:<BR></FONT>\n";
    Else:
                Print "<FONT FACE='Helvetica, Verdana, Arial' COLOR=";
            Print "'$shopping_cart_font_color'>My Selections:<BR></FONT>\n";
    Endif;
Endif;
// start microtable
Print "<TABLE WIDTH=100% BORDER=0 CELLSPACING='0' CELLPADDING='0'>\n";
Print "<TR><TD COLSPAN=2><IMG SRC='img/clear.gif' HEIGHT='10' WIDTH=";
Print "'$shopping_cart_width'></TD></TR>";
$items_in_cart=0;
WHILE ($row=mysql_fetch_array($result))
    {
    $items_in_cart++;
    $cart_id=$row["cart_id"];
    $item_id=$row["item_id"];
    $item_name=$row["item_name"];
    $item_price=$row["item_price"];
    $total=$item_price+$total;
    // allow the opportunity to review an item in the cart.
    Print "<TR><TD VALIGN=TOP>";
    Print "<a href='$PHP_SELF?review_cart_id=$cart_id";
    Print "&reviewbuy_item_id=$item_id'>";
    Print "<FONT FACE='Helvetica, Verdana, Arial' SIZE=-3 COLOR=";
    Print "'$shopping_cart_font_color'>$item_name</FONT>";
    Print "</a></TD>";
    Print "<TD VALIGN=TOP ALIGN=RIGHT><FONT FACE='Helvetica, Verdana,";
    Print "Arial' SIZE=-2 COLOR='#$shopping_cart_font_color'>";
    $item_price_str=number_format($item_price,2,'.',',');
    Print "$item_price_str</FONT></TD>";
    Print "<TR><TD COLSPAN=2><IMG SRC='img/clear.gif' HEIGHT='5' ";
    Print "WIDTH='$shopping_cart_width'></TD></TR>";
    }
If ($items_in_cart>0):
    Print "<TR><TD VALIGN=TOP>";
    Print "<FONT FACE='Helvetica, Verdana, Arial' SIZE=-3 COLOR=";
    Print "'$shopping_cart_font_color'>Total:</FONT>";
    Print "</TD>";
    Print "<TD VALIGN=TOP ALIGN=RIGHT><FONT FACE='Helvetica, Verdana, ";
    Print "Arial' SIZE=-2 COLOR='#$shopping_cart_font_color'>";
    $total_str=number_format($total,2,'.',',');
    Print "$$total_str</FONT></TD>";
```

```
            Print "<TR><TD COLSPAN=2><IMG SRC='img/clear.gif' HEIGHT='5' WIDTH=";
            Print "'$shopping_cart_width'></TD></TR>";
        Endif;
        Print "</TABLE>\n";
        // end microtable
}


// Start Browse Column
function start_browse_column()
{
global $browse_color;
global $browse_font_color;
Print "<TD WIDTH='100%' VALIGN=TOP BGCOLOR='#$browse_color' ROWSPAN=1>";
Print "<FONT FACE='Helvetica, Verdana, Arial' COLOR='#$browse_font_color'>";
}


// Draw Category Table
function category_table()
{
global $index_tab_color;
global $index_tab_font_color;
global $main_index_tab_color;
global $main_index_tab_font_color;
global $PHP_SELF;
global $category_id;
Print "<TABLE WIDTH=100% BORDER=0 CELLSPACING='0' CELLPADDING='3'>\n";
Print "<TR BGCOLOR='#$index_tab_color'>\n";
$result=mysql_query("SELECT * FROM categories ORDER BY category_name");
WHILE ($row=mysql_fetch_array($result))
{
$col_category_id=$row["category_id"];
$col_category_name=$row["category_name"];
If ($col_category_id==$category_id):
    $category_name=$col_category_name;
    Print "<TD BGCOLOR='#$main_index_tab_color'>\n<CENTER>\n";
    Print "<a href='$PHP_SELF?category_id=$col_category_id'>\n";
    Print "<FONT FACE='Helvetica, Verdana, Arial'";
    Print " COLOR='#$main_index_tab_font_color'>\n";
    Print "$category_name</FONT>\n</a>\n</CENTER>\n</TD>\n";
Else:
    Print "<TD BGCOLOR='#$index_tab_color'>\n<CENTER>\n";
    Print "<a href='$PHP_SELF?category_id=$col_category_id'>\n";
    Print "<FONT FACE='Helvetica, Verdana, Arial' COLOR=";
```

```
        Print "'#$index_tab_font_color'>\n";
        Print "$col_category_name</FONT>\n</a>\n</CENTER>\n</TD>\n";
Endif;
}
Print "</TR>\n</TABLE>\n";
}


// Inform the user of userid after registration
function inform_user()
{
global $register_form;
global $user_id;
global $user_first_name;
global $user_last_name;
global $user_mail_address;
global $user_credit_card;
global $user_password;
global $browse_font_color;
global $browse_color;
If (register_form!=""):
Print "<FONT FACE='Helvetica, Verdana, Arial' COLOR='#$browse_font_color'>\n";
Print "<H1>Please write this down!</H1>";
Print "<CENTER><TABLE BORDER=0 WIDTH=75% VALIGN=TOP CELLSPACING='0'";
Print "CELLPADDING='0' BGCOLOR='#$browse_color'>";
Print "<TR><TD><FONT FACE='Helvetica, Verdana, Arial' COLOR=";
Print "'#$browse_font_color'>Your user ID is:</TD>";
Print "<TD><FONT FACE='Helvetica, Verdana, Arial' COLOR=";
Print "'#$browse_font_color'>$user_id</TD></TR>";
Print "<TR><TD><FONT FACE='Helvetica, Verdana, Arial' COLOR=";
Print "'#$browse_font_color'>Your password is:</TD>";
Print "<TD><FONT FACE='Helvetica, Verdana, Arial' COLOR=";
Print "'#$browse_font_color'>$user_password</TD></TR>";
Print "</TABLE>";
Endif;
}


// Inform a user if he was successfully logged in or out.
function inform_auth()
{
global $login;
global $logout;
global $login_success;
global $uc_user_first_name;
```

```php
If ($login):
    If ($login_success):
            Print "<H3>Login Successful! Welcome,
                $uc_user_first_name!</H3><HR><BR>";
    Else:
        Print "<H3>Login Failed!</H3>";
        Print "Unauthorized access is prohibited and will be prosecuted. Please";
        Print " <a href='$PHP_SELF?create_account=1'>";
        Print "create an account</a>. If you already have a valid account, ";
        Print "please try again.<BR><HR><BR>";
    Endif;
Endif;
If ($logout):
    // Logout always succeeds unless there is a database problem.
    // It might be useful to remove the cookie from the user's PC.
    Print "<H3>Logout Successful! Feel free to continue
        browsing.</H3><HR><BR>";
Endif;
}


// Input Table Row Form
function row_form($field_title,$field_name,$field_type)
{
global $browse_color;
global $browse_font_color;
global $table_row_rows;
global $table_row_cols;
If ($field_type==""):
    $field_type="text";
Endif;
Print "<TR><TD>";
Print "<FONT FACE='Helvetica, Verdana, Arial' COLOR='#$browse_font_color'>";
Print "$field_title";
Print "</FONT></TD><TD>";
Print "<FONT FACE='Helvetica, Verdana, Arial' COLOR='#$browse_font_color'>";
If ($field_type=="textarea"):
    Print "<$field_type ROWS=$table_row_rows COLS=$table_row_cols NAME=";
    Print "'$field_name'></$field_type>";
Else:
    Print "<INPUT TYPE='$field_type' NAME='$field_name'>";
Endif;
Print "</FONT>";
Print "</TD></TR>\n";
```

```
}


// Admin the site
function admin()
{
global $PHP_SELF;
global $browse_color;
global $browse_font_color;
global $category_id;
global $table_row_rows;
global $table_row_cols;
$table_row_rows=5;
$table_row_cols=30;
Print "<CENTER><TABLE BORDER=0 WIDTH=75% VALIGN=TOP CELLSPACING='0'";
Print " CELLPADDING='0' BGCOLOR='#$browse_color'>";
Print "<FORM ACTION='$PHP_SELF' ENCTYPE='multipart/form-data' METHOD=POST>";
Print "<INPUT TYPE=hidden NAME='admin_add' VALUE='1'>\n";
Print "<TR><TD COLSPAN=2 ALIGN=CENTER>";
Print "<FONT FACE='Helvetica, Verdana, Arial' COLOR='#$browse_font_color'>";
Print "<H3>Add an Item</H3></FONT></TD></TR>\n";
row_form("Item Name:","item_name","");
row_form("Item Description:","item_description","textarea");
row_form("Item Price:","item_price","text");
// Make Category Pull-down
$result=mysql_query("SELECT * FROM categories ORDER BY category_name");
Print "<TR><TD>";
Print "<FONT FACE='Helvetica, Verdana, Arial' COLOR='#$browse_font_color'>";
Print "Category:</FONT></TD><TD>";
Print "<FONT FACE='Helvetica, Verdana, Arial' COLOR='#$browse_font_color'>";
Print "<SELECT NAME='add_item_category_id'>";
WHILE ($row=mysql_fetch_array($result))
{
$col_category_id=$row["category_id"];
$col_category_name=$row["category_name"];
Print "<OPTION VALUE=$col_category_id>$col_category_name";
}
Print "</SELECT></TD></TR>\n";
Print "<TR><TD>";
Print "<FONT FACE='Helvetica, Verdana, Arial' COLOR='#$browse_font_color'>";
Print "Select an Image: (optional)</FONT></TD><TD>";
Print "<FONT FACE='Helvetica, Verdana, Arial' COLOR='#$browse_font_color'>";
Print "<INPUT TYPE='hidden' name='MAX_FILE_SIZE' value=500000>";
Print "<input type=file name=image accept='image/*'></FONT></TD></TR>\n";
```

```
Print "<TR><TD COLSPAN=2 ALIGN=CENTER><INPUT TYPE=SUBMIT></FONT></TD></TR>\n";
Print "</FORM>";
Print "</TABLE></CENTER>";
}


// Add an item to the site
function admin_add_item()
{
global $category_id;
global $item_name;
global $item_description;
global $item_price;
global $add_item_category_id;
global $image_id;
global $image; // PHP-provided variable (temporary filename)
global $image_name; // PHP-provided variable (original filename)
global $image_size; // PHP-provided variable (in bytes)
global $image_type; // PHP-provided variable (mime-type: image/gif,image/jpeg)
global $PHP_SELF;
If ($image != 'none'):
    $image_data = addslashes(fread(fopen($image,"r"),filesize($image)));
    // insert mime type into images database and get an id #.
    $fields="image_type, image_data";
    $values="'$image_type', '$image_data'";
    $query = "INSERT INTO images ($fields) VALUES($values)";
    $result = MYSQL_QUERY($query);
    $image_id=mysql_insert_id();
    Print "<img src='$PHP_SELF?image_id=$image_id'><BR>";
Endif;
$fields="item_name, item_description, item_price, category_id, image_id";
$values="'$item_name', '$item_description', '$item_price', ";
$values=$values."'$add_item_category_id', '$image_id'";
$query = "INSERT INTO items ($fields) VALUES($values)";
$result = MYSQL_QUERY($query);
$item_id=mysql_insert_id();
If ($result):
    Print "Item ID#$item_id addition ($item_name) succeeded.";
Else:
    Print "Item ID#$item_id addition ($item_name) failed.";
Endif;
}


// Create_account
```

```
function create_account()
{
global $PHP_SELF;
global $browse_color;
global $browse_font_color;
// Start Create Account Form
// We recommend that this form is secured in secure server!!
Print "<CENTER><TABLE BORDER=0 WIDTH=75% VALIGN=TOP CELLSPACING='0' ";
Print "CELLPADDING='0' BGCOLOR='#$browse_color'>";
Print "<FORM ACTION='$PHP_SELF' METHOD=POST>";
Print "<INPUT TYPE=hidden NAME='register_form' VALUE='1'>\n";
row_form("Your First Name:","user_first_name","");
row_form("Your Last Name:","user_last_name","");
row_form("Your Mail Address:","user_mail_address","");
row_form("Your Credit Card:","user_credit_card","");
row_form("Password:","user_password","");
// OR row_form("Password:","user_password","password");
// Recommend you confirm password if you conceal what is typed
Print "<TR><TD COLSPAN=2 ALIGN=CENTER><INPUT TYPE=SUBMIT></FONT></TD></TR>";
Print "</FORM>";
Print "</TABLE></CENTER>";
}


// Review an individual item
function review_item()
{
global $review_item_id;
global $PHP_SELF;
global $browse_font_color;
$result=mysql_query("SELECT * FROM items WHERE item_id=$review_item_id");
WHILE ($row=mysql_fetch_array($result))
    {
    $item_name=$row["item_name"];
    $item_description=$row["item_description"];
    $item_price=$row["item_price"];
    $image_id=$row["image_id"];
    If ($image_id!='0'):
        Print "<img src='$PHP_SELF?image_id=$image_id'><BR>";
    Endif;
    Print
"$item_name<BR>\n$item_description<BR>\n<BR>\n\$$item_price<BR><BR>";
    Print "<a href='$PHP_SELF?buy_item_id=$review_item_id'>\n";
    Print "<FONT FACE='Helvetica,Verdana,Arial' COLOR='#$browse_font_color'>";
```

```
    Print "Purchase this Item";
    Print "</FONT>";
    Print "</a>\n";
    }
}


// Review the purchase of an individual item
function review_purchase()
{
global $reviewbuy_item_id;
global $review_cart_id;
global $PHP_SELF;
global $browse_font_color;
$result=mysql_query("SELECT * FROM items WHERE item_id=$reviewbuy_item_id");
WHILE ($row=mysql_fetch_array($result))
    {
    $item_name=$row["item_name"];
    $item_description=$row["item_description"];
    $item_price=$row["item_price"];
    Print "$item_name<BR>\n$item_description<BR><BR>\$$item_price<BR><BR>";
    Print "<a href='$PHP_SELF?delete_cart_id=$review_cart_id'>\n";
    Print "<FONT FACE='Helvetica,Verdana,Arial' COLOR='#$browse_font_color'>";
    Print "Delete this Item from shopping basket.";
    Print "</FONT>";
    Print "</a>\n";
    }
}


// Start Browse Column, but for search items
function search_column()
{
global $category_id;
global $category_name;
global $search;
global $lower_limit;
global $browse_font_color;
global $PHP_SELF;
global $search_categories;
If ($lower_limit==""):
    $lower_limit=1;
Endif;
$upper_limit=$lower_limit+4;
If ($search_categories=='current'):
```

```
        $query="SELECT * FROM items WHERE item_name LIKE '%$search%' OR item_";
        $query=$query."description LIKE '%$search%' AND category_id=$category_id";
        $result=mysql_query($query);
Else:
        $query="SELECT * FROM items WHERE item_name LIKE '%$search%' OR item_";
        $query=$query."description LIKE '%$search%'";
        $result=mysql_query($query);
Endif;
$num_results=mysql_num_rows($result);
$upper_limit=$num_results+$lower_limit-1;
Print "Displaying $category_name containing '$search' from $lower_limit to ";
Print "$upper_limit:<BR>\n<BR>\n";
WHILE ($row=mysql_fetch_array($result))
        {
        $item_id=$row["item_id"];
        $item_name=$row["item_name"];
        $item_description=$row["item_description"];
        $item_price=$row["item_price"];
        Print "<a href='$PHP_SELF?review_item_id=$item_id&current_category_id=";
        Print "$category_id'>\n";
        Print "<FONT FACE='Helvetica,Verdana,Arial' COLOR='#$browse_font_color'>";
        Print "$item_name \$$item_price";
        Print "</FONT>\n";
        Print "</a>\n";
        Print "<BR>\n<BR>\n";
        }
}


// Display the normal browse window.
function browse_column()
{
global $category_id;
global $category_name;
global $search;
global $lower_limit;
global $browse_font_color;
global $PHP_SELF;
// display photos first...
$query="SELECT * FROM items WHERE category_id=$category_id AND image_id>0";
$result=mysql_query($query);
$num_results=mysql_num_rows($result);
$max_pics=4;
If ($num_results>0):
```

```
      Print ("<BR><CENTER><TABLE WIDTH='80%' BORDER=0>");
      If ($num_results > $max_pics):
            $num_results=$max_pics;
      Endif;
      FOR ($x=1;$x<=$num_results;$x++)
       {
       $row=mysql_fetch_array($result);
       $item_id=$row["item_id"];
       $item_name=$row["item_name"];
       $item_description=$row["item_description"];
       $item_price=$row["item_price"];
       $image_id=$row["image_id"];
      If ($x%2 != 0): // if $x is odd
            Print "<TR><TD><CENTER>\n<a href='$PHP_SELF?review_item_id=$item_id'>";
            Print "<img src='$PHP_SELF?image_id=$image_id' BORDER=0 WIDTH=225>";
            Print "<BR><FONT FACE='Helvetica,Verdana,Arial'";
            Print " COLOR='#$browse_font_color'>";
            Print "$item_name \$$item_price</FONT></a>";
            Print "</TD>\n";
      Else:
            Print "<TD><CENTER>\n<a href='$PHP_SELF?review_item_id=$item_id'>";
            Print "<img src='$PHP_SELF?image_id=$image_id' BORDER=0 WIDTH=225>";
            Print "<BR>";
            Print "<FONT FACE='Helvetica, Verdana, Arial' COLOR=";
            Print "'#$browse_font_color'>";
            Print "$item_name \$$item_price</FONT></a>";
            Print "</TD></TR>\n";
      Endif;
      }
      Print ("</TABLE></CENTER><BR>");
Endif;
If ($lower_limit==""):
      $lower_limit=1;
Endif;
$upper_limit=$lower_limit+4;
$result=mysql_query("SELECT * FROM items WHERE category_id=$category_id");
$num_results=mysql_num_rows($result);
$upper_limit=$num_results+$lower_limit-1;
Print "<CENTER><TABLE WIDTH=60% BORDER=0>";
Print "<TR><TD ALIGN=CENTER><B>";
Print "<FONT FACE='Helvetica, Verdana, Arial' COLOR='#$browse_font_color'>\
Print "Displaying $category_name from $lower_limit to $upper_limit:</TD></TR>";
Print "</FONT>\n";
```

```
Print "</B></TD></TR>";
WHILE ($row=mysql_fetch_array($result))
    {
    $item_id=$row["item_id"];
    $item_name=$row["item_name"];
    $item_description=$row["item_description"];
    $item_price=$row["item_price"];
    Print "<TR><TD>";
    Print "<a href='$PHP_SELF?review_item_id=$item_id'>\n";
    Print "<FONT FACE='Helvetica, Verdana, Arial' COLOR=";
    Print "'#$browse_font_color'>";
    Print "$item_name \$$item_price";
    Print "</FONT>\n";
    Print "</a>\n";
    Print "</TD></TR>\n";
    }
Print "</TABLE>";
Print " </TD></TR>\n";
}


// Display bottom of Shopping Cart column
function end_shop_column()
{
global $session_id;
global $shopping_cart_color;
global $shopping_cart_font_color;
global $shopping_cart_width;
global $PHP_SELF;
global $session_status;
global $uc_user_first_name;
global $user_perm;
global $items_in_cart;
Print "<TR><TD BGCOLOR='#$shopping_cart_color' VALIGN=BOTTOM><p>";
If ($session_status == 1):
    Print "<CENTER><A HREF='$PHP_SELF?logout=1'><FONT FACE=";
    Print "'Helvetica,Verdana,Arial' COLOR='$shopping_cart_font_color'";
    Print " SIZE=-1>Logout</FONT></CENTER><BR>";
Endif;
If ($session_status > 0 and $items_in_cart > 0):
    Print "<CENTER><A HREF='$PHP_SELF?checkout=1'><FONT FACE=";
    Print "'Helvetica, Verdana, Arial' COLOR='$shopping_cart_font_color' ";
    Print "SIZE=-1>Checkout</FONT></CENTER><BR>";
Endif;
```

```
If ($user_perm > 0):
    Print "<CENTER><A HREF='$PHP_SELF?admin=1'><FONT FACE=";
    Print "'Helvetica, Verdana, Arial' COLOR='$shopping_cart_font_color'";
    Print " SIZE=-1>Add an Item</FONT></CENTER><BR>";
Endif;
Print "<a href='$PHP_SELF?create_account=1'>\n";
Print "<FONT FACE='Helvetica, Verdana, Arial' SIZE=-1 COLOR=";
Print "'#$shopping_cart_font_color'>";
Print "<CENTER>Create an account</CENTER>";
Print "</FONT></a>";
Print "<BR>";
Print "<FORM ACTION='$PHP_SELF' METHOD=POST>\n";
Print "<FONT FACE='Helvetica, Verdana, Arial' SIZE=-2 COLOR=";
Print "'$shopping_cart_font_color'>Your User ID:<br> ";
Print "<INPUT TYPE=text NAME='user_id'> <br>\n";
Print "Your Password:<br> <INPUT TYPE=password NAME='user_password'>";
Print " <br>\n";
Print "<INPUT TYPE=hidden NAME='login' VALUE='1'><br>\n";
Print "<CENTER><INPUT TYPE=SUBMIT VALUE='Login'></CENTER></FONT></FORM>\n";
Print "</p></TD>";
}


// Display bottom of Browse column
function end_browse_column()
{
global $browse_color;
global $browse_font_color;
global $company_name;
Print "<TD VALIGN=BOTTOM BGCOLOR='#$browse_color'><FONT FACE='Helvetica,";
Print "Verdana, Arial' COLOR='#$browse_font_color' SIZE=-2><CENTER>Copyright ";
Print "&copy 2000 $company_name</CENTER></FONT></TD>";
Print "</TR>";
}


// End Shopping Cart & Browse Table
function end_shop_browse_table()
{
Print "</TABLE>";
}


// Start of Program
// Note — NO PROGRAM STATEMENTS SHOULD EXIST OUTSIDE OF A FUNCTION
// BEFORE THIS SECTION!
```

```
init_db_variables();
set_color_theme();
connect_db();
If ($image_id != ""):
    display_image();
    exit();
Endif;
init_cookies();
logout_user();
register_user();
login_user();
read_user_info();
layout_page();
init_category();
header_table();
start_shop_browse_table();
start_shop_column();
delete_item();
buy_item();
print_shopping_cart();
divide_colv();
start_browse_column();
divide_lineh();
category_table();
divide_lineh();
inform_auth();
// Change browse window based on action:
If ($checkout!=""):
    checkout();
Endif;
If ($review_item_id!=""):
    review_item();
ElseIf ($admin!=""):
    admin();
ElseIf ($admin_add!=""):
    admin_add_item();
ElseIf($register_form!=""):
    inform_user();
ElseIf ($reviewbuy_item_id!=""):
    review_purchase();
ElseIf ($create_account!=""):
    create_account();
ElseIf ($search!=""):
```

```
        search_column();
Else:
        browse_column();
Endif;
// Display page footer
end_shop_column();
divide_colv();
end_browse_column();
end_shop_browse_table();
```

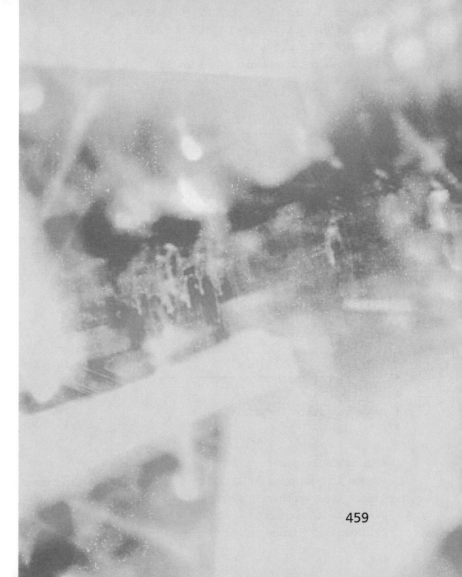

Appendix B

Dump File for Shopping Cart Application

459

```
# phpMyAdmin MySQL-Dump
# http://phpwizard.net/phpMyAdmin/
#
# Host: localhost Database : shopcart


# ----------------------------------------------
#
# Table structure for table 'carts'
#

CREATE TABLE carts (
    cart_id mediumint(9) DEFAULT '0' NOT NULL auto_increment,
    session_id tinyint(4) DEFAULT '0' NOT NULL,
    item_id tinyint(4) DEFAULT '0' NOT NULL,
    PRIMARY KEY (cart_id),
    KEY session_id (session_id, item_id)
);



# ----------------------------------------------
#
# Table structure for table 'categories'
#

CREATE TABLE categories (
    category_id tinyint(4) DEFAULT '0' NOT NULL auto_increment,
    category_name varchar(15) NOT NULL,
    PRIMARY KEY (category_id),
    KEY category_id (category_id),
    UNIQUE category_name (category_name)
);



# ----------------------------------------------
#
# Table structure for table 'images'
#

CREATE TABLE images (
    image_id mediumint(9) DEFAULT '0' NOT NULL auto_increment,
    image_type varchar(30) NOT NULL,
    image_data longblob,
    PRIMARY KEY (image_id)
```

```
);


# ------------------------------------------------
#
# Table structure for table 'items'
#

CREATE TABLE items (
    item_id int(11) DEFAULT '0' NOT NULL auto_increment,
    item_name varchar(30),
    item_description tinytext,
    item_price float(10,2) DEFAULT '0.00' NOT NULL,
    category_id tinyint(4) DEFAULT '0' NOT NULL,
    image_id mediumint(9) DEFAULT '0' NOT NULL,
    PRIMARY KEY (item_id),
    KEY image_id (image_id),
    KEY category_id (category_id)
);


# ------------------------------------------------
#
# Table structure for table 'sessions'
#

CREATE TABLE sessions (
    session_id int(11) DEFAULT '0' NOT NULL auto_increment,
    user_id int(11) DEFAULT '0',
    session_status tinyint(4) DEFAULT '0' NOT NULL,
    category_id tinyint(4),
    PRIMARY KEY (session_id)
);


# ------------------------------------------------
#
# Table structure for table 'users'
#

CREATE TABLE users (
    user_id int(11) DEFAULT '0' NOT NULL auto_increment,
    user_first_name varchar(15),
```

```
user_last_name varchar(15),
user_mail_address varchar(100),
user_credit_card varchar(20),
user_password varchar(30) NOT NULL,
user_perm tinyint(4) DEFAULT '0' NOT NULL,
PRIMARY KEY (user_id)
```

Index

D

N

The Global Knowledge Advantage

Global Knowledge has a global delivery system for its products and services. The company has 28 subsidiaries, and offers its programs through a total of 60+ locations. No other vendor can provide consistent services across a geographic area this large. Global Knowledge is the largest independent information technology education provider, offering programs on a variety of platforms. This enables our multi-platform and multi-national customers to obtain all of their programs from a single vendor. The company has developed the unique CompetusTM Framework software tool and methodology which can quickly reconfigure courseware to the proficiency level of a student on an interactive basis. Combined with self-paced and on-line programs, this technology can reduce the time required for training by prescribing content in only the deficient skills areas. The company has fully automated every aspect of the education process, from registration and follow-up, to "just-in-time" production of courseware. Global Knowledge through its Enterprise Services Consultancy, can customize programs and products to suit the needs of an individual customer.

Global Knowledge Classroom Education Programs

The backbone of our delivery options is classroom-based education. Our modern, well-equipped facilities staffed with the finest instructors offer programs in a wide variety of information technology topics, many of which lead to professional certifications.

Custom Learning Solutions

This delivery option has been created for companies and governments that value customized learning solutions. For them, our consultancy-based approach of developing targeted education solutions is most effective at helping them meet specific objectives.

Self-Paced and Multimedia Products

This delivery option offers self-paced program titles in interactive CD-ROM, videotape and audio tape programs. In addition, we offer custom development of interactive multimedia courseware to customers and partners. Call us at 1-888-427-4228.

Electronic Delivery of Training

Our network-based training service delivers efficient competency-based, interactive training via the World Wide Web and organizational intranets. This leading-edge delivery option provides a custom learning path and "just-in-time" training for maximum convenience to students.

Global Knowledge Courses Available

Microsoft
- Windows 2000 Deployment Strategies
- Introduction to Directory Services
- Windows 2000 Client Administration
- Windows 2000 Server
- Windows 2000 Update
- MCSE Bootcamp
- Microsoft Networking Essentials
- Windows NT 4.0 Workstation
- Windows NT 4.0 Server
- Windows NT Troubleshooting
- Windows NT 4.0 Security
- Windows 2000 Security
- Introduction to Microsoft Web Tools

Management Skills
- Project Management for IT Professionals
- Microsoft Project Workshop
- Management Skills for IT Professionals

Network Fundamentals
- Understanding Computer Networks
- Telecommunications Fundamentals I
- Telecommunications Fundamentals II
- Understanding Networking Fundamentals
- Upgrading and Repairing PCs
- DOS/Windows A+ Preparation
- Network Cabling Systems

WAN Networking and Telephony
- Building Broadband Networks
- Frame Relay Internetworking
- Converging Voice and Data Networks
- Introduction to Voice Over IP
- Understanding Digital Subscriber Line (xDSL)

Internetworking
- ATM Essentials
- ATM Internetworking
- ATM Troubleshooting
- Understanding Networking Protocols
- Internetworking Routers and Switches
- Network Troubleshooting
- Internetworking with TCP/IP
- Troubleshooting TCP/IP Networks
- Network Management
- Network Security Administration
- Virtual Private Networks
- Storage Area Networks
- Cisco OSPF Design and Configuration
- Cisco Border Gateway Protocol (BGP) Configuration

Web Site Management and Development
- Advanced Web Site Design
- Introduction to XML
- Building a Web Site
- Introduction to JavaScript
- Web Development Fundamentals
- Introduction to Web Databases

PERL, UNIX, and Linux
- PERL Scripting
- PERL with CGI for the Web
- UNIX Level I
- UNIX Level II
- Introduction to Linux for New Users
- Linux Installation, Configuration, and Maintenance

Authorized Vendor Training
Red Hat
- Introduction to Red Hat Linux
- Red Hat Linux Systems Administration
- Red Hat Linux Network and Security Administration
- RHCE Rapid Track Certification

Cisco Systems
- Interconnecting Cisco Network Devices
- Advanced Cisco Router Configuration
- Installation and Maintenance of Cisco Routers
- Cisco Internetwork Troubleshooting
- Designing Cisco Networks
- Cisco Internetwork Design
- Configuring Cisco Catalyst Switches
- Cisco Campus ATM Solutions
- Cisco Voice Over Frame Relay, ATM, and IP
- Configuring for Selsius IP Phones
- Building Cisco Remote Access Networks
- Managing Cisco Network Security
- Cisco Enterprise Management Solutions

Nortel Networks
- Nortel Networks Accelerated Router Configuration
- Nortel Networks Advanced IP Routing
- Nortel Networks WAN Protocols
- Nortel Networks Frame Switching
- Nortel Networks Accelar 1000
- Comprehensive Configuration
- Nortel Networks Centillion Switching
- Network Management with Optivity for Windows

Oracle Training
- Introduction to Oracle8 and PL/SQL
- Oracle8 Database Administration

Custom Corporate Network Training

Train on Cutting Edge Technology
We can bring the best in skill-based training to your facility to create a real-world hands-on training experience. Global Knowledge has invested millions of dollars in network hardware and software to train our students on the same equipment they will work with on the job. Our relationships with vendors allow us to incorporate the latest equipment and platforms into your on-site labs.

Maximize Your Training Budget
Global Knowledge provides experienced instructors, comprehensive course materials, and all the networking equipment needed to deliver high quality training. You provide the students; we provide the knowledge.

Avoid Travel Expenses
On-site courses allow you to schedule technical training at your convenience, saving time, expense, and the opportunity cost of travel away from the workplace.

Discuss Confidential Topics
Private on-site training permits the open discussion of sensitive issues such as security, access, and network design. We can work with your existing network's proprietary files while demonstrating the latest technologies.

Customize Course Content
Global Knowledge can tailor your courses to include the technologies and the topics which have the greatest impact on your business. We can complement your internal training efforts or provide a total solution to your training needs.

Corporate Pass
The Corporate Pass Discount Program rewards our best network training customers with preferred pricing on public courses, discounts on multimedia training packages, and an array of career planning services.

Global Knowledge Training Lifecycle
Supporting the Dynamic and Specialized Training Requirements of Information Technology Professionals

- Define Profile
- Assess Skills
- Design Training
- Deliver Training
- Test Knowledge
- Update Profile
- Use New Skills

Global Knowledge

Global Knowledge programs are developed and presented by industry profession-als with "real-world" experience. Designed to help professionals meet today's inter-connectivity and interoperability challenges, most of our programs feature hands-on labs that incorporate state-of-the-art communication components and equipment.

ON-SITE TEAM TRAINING

Bring Global Knowledge's powerful training programs to your company. At Global Knowledge, we will custom design courses to meet your specific network require-ments. Call (919)-461-8686 for more information.

YOUR GUARANTEE

Global Knowledge believes its courses offer the best possible training in this field. If during the first day you are not satisfied and wish to withdraw from the course, simply notify the instructor, return all course materials and receive a 100% refund.

REGISTRATION INFORMATION

In the US:
call: (888) 762–4442
fax: (919) 469–7070
visit our website:
www.globalknowledge.com